Such Anxious Hours

Wisconsin Studies in Autobiography
WILLIAM L. ANDREWS, SERIES EDITOR

Such Anxious Hours

WISCONSIN WOMEN'S VOICES
FROM THE CIVIL WAR

Edited by
Jo Ann Daly Carr

THE UNIVERSITY OF WISCONSIN PRESS

Publication of this book has been made possible, in part, through support
from the Anonymous Fund of the College of Letters and Science at the
University of Wisconsin–Madison.

The University of Wisconsin Press
728 State Street, Suite 443
Madison, Wisconsin 53706
uwpress.wisc.edu

Gray's Inn House, 127 Clerkenwell Road
London EC1R 5DB, United Kingdom
eurospanbookstore.com

Copyright © 2019
The Board of Regents of the University of Wisconsin System
All rights reserved. Except in the case of brief quotations embedded in critical
articles and reviews, no part of this publication may be reproduced, stored in a retrieval
system, transmitted in any format or by any means—digital, electronic, mechanical,
photocopying, recording, or otherwise—or conveyed via the Internet or a website
without written permission of the University of Wisconsin Press. Rights inquiries
should be directed to rights@uwpress.wisc.edu.

Printed in the United States of America
This book may be available in a digital edition.

Library of Congress Cataloging-in-Publication Data
Names: Carr, Jo Ann, editor.
Title: Such anxious hours : Wisconsin women's voices from the Civil War /
edited by Jo Ann Daly Carr.
Other titles: Wisconsin studies in autobiography.
Description: Madison, Wisconsin : The University of Wisconsin Press, [2019] |
Series: Wisconsin studies in autobiography | Includes bibliographical references
and index.
Identifiers: LCCN 2019011083 | ISBN 9780299324209 (cloth : alk. paper)
Subjects: LCSH: Wisconsin—History—Civil War, 1861–1865—Personal narratives. |
United States—History—Civil War, 1861–1865—Women—Personal narratives. |
Women—Wisconsin—Correspondence.
Classification: LCC E601 .S94 2019 | DDC 973.7082—dc23
LC record available at https://lccn.loc.gov/2019011083

*For my sister and fellow author, C. Ruth Daly,
and for George.*

Contents

List of Illustrations	ix
Preface	xi
Introduction: April 13, 1861	3
1 April 1861 to April 1862	9
2 May 1862 to April 1863	82
3 May 1863 to April 1864	120
4 May 1864 to April 1865	196
Aftermath of War: April 16, 1865	291
Notes	301
Bibliography	325
Index	333

Illustrations

Wisconsin map depicting locations of women whose writings are included in this volume	2
Wisconsin capitol building in 1861	11
Washing machine	43
Town of Mazomanie	75
1860 railroad engine	102
Town of Portage	127
Harriet Whetten, Civil War nurse	140
Lakeshore sketch by Annie Cox	174
Baptist church housing Wisconsin Historical Society rooms	181
Printing press	185
Winter farmyard	226
Patchin farmstead	296

Preface

In May 2014 I attended a program where authors discussed their books, all of which were based on the writings of Wisconsin men during the Civil War. Noting the lack of books containing the writings of women, I embarked on a five-year project to locate and share women's voices from the Wisconsin home front.

Other titles have been published on Northern women in the Civil War—Jeannie Attie, *Patriotic Toll: Northern Women and the Civil War*; Catherine Clinton and Nina Silber, *Divided Houses: Gender and the Civil War*; and Frank Moore, *Women of the War: Their Heroism and Self-Sacrifice*; and, on Wisconsin women, Ethel Alice Hurn, *Wisconsin Women in the War between the States*; Karen A. Kehoe, "'Not a Moment for Delay': Benevolence in Wisconsin during the Civil War Era"; and Kerry Trask, *The Fire Within: A Civil War Narrative from Wisconsin*. These works included only brief excerpts from the letters and diaries of Civil War women, used to illustrate the authors' viewpoints or to provide a third-person account. Two works—*A Quiet Corner of the War: The Civil War Letters of Gilbert and Esther Claflin: Oconomowoc, Wisconsin, 1862–1863* and *Postmarked Hudson: The Letters of Sarah A. [sic: E.] Andrews to Her Brother, James A. Andrews, 1864–1865*—give prominence to the words these women wrote during the war but are limited to the viewpoint of a single woman or couple during a single year of the war.

In this book, the voices of eight ordinary Wisconsin women—Emily Quiner and Annie Cox of Madison; Ann Waldo and Susan Brown of Winneconne; Margaret MacNish Patchin of Wyocena; Sarah Powers of Fox Lake; Mary Burwell of Oxford; and Rosabella (Belle) Augusta Arnold Sleeper of

Berlin—provide a narrative of the Wisconsin home front during the Civil War. Their voices are presented in transcriptions of writings at the Wisconsin Historical Society (WHS) Library and Archives for Ann Waldo, Susan Brown, and Sarah Powers; at the Wisconsin Veterans Museum (WVM) for Margaret Patchin; and at McCain Library and Archives at the University of Southern Mississippi (USM) for Mary Burwell. Emily Quiner's diary was the most accessible source document, as it has been transcribed and posted on the WHS website. Future access to Annie Cox's letters is threatened as they have not been transcribed and the brittle paper and ink she used are disintegrating. Revealing Belle Arnold Sleeper's voice was a challenge as her letters are housed in two separate folders under the names Bell Sexton and Augusta Sleeper. I was able to determine Belle's true identify by tracing the genealogy for Wiley Arnold and was able to bring her story together by comparing the handwriting and content of the letters attributed to Bell Sexton and to Augusta Sleeper. The archives for Annie Cox, Ann Waldo, Susan Brown, Sarah Powers, Mary Burwell, and Belle Arnold Sleeper also contain letters from their spouses, other family members, and friends. These additional letters provided important context for understanding these women and the role that their writing had in their lives.

Writings were selected to provide a narrative of the Wisconsin home front beginning with the surrender of Union forces at Fort Sumter and ending with the surrender of Confederate forces at Appomattox Courthouse. The writings of each woman were sustained over a period of time ranging from two months to two and a half years. The longest contribution is provided by the diary of Emily Quiner of Madison. The remainder of the primary material comes from letters that provide the perspectives of women ranging in age from eighteen to forty-three, living in cities, villages, and farms, writing to sisters, friends, fiancés, sons, and husbands. The letters reflect both the dominant ethnicity and the settlement patterns of 1861–65 Wisconsin. All the letters are from Caucasian women who lived in the most heavily populated areas of the state, from Wyocena in central Wisconsin to Madison in south-central Wisconsin. I regret that I was unable to find any primary materials written by any of the 1,171 African American or 1,017 Native American women identified in the 1860 US Census (or from the approximately five thousand Native women who lived on reservations or were from First Nations not counted in the 1860 census).[1]

The diaries and letters that may have been written by Wisconsin women of color may have fallen victim to the same circumstances that contribute to the relative scarcity of Civil War–era diaries and letters from women of the North. Women of the North may not have written as many letters as the men at the front (estimated at forty-five thousand letters per day) as these women's lives were filled with not only their own responsibilities but also additional responsibilities caused by the absence of family members. Recipients at home lovingly preserved letters from the front, whereas soldiers often burned their letters from home before a battle. The letters that Northern women wrote did not receive high priority on the trains and riverboats bearing soldiers and supplies to the front, and thus some were never delivered.[2] Letters that were sent south did not always reach their intended recipients as soldiers moved to new locations.[3]

The letters contained in this volume include letters between civilians (Annie Cox); letters returned home as part of the recipient's final effects (Sarah Powers, Ann Waldo, Susan Brown); and letters sent to an individual who was primarily in a single location during the war (Belle Arnold Sleeper). Mary Burwell and her husband, Andrew, made an agreement to preserve their letters so that they might share them after the war; his role as a cook who was not directly involved in battle may have enabled him to save Mary's letters. I have not determined how Margaret Patchin's letters were able to escape destruction at the warfront.

Most of the primary materials contained in this volume are based on transcriptions of women's writings (Emily Quiner, Ann Waldo, Susan Brown, Margaret Patchin, Sarah Powers, and Mary Burwell). When possible, I compared these transcriptions to the original materials and made alterations if the transcription did not fit the context or the transcriber had indicated that the original was illegible. I transcribed the letters from Annie Cox and Belle Arnold Sleeper from images of the original materials. I maintained the original spelling or misspelling unless the spelling obscured the meaning of the letter (this was especially true for the early letters of Margaret Patchin, whose "creative" spelling often made her thoughts difficult to decipher). Although most of the writings have been used in their entirety, I have excerpted some letters because of their length (indicated with an ellipsis) and I have omitted some of Emily Quiner's diary entries when they provided little information (indicated with an ornament).

Thanks to the staff of the WHS Archives for permission to include the writings of Emily Quiner, Ann Waldo, Susan Brown, and Belle Arnold Sleeper and to the WVM for permission to include the writings of Margaret MacNish Patchin. Annie Cox's letters are included in the Allen Family papers held by the Newberry Library, an open access institution. Permission to use Mary Burwell's letters was provided by the McCain Library and Archives at USM. Jean Bastian, Sarah Powers's great-granddaughter, granted permission to include Sarah's letters that were transcribed into a volume held by the WHS Library. Complete citations for all of these materials can be found in the bibliography.

Library and archives staff were invaluable in the writing of this book. I give special thanks to Andrew Heckroth and Annie Ottman of the WHS, who not only brought me the books but also shared many conversations with me as I was researching and writing this book. Thank you to the staffs of the WHS, WVM, SMU, and the Newberry Library in Chicago, particularly Jennifer Barth, Lee Grady, David Clerkin, Lisa Saywell, Laura Hemming, and Carmella Hatch of the WHS; Russell Horton of the WVM; Cindy Lawler and Andrew Rhoades of USM; and Tyne Lowe and Lisa Schoblasky of the Newberry Library. Thanks also to Steve Drake of the Middleton Area Historical Society, who helped me to locate Emily Quiner's school; to Terry Pease of Wyocena, who shared information about the Patchin family; and to Bobbie Erdman, director of the Berlin Historical Society, who provided information on places Belle Arnold Sleeper spoke about in her letters. Special thanks to Linda Endlich, who provided the map of women in this book. The editorial team at the University of Wisconsin Press provided insightful and generous support as my interesting idea became a book that honors and cherishes the contributions of Wisconsin Civil War women.

Deep and loving appreciation is extended to my parents, who inspired my love of history, and to siblings and other family members, who listened patiently to my many anecdotes about the Civil War. Last, thanks to my children and grandchildren Amelia, Jasun, Carmen, Wyatt, Elisa, and Konnor, and especially to my grandson Gavin, whose interest in history assures me that the Civil War will continue to be studied by future generations.

Such Anxious Hours

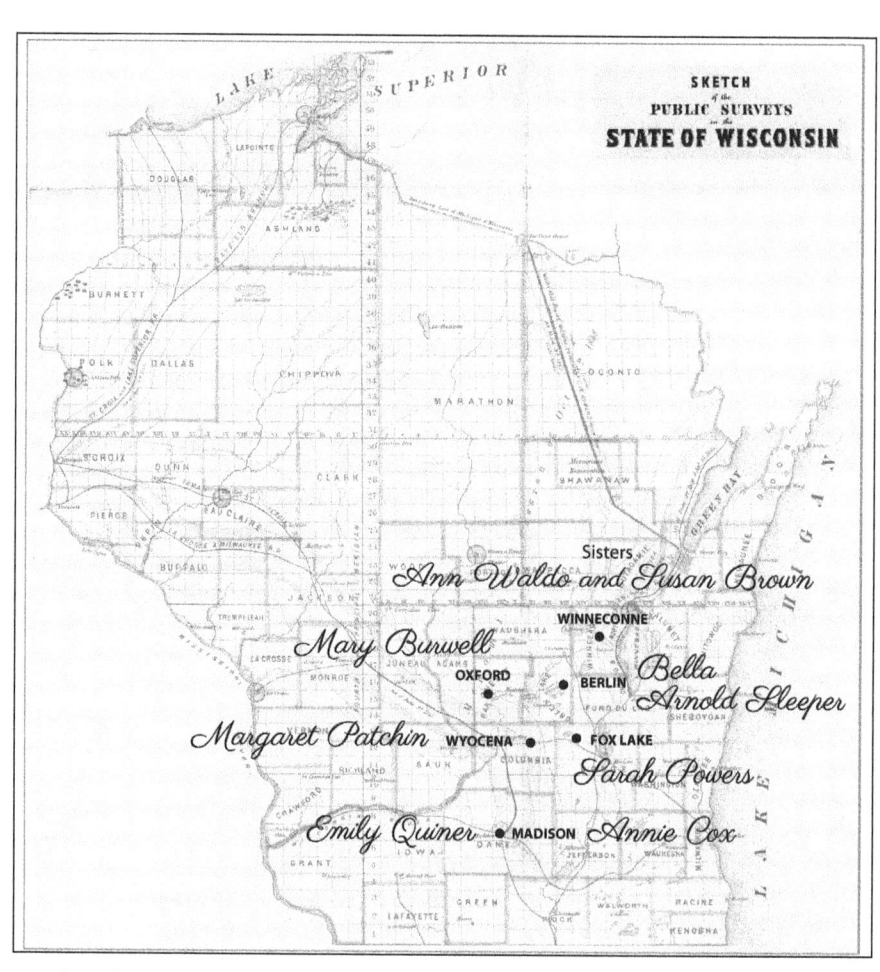

Emily and Annie, Susan and Ann, Margaret, Sarah, Mary, and Belle lived in Wisconsin cities and towns and on farms. (Artist: Linda Endlich; map courtesy of David Rumsey Map Collection, www.davidrumsey.com.)

Introduction

April 13, 1861

The sun's rays spread softly across cities, towns, and farms as the women of Wisconsin began their daily routines, safely ensconced in their homes and surrounded by their families. By the end of that day the surrender of Fort Sumter in South Carolina had plunged their nation into war and changed the lives and histories of each of these women.

When 42 percent of the Wisconsin's adult male population was called into service, women became the majority adult population.[1] Women were also called to service as they expanded their domestic roles to support the troops and assumed the responsibilities of the absent men.

The story of Wisconsin's soldiers in the Civil War began soon after the news of the surrender of Fort Sumter reached Madison. The Wisconsin legislature had adjourned the previous Saturday, but Governor Alexander Randall immediately called the legislature back into a special session to respond to President Lincoln's call for each state to provide troops to put down the insurrection. On Tuesday, April 16, the legislature approved Lincoln's request for a single regiment of 780 men from Wisconsin and issued bonds to support the war.[2] Over the next four years, Wisconsin would send eighty thousand soldiers to the front and spend $12 million.[3] Wisconsin soldiers' first engagement in the war was at Falling Waters, Virginia, on July 2, 1861, and their last was at the capture of Jefferson Davis on May 10, 1865.[4] The war brought honor and acclaim to many Wisconsin troops, including those of the Iron Brigade who fought at Bull Run, Antietam, and Gettysburg.[5] The war brought pain and suffering to families throughout

Wisconsin as fifteen thousand of Wisconsin's soldiers were wounded or disabled and eleven thousand died from wounds or disease.[6]

The story of Wisconsin women in the Civil War also began soon after the fall of Fort Sumter as women gathered to sew flags and clothing and to assemble supplies to sustain their soldiers. The women's stories of the Wisconsin home front in the Civil War were recorded in their diaries and letters. Some women sought greater understanding of the turbulence of the war years by recording their activities and thoughts in diaries. In these diaries, women could record their personal history of the war, take pride in their own home front contributions to the war, show the daily patterns of their lives, and have a safe place in which to share their perspectives. These diaries offered a place in which the writer's "view on the universe matters."[7]

As men departed for the front, many women reached out to their soldiers and to one another through their letters. The letters sent to soldiers at the front served many purposes. Some sought soldiers' advice and approval as wives were thrust into making financial and farming decisions on their own. Others offered counsel and prayers that the soldiers would not succumb to the temptations of liquor, prostitution, and other vices. Some letters served to keep soldiers bound within their families and communities by recounting tales of young children growing up without their fathers and by sharing news and gossip about friends and neighbors. Others connected soldiers to the war beyond their regiments as the outcome of battles in other arenas reached the Northern states more quickly than it reached some soldiers in the south.[8] Still others expressed frustration and bewilderment at the restrictions that military service brought to the independence of the freedom-loving Wisconsin soldiers. Some letters expressed concern and worry that the recipient would lose his life as well as his independence. The letters sent to friends and family at home shared war news, both national and personal, and served to reduce the loneliness and fear that the war had brought to their lives.

Relatively few of the letters and diaries written by Wisconsin women have survived the ravages of time, especially measured against the volumes of letters and diaries from Wisconsin's Civil War soldiers. Among the surviving documents are the writings of Emily Quiner and Annie Cox of Madison; Ann Waldo and Susan Brown of Winneconne; Margaret MacNish Patchin of Wyocena; Sarah Powers of Fox Lake; Mary Burwell of Oxford; and Rosabella Augusta (Belle) Arnold Sleeper of Berlin. Their diaries and letters shared their opinions about the war, their worries about loved ones, and their contributions to the war. This volume reveals their story of the Civil War in the words they recorded more than 150 years ago.

Emily Quiner and Annie Cox were among the 6,648 residents who called Wisconsin's capital city of Madison home.[9] They were the same age and mentioned many of the same places in their accounts of the Civil War years, and both were acquainted with Wisconsin state senators. Despite these similarities Annie and Emily did not mention each other in their writings, for they differed greatly in social status. Emily knew state senators and other officials as her father's equals; Annie was acquainted with these individuals as the stepdaughter of an itinerant carpenter whose family worked for its keep in the homes of others.

In 1861 Emily Quiner was a twenty-one-year-old part-time schoolteacher and university student who lived with her parents and her siblings Fannie (twenty-two), Maria (nineteen), Ellen (fifteen), Kate (thirteen), Alice (eleven), and Charles (eight).[10] Emily's father, E. B. Quiner, was the former publisher of the Watertown *Democratic State Register*. Mr. Quiner had changed his political leanings and in 1858 moved with his family to Madison, where he served as the clerk to the state legislature and then as secretary to the governor. During most of the war, Emily and her family lived in a home on Main Street between Carroll and Henry Streets.[11]

In 1861 Annie Cox, an aspiring artist, was the twenty-one-year-old daughter of Michael Poad, a miner from Cornwall, England, and Elizabeth Baker, originally from Boston. Elizabeth left Michael shortly after Annie's birth and was granted one of the first divorces in Wisconsin.[12] Elizabeth subsequently married Charles J. Cox, Annie's Pa. During much of the war, the Cox family lived on the corner of Mifflin and Canal (now Hancock) Streets, three-quarters of a mile from the Quiner family.[13] Annie's family also included her fourteen-year-old half-sister, Florance.[14]

The mother of Susan Brown and her younger sister, Ann, had passed away in 1834, when Susan was six and Ann was only a year old. When their stepmother treated the sisters with cruelty and neglect, Susan took responsibility for Ann, helping other girls with their arithmetic in exchange for food. By the age of fifteen Susan had learned to sew from her Uncle Joseph, who was a tailor, and had also begun teaching school. When Susan married Waldo Brown, on June 1, 1847, she exacted a promise from him that he would also provide a home for her sister.[15] While living with Susan and Waldo, Ann met and married her brother-in-law's cousin Morris Waldo. Ann and Morris moved to Ripon, where their daughter Della was born in

1858.[16] Susan Brown was a housewife, schoolteacher, and mother to two sons, Willis (thirteen) and Edward (four).[17] Susan and her family lived in the town of Winneconne, population 1,184, which had been established when the Menomonie people were forced off their land in 1852.[18] When the war began and Morris Waldo went off to war, thirty-four-year-old Susan again welcomed her younger sister into her home.

Margaret MacNish Patchin and her husband, Augustus, were farmers near the town of Wyocena, population 1,352.[19] When the war began in April 1861 Margaret was forty-three and pregnant with her eighth child. Her three oldest children had died when they were young, but her sons James (seventeen), Elbert (twelve), Orlo (ten), and John (eight) survived and assumed many of Augustus's farm responsibilities when he enlisted. Margaret had little schooling, and her letters often spoke of the challenges she faced in writing to her Augustus.[20]

Twenty-seven-year-old Sarah Powers and her thirty-four-year-old husband, Norman, had been married for six years in 1862 and farmed near the village of Fox Lake, where they lived with their children, Milton (five), Sarah Adelaide (four), and George (born in 1861). When Norman enlisted, Sarah moved with their children to Fond du Lac to live with her parents. This move was a substantial change in environment for Sarah. The village of Fox Lake had a population of 1,467.[21] In contrast, Fond Du Lac, the major trading center for the Fox Valley, boasted a population of 5,547 as well as gristmills, a post office, four elementary schools, and a high school.[22]

Twenty-one-year-old Mary E. Swannell was living on a farm in Marquette County with her parents when the war began in 1861. Within a few months she married Andrew Burwell, and they moved to a farm near what is now the town of Endeavor, where their daughter, Lucy, was born in 1863. After Andrew's enlistment, Mary Burwell returned with her daughter to family in Oxford, making occasional trips to her own farm. Oxford, with a population of 625, was also in Marquette County.[23]

Rosabella (Belle) Arnold was eighteen years old in 1861 and living in Berlin, Wisconsin, with her mother and brothers. Her older brother, Wiley Arnold, was a good friend of Charles Bennett Palmer, who worked at the *Berlin Courant*, where Belle was employed as a typesetter.[24] At the beginning of the war Belle enjoyed gossiping about the people in her community of 1,450.[25] During the early years of the war Belle married Hiram Sleeper. As the war progressed, Belle's carefree life changed as Hiram, her brother Wiley, and her friend Charles joined the Union Army.

These eight women were among the 775,881 residents of Wisconsin in its twelfth year of statehood, a population that included 1,171 African Americans and 1,017 "civilized Indians" who lived among the predominantly Caucasian population of the state.[26] Most of Wisconsin's population lived in the southern third of the state. Much of the northern two-thirds of the state was regarded as frontier land, despite the presence of reservations where members of the Ojibwa, Menomonie, Stockbridge Munsee, Iroquois, and Brotherton peoples lived.[27] None of the residents of these reservations were counted in the census, and members of the Winnebago (Hoocąągra) and Potawatomi nations were not counted at all as they were not considered "civilized Indians."[28]

The voices of Emily and Annie, Susan and Ann, Margaret, Sarah, Mary, and Belle emanate from the diverse environments of Wisconsin and from their differing experiences of Civil War life. Emily Quiner's diary, begun the day she learned of the fall of Fort Sumter, served as a place in which she could "clarify, conceptualize, and evaluate" her experiences as well as find a place of confidence and privacy in the crowded households of her own family and of the Carey family, with whom she boarded during her time as a schoolteacher in Madison.[29] A single young woman in an upper-class household, Emily used her diary to discuss her volunteer efforts for the Union cause as well as a life of picnics, lectures, and visits with friends; she also revealed an unfulfilled desire to make a difference in the world.

Annie Cox's letters to Gideon Allen provided her with a vehicle in which she could express her strong, well-articulated opinions on the war, slavery, and myriad other topics. Her letters also show her common bond with Gideon Allen; they were each burdened by a lack of opportunity and by their families' financial positions.

The remaining letters were written from the women at the home front to their loved ones at the warfront. In contrast to the letters written from the warfront, which were often shared with other family members and friends and with the local newspaper, the letters written from the home front were addressed to a single individual, and thus the correspondent was freer to reflect her own personality and needs. Mary Burwell and Ann Waldo's affectionate letters to their absent husbands attempted to bring their soldiers into the day-to-day activities of their household and to sustain the loving relationships that were the foundations of their marriages. Susan Brown's letters to Ann and to Morris Waldo were reportorial in nature as she shared news of family and neighbors while also revealing the heavy burdens she carried for the combined Brown and Waldo households. Sarah Powers's letters to her Norman reflected a desire to bridge the miles between them while also expressing her deep frustration when he, failing to receive her letters, experienced the despair of loneliness. Margaret MacNish Patchin led an isolated existence on the farm, and her letters shared her feeling of abandonment when Augustus went off to war. As the war progressed, her skill as a correspondent increased, and she gained new confidence in her abilities as a farmer. Belle Arnold Sleeper's letters reflected the changes the war had brought in her life as she moved from being a lively, free-spirited young girl to her life as a newly married wife desperate for news from her soldier husband. Taken together, the writings of these women offer a diverse narrative on the role, challenges, and contributions of Wisconsin women on the Civil War home front.

CHAPTER I

April 1861 to April 1862

On Sunday, April 14, Madison residents gathered on Pinkney Street for the reading of a telegram announcing the surrender of Fort Sumter.[1] The next day Emily Quiner began a diary of her experiences during the Civil War. For the next two and a half years, this diary reflected Emily's thoughts and involvement in the war as well as everyday life in Madison, Wisconsin.[2]

During the first days of the war, Emily was greatly involved in the war effort; she raised money, participated in patriotic gatherings, and sewed a flag for the troops to carry into battle, a demonstration of her patriotism and domestic prowess.[3] By April 22, Emily began balancing the new demands of the war with her ongoing responsibilities as she prepared to teach the summer session at a school in the town of Madison, where she boarded with the Carey family.[4]

In her first diary entry, Emily revealed "her war-like feelings," which were echoed in Wisconsin governor Alexander Randall's call for troops: "Let the President call for 100,000 more men, Wisconsin will not be content to furnish one regiment alone."[5] Governor Randall also recognized the necessity for women to play a role in the war and issued a letter on April 22 to the "Patriotic Women of Wisconsin," calling on them to prepare lint and bandages for the soldiers. Governor Randall's letter also noted "that when the occasion calls, many, very many Florence Nightingales will be found in our goodly land."[6]

During April 1861, the Union and Confederate governments and citizens made decisions that would shape the events of the next four years. Robert E. Lee, one of the 286 out of a thousand active army officers to resign their commissions in the US Army to serve the Confederacy, declined Lincoln's offer to command all Union forces and soon assumed command of all of Virginia's army and naval forces.[7] On April 20, Lincoln made the strategic decision to blockade all Southern ports, greatly curtailing the ability of the Confederacy to obtain both military and civilian supplies.[8]

EMILY

April 15, 1861: News came this morning that Fort Sumpter [sic] had been taken by the Southern forces under Gen. Beaureguard [sic], it caused a good deal of excitement here, though it had been daily expected for some time before Anderson surrendered after a gallant defense and when the fort was in flames, he left it with seventy-five men, his entire command was infuried, his colors flying and band playing Yankee Doodle. His opponents it is reported had forty killed and one hundred wounded.

The Wisconsin Legislature were to have adjourned this morning at nine-o'clock and many of them left here on Saturday, as soon as the telegraph came. The Governor recalled the members and ordered a new sitting to consult on the question of putting the State on a war footing. We went to the Assembly Chamber at seven. They seemed to be discussing the question in a general manner among themselves, on motion of Judge Spooner a Committee was appointed to consult on the matter, and the assembly adjourned until seven o'clock PM.[9] War seemed inevitable and every one seems to be willing to do their best in their country's service.

I have an invitation from Lottie Lattimer to Mrs. Bliss' to-night, but cannot as I am to have company. George C. Smith, Miss Rogers, Misses Bodwells, and Mr. Newton came in the evening. Had a pleasant time, talked about the news of the morning and got war like in our feelings. Patriotism is a great ingredient of Northern blood and I think our country has nothing to fear in regard to the loyalty of her sons and daughters. Mr. Newton is a democrat and the rest of us being Republicans, we had quite a war of words. After our friends were gone, we talked of the events of the day for a while and then retired.

April 16, 1861, Tuesday: This morning we went to the Senate Chambers to hear the debate on the war bill. The resolution to put the State on a war footing passed the Senate and was carried into the Assembly, where it was again discussed by many members and passed. The bill in relation to bank currency was taken up and also discussed, a Committee appointed and the Assembly adjourned until tomorrow morning at nine. There were several

The entrance to the capitol in 1861, from the corner of Main and Carroll near the Quiner family home. (Wisconsin Historical Society, WHS 23459)

ladies in attendance this morning, Kate Kavenaugh and Fannie, went into the country this afternoon. Maria and I went up town, went to Klanber's and to Bliss Book store, purchased the book in which I am writing. Fay Hubbard said I would never write it half through, that I would get tired of it in two weeks. I told him I should not, that I should write every day, and that every entry would be longer than the one preceding it. He said it would be a marvel if I did and it remains to be seen which was in the right. We came home in time to see Kate and Fannie start for the country. Preparations are making to send the regiment ordered by the President for the protection of the Federal Government. The Assembly this morning voted 200,000 dollars for war purposes and Col. Hood said that two Garrison companies in Milwaukee had already offered their services, all are waiting anxiously for more news.[10]

We went to the [Temperance] Lodge in the evening. Maria went with me and stood in the ante-room until recess.[11] We had two candidates inducted. Mr. Craig was gone, and the news of the day took away the interest of the meeting somewhat and we adjourned early.[12] There was a sociable appointed for the coming evening and as the Committee had done nothing in regard to preparations, we took it in hand, and arranged a program impromptu. It recessed to be a good one. There were several strangers in tonight. Adjourned to meet again in Lodge [indecipherable] on the next evening. Mr. Krupp came home with us. He seems very lonely without Fannie & Kate. Got acquainted with Mr. Bristol, a student of the University. He was instated tonight. He seems very pleasant and intelligent.

April 17, 1861, Wednesday: The legislature met this morning and as there was no further business adjourned sine die [without assigning a day to meet again]. The Governor's Guard tendered their services to the Governor and were accepted amid hearty cheers. The Star Spangled Banner was then sung by the entire company. I shall copy it to preserve my remembrance of this day.[13]

The song was greeted with tremendous cheers and the members of the Legislature parted to go to their homes, with a determination in their hearts to do all they could for the cause of their country. We heard today of many friends who had enlisted to join the companies who are going to the seat of war. The sociable this evening was well attended. Maria went with me. We had a good resume. Dr. Cass read a poem entitled The Tragedy by T. B. Aldrich, which was beautiful. Miss Crocker recited Joan of Arc at Reims which was very appropriate to the occasion. I recited Ralph Farnham's last dream which called forth hearty applause, and caused more tears. It is so beautiful I shall copy it.

Mr. Baker then read, The "Charge of the Light Brigade." A toast was given by Mr. Purple "Our country free now and forever" responded to by Dr. Brisbane. One by P. G. Scofield "The Good Templars [?] Volunteers" responded to by Mr. Hastings he spoke feelingly and brought tears to many eyes. Mr. Fox sang several patriotic pieces and we came home at half past eleven. Mr. High came home with us.[14]

April 18, 1861, Thursday: An unpleasant day, and my spirits down to zero, we still have news from all quarters in the South. Heard today that a vessel laden with bacon and also one with ammunition had been seized on its way down the Mississippi by the Union men.[15] Went out this afternoon to Rosa's staid there a short time, went up town with. Got some ribbon to make red, white and blue cockades. Mr. Williamson gave me the ribbon. Rosa came home with us and we made the rosettes, wore them to the patriotic meeting in the evening. A large crowd present in the Assembly hall, the meeting was for the purpose of raising funds to support the families of the volunteers. Nearly 8,000 dollars was subscribed. The meeting was very enthusiastic. The volunteers marched in amid tremendous cheers. The band playing Yankee Doodle and the crowd sang Star Spangled Banner. The meeting adjourned to meet again in one week.

April 19, 1861, Friday: Went to Dr. Brisbane's with mother. Meet [sic] Will, he said that news had first been received that there had been fighting on the Baltimore Railroad, that the Southerners had some of the track, and the mob assaulted troops in passing through Baltimore. Three persons were killed, the President had issued orders for double the number of troops. Saw young Mrs. Brisbane at home, said her husband had gone to enlist, felt very badly about it. I pitied her very much.[16]

Saw Lottie Lattimer said she was going to have a cockade. Mrs. Bliss bought ribbon for rosettes for shoes and collars. I have seen several ladies with them in the skirt.

Came home and spent the evening alone.

April 20, 1861, Saturday: Went this afternoon with Maria to get up a subscription for a flag for the Third Volunteer Corp, met with good success, raised 84 dollars together with what the School Choir gave.

Went in the evening to the City Hall to see the Governor's Guard drill. They are a very good-looking company and will be Company A in the first regiment. Saw several of the volunteers from Madison and bade them farewell as I shall not probably speak with them again.

April 21, 1861, Sunday: Went to church this morning at the Baptist Church. There was a sermon preached in the Episcopal Church by the pastor, Mr. Britton, to the volunteers who attended in uniform. The discourse is said to have been very appropriate and impressive. I would like to have gone but thought I must go to my own church. Dr. Brisbane's son preached in uniform. Went to the Congregational Chapel this afternoon. Do not like Dr. Baylor as well as our minister. Came home and wrote in my diary, read aloud from *Gold Fool*, and 'Emerson's Conduct of Life.' Dr. Brisbane, Jr. preached in the evening to volunteers. Pa and Ma went with us as we were starting. Mr. High came for Maria, she had gone and he accompanied me. A large crowd in attendance. Choir sang Star Spangled Banner. As the people were going out Dr. Brisbane announced telegraph news from Fort Pickens. The rebels were defeated with loss of three hundred men. The audience received this with three hearty cheers. The volunteers formed in a line and marched from the church and down the street to the sound of muffled drums. Found Miss Kavenaugh and Fannie at home and also Kate's brothers all very much excited about the war news, sat and talked an hour or two before going to bed.[17]

April 22, 1861, Monday: Commenced cleaning house. Went up town and then Dr. Kayes took me out to my schoolhouse. Went to Mr. Danning's, Mr. Tenney's and Carey's engaged board for the summer at Carey's, saw the schoolhouse, going to commence teaching a week from today. Came home. Went in the evening to Governor's Guard drill.

April 23, 1861, Tuesday: Cleaned the parlor. Went in the evening to the Lodge, had the blues could scarcely keep from crying all the evening. Dr. Brisbane, Jr. & wife initiated. She is very sad about his going and scarcely expects his return. While Brother Walters was making remarks on the dependence of brothers to the war she fainted, and when she recovered was taken home. Choir sang Star Spangled Banner and Red White & Blue.[18]

All felt very sad at parting with our friends perhaps never to see them again. Nomination of officers.

April 24, 1861, Wednesday: Went up town at seven o'clock, came home and got ready to go with the rest to the Capitol where the members of the order and the officers of the Guards were presented with rosettes of remembrance and bade God Speed in the cause of freedom. Went at twelve to the depot to see the Companies leave for Milwaukee, the rendezvous of the regiment. An immense crowd collected procession of the military, five Companies, Carriages, & came at 1 o'clock. Denin sisters sang Star Spangled Banner. Keyes and others addressed the volunteers, and then the friends took leave of them. They entered the cars, and were bound away amid cheering, waving of hats and handkerchiefs, and cries of "God Bless you" from every side. It was an affecting and interesting scene. Cora Williams came home with me. Went down to the lake in the afternoon.

April 25, 1861, Thursday: Cora & Hattie, and two or three other girls came to spend the afternoon with the children. Went up town. Met Lottie and Miss Taylor went up to the cupola in the City Hall. Randall Guards drilling stopped a while to see them. [indecipherable, paper torn] to see Miss Fernandez, she was not at home. Came back to tea, and then went and got a basket and called on Nancy McConnell, not at home. Saw Bob, stopped a few minutes at the gate. Came home and went to bed. Adjourned meeting of citizens tonight.[19]

April 26, 1861, Friday: Getting ready to go in the country some and mended all the forenoon, a warm, pleasant day. Went out to make some calls. Conversation on the State of the country, entirely.

April 28, 1861, Sunday: Went to church, a beautiful Spring morning. The air fragrant and calm. Just such a sweet Sabbath—as I dearly love. Dr. Brisbane preached a beautiful sermon from the text "Passed my Fathers are one &c" [Matt. 23:69]. We staid at home in the afternoon, Dr. Brisbane preached to the volunteers in the evening and the choir sang the "Star Spangled Banner." Sat up until eleven o'clock to finish "Miss Gilbert's Career."

April 29, 1861, Monday: The school seems to be a very pleasant one, and I think I shall like it much. Was a good deal disappointed in not having a room by myself [at the Careys' house, where she was a boarder]. I am so tired of noise, and confusion that when I get home I want to sit down quietly with my own thoughts, but I shall try and get along as well as possible under the circumstances.

April 30, 1861, Tuesday: Rose at six, breakfasted, and went out in the yard, a pleasant day. Crocheted nearly two hours and then went to school. Got everything into sunny order today. Had no trouble whatever. Went to tea. It looked some like rain. I walked home, got there just as the family had finished tea. Went to the Lodge, had a pleasant time. Left before close. Mr. Baker came home with me. Found Lottie & D. Fernandez at home sewing on Mrs. Bliss's flags they remained late. Pa came home, had a good deal of fun about the "Home Guards." Promised to come home Thursday night to help finish the flag.

The State Fair grounds outside of Madison were transformed into Camp Randall, the training site for seventy thousand of the eighty thousand Wisconsin's troops.[20] The conversion of the State Fair grounds to a military camp was a slow process, and some felt that the man responsible for this change, H. A. Tenney, was getting rich at the expense of the soldiers.[21]

Emily also experienced a transition this month as she began her teaching responsibilities. Her war effort increased as she joined with other Madison women in sewing shirts for soldiers with the assistance of a new technology—the sewing machine. The integration of sewing machines into the production of clothing made the large-scale production of shirts possible by reducing the time needed to make one shirt from fourteen hours for one sewn by hand to one hour for one made on a machine.[22] Governor Randall sponsored a dinner for the women who were sewing shirts for the soldiers and acknowledged the unusual nature of the contributions of the "Patriotic Ladies of Madison" in a letter. In his letter he stated, "It is not the business of your sex to mingle in the severer strifes of the thronging heaving world" and acknowledged women's role in providing "comforts and necessities for the gallant sons of our beloved State."[23]

May 1, 1861, Wednesday: The several companies composing the 2nd infantry regiment commenced coming in today, one from La Crosse, and another from Portage came this afternoon. They are to Camp on the fairgrounds. The barracks are not quite ready and they will remain in town until they are.

May 2, 1861, Thursday: Went to school as usual. Nothing of importance occurred aside from the regular school exercises. Came home, after tea. Found Mrs. De Mott here. She staid to tea, and Ma & she went up to the Assembly Chamber to work on the shirts for the soldiers. Maria and I went up and staid about an hour and then to Mrs. Seymour's to sew on the flag. Lottie, Kate, Laura, & Addie Ripley were there. We worked until ten o'clock and then the boys i.e. Chappell, Gay & Sam came. We finished the stripes and fourteen stars on each side, listened to some singing by Vesey and came home at 1 o'clock. Fay came with us.

May 3, 1861, Friday: Awoke this morning to the pleasing consciousness that it was raining heavily with not the slightest prospect of cessation. Hoped that some of my friends would remember me and offer to take me out, but who ever was in luck on a Friday? Put on a thick hood sail & took my umbrella and started.

Of all the walks I ever took this was certainly most cleansing. It rained and it blew and between my umbrella and basket and bedraggled skirts, and a three-mile walk in the rain, I fared poorly and was completely exhausted when I came in sight of the schoolhouse. I walked on the railroad track and reached the end of my journey in a condition utterly indescribable. Laid my dress by the fire and sat all day in school with wet feet, wet skirts and head throbbing with pains. About eighteen scholars present. After I reached the schoolhouse it stopped raining and after hailing a few minutes commenced snowing beautifully and continued for an hour. Went to tea, intended to have gone home tonight, but was too tired. Went to bed early. I cleaned up and there was a prospect of a pleasant day on the morrow. Have heard no war news today. Two more companies arrived. One of the men from Portage broke his leg.

May 4, 1861, Saturday: A pleasant morning, breakfasted early and about half past seven started for home. The walking very bad, meet [sic] Mrs. Allen and Miss Phelps going up town to work on shirts for soldiers. Got home at eight o'clock very tired rested a little while, got ready and went with Ma & Fannie to the Assembly Chambers. It was crowded and presented a busy spectacle. There were ten sewing machines in operation. Staid until 1 o'clock, went to dinner and then back in the afternoon. There were a great many present this afternoon and we accomplished a good deal. The President of the meeting said there would be no necessity of working tomorrow. We met again in the evening, and altogether finished about thirteen dozen today.

May 5, 1861, Sunday: Rainy and cold again, got ready for church. Dr. Brisbane preached from the first chapter of Genesis. When the services were over found it storming violently. Mrs. Craig got us umbrellas and we started home got as far as Mrs. Wise's. Mrs. De Mott was with us. The wind blew so hard that we could not keep an umbrella up and we went into Mrs. Wise's for shelter took dinner there staid an hour and came home in the rain, 2nd time I have been "out in the rain" this season. Finished reading "Bittersweet" very good. Went to bed at four o'clock, sick.

May 6, 1861, Monday: Walked to school. Very tired when I got there glad to find a warm fire. The wind blew violently all day. Went to Mrs. Carey's at night.

May 7, 1861, Tuesday: Cold and storming worried all day for fear it would storm so that I could not go home tonight, rained all the afternoon. I went home to tea, had concluded not to go home, however it cleared off after tea and I started home. Went to the Lodge. There were fifty-two of the members of the Randall Guards inducted. It was a sight worth seeing, fifty-two young men binding themselves to abstain from everything which could intoxicate. I sincerely hope those pledges will be kept and that this terrible curse of soldiers in all lands will have no power over them. The officers for the next quarter were installed. We came home at eleven o'clock. Mr. High came home with Fannie and I came along.

May 8, 1861, Wednesday: A beautiful morning. Rose at 6 got ready and started for school at half seven, had a pleasant walk. It seemed almost cruel to call the children into the schoolroom. The girls brought me some beautiful violets. Went home with Hattie Carey tonight. Her mother is a very nice woman. We went up to the quarry after sundown and climbed to the top of the hill. Mrs. Carey brought home a poor little lamb which had been bitten by the dogs. It was a pretty little thing. The children are going to take extra care of it, make it live if possible.

May 9, 1861, Thursday: Got up at 6, had breakfast. Went up to the top of the hill with the children to get flowers. Grand quantities of Passion flowers or Rock Lillies as they call them here. The scholars came from all directions and we had plenty of flowers for one day. Kept some of the scholars tonight to get them tea, many staid till five. Went to tea. Afterwards went home. Was dreadfully tired, dressed myself and went up to the Assembly Room sewed a while. Went home and to bed.

May 10, 1861, Friday: Went to school. Cold and windy & raining. After walking three miles did not feel very smart. Scholars did very well today.

May 11, 1861, Saturday: Sick this morning. Felt hardly able to sit up. Before I went to school the Lieutenant and Orderly Sergeant of the Beloit Rifles came to Mrs. Carey's after butter, said that they had had none for a week.[24] Came again in the afternoon, got a loaf of bread & some milk. We went up on the hill this [indecipherable] to get flowers. Nellie, Hattie & Esmosette Stoel [?] came out this morning and staid all day. Went into the Camp [Randall] ground tonight. Saw the men's seven barracks &c. and the soldier's arrived. Walked home, dressed, went up to the Assembly Room and had a good time. The Governor gave a supper to the ladies who worked on the shirts. The table looked very nice indeed. The band played Yankee Doodle and all the other patriotics.

May 12, 1861, Sunday: Went to church. The Randall Guards were there in uniform. They are a fine looking company. Went to hear Dr. Baylor in the evening.

May 22, 1861, Wednesday: Walked out to school, a beautiful morning. Staid to hear some lessons, sweep the schoolhouse too and as I was going home met Lottie, Rosa & Maria with Mr. Baker and Mr. Rockwell, coming after me. Went to Mrs. Carey's, rested a while, and then started for the boat, had a pleasant row home. Got windy and went to the sociable in the evening. The Red, White & Blue Lodge [Masonic] was organized, and they hold their first meeting at Camp Randall on Thursday next, there was about 120 members. Had a pleasant time. Came home about half past eleven. Mr. Baker home with Rosa & I.

May 26, 1861, Sunday: Went to church, Dr. Brisbane preached a splendid sermon. It cleared off beautifully during service. Came home, read till three o'clock and then went to Bible class. Mr. Bray came along with us said he was going out to Camp Randall as we were all going concluded to go together started about five o'clock. Got as far as the corner of State Street when it began to rain and we very reluctantly retraced our footsteps. It rained all the afternoon and evening, and prevented our going to church.

May 27, 1861, Monday: Went to school as usual. Nothing unusual happened today the old routine of school duties which get so tiresome sometimes went on as ever. Went home to Mrs. Carey's at six, having staid to sew on the flag, we have got it almost done, took some stars home to cut, went to bed at eight.

May 28, 1861, Tuesday: A pleasant day. The country has put on its robes of beauty and everything is beautiful indeed. June that queen of months is approaching crowned with flowers and beautiful with waving branches and graceful foliage. How I love this month, so fresh and beautiful, as the blighting heat of summer has despoiled its springtime verdure. I walked home tonight and enjoyed it much. Went to the Lodge had a pleasant time. Sociable appointed for tomorrow night. Mr. Gray offered to take me out in his boat tomorrow morning. Mr. Baker came home with me & Mr. High with Fannie.

May 29, 1861, Wednesday: Had a nice boat ride this morning. It was very pleasant indeed. Fannie & Maria went with me. Maria went to school with me and staid all day and walked home with me tonight. People are talking now of the tragic death of Col. Ellsworth. This noble young commander of the Chicago Zouaves, shot in Alexandria by one of the rebels, Jackson by name, while in the act of trampling upon a secession flag taken from the top of his [Jackson's] hotel. The death of this brave young commander was speedily avenged by one of his men by the name of Brummell [sic: Brownell] who run him through with his bayonet killing him instantly. Great excitement prevailed and his regiment have sworn by every hair of his head to avenge his death in that of thousands of his murderers, his body was embalmed and buried with [indecipherable] ceremonies, and the nation mourns his loss. We went to the sociable, had a pleasant time.[25]

May 30, 1861, Thursday: Went to school in a boat this morning. Staid tonight to sew on the flag, finished sewing around the stars. Went to Mrs. Danning's. They all went out to see a neighbor but I and the children. We talked until nine o'clock, and then went to bed.

May 31, 1861, Friday: Cora and I had a nice ramble this morning over the farm. Went to see the sheep & horses, and goslings. Through the woods, Mrs. Danning's farm is one of the finest in this vicinity and very pleasantly located full of slopes and undulations and very nicely kept. Mrs. Botkin came to Mrs. Danning's this morning she is a very nice old lady, her sister was with her, she has her maiden sisters living with who are over sixty years of age, she asked me to call, and I shall some time.

Mr. Tusoill, the school superintendent came to see me this afternoon, and gave me my certificate. I was to go home in a boat tonight but it looked so stormy that I concluded I would not wait and started in with Mrs. Maxwell on a load of lumber. When we had got almost to town, met Fannie & Mrs. Craig in a buggy going after me. I exchanged news and we went back to the Camp, drove around a while, and then came home.[26]

June 5, 1861, Wednesday: Ma went with me to school had a pleasant ride. A meeting tonight to arrange a picnic for the soldiers. Mr. Smith said he would come for me and I concluded I would go in.

Went to the meeting. They appointed me as a committee to bag provisions which very agreeable task I shall escape by being a school marm.

June 8, 1861, Saturday: Went over to Mrs. Wise's this morning, got some flowers & also went to Mrs. Sulmons's afterwards went to the store. A warm day for the premier. We went down to the Camp in the Omnibus, when there went through to the mess hall, worked three hours getting the tables ready, they looked very nice indeed, and we had an surplus of provisions. We had a speech from Col. Boon in behalf of the soldiers, one from Mr. Baylor in behalf of the Ladies, and several others gratis. The soldiers there cheered "the ladies," "The Star Spangled Banner" the Union, and almost every thing else. They then sang "The Star Spangled Banner" and as there are some fine voices among them it sounded well. The Cornet Band enlivened the whole with excellent music. After the soldiers had retired, the Guard came in and were served by the Ladies, also the Band. The remains of the repast were divided among the soldiers who expressed themselves highly gratified by the attention shown them. I said they should never forget it. We remained on the grounds awhile after services and then came home tired enough.

June 12, 1861, Wednesday: Walked to school Charlie [Carey] went with me. Had the 'blues' terribly this morning. Went to Mr. Kellogg's to tea. Went over to the school house after tea and assisted in raising the flag. We had quite a celebration gave more cheers for the S. S. B. [Star Spangled Banner] & had a patriotic time generally. It looked finely and is quite an item in the neighborhood. Staid at Mr. Kellogg's tonight. Saw them milk the cows. Had more skim milk. Grandma Kellogg recited some forty of her own compositions about the war she is eighty-five years of age and it really showed extraordinary prowess of mind for one so old.

June 13, 1861, Thursday: Looked out this morning and saw my flag floating in grand style. Went to Mrs. Carey's tonight.

June 14, 1861, Friday: Wind blew terribly this morning, found my flag had lowered itself without saying by your leave, took it down. Wind blew dreadfully all day.

∽

June 17, 1861, Monday: Went to school this morning, and when almost there discovered that I had left my key it was too far and too late to go back and I thought that I would make the best of it and so got in at the window. It was very amusing to see the scholars hopping out and in at the window all day but I kept on a sober face and they did not say anything. Went home at night after the key rode home with Mr. Maxwell.

June 18, 1861, Tuesday: Walked to school this morning. Lottie went with me, and we walked home at night, found after we got home that Fannie & Mr. Craig had gone after us in a boat. Went to the Lodge, Mr. Craig said they waited for us an hour and a half. Had a pleasant time. Mr. Baker came home with me & Mr. High with Fannie.

June 19, 1861, Wednesday: Mr. Craig carried me out to school this morning. Maj. Crocker and Fannie went with us. Came after me again at night. Went to the Sociable, staid an hour or two and came home accompanied by Mr. Miller. Made arrangements for a picnic on Saturday.

June 20, 1861, Thursday: Started with the intention of going in the boat when we got up town found that our timer was slow, we were half an hour too late, and so had to walk to school. Went to Mrs. Pierson's to stay tonight. Went out and found some strawberries.

June 21, 1861, Friday: This is a week of mistakes with me. Mrs. P. had no timepiece and as we waited for the nine o'clock train of cars and they did not pass I found myself at the schoolhouse at half past eleven. I was as much provoked as ever in my life but that did no good and as we were to have a picnic in the afternoon, I sent the children home to get ready. We started at one o'clock and after sundry delays in calling for scholars &c we arrived at our destination, and met Fannie's school just coming out.[27] We had a pleasant time on the bank of the lake, a ride in a boat, a supper under the trees, and a general frolic and then adjourned tired enough. Maria & I went up to Mr. Carey's and were glad enough to get a ride home.

June 22, 1861, Saturday: A breezy delightful day, although rather warm. This is the day of our picnic. Started at nine A.M. for the rendezvous, and after searching for various articles and a good deal of fixing we embarked for picnic point. We had a splendid row over, and saw quantities of fish on the other side of the point did not succeed in catching any, found a poor little squirrel in the water half drowned, laid in the sun a while and he soon found his senses and ran off. Went over to McBrides leaving Mr. Baker fishing. Got some cream, a pail of water, and some flowers and started back home again.

Mr. Baker, Maj. Crocker and Maria went out to fish. The rest went to walk and I not having any special desire for either chose myself sentinel and sat down to guard the provisions had a nice time by myself till obliged to defend them against a company of cows, who were determined to investigate the contents of the water pail and baskets. When they returned made preparations for dinner which we took at the fashionable hour of five after having the misfortune of having the ice water spoiled by the obtrusive nose of a cow which stole upon us in an unguarded moment. We had plenty of strawberries with cream, besides everything else nice, and after supper had the pleasure of ministering to the wants of two weary fishermen who had been out all day without water, i.e. the brother of our Governor and Will Atwood. After dinner had literary entertainment interspersed with jokes, laughter, gooseberry picking, machine poetry making, teetering [indecipherable] &, started after sundown for home, made the waters sing with our shouts & laughter. Maria sang her echo song, and we heard a beautiful echo. The full moon was about an hour high as we rounded the point and we had no idea of going home, and accordingly took a beeline for Gooseberry point. The evening was perfectly delightful and I never enjoyed myself better. We arrived at home a little before twelve tired enough.

June 23, 1861, Sunday: Rose this morning with a dreadful headache. Got ready for church, heard Dr. Brisbane. Went to hear the Baccalaureate address [at the University] in the afternoon and to church in the evening.

June 24, 1861, Monday: Mr. Craig took me to school in the boat this morning. I went to the store and then to the lake, when I arrived there I found that I had forgotten my key and soon made the disagreeable necessity of going back for it. I got to school about 9 ¼ o'clock.

June 25, 1861, Tuesday: Went to school as usual. Very warm & sultry all day, and just as the last scholar took his departure clouds began to gather the wind rose and we had a most splendid thunderstorm. I was alone in the schoolhouse and sat by the window to look, listen and wonder & as the flash succeeded flash the rain came in cascades accompanied by the loud peals of thunder, I felt God's awful presence in my very soul. I love a storm when alone, and the wilder it rages the greater the fury of contending elements, the higher and fuller the pleasure I experience. In about an hour and a half the storm abated and it being Tuesday night, I started for home. The air was cool and fresh, and had such an exhilarating effect on my spirits that I walked home in a very different frame of mind from that which I possessed at the close of school. Found Mrs. Craig in the parlor when I arrived, they all laughed at me well for walking so far in the wind. We had ice cream and strawberries, and afterwards went to hear the eulogy on the "life & character of Stephen A. Douglass" by Prof. D. B. Reed.[28] It was very good. We had intended to go to the Lodge after the eulogy but it closed before we were released and therefore we did not go.

June 26, 1861, Wednesday: Today is the annual commencement of the Wisconsin University. I would like very much to go but cannot. Walked to school. Went over to Mr. Tenney's after tea. They were just eating their supper of green peas and new potatoes, and I complied with their request to sit down also.[29]

June 27, 1861, Thursday: Walked home tonight to attend the Horticultural Exhibition at the City Hall. It was fine, I did not go until late. Saw several old friends and enjoyed myself well, left them dancing to the music of the fifth regiment band. Major Larrabee was there. He is an old college friend of Pa's and I saw him for the first time.

June 28, 1861, Friday: Walked out this morning. We raised the flag the second time tonight. It is upon a pole this time and I think it will stay there. Went over to Mr. Maxwell's tonight with Mary, the little Mary got asleep and I brought her part way home, which pleased her mightily.

July 4, 1861, Thursday: Wakened this morning by firing of guns and ringing of bells. Saw the procession go by our house at twelve o'clock, the chief features of which were the thirty-four girls in red, white, & blue to represent the States & nearly two thousand soldiers representing the Fifth & Sixth regiments quartered here.[30]

Went up to Ski Park a little while, heard the Declaration read and the commencement of the nation, came home and a short walk in the evening finished my outdoor performances for the day. This Fourth is an important one to us all, and who could look upon the two thousand brave men who passed through our streets today volunteers to defend our liberty and not feel his patriotism swell within him. Our country is shrouded and darkened by this cloud of civil war but trusting in God as our help and strength and as the supporter of the cause of right we shall yet see the clear sky over our heads and the light of peace and fraternity bearing upon us. Mr. High spent the evening here.

July 5, 1861, Friday: Fannie & I having adjourned our schools till Monday, we set about enjoying our vacation in the most miserable measures possible. In the first place it was very warm. Fannie went to bed as soon as she finished her breakfast and we saw her only at intervals during the day. Celia & Maria & I decorated the parlor with oak leaf wreaths, cherries, and flowers. It took nearly the whole forenoon to arrange them to our satisfaction. Then we concluded we would have a "party" and I made invitations for half a dozen friends to "drop in." Lottie Lattimer & Kittie Hubbard called in the afternoon and were treated to cherry pie. Only four of our guests came. We went down to the lake shore, sat on a boat near the lake, sang, recited, talked, laughed, and came home, finished the evening with ice cream & cake.

July 6, 1861, Saturday: Went up town this morning, came home and sewed till eleven. Mr. Craig called and said that the committee was going across the lake to select a suitable place for a picnic and that he would call at two for us. It was very warm when we started, but when on the water, very cool and pleasant. Went over to "Sugar Bush" rambled around awhile and concluded that that would not do, and embarked for McBride's point. The lake was very rough and the waves occasionally washed over the stern of the boat where I sat so that I was completely wet through, it was so pleasant however I did not mind that. We went up to Mrs. McBride's who gave us a drink of water and all the ripe currants we could eat, besides a beautiful rose apiece, we again sought the shore and ate our luncheon seated and chatted for an hour, and then started for home. The lake was rough but we were not afraid and I rowed with one oar all the way home. Went to the Committee meeting at Mr. C's office, got home at ten tired enough.

July 16, 1861, Tuesday: Mr. Craig came for me today before school was out. I was sick and as always is the case at such times the children were more disorderly than usual. I was almost discouraged. I love my scholars dearly and I do not believe there is one who would willingly cause me pain but they are thoughtless and often seem unkind and ungrateful, but I will try and have patience with them. Went to the lodge, saw Eunice Hastings who has just returned from school, just as saucy and just as ever. There were a good many soldiers present, and we had some good speeches. After the Lodge Mr. Miller took us to ride, it was very pleasant being a bright moonlight evening.

July 17, 1861, Wednesday: Rained in torrents this morning could not go to school. Fannie was at home also and we had a good time till it stopped raining about eleven o'clock, and then we went up town, went to the store. Made arrangements to go out to Camp Randall tonight in the boat. I went with Fanny to her school this afternoon. I believe visiting schools is worse than teaching. Our boat ride tonight ended in a rain down and we staid at home. Mr. High and Mr. Craig came and we spent a very pleasant evening.

July 18, 1861, Thursday: Went to school in the boat. Came in at the soldier's picnic at Camp Randall, & home.[31]

News of the first major battle of the war at Bull Run (Manassas) brought "a chill" to Emily's heart as she learned that 2,700 Union soldiers were killed, wounded, or missing. The July 21 First Battle of Bull Run (known to the Confederacy as 1st Manassas) presaged the long and bloody struggle ahead. Union forces, routed by Confederate troops, made a disorderly retreat to Washington. Although victorious, the Confederates also sustained major losses, with 1,900 killed, wounded, or missing.[32]

Despite Emily's protestations that the news of war had brought a "chill to her heart," her diary entries from late July through August reflect a widespread lack of interest in the war during this time period as the state failed to reach volunteer enlistment quotas and began offering financial incentives to enlist. For the first time in the nation's history, men faced the threat of being drafted if there were not enough volunteers.³³

July 22, 1861, Monday: Went to school in the boat this morning. School about as usual. Went home with Ella Hill. After tea we went after flowers in the meadow and up on the hill got a lot of grass to crystallize. When Mrs. Hill's paper came, the news struck a chill to all our hearts. The telegraph announced the total rout of our troops at Manassas Junction and that between four and five thousand were killed and many taken prisoner. Our 2nd Regiment were in the engagement. Real loss in killed and wounded and taken prisoner not ascertained. Hopes are entertained from the usual exaggeration in such cases that it will turn out better than was supposed.³⁴

July 23, 1861, Tuesday: Went to school this morning as usual. About three o'clock Ma & Nellie, Charlie & Mrs. Carey came out and remained until school closed when we went over to the Lake and came home in the boat. It was very pleasant. Last night news confirmed and scarcely modified except that the losses of our men had been over extended, stragglers coming into Camp in numbers. The 5th & 6th Regiments were ordered to march. Went to the Lodge with a severe headache. Some of the Zouaves were present.

July 24, 1861, Wednesday: Found myself unable to go to school this morning. Fannie kindly offered to go in my place. Lay in bed all the forenoon and in afternoon read some. Fannie came home at night thoroughly tired out. Telegraph tonight; reports that more than two hundred men killed on our side to two thousand of the rebels. Defeat owing to General Patterson's delay in reinforcing us.

July 27, 1861, Saturday: Mr. Craig called this morning to see about the arrangements for going to Fond du Lac next week to the teacher's Association. I wanted to go very much, but want of money and other reasons will keep me at home or rather at school. News tonight nothing of importance. Telegraph reports somewhat more reliable, state the number of killed and wounded to be much less than at first supposed. Our 2nd Regiment lost about forty men. Gen. Patterson has been superseded by Gen. Banks, and

Gen. McClellan has taken Scott's place as commander in chief of the American forces that noble old General being too old to sustain the duties of so arduous an office he will remain however as McClellan's advisor.

July 28, 1861, Sunday: A bright pleasant morning. The 6th Regiment started for Chicago at nine o'clock. Pa went with them. Went to church Rev. Mr. Harwood from Cincinnati preached. Annie Main sang in the choir, she has been gone two years. Services at the Church this afternoon but I did not go. Went to the Congregational Church this evening.

August 4, 1861, Sunday: Woke this morning with a dreadful headache. It is warm as ever and it seems almost impossible to exist. How I pity our poor soldiers several degrees farther south under the burning sun. I hope there will be no more fighting done while the weather remains so warm. I did not go to church this morning being pretty sure that the weather and my headache would do away with all devotional feelings. Finished reading "Tom Brown at Oxford" today, read ditto at Rugby last week, it is very fine and gives one a good idea of English schools and English scenery. The name of the author is Hughes I believe though I am not certain.

August 9, 1861, Friday: Tired to death this morning, but had to go to school. Only 16 scholars the least I have had this summer. This week makes fifteen weeks that I have taught. Went home after school and washed me and washed my hair, and then went over to Mrs. Tenney's. In the evening Eddie & Sinclair Botkin came over and stayed till about ten o'clock.

August 13, 1861, Tuesday: Went to school, but few scholars on account of harvest. Walked home tonight. Went to the Lodge. Elected delegates to the Grand Lodge. Fanny was one, Mr. Hastings read an extra tonight containing news of the battle at Springfield yesterday. Gen. Lyon killed.[35]

August 15, 1861, Thursday: Not home. Nothing unusual occurred today. Report of death of Gen. Lyon confirmed, also of rebel General McCulloch. Sen. Price also rebel severely wounded. Our forces forced the enemy to retreat and camped on the battlefield. Rebel loss estimated at 8,000 killed and wounded, they had 28,000 engaged, we only seven thousand.

August 21, 1861, Wednesday: Did not go to school, but to Teacher's Examination instead. There were twenty-five teachers to be examined. Mr. Pickard and Messrs Sterling Bliss and Fox were the examining committee. Went to call upon Mrs. Mercer at Mr. Mason's after it was over. Were going boat riding tonight but were prevented by the rain.

August 23, 1861, Friday: This is the last day of school. Rose this morning after breakfast went over to Mrs. D's staid a little while and then went to school had a very pleasant day but the tears would come in my eyes on discussing each class for the last time. We parted to meet again in the morning. Went to Mr. Maxwell's to tea staid a couple of hours and then went home. Eliza Tenney was there, we played games all the evening.

August 24, 1861, Saturday: Rose early this morning a good deal anxious about scale of the day's arrangements. Started with Ella, Eddie [Carey], Eliza Tenney, George & Mary [Carey] for the schoolhouse. Found the greater part of the children there. We went to the grounds Mr. Danning had very kindly fixed up some seats, and a table, also a couple of swings. They turned out very well. There were about seventy-three old and young, and all seemed to enjoy it very much. We had a nice supper, everything passed off in an orderly manner. Fannie and Mr. Craig came after me, and after bidding them all goodbye I felt that one more episode of my life had passed, that my influences there for good or evil, was ended. The children all seemed sorry to part with me, there were tears in many eyes, and one little girl sobbed all the way home and would not be comforted. God bless them all I love every one of them, although some of them have given me trouble and they have often seemed ungrateful for all my care and patience with them. I have passed a pleasant term among them, and sincerely wish them well in this world and the world to come, and hope that I may have done them some good. I was very tired at night, and after collecting my things, we started for home, we had a mile to walk to the lakeshore. We had a picnic of our own on board, and after a very pleasant ride reached home about nine.

The soldiers of the first Regiment returned today, and were enthusiastically received by the people they were welcomed at the depot, and provided with a dinner in one of the buildings, and in the evening were received by the ladies at the Assembly Room. They had a very pleasant time, most of them will re-enlist for the war.

August 25, 1861, Sunday: Found on awakening that I had not fully recovered from the effects of the picnic. Went to church, Dr. Brisbane's son, one of the returned volunteers, preached this morning. Did not go this afternoon to church.[36]

August 26, 1861, Monday: Woke this morning with a strange feeling of loss, did not seem possible that I was not going to school, however I managed to get along very comfortably. I have a great deal to do this fall, and must improve every moment.

August 29–30, 1861, Thursday–Friday: Went up town this morning, Mr. Craig offered to take me out to Mr. Tenney's this afternoon, as I wanted to go. We started that is, Fannie & I & Mr. Craig about 3 P. M. and they sat down among the trees near the railroad to wait for me. They promised to wait until seven o'clock before they launched. I was overtaken by Sinclair Botkin who came up through the woods, and he & I surveyed a new road through Mr. Carey's cornfield it was not altogether straight. He very kindly helped me over the intervening fences, and I arrived at Mr. Carey's in safety. I took tea there and then Ella and Mrs. Carey accompanied me to Mr. Tenney's. They had a house full of company, and Mr. Tenney did not get home until seven o'clock, and by the time I had my business with him arranged it was eight o'clock, and altogether too late to meet my friends at the boat. It being very dark I thought it likely that they had gone home long before Sinclair & Alex Botkin came over to Mr. Tenney's and Mrs. Mesees invited us all over to their house to spend the evening. We had a very pleasant time, playing Proverbs & c.

August 31, 1861, Saturday: Rose early, after breakfast went out to the barn to hunt for eggs, got seven in all, I had to go to Mr. Danning's, and so walked up as soon as possible after breakfast, it was something over a mile. Mr.

Danning said I might ride on a load of wheat with him if I chose which I did accordingly. Ella & I went over to Mr. Tenney's after Eliza who with Ella was going home with me. We started about nine o'clock found it very warm and dusty, got into town a little after ten, the girls staid all day. Eliza's father came for her in the evening. Ella staid all night.

September 2, 1861, Monday: Rained all day, until late in the afternoon, about 3 o'clock I went up to the Hall to help trim it for the reception of the Grand Lodge, it looked very nice indeed. After tea Maria & I started to accompany Ella part way home, it grew dark by the time we reached the Camp ground and Ella did not dare go home alone through the woods and I did not dare go alone back to town, so we all went on. Staid all night and came back in the morning.

September 12, 1861, Thursday: Nothing of importance today. We got no telegrams of importance. Our Regiments here, the Seventh & Eighth are filling up and will probably leave next week.

September 13, 1861, Friday: The Methodist Conference is in session here, went to the Church in the evening and heard the Rev. Mr. Tilton of Janesville on the State of affairs in the County, his text, " Every soul must be obedient to the higher powers" & c., was well treated indeed. I think I never heard a better discourse on the subject.

September 14, 1861, Saturday: Went up town this morning. We were all very much surprised by a visit from Cousin Augustus tonight. We were all very glad to see him I have not seen him since we were little children.

September 15, 1861, Sunday: Went to church this morning. One of the Methodist ministers preached. Augustus came before Church but did not accompany us, went again in the afternoon, and after that Augustus went with us to walk, until teatime. Went to church at the M. E. Church in the evening, found it crowded so much so that some of the contents ran over into the street, and dispersed to other churches, we were fortunate enough to obtain a seat.

September 17, 1861, Tuesday: The cloth for making shirts for the soldiers came in today, and we commenced making them. There are twenty-five thousand yd's to make up. Went to Lodge tonight.[37]

September 18, 1861, Wednesday: Augustus went yesterday, still making shirts. I like it very well. Had a picnic for the soldiers at the Camp today, we went up, it passed off pleasantly. The Seventh Regiment go Saturday.

September 19, 1861, Thursday: Worked all day on the shirts, went to the Horticultural Exhibition in the evening. It was very pleasant.

September 20, 1861, Friday: Made 10 shirts today. Maria & I and the machine that is.

September 21, 1861, Saturday: Shirt making still, finished ten today.

September 22, 1861, Sunday: Went to church today, a beautiful morning, heard a good sermon from the old text, "Enter in at the Strait Gate & c. I hope it may do me good" [Matt. 7:13], went again in the afternoon, a stranger, a member of the Conference, preached. Went in the evening to hear Dr. Baylor.

September 23, 1861, Monday: Rose early, sent off the shirts made Saturday and got ten more just as we got nicely at work one of the machine springs broke, and so delayed us somewhat in getting it mended. We finished our ten however by six o'clock. I went to a committee meeting at Mr. Miller's. We staid until ten, had a pleasant time and all came as far as the gate with me.

September 24, 1861, Tuesday: Had no work this morning, sewed on Ma's dress. Went to the Lodge. Dr. Brisbane was here and went with us. Our committee reported, and was received with satisfaction. We played Grab at recess, had a pleasant time. Fanny went home early. Mr. High came with me.

September 26, 1861, Thursday: This was the day appointed by the President as a day of fasting and prayer. Services in all the churches, places of business all closed, Dr. Brisbane preached, prayer meeting before and after preaching.[38]

September 27, 1861, Friday: Went up town this morning, a very cold cloudy day, sewed until four o'clock and then went out in the country to Mr. Carey's, stopped at Mr. Maxwell's on the way. Mrs. Carey and Ella were making pies for the soldiers in the evening and I kept them company and looked on. They made thirty-four in a little more than an hour.

September 28, 1861, Saturday: Got up by candle light this morning. Very cold. Ella was coming to town. We started at seven o'clock. Stopped at the Camp ground, went to Mr. Tenney's office, then to William's staid where he treated us to candy and grapes, we walked about a little and then walked into town. Ella went to take her music lesson after which we went to Curtiss's and had our photographs taken. Mrs. Wise and also Kate Kavenaugh & Kittie Hubbard called in the afternoon. Mr. C. came and spent the evening.

◦∽

October 1, 1861, Tuesday: Rained incessantly all day. Could not go to the Lodge.

October 2, 1861, Wednesday: Still raining. How I pity our poor soldiers in Camp. It is so cold and wet I think they must suffer.

October 3, 1861, Thursday: Still rainy & cold. In the house and sewing all day. Mrs. Fairchild came over this evening.[39]

From October 6 to 28 and again from October 29 to November 4 Emily did not write in her diary.

October 28, 1861, Monday: We have been moving and I have not seen my diary for a long time. I take it up now with something of the feeling of welcoming an old friend. I am to be at home this winter, how many of the records made here will be worthy of the time spent time alone can prove. I hope that I shall not have cause to chide myself for time misspent or opportunities misimproved. We have a meeting at our house tonight for the purpose of organizing a Society of young people to send articles of comfort and necessity to our sick and wounded soldiers in the hospitals. It seems to me a work of importance as they so very much need our aid and I hope that we shall accomplish something.

November 5, 1861, Tuesday: The gathering last night was not large but we organized under the name of "The Young Ladies Relief Society" and appointed the following officers: Emily Quiner, President; Hattie Benedict, Vice President; Addie Purple, Secretary; Minnie Baylor, Treas. Also the President, Vice President, Secretary & Treasurer Soliciting Committee for the various wards. Adjourned to meet next Monday evening at Addie Brisbane's. Went to the Lodge, James High came home with me.[40]

November 6, 1861, Wednesday: Went up town this morning, Ella Carey came while I was gone staid until afternoon had a committee meeting in regard to the sociable here tonight.

November 7, 1861, Thursday: Attended the Ladies' Aid meeting at the Hall, wound two skeins of yarn and raveled a square of linen for setons.[41]

November 8, 1861, Friday: Went out this morning on the Soliciting Committee, took me nearly all day, had good success. Tired enough tonight. Staid at home.

November 9, 1861, Saturday: Went up town got some yarn to knit stockings also some needles for [indecipherable]. Went out in the afternoon to collect bundles.

November 10, 1861, Sunday: Went with Pa to the Camp to hear Capt. McLeod of the 8th Regiment preach. It was cloudy and cold when we started, but the sun came out beautifully in a short time. The preaching was in the Hall of Fine Arts and we had empty musket boxes for seats. The sermon was very fine and the attendance good. After the sermon Pa introduced us to Capt. McLeod, and also to Lieut. Moore of the same company. They seemed to be very fine men indeed, as we came out of the building the scene from the hill was picturesque indeed, with the bright sunshine (the first we have had for nearly a week) shining sweetly over Camp and city, lake and hill. We took a walk around the tents stood a while to see them fall in for dinner and the march thereto, and then came home. Went to the Baptist Church in the afternoon, and Congregational in the evening.

November 11, 1861, Monday: Went up town this morning, and to the Society at Addie Brisbane's in the evening. There was a good number present, and we did a considerable amount of work, had a pleasant time. Addie treated us to pumpkin pie. Adjourned to meet at Addie Purple's.

November 12, 1861, Tuesday: Went to the Lodge installation of officers. I was installed as Treasurer, had a Committee meeting at recess.

November 14, 1861, Thursday: Went up to the Ladies' Aid Society to Addie Purple's in the evening to rehearse. Mr. Baker called for me. Mr. High being present, we rehearsed our charade several times, and adjourned to meet at our house tomorrow night.

November 15, 1861, Friday: A pleasant day. Been at work all day sewing. Mr. High and Mr. McHenry came tonight but the rest of the corps dramatique were not on hand, and so we had no rehearsal. They staid about an hour and a half, after they were gone Mr. Craig came, and spent the remainder of the evening.

November 16, 1861, Saturday: Today passed with the usual round of morning duties, a trip up town after a pattern for soldiers mittens, and a visit to Camp in the afternoon. Came home cold and tired and knit until twelve o'clock on the mittens.[42]

November 17, 1861, Sunday: A pleasant day, went to church, had a good sermon, Dr. Brisbane announced that he was about to leave as having received an appointment as Chaplain in the 2nd Cavalry Regiment. We are very sorry to lose him, Mr. Craig said he would call for us to go to Camp in the afternoon. He came at one o'clock and we had a pleasant walk, when we got there found the services would not commence for an hour sat down and waited. Mr. Britton preached and the band played, and we had some good singing by the congregation, after the services Mr. Craig took tracts (temperance etc.) to the Chaplain to distribute and then we went to find some of our friends for whom we had some papers, found Will McConnell, gave them to him and told him to share them with Wells High when he came. Mr. Craig staid to tea and we went to the Congregational Church in the evening.

November 21, 1861, Thursday: Went to the Ladies Aid Society. They were making slippers. Went to Mrs. Rowe's and then home.

November 22, 1861, Friday: Went out collecting bundles, came home found that Addie Purple had been here to inform me that James High would not be in town, so that we could not go on with our charade in consequence.

November 23, 1861, Saturday: Mrs. Rowe called this morning to see me in regard to the Sociable. Mrs. Martin called this afternoon. We were very agreeably surprised to see Cousin Augustus this evening. He came from Portage City.

November 25, 1861, Monday: The Society met here in the evening. Pa's got a buggy this afternoon and took me around to collect my bundles. We had quite a gathering in the evening and a pleasant time. James High was here and informed me that he would stay and take part in the charade. I told him that I should have nothing to do with it.

November 26, 1861, Tuesday: Went up town this afternoon with Addie Purple to get some batting for the Comforter we are to tack today, got enough for one came home and got one ready to tack and that was all. Addie staid to tea, Mr. High came for me to go to Exhibition of the Myrmidons Society of the University. Went to the Lodge afterward, got very much provoked at some of the members, and came home in no amicable frame of mind. Bid Mr. High goodbye for four months.[43]

November 27, 1861, Wednesday: Pa's got a carriage this afternoon and took me out riding. It was very cold but we wrapped up warm and were not at all uncomfortable. We went out to Mr. Tenney's and from there to Mrs. Reynolds' got home about six o'clock. Fannie was sick and I taught school for her this morning. Went to Sociable.

November 28, 1861, Thursday: Today is Thanksgiving, went to Church in the morning, had dinner at four in the afternoon, had an invitation to a surprise party at Mrs. Miller's played cards in the evening until time to go, had a very pleasant time, our oyster supper & c. came home at twelve.[44]

November 29, 1861, Friday: Augustus started for home, this morning. I was sorry to have him go, it seems lonely without him, he is so lively and pleasant,

April 1861 to April 1862   37

we all like him very much. Commenced a course of study today, Rhetoric, Algebra, Geometry and Arithmetic studied till twelve.

∽

December 2, 1861, Monday: Cold but pleasant. Sewed all day. Went to Society at Hattie Benedict's in the evening, the members present was smaller than at any time since our organization but the amount of work accomplished was very creditable. I am very anxious to get one box started, as our poor sick soldiers in the hospitals are very much in need of the articles. Meeting adjourned to meet at Addie Ripley's.

December 3, 1861, Tuesday: Maria & I tried our skill at the washing machine today it worked wonderfully and we thought some of taking in washings first for the pleasure of working it, but concluded on hanging out the clothes and coming in with frozen fingers that we had had enough for once. Went to the Lodge tonight. Came home with the blues.[45]

December 4, 1861, Wednesday: Went up town a beautiful day with the air of Indian Summer, a hazy dreary fragrant air if it had not been for a foot or so of snow which lay upon the ground I could have fancied it October. I was out the greater part of the forenoon, came home went up in the afternoon to get a box for our goods, Mr. Sprague gave me a nice one, and I had it sent to Addie's. Went up to see her staid an hour and home again. Received a letter from Pa just like him, full of fun and frolic. Spent my evening at home.

Seventy-three miles north of Madison, another young Wisconsin woman, only five years older than Emily, had a much greater personal involvement in the war than Emily did. Ann Waldo's life was different from Emily's in many ways. She was a wife and mother and a woman who had known poverty and neglect. Ann's husband, Morris, had enlisted in the 1st Cavalry on November 2, 1861, and was first stationed at Camp Harvey, in Kenosha. Like many women whose husbands were away at war, Ann moved from their home when her husband departed. Her initial letters described her attempts to collect debts owed to Morris so that she and her young daughter, Della, could afford the basics of life. The challenges Ann faced in supporting herself and her daughter and in finding a home while Morris was away at the war stand in marked contrast with Emily's life of sewing and sociables, reading and chess. Ann's peripatetic existence during this time caused her additional pain as the cherished letters from Morris were often sent to the wrong post office. Early in the war Ann went to Missouri to nurse her ill husband back to health, an action that had a lifelong impact on her family.

ANN

From Ann Waldo at Ripon to Morris Waldo at Kenosha, Wisconsin, Wednesday evening, December 4, 1861

My dear husband,

Your favor of Nov. 15th was rec'd this morning (ten days after it was written) and I had almost despaired of hearing from you. Della and I are well and also the rest of the friends. The day I left you I went home with our folks as George and Juliet had not gone home yet, staid 'til the next day, and then went to George's, staid there until last Saturday, and went to Pa's again and staid until this morning and got him to bring me here today (to Silas's) so that I can get business arranged to go to Winneconne Saturday if the snow don't go off. But it has thawed all day today and the sleighing is almost gone in town now, so I expect to have to run in the road or go on foot, or stay two or three weeks longer.

I have staid longer now than I want to, out to our folk's and George's, for my things are so scattered about I want to get settled somewhere. Besides, I don't want to visit folks to death when it is only a matter of convenience. Silas and his family are going to his father's next Monday to be gone a week or more, so I expect to go back on the prairie again. I have not got that money yet of Silas. He said he had the money for me last week but there was so much talk about banks failing he did not like to keep it on hand and he thought I would not want to, so he used it. I think he intends to get the money of his father but I don't know.

Silas is going out there to draw off grain for his father as his father has been sick and has no one he dares trust his team with. I got Silas to present that due bill to Mr. Cramer tonight and he said the agreement with you was that he was not to pay it 'til the middle or last of the month and he could not possibly pay it before the middle.

I sent you a paper a week ago stating that the wives of Cavalry and Artillery soldiers received nothing from the state. Did you receive it and if so what did you think of it? You see I have accomplished nothing so far by staying. I think it was quite too bad you had to go off without so much as a good-bye for your wife and daughter. You might as well have told me that when I started. I am sorry about your needle book but I had no idea that you were going away without seeing me again. Did you get that money of Mr. Lanning? When will you be back do you think? Silas says he heard there was several of those boys coming back next week.

Do you have clothes enough to keep you warm [during] the cold nights we have had lately? Make yourself as comfortable as possible. Silas said last evening's paper stated the government had already more troops than they wanted and that the Cavalry's forming would have to disband. God grant it may be so. Write often and I will answer as soon as I receive them and as much oftener as I have anything to write. It is ten o'clock and I am keeping Silas up so I must stop. Direct your letters to Ripon until you hear from me again as I expect to live on charity some time longer, though very much against my will.

Good night,
Ann

Emily

December 5, 1861, Thursday: A warm pleasant day, Mrs. Mercer came in the forenoon and staid until the time for the meeting of the Aid Society at the Assembly Room. The Ladies' sent off their first box today, well filled. I hope it may do much good, and alleviate some of the suffering growing out of this terrible war. There is now some hope felt that it will soon end, if it does it will have cost already a fearful price, in broken hearts and desolated homes. God grant there be not many more. Mr. Craig came this evening to teach us to play Chess. I like it very much, and hope some time to be a skillful player. After he had gone Fannie & I had a game of backgammon for fours and then went to bed.

December 6, 1861, Friday: This morning the snow had nearly disappeared; the air was misty warm & soft as spring. I felt a sort of house cleaning propensity come over me and after sweeping and dusting the rooms, making beds I found myself up to elbows in suds cleaning shelves in the pantry. Scraped lint in the afternoon. Played a game of chess with Fannie when she came home, scraped some more lint, read several chapters of Dicken's *Great Expectations* aloud for the edification of Ma & Marie and at this present moment am writing in my room 11½ o'clock P. M. without a fire and entirely comfortable notwithstanding the "rain dripping on the panes and sixth of December too!" I have an odd fancy to describe my dress tonight, that I may remember myself all Decembers to come as I sit here tonight. First dress dark delaine [delaine is a lightweight fabric made of wool or wool and cotton] close sleeves and cuff's, white apron cut round with ruffles, linen collar embroidered in prints as is the present style, black velvet bow in front, belt with buckle, a la Zouave and hair combed straight back from my bun classic brow over my ears, fingers dabbed in ink.

ANN

From Ann Waldo at Ripon to Morris Waldo, Co. 1st Reg. Wis. Cavalry, at Kenosha, Wisconsin, December 8, 1861

My dear husband

I was so fortunate yesterday as to receive another letter from my husband and as that same husband seemed to be suffering from a fit of the blues because he did not hear from his other half, I have seated myself to spoil another sheet of paper, although it is but four days since I committed my most important ideas to paper and mailed them to you. You seemed to censure me very much for not writing sooner but you will see by other, that I answered yours as soon as I received. I thought if you did not care enough about hearing from me to write it was not worth while for me to go to the trouble to write but it seems that the fault was not yours but the fault of the mail that took ten days to bring a letter from there to here.

George C. was in town yesterday and I hailed him as he came back past Giles to get a paper safe home with him He was in a double wagon and no seat and no umbrella and a drizzling rain. But by putting a board across the top of the box, he made a seat and we started. It was not a very pleasant trip but there was no other alternative as Giles' folks are going away Monday and it would have left me in the street.

I suppose if I would take a peep at you today, I should see you strutting about in your new uniform. I should be very happy to see you even without anything on, though I'll hope you will not be driven to that extremity.

There is a great deal said in these parts about the Cavalry regiments disbanding. The Milwaukee papers last week stated that telegrams had been rec'd there, that all cavalry regiments that were not full must be mustered out of service unless they were willing to go in as infantry, as there was already more cavalry than was needed. Did you hear anything about it there? I presume the privates do not know much about their designs. If they go as infantry, you of course will not go, for I shan't let you. I shall be very glad if we can get a furlough to go East I want you should go, and I want to go with you. But if you cannot go, perhaps I had better not go, for I feel as if you were earning your money at too great of sacrifice of home comforts for me to spend anything that is not absolutely necessary. I think if that Regiment don't disband so that you will come home, I had better try and get a school another summer and take Della with me. How long do you suppose you will stay at Kenosha? Be sure you do not put off getting a furlough till the regiment gets ready to move, so that it will be too late and I shall not see you at all, for I must see you again before you leave the state.

Is H. Lagrange Major of that reg.?[46] And is he there at Kenosha? Have you got an overcoat that will keep you warm? I do not see any prospect of my getting to Winneconne very soon. I shall have to wait until Giles get back and that will be a week or ten days & I don't know how much longer on account of the roads. If we should go east in Jan., I don't think I had better get any groceries of Mr. Ferrington for that bedstead will pay one month's board.

I have made Della's cloak out of my black cape and it is very pretty. I got me a delaine dress at Mr. Bowen's on that order I had. I will put a piece of it [in this letter]. I came very near being to a party last night. George went out about ten o'clock and hitched them on, to go after Dr. and I came in and concluded there was no immediate hurry and put them in the barn and let them stand all night with the harness on and he went to bed. I believe it is postponed indefinitely but will come off before many days.

I don't see but I am in for it, as the saying is, I don't think much of the idea, but I don't see how I can help myself. I might as well have hired my board here if I had known I had got to stay so long.

If you should go East, what time do you think you will go? Probably I shall have to wait till the middle of Jan. for that last order of Mr. Cramer as he said there they were to be a month apart and he cannot give the last one until the middle of Dec. I don't understand how V.A. Groesbeck's name could have been on the paper I sent you. If I sent the paper I meant to, which was a Berlin [Wisconsin] paper with a paragraph marked in it which I wished you to read. I took the paper from George's to Giles and may have taken it down and taken up his through mistake.

I guess you will think I have written a long letter about nothing, but that was all I had to write and thought you would have plenty of time to pick it out.

Write every week without fail and you may as well direct to George's care (but write your care with an (e) on the end of it, and spell Carlings right). I don't care anything about the spelling on the inside for that is only for my eyes. Now don't be offended, will you. Take good care of yourself, and make yourself warm and comfortable if possible. Accept a heap of love from Della and I and may God bless you.

Your affectionate wife,
A.E. Waldo

Much obliged for the paper you sent me last week.

EMILY

December 9, 1861, Monday: We washed today with our new machine, it works admirably, though I would prefer one which would wash without assistance. Went to the Society at Mrs. Ripley's. We rolled a great many yards of bandages and also pieced some calico for comforters had a pleasant time. Adjourned to meet at Mrs. Griffin's next Monday evening.

December 10, 1861, Tuesday: Sewed all day. Went to the Lodge in the evening, quite a large number present had a very pleasant time talked about getting up an impromptu sociable tomorrow night. Promised to recite something.

December 11, 1861, Wednesday: Sewed, swept, dusted and cleaned this morning, spent a few minutes looking for a piece to recite—found one but had no time to learn it until about six o'clock. Addie Riply & Miss Balkin came this afternoon to tack comforters. We tied two & got another ready to tie. Went to the Sociable. We had some nice recitations & tableaus also an impromptu charade everything went off well and we had a pleasant time.

December 12, 1861, Thursday: Played Chess with Fannie this morning. Sewed some. Mrs. Wise & Mrs. Fairchild called this afternoon. Started about three o'clock to go out to Mrs. Carey's. It was very pleasant. They all seemed glad to see me. After tea we went to Mr. Tenney's stayed a little while & Mrs. Tenney & Wife Church came back with us. Found Sinclair Botkin at home had a pleasant evening. Kept country hours eating at half past nine.

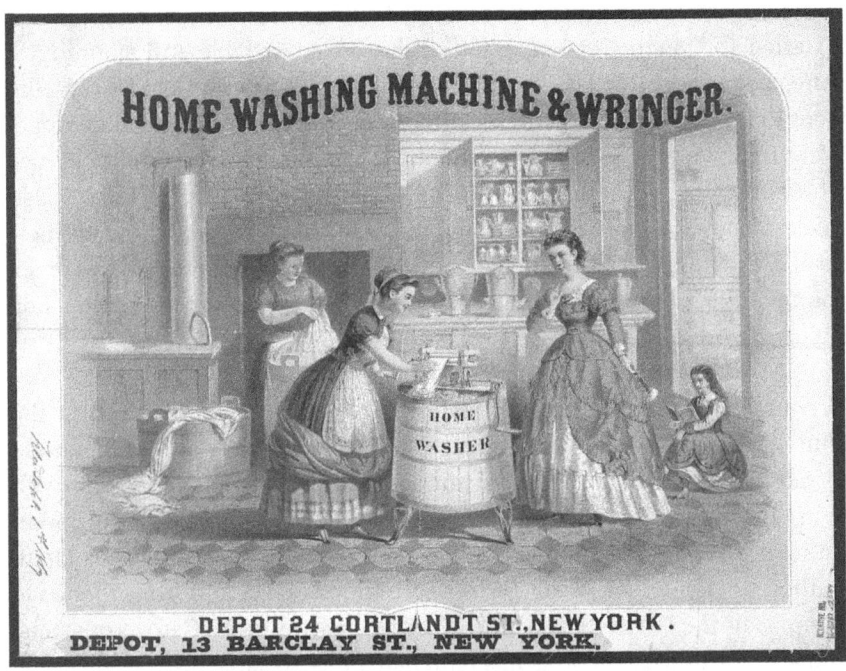

Emily would have preferred a washing machine "that washed without assistance." (Library of Congress, https://www.loc.gov/item/96510205/)

December 13, 1861, Friday: Had our programme for today mapped out yesterday. Rose at 5 ½ this morning not because I wanted too, but I being in home must conduct myself a la Rossian. I knit all the forenoon and a long one it was. After dinner Ella & I sallied out for a visiting tour. We first called on Miss Sinclair, found her alone Mrs. Botkin having gone away. Staid a short time, called at Mrs. Petherick's, she entertained us very pleasantly showing us books & pictures brought from their old home in England, among which was an splendid painting, of the family nearly life size. It was very beautiful and I shall never forget it. Mrs. Petherick is a lovely woman, a lady even in the poverty which now surrounds her. From there we went to Mrs. Danning's & Mrs. Kellogg's and spent the remainder of the afternoon at the school house. Like Mr. Allen very well think he might keep better order in school, he walked as far as Mr. Carey's with us asked me to come out to spelling school sometime think I shall. Went up to Mr. Tenney's to spend the evening found Sinclair there. Eliza was at home played euchre. Went home and to bed.

December 14, 1861, Saturday: Rose at a ridiculously early hour. At ten Ella & I started for town. Got home found the breakfast table still standing & coffee hot ate a 2nd breakfast. Ella came to dinner. After which she & Nellie went to Mr. Laskin's to spend the afternoon & I went to the Band of Hope. Went up town first in time to see all the Reg's march to the Capitol House where the Gov. addressed them. The Governor elect [Louis Harvey] also made a speech. Poor fellows I fear many of them are marching to their deaths, they are as fine looking soldiers as one would wish to see, five or six young ladies came in the evening and we had a dance in the parlor. Ella staid with me.

December 15, 1861, Sunday: Rose late this morning went with Ella to the church of the Messiah, Mrs. Mercer & Mrs. Tenney were there. They were to ride home and Ella pressured me to go and come back to Camp with them in the afternoon it was a beautiful day Sinclair & Wallace Botkin came in while we were at lunch and staid an hour or so. Wallace is a Lieut. in the 12th Regiment. Went for Mrs. Tenney & Eliza and from thence to Camp. Saw the Dress Parade, & Mr. Tenney took us to Dr. Carey's quarters, and afterwards to Lieut. Mason's tent, had a very sociable time. Rode home with Mr. Main, found Mr. Craig in the parlor staid and went to church with Ma & Fannie, Miss Crocker called for me & we went to the Congregational Church. Heard a good sermon.

ANN

From Ann Waldo at Fairwater to Morris Waldo at Kenosha, Wisconsin, December 15, 1861

My dear husband,

   Now make up your mind you are going to have something interesting to read for I have a headache and am too tired to write, but I thought you would be more disappointed to receive no letter than to receive a poor one. Ruby has been quite sick all day was taken last night in very severe pain and has not been able to sit up more than an hour today. Nettie went to Mr. Sweets yesterday and did not get back until tonight so I have had to be chief cook and bottle washer. George & Juliette and the children were here to supper so I had plenty to do.
   I have had the greatest time entirely this past week to get my mail. George C. sent down by Mr. [illegible] Thursday and there was nothing

there for me. Pa went down Friday and came back by the way of George's and I sent down by him he [illegible]. Giles she called to him, and told him there was a letter and some papers there for me and to call when he came back for them. About an hour before they started for home they saw her downtown and she said she was going home in a few minutes when they got there the house was fastened and she was not there.

Then they drove back downtown and looked all over for her and George couldn't find her and had to come home without them. So you may suspect that your dear wife was rather out of patience to think they did not leave my mail in the office and then I should have got it Thursday. I was so disappointed I could have cried if it would have been of any use to think it was there and I couldn't get it. The roads were so bad they could not go last week, but they were going to start next Mondays for his father's. I came home with Pa Friday night and he is awake all night nearly thinking about it. Here I still have 3 weeks for nothing and they still want any next week and were or were gone a week or ten days my trunks were there and I should have to wait till they get back and I was determined I wouldn't do it. Pa got up yesterday morning and asked me if he would let George take one of the teams and go to Ripon with me. He said yes and off we went then in the first place and had the pleasure of reading my letter. Then I got George to take that one bill and go & see if he could get order of Mr. Craner. He had gone to Eureka so I couldn't do that. I didn't want to go without it for I needed some cotton flannel and cloth for Della some drawers and & c. Giles said he hadn't got a cent of money, but he had a due-bill at Bowens of $6.86 if I could use that he wished I would, so I took that & got what I needed which came to $5.17 & gave him back the rest, .42 cts of it was for Nettie. She sent the money by me, so I got what she wanted on the due-bill and got the money as I had but 10c and two postage stamps. I don't know whether I did right to use that due bill of Giles, but he said it was impossible for him to get any money, but he could and would get it just as soon as he could and send it to me. I let Giles take those due bills against Mr. Craner. He says he will try and get the orders off him as soon as possible and will get them into due-bill for me and then I can use them anytime.

Mr. Grent did not come after me this morning (Monday) and I was very glad of it. Nettie and I have been doing a huge washing and I expect to go down to Winneconne tomorrow and will mail this in Ripon as we go through there.

Emily

December 16, 1861, Monday: Went up town this morning. Mr. Findley promised us a package of [indecipherable] for our box and Mr. Gilman wine slippers. Went to Flora's in the evening. Meeting adjourned to meet at Addie Purple's two weeks from tonight. We are going to send our box next week & commence on another at our next meeting.

December 17, 1861, Tuesday: Miss Crocker came this morning with Mrs. Johnson's baby she staid all day. Sent the baby home at noon she & Fannie played Chess in the afternoon. Maria & I and the machine did the washing. Maria went into the country in the afternoon. Went to the Lodge in the evening. A good many soldiers present, had a good many speeches, the evening passed pleasantly.

December 18, 1861, Wednesday: Expected company in the evening baked all the morning. Went up to Camp with Pa & Ma this afternoon. Went to see Dr. Carey about sending our box with the 12th and concluded to do so. Found Mrs. Wise at home on our return. Mrs. De Mott & Mrs. Davis also came to tea, & Mr. & Mrs. Carson in the evening. We had coffee which so exhilarated Fannie & I that we could not go to bed and so sat down to play chess, after they were gone played one game which lasted nearly three hours.

December 19, 1861, Thursday: Three or four young ladies came in the afternoon to tie comforters. We tied three they stayed in the evening & Mr. Craig & Mr. Smith came in the evening.

Ann

From Ann Waldo at Winneconne to Morris Waldo at Kenosha, Wisconsin, December 22, 1861

To "My dear husband"

Excuse this mammoth sheet of paper, as I have nothing smaller but I will try to stop before I get it full as I suspect my former lengthy letters <u>have never been read</u>, as I touched several subjects, requiring an answer, which you do not allude to at all in yours.

Well here I am in Winneconne. I came here last Tuesday and a beautiful day it was, nearly as warm as May, found everybody and his wife all well, but the dullest, desolate place was ever in, even worse that it used to be, there is no tavern at all kept here and scarcely anything else. (Mac has gone into the Swart house.) I would not live here again if they would give me the whole town.

I found a letter waiting for me here from Orange [Ann and Susan's half-brother], as he did not know we had left town. I will send it to you with this and want you to be sure to answer it. I expect they have taken your name in vain ere a considerable, as Susan says. Waldo was in to Mrs. Owens one day and he never saw a woman in such a rage as she was about you, she said you had better never show your face to her again. She said Mr. Waldo talked about Mr. D.P. Smith being a <u>mean man</u>, and Mr. Waldo was so much <u>meaner</u> than Mr. Smith as a man <u>could be</u>, the way he served them, she said you had ruined them, enlisting, and leaving that machine for <u>them</u> to pay for.

Rufus tells that the machine belongs to him, so I want to know how much you received for your fall's work. Waldo told Mr. Rowley, that you expected R. to pay him something on your account. Mr. R. asked Rufus about it and he told him that all he had collected of D. Moscrip [indecipherable] belonged to him. Rufus told Waldo he thought it was pretty well that Mr. Rowley was dunning him for Mott [a nickname for Morris] when Mott was owing him (Rufus) so you see how much you can depend on anybody.[47]

Are you owing Mr. Stacy anything, he is owing Waldo nine shillings and he says you are owing him and wants to turn it. How much do you owe him if anything? Tom Pierson has been dunning Waldo for you, he claims that you owe him $2.00, he seems to have forgotten the load of hay that you drawed for him. Mr. Max claims that you owe him for those bob as he told Waldo that he only took that note against Wood on conditions that he could not collect it. They thought they had better wait till I came to see if I couldn't get it of Mrs. Wood. I am not going to take that note on my hands and try to collect it of her. You <u>must</u> get a <u>furlough</u> and come up here any way. You don't mean to leave the state without my seeing you, do you?

[Fragment of letter missing] . . . family. Have you got any boots yet and are your clothes warm and comfortable and do they <u>fit good</u>? I feel almost sick today, but nothing <u>serious</u>. I think my <u>aches</u> will be better in a day or two. Your last letter was forwarded from Ripon here and I received it Friday night. I purchased $3.40 worth of groceries at Mr. Farrington for Waldo's folks when I came here and I gave Pa an order for $2.00 for bringing me up here. He did not charge me anything but I thought they had carried me around here so much I wouldn't have come for nothing. He had to stop and feed on the way and I know he had to borrow money to bear expenses on the road. Well I must stop or I shall have this letter as long as the others.

Della says she want to see her Papa very badly, and she has got a kiss saved for him.

Your affectionate wife.
A.E. Waldo

Emily

December 23, 1861, Monday: Went up town this morning, & to Addie Purple's in the afternoon. While there Geo. C. Smith came for Addie & I to go to Sun Prairie to visit with a Lodge, I came home and we started about 4 o'clock. We were to stop at Mr. Bush's and get some supper, but were late and so went on got there at half past seven and went directly to the nerve of operations staid until about two o'clock in the morning, then went to Mr. Bush's who with his good wife Emily entertained us at this unreasonable hour and then started for home where we arrived about 6 A. M. tired enough.

December 25, 1861, Wednesday: The day passed as Christmas days are wont to do. Passed most of the time in the kitchen had a nice dinner. Went to the Sociable in the evening had a very pleasant time.[48]

December 26, 1861, Thursday: Sewed part of the day, played chess with Fannie went up to Addie Purple's to help pack our box found Mr. Sprague had not sent it came home again spent the evening at home.

December 29, 1861, Sunday: Went to church. Dr. Howard preached a very good sermon, though a long one. It was very cold. Wrote and sewed all the afternoon, finished "Willette" and commenced "Aurora Leigh" a Christmas gift from Fannie. I like it very much, went to church in the evening.

December 30, 1861, Monday: Went up town first thing this morning to get a box to put our goods in for the soldiers got one at Bartels. Pa got a dray and sent it up for me and in the afternoon Addie & I packed it—we had just enough to fill it nicely. I packed my box of jellies, and they are all ready to send. The Society met at Addie Purple's. We had a very pleasant time with no work to do, adjourned to meet again at Hattie Garvey's.

December 31, 1861, Tuesday: At home all day. Went to the Lodge tonight. Lodge adjourned early. Some of us staid to watch the New Year in, had a splendid time danced away & c. came away after midnight.

January 1, 1862, Wednesday: New Year's Day, pleasant but cold, went out to bring in some clothes from the line nearly froze my fingers so began the New Year's. Received several calls, staid at home in the evening.

Emily Quiner and Ann Waldo's writings during the remainder of this early winter reflect the very different circumstances of their lives. After a few quiet days, Emily resumed her work with the Aid Society and filled her time with reading and lectures. Although Ann was once again living under the protection of her older sister, her money worries increased due to fear that Morris would not receive pay for his service, a fear that was bolstered by rumors of what had happened to other regiments. She kept Morris connected to home by sharing her pride in their daughter's accomplishments and by updating him on local gossip. Ann took comfort in their ability to write to each other frequently while Morris was still in the state but worried about whether they would be able to keep up a regular correspondence after he was sent to the front. Eager to see her husband, Ann Waldo again asked whether he would receive a furlough before leaving the state and began to explore the possibility that she could come to Kenosha to visit him at camp. This would be long journey for Ann, as Kenosha is 133 miles from Winneconne.

At the federal level, the role of African Americans in the Union Army began to be explored when James Henry Lane, a senator from Kansas, encouraged slaves to run away from their masters. In January 1862, he proposed that he lead a brigade into the South to free slaves. Lane had the backing of General George B. McClellan, the leader of the Union Army, for this endeavor, but Lincoln insisted that all orders had to come through Lane's commanding officer, and that put an end to Lane's plan on February 13, 1862.[49] President Lincoln began to express concerns about McClellan's failure to move against the Confederate forces. These fears were echoed by Ann, who commented on the reluctance of the Union commanders to take action against the Confederacy.

ANN

From Ann Waldo at Winneconne to Morris Waldo at Kenosha, Wisconsin, January 1, 1862

My dear Mr. Waldo

That letter that I had been looking for until my eyes ached, came to hand yesterday which very much pleased your humble servant.

The locket enclosed came safely & I think it contains an excellent likeness of M.A.W. The locket is very pretty but I sorry you did not get a smaller one, so she could have worn it on her beads sometimes. This will be too large for her to wear for years to come. She says, "Tell Papa thank you and I will be a good girl." Now for myself I have a great mind to be jealous of you sending your likeness to a young lady and neglecting poor I, but I won't on condition that your send me that pin that I engaged (not now but when you get the money to spare). If you should not get your pay long before the Re. starts to give me time to come and see you, I want you to be sure and send me that. Now I have heard of an old saying somewhere that beggars should not be choosers, but I guess that is out of date now. At any rate I will be an exception to the rule. I want a miniature pin, that the center revolves so that it can be worn with the gold side out to look like a plain gold pin, or with the miniature out. In one side, I want the likeness of a certain good looking soldier that is a teamster in Co. E. (don't send me Capt. Atwell's likeness). Now you will get it for me, won't you, as you have never purchased me any jewelry you can afford to treat me to that.

I want a nice one, if I have any. You can send it in a newspaper by cutting a hole in the paper after it is folded the shape of the pin and putting it in. Isn't this an interesting subject?

But I am going to send this by Mr. Stacy & and it won't cost anything. You will get it so much sooner. I THOUGHT I would send a line by him. I do hope you will get your pay in time so that I can come down there, but it would not pay for me to go just a day or two before you started. It would be too much expense for the time I could stay.

Della has learned all her letters & yesterday I invested ten cents in a first Reader, for her. She is getting along nicely. I have sent to Omro by Waldo today to get her a little slate if there is any small ones there. For she is all the time getting the scholar's slates & I am afraid of her breaking or scratching them. There is no small ones in town here.

My little sheet of paper seems to be getting full. I never know when to stop writing to you even if I have nothing to write. I purchased 12 sheets of paper the other day and that daughter of yours got to play in the ink and spoiled 4 sheets of it. So if you receive blotted paper, you can account for it. It is noon now. Susan is paring potatoes for dinner & Della has got her book, hearing her Aunt Susan spell.

According to a paragraph I have clipped from the Daily Wisconsin, you will not be likely to go in Lane's Expedition as a teamster. I will enclose it. What was the price of Della's locket?

[Letter continued on another sheet of paper] You see I <u>must</u> send two sheets of paper, even if there is nothing in them. It seems that I shall not be able to send this in the way I had intended as Mr. Stacy left town yesterday. What in the world is there that Giles Clark can do there? They say he has gone too. I wish there was something that the poor man seems able to do for there is need enough of it and there is nothing he can do here. O dear, how we do want something to read here. I have counted the hours almost until the <u>North Western</u> would come and so this morning it came and only ½ sheet at that. That constitutes our week's reading. I am out of sewing so I'll have plenty of time to read and notice it all the more, do send me something to read. Now don't complain if my letters are not very interesting, for I have not a single idea in my head more than when you were here. Nobody goes out of town and nobody comes in (to town I mean). So I have no means of knowing anything. I am not sure but you would be jealous if you knew how much I admire a certain gentleman's likeness that was sent to my daughter the other day, in fact I am quite in love with it. It is so very correct, it looks like it might speak, to tell the truth. I don't think I ever saw a gentleman <u>I liked any better</u>. But if you are very jealous and will send me your likeness as I specified, (don't forget to read that part of my letter), I will promise not to look at that so much. Waldo got a little slate to Omro yesterday for Della for 9 cents, not a very heavy investment. We have plenty of snow now and the weather today is quite cold, in fact it was so cold last night, it froze between <u>me</u> and my <u>husband</u>, strange wasn't it? I shall not go home with Mr. Vedder next week for I have not give up all hope of going to Kenosha yet. If you should be so fortunate as to get your pay before the Regiments are ready to start.

Monday morning

How I do wish I knew what the contents of your next letter would be, for I would like very much to go home with Mr. Vedder tomorrow and stay a week or two until Susan's school is out, but I dare not go for fear you may send for me to come to Kenosha and I should not get your letter or be here to go. Rufus received a letter from Mr. Vedder Saturday saying he would deliver a temperance in town this evening so he will be here today. He thinks the lodge is in running order, yet: he sent Rufus the password awhile ago. (I have been making beds and my hands are so cold I cannot write.) (I think they must be picking feathers in the celestial regions this morning by the way the feathers fly in the air.) Mr. M. got back from Oconto yesterday and he did not see those fishermen. He went within three miles of them and was going to see them but he was told it would be of no use as they had no fish or anything else, so much for that debt. I am knitting another pair of socks for my soldier, but I don't know whether he will be able to get them, but I don't think he can need them very badly at present. Can you keep warm these cold nights, I can't. I'm awake part of every night. I am so cold I can't sleep. I am very sorry Dr. Johnson is in such poor health, tell me how he is in the next letter when you write.[50]

Yours in haste,
Ann

EMILY

January 6, 1862, Monday: The State officers were installed today. We went up into the Assembly Room there was such a crowd that we could hear and see nothing. Went up town and then home. Addie Purple came for me to go up town with her. Went to Hattie's in the evening, a good many there, made arrangements to meet tomorrow to consult about a festival, and then some of us went to the Governor's Reception at the Capital, staid until about twelve, and then came home.[51]

January 7, 1862, Tuesday: At home all day. Society met this afternoon. Concluded to have our festival on Friday evening. Appointed committees and adjourned to meet at 4 o'clock tomorrow. Went to the Lodge tonight.

January 8, 1862, Wednesday: Maria & Addie hired a sleigh and started out soliciting this morning. Miss Chapman & I ditto, went all day came home wet cold and miserable, met in the evening to roll up the articles for the "Grab bag."

Ann

From Ann Waldo at Winneconne to Morris Waldo at Kenosha, Wisconsin, January 8, 1862

My dear husband,

Although I have already written you once this week I am just going to scribble a few lines more. I was beginning to feel quite uneasy because I did not hear from you until the Omro [mail] came yesterday and was kind enough to bring me a letter from you (I'll think it came very quickly) though I cannot say I feel much better now. For I think my dear husband wrote as if he was rather low-spirited. I should be very sorry to think that you were obliged to step and put up with camp life, if you felt as if you would rather be somewhere else.

Morris, do take care of that cold of yours. Do not let it get seated on your lungs. You know your father died of consumption and you may inherit a predisposition to it. Get Dr. Johnson to prescribe for your cough. Now do something for it right away, won't you?

What about my coming to Kenosha? Did you mean that I should go east then? It would suit me just as well to not go east until navigation opens. I have more sewing that I want to do before I go than I can get done before you will want me to come to Kenosha, and we have money due us that I can not get as soon as that & I think that we had better stay until our business is all settled. I know that it will be an extra expense to go to Kenosha and come back, but perhaps we go east enough cheaper when the boats run to make up the difference. At any rate you will have more money paid by that time. I feel quite contented here now & as long as I do I may as well stay, as I shall have long enough time to go East & I don't want to hurry so to get ready. If I have an opportunity I shall go to Mr. Bedelers and stay a week or so this winter. I wrote to Amelia this morning about those chairs, to see what arrangement Mr. Steele has made about them. I also wrote to Mr. Groesbeck to know if Giles had got those orders of Mr. Crevey.

You must excuse this writing, as this is the third letter I have written this morning, thanks to my husband's generosity as I had but 11 cents left. I could not have been so extravagant if he had not sent me a remittance. Barstow Cavalry is now ordered to Fort. I do expect your Reg. will be sent there too. A. McIntyre gave Waldo Mr. Mants duebill the day you went away. I spoke to her about it & she said she would write to Mr. Mant about it.[52]

Do take care of that cold. Write Sunday without fail.

I will try and hold myself in readiness to come to Kenosha anytime you send for me for if I go there and come back again before I go East. I can go anytime. Goodbye.

Ann Winneconne

Emily

January 9, 1862, Thursday: Maria & Addie went out again this morning and I did up a little begging and then went up to the Hall, worked all the afternoon came home very tired.

January 10, 1862, Friday: Went up to the Hall this morning early washed dishes, swept, dusted, and worked all day, got everything in good order by seven o'clock, and then went home to dress did not have as large an attendance as expected receipts about eighty dollars, had a pleasant time, a nice dance and came home about two o'clock AM.

January 11, 1862, Saturday: Had all the ruins of the last night's banquet to straighten out and put in order, worked at the Hall all day, we had a Society Festival in the evening. Met Mr. Combs, Sen.'s Brown & Hazleton tonight had a pleasant time.

January 12, 1862, Sunday: Went to church today feeling very stiff & sore, heard a good sermon staid to Bible Class wrote all the afternoon read a little of Aurora Leigh went to church in the evening. Terribly cold, glad to get home.

January 13, 1862, Monday: Sewed all the forenoon. In the afternoon Mr. Campbell called I went up town came back. Addie Purple came spent the afternoon staid in the evening. Mr. Craig, Mr. Campbell & Mr. McHenry came also, had a pleasant time played chess, backgammon checkers & c.

January 14, 1862, Tuesday: Mr. Campbell & Mr. McHenry called this afternoon to see about some of the Festival arrangements. Went to Lodge tonight.

January 15, 1862, Wednesday: Washed today. Cold and snowy. Don't like housework, such weather as this snow or in any weather. Maria & I went out in the afternoon to call upon Kate & Annie Kavenaugh & Kittie Hubbard, found them at home said they had a splendid time last night went to Mrs. Reynolds and were provoked that we did not go. I went to Addie Purple's tonight to rehearse a Charade we are to perform next week.

January 16, 1862, Thursday: Sewed all day. Went to see Tom Thumb in the evening. Liked the exhibition very well bought a Photograph of the little gentleman. His experimentations of statuary I thought very fine.[53]

January 17, 1862, Friday: Worked in the kitchen all the forenoon helping Ma weigh and pack port, first experience in the business, did not like it at all. Ma said that any who even expected to be a housekeeper should not fail to learn this important branch of business, couldn't see how the remark applied to me, I have no expectations. Fannie & I went to the Round Table at Mrs. Williams's tonight for the first time this season. It was very pleasant made some new acquaintances, and met many old ones. Came home in a rainstorm.

January 18, 1862, Saturday: Did not feel very well today. Sewed all day. Mr. Purman & Mr. McHenry came to rehearse the charade. Addie did not come Maria took her part and we went through it once to our entire satisfaction.

January 19, 1862, Sunday: Went to the Congregational Church this morning, and then to ours to Bible Class. Came home made a fire in our room swept & dusted and then read Lalla Rookh until done. Wrote a letter to Gus and then went to church. Came home wrote in my diary read awhile and then to bed.

January 20, 1862, Monday: Sewed and did housework all day. Went to hear Bayard Taylor lecture in the evening. Liked the lecture very much, it was on American Peculiarities. He spoke to a large audience.[54]

January 21, 1862, Tuesday: Went up town this morning. Sewed in the afternoon went to Lodge in the evening. Several Senators initiated this evening, made arrangement for a Sociable tomorrow evening.

January 22, 1862, Wednesday: Addie Purple & I went up this morning to arrange the room for the Sociable tonight. We put up the curtains, arranged the stage & c. and then went home. Had Recitations, music, charades and tableaus, and a pleasant time, danced a little afterwards.

ANN

From Ann Waldo at Winneconne to Morris Waldo at Kenosha, Wisconsin, January 22, 1862

With the utmost pleasure I again seat myself to answer the very welcome letter rec'd yesterday from my dear husband. I am sorry you were disappointed in not getting your pay as soon as you expected, for I had got my mind up to come and make you a visit this week. But perhaps it is all for the best. But are you not afraid that your Reg. may not get your pay at all? I have heard that the paymaster has been to Milwaukee and Racine paying off those troops and it seems very strange he should go right past you and pay off the others. Seems to me that looks a little as if they were intending to disband the Reg. I hope not, for as long as I have made up my mind to your going and we have sacrificed so much and so broken up I feel it would be better for you to go, though I would not like to go in any other Reg.

It will be too bad if we have to lose all the time you have been there and do not get any pay for it. If you should like to get your pay and should be ordered South I should very much like to come down there before you go and will be ready to come any time at one day's notice. But if you think it would cost too much and would not be best for me to come, you have only got to say so.

I rec'd a letter from Giles Monday. He said he had seen Mr. Cramer and he could not pay those orders now and would not specify any particular time when he would pay them. But he said Mr. C. said I need not be troubled about them. He would pay them as soon as he could. Giles said he would try and pay the balance of that order on the store if I wanted it, but as we do not need any store pay at present I shall not go out.

Larson received a paper from Maggie the other day containing the marriage of Mr. Andrew Cullings to Miss Amanda Barnard (on Christmas Day). Larson also rec'd a letter from Converse and Adeline yesterday. All well as usual. They said they had heard that Ellen Waite Johnson had become converted and had talked and prayed in public. Also that Horace Waldo had become pious and that David Waldo's son Johnny had become deranged through a religious excitement for they were going to take him to a Lunatic Asylum.

The recruiting officer you mentioned came to town Monday. He went to see young Gunner yesterday and I believe he is going to enlist and I believe

Pat. Early thinks of enlisting. That does not look much as if there was a prospect of disbanding.

Mrs. Tucker called here Monday for that order on Mr. Ferrington. She said the order was for $11.00 and I told her that you told me $10.50 but as Mr. F. was only owing $10.17 I could only give her an order for that am't. She said when they got your bill and looked it over there was the making of 8 doors charged to them, and as you only return 7 doors and pay them for lumber for the other, you must owe them for the making of one door. I told her I would mention it to you as I presumed you had forgotten; it was so long ago, but it is probably all right. But how much was it $10.50 or $11.00. She seemed to think it rather hard they should have to be the expense of staying out over night and hiring a man to stay there while he was gone.

I think it is rather hard but you must direct them what to do. I mentioned the nails and she said they would pay Mr. Clark for them. So that will make a difference in what you owe Mr. Clark. How much was it without that? I mean to propose to Mr. Tucker to let Waldo take his team and he will go and get the doors without costing Mr. F. anything.

The Rev. Mr. Chittenden, a younger brother of your Capt called here yesterday afternoon to ascertain whether we were sheep or goats [Matt. 25:32–33]. He said Mr. A Harris was trying to get up a revival here and had invited him to assist him. Mr. C. preached last evening and is to preach again this evening. I fear it is a barren field to labor in. I am sorry to hear of Dr. Johnson's illness. Hope he was better soon.[55]

Mrs. Morton and George have gone with Rufus' team, down south somewhere, on a visit. I believe not into Secessia, however. They were expected back yesterday or today.

We do not know what Mr. White has done about that note, but will go to ask him before I seal this letter.

I expect a letter from you regularly every Tuesday. Do not disappoint me. I do not write Lindas lately, as I have nothing to write them, and think it is better to wait until I receive yours as it comes so early in the week.

Della is very anxious to learn to read. She comes every day with a book teasing me to learn her to read. She stands here now teasing me to tell her what the letters are and will not take no for an answer. She knows several of the letters now and I am getting over my hurry in sewing so I must take time to teach her. She is so anxious. She says, "Why won't you take time to learn me to read, mama, as Aunt Susan does the little girls."

I must not write any more as this will be too late for today's mail & and I expect somebody will be looking for it pretty anxiously, even if it is not very interesting, so good night.

Ann

M. M. says he has done nothing about note. Mr. C. has been in town several times but has not been near here.

Emily

January 23, 1862, Thursday: Washed the forenoon went up to the Hall to arrange matters a little found Mr. Bowers and the Janitor there. They had straitened everything out nicely so that we had nothing to do but talk. Mr. Picken came up and helped us. The Relief Society met at our house tonight. We hemmed towels, talked, and played some, Society adjourned to meet here again on Monday evening next.

January 24, 1862, Friday: Sewed all the forenoon, got ready to go to Oakland this afternoon. Started at one o'clock Mr. Craig & Geo. C. Smith with us. Had a pleasant ride though rather cold sleighing excellent arrived at Mr. Smith's about 6 o'clock, had supper and drove to a festival which we had come to attend. Found the Hall crowded tables spread and everybody enjoying themselves. Had plenty of oysters, chicken pie, and such creature comforts as well as more intellectual gratifications. Got back about one o'clock. I made several pleasant acquaintances among which were Mr. Pardy, Miss Hunt & Mr. & Mrs. Bowers. Went to bed at half past two thoroughly tired.

January 25, 1862, Saturday: Rose about nine o'clock this morning. Had a nice breakfast with country cream in our coffee, spent a pleasant forenoon and after dinner started for Madison where we arrived about eight o'clock very cold and tired.

Ann

From Ann Waldo at Winneconne to Morris Waldo at Kenosha, Wisconsin, January 26, 1862

My dear husband,

I have not one word of anything to write but I do want to see you awfully. And as I cannot have that pleasure, I must content myself with scribbling over this sheet of paper & then punish you in picking it out. Susan and I attended church this forenoon and afternoon. Mr. Chittenden preached this P.M. He has been in town the last week, labouring with Mr. Harris and Robertson for the salvation of souls, but I fear they have cast their bread upon the waters [Eccles. 11], with no immediate prospect of a return. I rec'd a letter from Amelia the other day in answer to the one I sent her two weeks ago. It contained the money for those chairs, $4.00 though it seems Abner nor Amelia knew anything about the arrangement until she received my letter (which I thought was very probable). Abner was not at home so Amelia went right over to see Mr. Steele. She said he acknowledged he had been rather negligent about saying anything to them about it, as he supposed I had arranged with them. Fortunately Abner came home sooner than expected and still more fortunate, had the money, though she said she was not very pleased with the transfer of his creditor without his knowledge.

I took the money and paid Mr. Rowley $3.28, one dollar on the old account & the rest for Della's dress and trimmings. Mr. R. Said he spoke to Dan. M. about that order on him and D. said he would see Rufus and if he had no objections he would pay it to him. I think that is pretty well. Who do you suppose Rufus thinks he is. I told Mr. R. that Rufus had already received more than half & had no claims on the remainder. If I were you I would send a line to Dan forbidding his paying it to Rufus and requesting him to pay it to Mr. Rowley.

Tuesday morning

Well here I have delayed this letter waiting for the one I expected from my husband this afternoon but don't know whether it will come or not. What a privilege it is to be able to hear from and write to you every week. What shall we do when you get away down toward [illegible], if that should be your destination for there has been no mail route in that vicinity for months. I shall not probably be able to hear anything from you or you from me after you get beyond Kansas until your return, should you be so fortunate, which may God grant.

You will probably have the pleasure of Mr. Stacy's company among you next Monday as he goes to Ripon Sunday. The recruiting officer that was here has got him on his old enlistment by a little flattery and a little scaring as Waldo says Giles Clerk gave him a hint to make Mr. G. believe he had some papers for him. He has promised him that he shall draw pay from the time he enlisted.[56]

Mr. G. has sold his shop, coal and tools to I.P. Hercox. He (Mr. H.) has also bought out John Larson. He has gone down below Oconto. Mr. H is going to keep a man in his shop over there too. I have heard he is going to move over the in town. They are having the scarlet fever out on the prairie. Mr. Vosburgh of Vinland buried two daughters a week ago Sunday with it. I was quite unwell yesterday with a diarrhea & pain in my back under my apron, without any cause whatever. But I took one of those powders I took out of your pocket when you was here and that cured me so I feel as well as normal today. Waldo woke me this morning rattling the door, trying to get in to build a fire as usual. I got up and went to the door and found it fastened with a stick over the latch and the mystery is how did it get there. Willie and Eddie [Susan's sons] went to bed before I did and after I got to bed Waldo came and shut the middle door and I was certainly not out of bed again 'till he woke me this morning. Willie knows nothing about it, so one of us must have got up would fasten it.

Waldo has just come from the P.O. and reports no letter for me but the Omro mail will be in soon and then I hope for better success. You say you go morning and night after the m-a-l-e. Do you go after the female too?

You say you have a file of "litters" to distribute. What are they litters of usually? I am very glad of the papers you send me and do send me paper as often as you can for we have nothing but the Oshkosh paper to read in the whole week. I wish I could take the Milwaukee Sentinel for three months at least. I could get the tri-weekly Sentinel for 3 months for $1.00. We are so destitute of something to read, do send me something.

How does that engraving of your camp prosper? I have not rec'd one yet. I do want to come down there very much before you leave. I shall feel very disappointed if I can't & I think you will feel as quite as much so.

We have all the snow we need for sleighing and rather more. For it snows nearly every day. Have you seen that cap for Eddie since you went back there? I ought to empty the bookcase but do not know what to do with its contents.

What are you going to do with your harness? Is Mrs. Hunt there yet? The name of the recruiting officer that was here was Adams so it could not have been the one you spoke of as his name was Wood.

I wish there could be something done about that note Mr. White holds, for that is drawing no interest & he will charge you interest until it is paid & it will take the whole note to pay him. Mr. McIntyre has gone to Oconto. I have sent an order on those fisherman but I have no idea it will be of any use for Willis says they are not doing as well there as they were here. Every one that owes us seem to take their own time to pay it. Waldo exchanged that half-dollar with Mr. Lansing the next time he went to Omro.

Wednesday morning and no letter for poor me.

I dreamed last night that something had fallen on your foot & broken it. The reason you had not written to me this week, you were not able to but I hope Ross-O-Moore that "dreams always go by contrary's, my dear." Amelia wrote that Abner preached at Black Wolf once in four weeks & that next Sunday was his day & he would return this way & she wished me to return with him & make him a visit. But I want to see my husband more than all of the world beside, and unless I am satisfied before that time, then I shall not be able to go to Kenosha.

I shall not go there. I have so many things to talk with you about besides writing to you everything I know. I have got some smaller paper to write my letters on. Ain't you glad?

I am going to send this today so that you shall not be disappointed & I know there is some reason for my not getting a letter yesterday, for I know Mr. W. has not forgotten me.

Della is well and has learned half her letters.

Your affectionate wife.
A.E. Waldo

Emily

January 27, 1862, Monday: Washed today. It stormed violently all day. The Relief Society was to have met here but no one came on account of the storm Mr. Smith came and we played backgammon & checkers all the evening.

January 28, 1862, Tuesday: Sewed all day. Went to the Lodge in the evening. Had a pleasant time. Mr. Scofield accompanied me home.

January 29, 1862, Wednesday: Sewed in the forenoon. Went up town with Addie & Maria in the afternoon. Went to Hannah Chapman's in the evening.

January 30, 1862, Thursday: Staid at home all day. Went to the Senate in the evening to hear a lecture before the State Historical Society.

January 31, 1862, Friday: Sewed all day. Staid at home in the evening. Cousin Joseph came down from Camp Randall & spent the evening.

February 3, 1862, Monday: Stayed at home all day. Went to the Society in the evening. Had a very pleasant time, made sheets & pillowcases, played games afterward, among which was "Brother I'm bobbed!" under direction of Mr. Purman.

February 4, 1862, Tuesday: Went up to the Assembly Room with Ma. The body was in session, staid till adjourned. Went to Lodge in the evening. Was appointed Assistant Sec'ry much against my will. Mr. Scofield came home with us.

February 5, 1862, Wednesday: Rose feeling quite ill this morning did not go to bed again on account of sleigh ride tonight. We started to Sun Prairie about five o'clock. Had a splendid time. About thirty of us went to the hotel and took supper and started home at about eleven o'clock.

February 6, 1862, Thursday: Went up to the Legislature this morning staid about an hour. Went to the lecture in the evening by Prof. Denton subject Geology, it was very interesting indeed.

February 9, 1862, Sunday: Went to Church this forenoon. Staid to Bible Class. Hattie Benedick, Maria & I concluded to stay and attend the Band of Hope meeting in the afternoon which we did. Ma sent us a lunch by Charley. Wrote & read in the afternoon. Went to Church at the Congregational Chapel in the evening.

ANN

From Ann Waldo at Winneconne to Morris Waldo at Kenosha, Wisconsin, February 9, 1862

My dear good old husband,

"Wait until the good time coming, comes."

Well now, prepare yourself for another infliction from the pen of your spouse, and if not particularly eloquent, I trust you will find an interesting auditor. Firstly as D.W. would say, I was very glad to receive those Photographs which I think are very good representations of my soldier.

I am sorry the prospects of your Reg. are not more encouraging. I have given up all idea of coming to see you before you leave the state, which I had certainly hoped to do. But there are many worse situated than we, those that have large families depending upon them with no means of support, except what is due them from the army. I hope something more encouraging may transpire soon.

Maggie came here with Mr. Vedder last Monday & Waldo is going to take her home tomorrow, & Della and I intend going with her. I don't know how long I shall stay, as I shall leave to Providence to get back. I rather dislike to go on that account as I may have to stay longer than I shall want to as Abner is away lecturing all of the time will be engaged constantly until the last of March.

If you received the paper I sent you yesterday, I shall receive your next letter at Koro. I hope so for I shall hate to go without a letter next week.

Miss Ellen Vedder was married two weeks ago tomorrow to a Mr. Geo. Wakefield, a young man that lived in that vicinity. Waldo came from Uncle Pete's yesterday; he went out with a load of lumber for Mr. Steinsburg to sell. He saw Pa & David in Ripon a minute. All well. Juliette has another daughter several weeks old. Mr. and Mrs. Morton visited here yesterday. Mr. M. had a head cold; they are well otherwise.

Has Giles Clark found any employment yet?

It seems there is to be no such thing as Lane's expedition as he is only a Brigadier-General under Hunter. I thought strange if they allowed a man to take command that would be likely to hurt the rebels. We have too many traitors North to ever hope to conquer the South. But I suppose "All's well that ends well."

It is getting dark and as I have nothing to write I will not occupy any more time or paper writing it.

Hoping to hear from you soon, I remain
Your affectionate Ann

How many photographs did you have taken? Have you sent any to any of the rest of your friends? Too bad the pasteboard is cut off so closely around them.

Emily

February 10, 1862, Monday: Worked in the kitchen in the forenoon. Went up town and purchased cloth for some nightshirts. Ma & I cut them out to be in readiness to spare this evening. Fannie & I went to the lecture I left Maria President pro tem. We returned home about nine o'clock had a pleasant time. The Society adjourned to meet next week at Miss Chapman's.

Ann

From Ann Waldo at Koro to Morris Waldo at Kenosha, Wisconsin, February 16, 1862

My dear husband

Again I find myself under the necessity of answering the letter I did not receive. But I suppose it is not the fault of my dear husband, but myself in not sending you word sooner than I was coming here, but I hope to receive one here this week.

I read a letter in the Berlin Courant from some one in your Reg. written last Sunday, so that informed me in regard to what you were doing or rather not doing. I think as the writer of that letter did. If that Reg. is needed why not go into service immediately & if they are not needed, then let them disband at once and not be any longer an expense to government. As our treasury is already empty it seems a pity to keep so large an army doing nothing. I hope there will be something definite decided on soon.

Waldo got Mr. Stansbury's horse & brought Maggie, Della, and I here last Monday. We stopped at Wausau on the way and had Mr. Gibson extract a tooth for me as it had ached so severely. I was afraid to come away without having it out. I wish you could have looked upon our adventure last Tuesday evening. A man from 20 miles from Berlin (an acquaintance of theirs) came here last Monday with an Ox team & left his team here while he went to Ripon on foot. He had a daughter that he had been visiting in Ripon some time that was coming home with him, so Amelia promised him that their boy that does chores here might take his oxen and meet them at the cars Tuesday evening. The man said the cars got to Berlin at 10 o'clock so Amelia and Reggie thought it would be a good time to go and spend the evening of Ella, as they had not called on her since she went to housekeeping (they live in the 2nd house toward the depot, as her husband has taken her father's farm and live in their old house they put up last fall).

Well I went there with them and we staid there till 9 ½ o'clock and then started with our ox team for the depot. We got there and turned the team around and commenced waiting for the cars. The moon shone so that it was as light as day. There we sat in the sleigh singing songs and making ourselves as comfortable as possible until we began to get chilly and rather sleepy. Then Amelia and Maggie got out and ran about ½ mile and back on the track trying to warm their feet. But I sat still thinking I should be colder for getting out in the snow than I should be to sit still.

Finally when we had concluded to wait no longer, we were getting so cold, we heard the whistle and when they came and inquired what time the cars left Ripon, they said about 11 o'clock, and there we had been waiting since ½ past nine.

I shall have to stop writing for I am not well today, having trouble with a very hard backache. Besides my headaches so I can't hold it down to write it makes me so dizzy.

Della says send a kiss to papa, but I would much rather deliver mine in person.

Monday morning

I will make another attempt to finish this letter, tho I don't feel like writing anything very interesting this morning. But hope to feel better in a day or two. Della has had a very bad cold since she has been here. She has had a severe cough and some fever, but is better now.

Howard has the mumps so I expect Della will have those soon. Tomorrow evening we are all invited to a party at Mr. Wakefield's (Ella's father in law). Maggie and I attended a knitting bee at the soldier's aid society last Wednesday. We were invited to a party at Adams the same evening but as we could not get back until the team came we did not get there until they were eating supper between nine and ten.

Mr. Bell called here yesterday on his way to Berlin at Waldo's request to let me know I could have an opportunity to ride to Winneconne with him this morning. He has not come along yet but I have decided not to go. I am all out of knitting and sewing, and I am in no hurry to go back. That is not such a delightful neighborhood to be in and I have not finished my visits here yet. Old Mr. Vedder's Adam and Mr. Steele's people are all expecting me to visit them.

How I do wish I knew what you were going to do and how I want to see you. If you do not go into service I hope they will release you in time to come home so that you can do something this spring. In fact I had much rather you would not go, if you could get away from it honorably. God knows there are too many traitors in high places that think nothing of continuing the war as long as profitable, in order that they may line their pockets at the expense of our poor bankrupt government.

I find it is the very general opinion (among Republicans even) that Lincoln and McClellan are neither of them the right men in the right places, and that a great deal of information is conveyed to the rebels through Mrs. Lincoln, whose friends and interests are too much in secession for the good of our country.

Perhaps it may be the case with your Reg. that your Col. is keeping the Reg. together as long as profitable in order that he may draw pay even when he knows that it is never intended to go into service.

God grant that there may be a stop to this "masterly inactivity" and that speedily.

How is your health now and how do you feel in spirits? Poor fellows, it is too bad to be kept so and not know what you are going to do. How I do wish I could see you and have a good talk with you. Though writing is better than nothing it don't half satisfy me for I have to ask all of the questions and have no one to answer them.

I don't know when this letter can go, for they have not mail, only as Mr. Carter goes to Berlin which is usually once or twice a week. I think now I shall not go to Winneconne until Mr. Vedder goes to preach to Black Wolf again, which will be two weeks from yesterday, unless I hear something from you which changes my mind. So you will please direct to me here next week, but further than that date cannot sayest.

I was very very sorry to not hear from you last week but I presume there is a letter to Winneconne for me. But Waldo's folks did not think to send it by William.

Della got hold of one of my letters a week or two ago after I read it. Says she, "Mommie, if you ain't careful I shall read all of your privates." I sent her away from the supper table last night to put on an apron. When she came back, she says, "Excuse me a little. I've got on a dirty apron." She is a dear little girl and a great deal of company for me.[57]

Your wife,

Ann

Emily

February 17, 1862, Monday: This morning we received official accounts of the taking of Fort Donelson by our troops and the capture of fifteen thousand rebels composing the garrison also many pieces of cannon. It caused great rejoicing here, thirty-four guns were fired and every one felt great hopes of the speedy triumph of our men. We received additional telegraphic news during the evening stating that five thousand more prisoners had been taken among whom were Buckner, Johnston & Pillow. The Society met at Miss Chapman. The rooms were full, had a very sociable evening.[58]

February 20, 1862, Thursday: A splendid day. Went up town this forenoon to purchase articles for the use of the sick in Camp. Took a long walk this afternoon felt dreadfully blue. Went to hear Mrs. Swishelm at the Senate Chamber in the evening.[59]

February 22, 1862, Saturday: Went up this morning to help celebrate the day by listening to Gov. Harvey's presentation speech to the Regiments on giving them the colors. Could not get near enough to hear a word he said. Went over to the Assembly Room and worked an hour to hear Judge Davis read Washington's Farewell Address. Came home too tired to go in the evening to the address.

February 24, 1862, Monday: Went up town this morning & to the Society in the evening it met at Miss Benedicts. We made & rolled bandages all the evening. There was quite a number present. Society adjourned to meet at Miss Dodge's next Monday evening.

February 25, 1862, Tuesday: Sewed all day. Went to the Lodge in the evening. A large number of soldiers were present as well as a delegation from Sun Prairie Lodge. About twenty- five persons were initiated. We spent a very pleasant evening.

Despite the issues with the mail catching up with her in Koro, Ann was able to make the trip to Kenosha and was there when her sister, Susan, wrote to her about their neighbors in Winnecone and expressed her surprise at Ann's location. Susan's sense of responsibility contrasts with Ann's decision to follow her heart and be with her husband. While Ann remained with Morris in Kenosha, Susan was faced with financial worries and asked whether some of Morris's pay could be used to hire help on the farm. She also asked Ann to consider taking the upcoming teacher exam to try to qualify as a teacher and in that way contribute to the combined Brown/Waldo household.

SUSAN

From Susan Brown at Winneconne to Ann Waldo at Kenosha, Wisconsin, February 27 [?], 1862

My dear Ann,

Yours of 2/25 was received today. I answer it this evening that I may have the letter ready when I have an opportunity to send the box. I will pack it also this evening.

I was somewhat surprised to hear that you are well at K. and presumed you enjoy yourself finely. My school was out last Wednesday week since which time I have been very busy sewing. I was intending to go to Ripon next week with Mr. Tucker's team & have you to keep house but it seems that was a miscalculation.

There has been some mortality in the place & vicinity since you went away. Mrs. Metham in Poygan has lost three children since the first of this month. An old man that lived at Mrs. Bock's died one day last week quite suddenly (his sobriquet was Beauregard). Walter Lake died Monday night, quite suddenly, he had a scarlet rash, after that the chicken pox, and when nearly well took cold and bloated very much but was dressed and around the house on Monday nearly all day but I do not think they were careful enough about his taking cold.

Old. Mr. McCauley will be buried tomorrow. He has had two or three strokes of palsy within the last two or three weeks. It is not however sickly here. William Roche was married to Mrs. Weston, that Irish widow, last Friday at Oshkosh. Report has come from Kenosha here that Dr. Johnson is engaged to be married to Miss Phittenden of Ripon.

Mrs. Guman has been down here and staid a day or two. Did not go to Mrs. A.C's, as at Mrs. Owen's and Mrs. Webster's. I went over in the evening to see her. She had left her baby at home with Ida. Mrs. Frank Webster has a new daughter. Mr. Gable at Weyauwega was killed very suddenly last

Saturday morning by the falling of a tree. It broke his neck and one of his legs three times.

This letter seems to be principally filled with casualties. Waldo made some kind of a trade with Mr. White and is to have three ounces of zephyr worsted. I thought that was so much it ought to go toward making me a hood but his colors are not suitable. I send you a couple of samples of the darkest colors. How do you think it will do? How much of that color would it take and how much pink? I suppose I might color it but I don't know.

I must stop and pack your box for Waldo says Myron Rowley is up and is going back early in the morning and will carry your box to the Express Office tomorrow night but I shall put this letter in the office this morning. Waldo thinks it the best way if not the cheapest to send by express.

It is after nine o'clock, Waldo has been down to get Willis to mark your box cover but he hadn't much to do it with.

It is so cold here I must stop. Eddie wanted I should say something about his cap and tell you how uncouth Willis is. Willis says there is no need as you know all about it now. Write when you receive your box. How did you hear of Mr. J. Ridney?

Yours truly,
Susan

I was much obliged for the picture.

EMILY

March 1, 1862, Saturday: Mrs. Mercer brought me home this evening, it was very cold. I sewed all day. Mr. Scofield came in the evening to have us attend an extra session of the Lodge this evening for the purpose of instituting a Lodge in the 16th Regiment. There was a good many there. Mr. Purman Lieut. in the 16th was chosen Monthly Chief, and about forty persons became members of the Lodge. We had some good speeches and pleasant time generally.[60]

March 2, 1862, Sunday: It commenced raining rapidly this morning about church time we went however, and heard a good sermon read and wrote in the afternoon. Did not go to church in the evening.

March 3, 1862, Monday: A cold stormy day. Went to my German recitation in the afternoon. Only Mr. Craig there, the girls did not come on account of the storm. Miss Crocker & I played backgammon until eight o'clock, and then went to the lecture, but found the lecturer missing, the storms having blocked up the roads and prevented the cars from arriving on time. He came however about nine o'clock. The subject was Phrenology. The speaker O. S. Fowler.

March 4, 1862, Tuesday: At home all day, went to the Lodge in the evening. After the Lodge closed the members adjourned to the American House where an oyster supper had been provided by S. D. Hastings and others in this office and spent a very pleasant evening together. We bid our soldier brothers farewell as they will probably go this week.

༄

March 11, 1862, Tuesday: Went up town this morning and to Lodge in the evening. Bade Lieut. Purman good bye as the Regiment goes Thursday. We shall probably never meet again but I wish him all good and it would do me good to see him again for the sake of the pleasant hours we have all spent together. But this cruel war is taking many friends from our sight forever. God grant it may not be long.

༄

SUSAN

From Susan Brown at Winneconne to M. A. Waldo, Co. E 1st Wis. Cavalry, at Kenosha, Wisconsin, March 11, 1862

My dear Ann

Yours of sometime (I've forgotten when) reached me last Saturday so you perceive I am a very faithful correspondent. We are all well of course and everything here moves on about as usual. I think I can tell you a better way to get from Ripon here than you spoke of.

The cars come into Omro every day and when the forenoon train comes in, the mail-carrier comes over here in a sleigh, he has purchased a pair of Ponys. The mail gets here before noon so the train must leave Ripon very early in the morning.

I am glad to hear that you are enjoying yourself so much. I have not been out much since school closed. Visited at Mr. Ferris's and Mr. Heicox however.

Louis Johns looked at the cradle and said he could not possibly give more than $1.00 for it as the willows were somewhat broken. Waldo wished me to write you about it, but I told him the baby would outgrow the cradle before we could get an answer and told him I would take the responsibility of selling it for that as I thought if you wished to sell it you would rather do so for that than not at all.

Waldo did not give Mr. Rowley that note from Morris for he said Mr. R. said it was all right as Mr. Moscrip had promised to pay it as soon as he could.

I was reading in the last Northwestern that our County sup would be in Winneconne the 1st Monday in April to examine the teachers of Poygan, Winchester, Winneconne, and some other town. Would you like to be present? Oh, what about that school in Koro?

I intended to have told you that the newspaper in the bottom of your box was sent to you from So. Rutland (N.Y. Reformer) by Henry Anderson. I guess tho' I am not sure Mrs. A's obituary notice.

I sent you a letter from Waupaca County. As I knew what it contained I took the liberty of removing the envelope before sending it. If you purchase a summer dress for me I would like something besides a white background. I was thinking of a buff background when I thought of getting calico with a set flower in it but you can judge better than I, only not too much white in it.

Windsor's address is Springfield, Oxford Co., Canada West.

If Morris should get his money now Waldo would like to hire some providing he could wait a year or more for his pay. He has sold hay enough to meet the small sums he had to pay, and we should not want any but that our ancient enemy, Mr. Abell is going to begin again before the first of April and Waldo though if he could raise part of it perhaps he might compromise. As Mr. A offers now to pay the cost it would be cheaper for Waldo than to let it go.

I had a letter from Mrs. Kirkham the other day in which she scolded me very much about you. Says she will send you Henry's photograph if you write to her. I can think of nothing more now. I will lay it by until morning. Answer this as soon as convenient.

Eddie says tell Aunt Ann I'm a naughty boy.

With much love I remain.
Affectionately
S. M. Brown

I see by the papers that there is another regiment in Kenosha and therefore I shall specify cavalry on the envelope.

EMILY

March 13, 1862, Thursday: Ella & I had intended to go to Camp this morning to see the 16th Regiment off, but they started too early and therefore we did not go. Ella went home about ten. I sewed all day had company in the evening.

March 15, 1862, Saturday: In the kitchen all the forenoon, up town in the afternoon. Finished John Halifax this evening. I like it very much. It is the most plain common sense and yet charming story of house life & love and trials I ever read.

March 16, 1862, Sunday: Went to church this morning. Mr. Howard preached on the text "We are fearfully and wonderfully made" [Ps. 149:14], he preached a very good sermon. Wrote and read all the afternoon, read Tennyson's "Maud" and "In Memoriam" and wrote a communication for our Lodge Paper.

March 17, 1862, Monday: At home in the forenoon, went to my German lesson in the afternoon. The Young Ladies Relief Society met here this evening. I made my report as President of the Society and we concluded we would have no more meetings. We played Chess and backgammon, and had a good time.

March 18, 1862, Tuesday: Went up town today. To lodge in the evening. We had quite a discussion on Temperance questions tonight and I got considerably excited.

March 25, 1862, Tuesday: Went up with Gus to get Maria's picture taken, got a very good one. Met Sen. Browne and Sen. Hazelton at the Gallery. Went to the Lodge in the evening, read the paper it was pronounced the best ever read in the Lodge.[61]

March 26, 1862, Wednesday: Went up with Augustus at nine o'clock this morning to get the children's likenesses taken as he was anxious to have them all. He went this morning. I was sorry to have him go, he seems like one of the family. Went to Miss Crocker's to a candy party this evening, we had any quantity of fun & candy. The Turner girls came home with us and remained all night.

～

March 29, 1862, Saturday: Sewed all day. Went to the Senate Chamber to attend a lecture on elocution by Prof. McCafferty [?] of New York.

March 30, 1862, Sunday: Dr. Howard preached his farewell sermon this morning. I am very sorry he is going.

March 31, 1862, Monday: At home in the forenoon. Went up town and to my German lesson. Wendall Philipps [sic] lectures tonight on the war. I had a headache and did not feel able to go. Ma & Fannie went.[62]

～

As the war neared the end of its first year, the horror of war touched Emily's life when both a friend and a cousin were fatally wounded in battle. Emily made another trip to Camp Randall hoping to see the arrival of Confederate soldiers who had been captured when Island No. 10 in the Mississippi River fell to Union troops (including the 8th and 15th Infantry regiments and the 5th, 6th and 7th Light Artillery). Of the 1,200 prisoners temporarily housed at Camp Randall, 140 perished. They are buried at Forest Hill in Madison, the northernmost Confederate cemetery. Because of the lack of medical facilities at the camp, the surviving prisoners were transferred to Chicago in May 1862.[63]

The Waldo/Brown family had not yet experienced a casualty of war despite Morris Waldo's deployment to Missouri. Susan Brown's letters continued to discuss her responsibilities and to express bewilderment at her sister's plans for the future. In a letter written late in the month Susan's pride in her own intellect shines as she details her exemplary success in completing her teacher's examination.

Citizens throughout Wisconsin were stunned when their new governor, Lewis Powell Harvey, drowned as he was returning North after delivering supplies to Wisconsin soldiers at the front. Following the Battle of Pittsburg Landing (Shiloh) on April 6 and 7, Harvey had issued an urgent call for supplies, and he left on April 10 to deliver them to Wisconsin soldiers in need. He began his return voyage up the Tennessee on the steamship *Dunleith*.

While awaiting transfer from the *Dunleith* to the *Minnehaha*, Governor Harvey lost his footing and fell into the river between the two boats. His body was found several days later about sixty miles downriver.[64] Edward Salomon succeeded Harvey as governor. One of his first actions was to declare thirty days of mourning and to set aside May 1, 1862, as a "day of public rest and cessation from business."[65] He also issued a call for more troops and received an overwhelming response from volunteers—enough to staff fourteen regiments.[66]

Governor Harvey's widow, Cordelia Harvey, continued her husband's charitable work and was named the "State's Sanitary Agent." After visiting ill and wounded soldiers in the hot and humid Southern climate, she determined that they would recover much more quickly if they were transported to the North. In 1863 she convinced President Lincoln to support this idea, and Harvey Hospital was established in Madison.[67] The lack of Union general hospitals meant that one-third of wounded soldiers languished in field hospitals awaiting beds in general hospitals. By 1863 the Union had 151 hospitals, with a total capacity of 58,715 beds; by 1865 there were 204 hospitals, with beds for 136,894.[68]

April 3, 1862, Thursday: Mr. McKinney came this morning to remind us to go to Mazomanie tonight to a Festival. Concluded to go.

April 4, 1862, Friday: Started yesterday at seven o'clock on the cars reached Mazo [Mazomanie] about nine, went to the place appointed had a splendid supper, stayed a short time and sang "John Brown" and some other things and then were invited to adjourn to the Hall where the dancing was to be. It was a large factory building. We danced until two o'clock, when a gentleman very kindly invited us to go home with him and pass the remainder of the night, about a half a dozen went with the rest preferring to stay. We danced until four o'clock when the musicians were so tired that they would play no longer, and then we promenaded the remainder of the night, at daylight we adjourned to the hotel. The rain having ceased the landlord made us a fire, and we procured water, washed and made ourselves comfortable, had breakfast, visited the bowling alley, took a walk down the railroad track, climbed a very steep and high hill, three-quarters of a mile from the hotel, went back and found it was time to take the cars. Had a splendid time coming home where we arrived at eleven. I went to bed where I remained until five o'clock. Mr. Craig came in the evening.

The town of Mazomanie, where Emily had a "splendid" evening. (Wisconsin Historical Society, WHS 27213)

April 8, 1862, Tuesday: Good sleighing this eighth of April. Snowed almost all day. Ironed and baked, worked in the kitchen most of the day. Went to the Lodge in the evening. Had quite a discussion in regard to the propriety of using liquors for culinary purposes. Mr. Hastings and Joseph Pickard also Mr. Scofield spoke on the question.

April 9, 1862, Wednesday: News of a terrible battle at Pittsburgh [sic] Landing came this morning. Wisconsin is said to have had six regiments engaged. The reports say we have lost 20,000 killed and wounded the rebels 10,000, but it must be exaggerated. Much anxiety is felt in regard to the Sixteenth Regiment reported to have been taken prisoners by the enemy at the commencement of the engagement. The battle occurred on Sunday and Monday resulting in the total rout of the enemy with terrible loss. Went to my German lesson staid afterwards and played a game of chess with Miss Crocker. Came home accompanied by Miss C. and we all went up to the Assembly Chambers to assist in preparing and packing articles of necessity and comfort for our wounded. There were a great many persons present, and a large amount of work was done. Gov. Harvey goes tomorrow with wagons and supplies. I went home with Miss Crocker played chess until tired and then went to bed.[69]

April 10, 1862, Thursday: Came home this morning sewed and crocheted all day. Stayed at home and played chess in the evening. News today is that our loss is about 10,000, enemies 15,000 and this a moderate estimate.

April 11, 1862, Friday: Ironed this forenoon baked and made myself generally useful. Got my German lesson and went to recitation. Afterward Mr. McHenry invited me to go to a hop on the armory. Did not feel much like dancing went however, had a pleasant time came home at 12 ½ o'clock.

April 12, 1862, Saturday: Rained incessantly today, much to my disappointment as I wished to go out. I packed two comfortables this forenoon, crocheted all the afternoon, read a little aloud from *Widow Beddott*, played Chess in the evening, crocheted & read, did not retire until one o'clock. News tonight that our Sixteenth were not taken prisoners as at first supposed, they were among the first in the engagement, and captured a Battery commanded by Beauregard in person and depriving him of an arm. They are much praised for their courage and determination. Our Tenth was not in this battle but in one at Yorktown on Monday, where they fought splendidly and covered themselves with glory. We are all very anxious to hear from our wounded and to know whom of our friends we shall see no more on earth.

This war is a terrible thing, but we hope soon by the blessing of God it will be brought to a close and bloodshed and horror no longer blight our fair land.

༄

SUSAN

From Susan Brown at Winneconne to Ann Waldo c/o Morris Benton Barracks, St. Louis, Missouri, April 13, 1862

My dear Ann,

Yours of March 24th was rec'd. on the ensuing Saturday but I had previously heard by the way of Mr. Morton that you were intending to go to St. Louis. I had intended to have this written before but have delayed it from day to day but still I think this will find you there. We are all well of course. I fear I shall not make a very interesting letter of this for it does not seem to me that I have much to say, however to begin. Almost everything in our village remains in "Status Quo." Mr. White has gone into the hotel with Mrs. Wood for Maid of all work hiring one of the children boarded at Mr. Tucker's. James Thompson's health is very poor. Mrs. A. Mc. told me she did not think he would live until summer. Dr. Lindau says he may live a year or two. His father has been sent for and is here now, and intends taking him to Ohio with him should he be able to go when warm weather comes. We are having a very dismal weather this month—it either rains or snows everyday almost. There have been a few cases of scarlet fever in town and is now. No one imminent danger but little Mary Scott, she has been sick a month I should think and I fear she will not recover, but I think her mother did nothing for her only what Dr. Brown told her to. He experimented a few days and gave her up. Since then they have had no physician and she is lingering along but I think will not recover. It is too bad. We have a letter or rather have two letters from Convers since you wrote, on business of course. Contained but little news. Celinda Waldo has a new son. I saw the death of Miss. Sarah A. Holcomb in the Reformer last week, aged 29 years. I think they must not have counted (as Aunt Mary would say) the seven years she was lying sick. (consumption her disease)

Elias Hill died several weeks since in Kentucky of brain fever. It is supposed or rather I think it is known that two or three persons from this vicinity were captured in the regiments that were captured last Sunday near Corinth. Gilbert Fish and Mr. Condonen. It is not ascertained here yet whether the 14th Reg. was engaged.[70]

I have received a letter from Thomas P. Mathews in which he says they are about moving onto the Goodrich farm. He has been lumbering some this winter. He says he has got about two hundred thousand logs. He also had a new son (Dec. 26th) which he says Aunt Mary thinks a fine a child as Eddie was which he says comprehends all that necessary to say. Waldo sends Morris a town meeting ticket with the names of those persons elected on it. Court starts tomorrow and Waldo has heard nothing officially from Mr. Abell. Perhaps it was not convenient for him to pay the cost which he told Waldo was about $30.00. So we have until July I suppose. How soon do you think your time will expire in which you have to redeem those lots. I see in the County the lands are to be sold the 13th of May. Perhaps in all counties it is the same. I do not know.

I am very busy sewing, have made myself a calico dress.

Yesterday was the first boat up, the Wolfe. She went into Lake Poygan and was obliged to return on account of ice, but she brought a barrel direct to Mr. Walt Brown of Kenosha. I suppose Eddie was much pleased to see his military cap. He wants to wear it all the time. Our teacher's examination comes off tomorrow.

You said nothing of Della, I suppose she is with you. Are you housekeeping there yet and when do you intend to return? If you are already gone, tell Morris to answer this letter. If not write me soon yourself and not wait as long as I have done.

Yours truly,
S.M.B.

Emily

April 14, 1862, Monday: Raining & unpleasant, nothing of importance occurred aside from the usual routine. Nothing new by telegraph. The list of killed and wounded not yet made out. Heard from Mr. Hadley of the death of Capt. Pease of the Sixteenth—he was an old acquaintance of ours and engaged to May Hadley. Heard also that Lieut. Purman was dangerously wounded. Miss Crocker came to play Chess tonight, Mr. Gillett came and spent the evening.[71]

April 18, 1862, Friday: Heard today that Cousin Joseph was wounded in the arm. We do not get full list of killed and wounded as yet. No news of importance from the rest of ours. Went up town this afternoon. Took a long walk. It was very pleasant.[72]

April 20, 1862, Sunday: Went to the Congregational Church this morning Dr. Baylor's subject was "Special Providences." Took a walk out to the Camp in the afternoon to see the Rebel prisoners come in, they were to come at five o'clock. Got out there and found that they were not coming until half past seven. Concluded not to wait. Maria & I went to the Methodist Church in the morning.

SUSAN

From Susan Brown at Winneconne to Ann M. Waldo at Kenosha, Wisconsin, April 20, 1862

My dear Ann

I wrote you last Sunday but having been so dilatory before and having rec'd a letter from you I make haste to answer it. I hope this may not find you there. I think you ought to hasten away with Della as soon as possible. Your housekeeping must be on rather a primitive scale. You will probably arrive at Ripon when our people are doing their spring work, but you can come to Aunt Margaret's in the cars, and from Eureka in a steamboat, although Waldo says now that the drive would not get to Butte De Mortes in time for the boat up the River. Don't you think of paying the taxes on those lots in time to save them? As I wrote you last Sunday, I have not much to write today. I rec'd. a letter from Emily Brown this last week. She was at Conver's visiting, on her way to Mass. She speaks of Anna as being very kind to her mother and being a very good girl. I mentioned last Sunday I think that, the teacher's examination came off Monday and Tuesday. I went there Monday morning to see the elephant. The schoolhouse had been cleaned and looked quite respectable. There was quite a gathering there before Mr. John Mingers made his appearance in company with two other gentlemen. (Let me promise that I think he looks about as taking or rather had about as taking an expression to his countenance as Lucian Clark.) Shortly after his arrival, he requested each teacher to occupy a separate seat as the exercises were to be written and no teacher was to have any communication with the other. The spectators were to take one side of the house and teachers the other. It required but few minutes for me to decide which I would be. So I took a separate seat and rec'd. a card [with] the questions on it. I was expected to answer in writing. If every question was answered perfectly, we were marked ten. If missed one or two, marked nine. If two but not four eight but falling below or not marked six on each branch you were not entitled to a certificate. We had 50 minutes in which to answer the questions on the card. The first subject was Reading i.e. questions on the rules of reading. The two gentlemen who assisted passed out the cards. Not a word was spoken but everyone went to writing. (Sarah Brown has been here two or three hours and so interrupted my story I do not know how to proceed.) I must tell you all about it when I see you. Suffice it to say Miss Sarah Fish left before she began. Sarah Brown said S.F. told the gentlemen who brought the cards <u>she</u> was not accustomed to answering such silly questions. I suppose she thought they were too inquisitive inquiring into the why and wherefore of everything. Miss Olive left discouraged about the middle of the first afternoon. About 14 remained in the class until the close, and when the case was summoned up the 2nd afternoon it stood something like this—1st S.M. Brown having been marked 4 10's, 1 eight and 1 seven; 2nd—Mr. Lester having 1 ten—I don't know the rest. 3rd—William Robertson (elder's son): had 1 nine, none higher; 4th Birch Ellis; 5th Sarah Brown; 6th Mrs. Harrington; 7th Delia Specs; Miss Gibbs so low her score was under consideration, Miss Gidding no certification, Two Miss Browns from BDM, not any; one or two from Poygan, not any, 1 from Winchester—not any. W.R. teaches here this summer. I did not care for that—my standing was higher than that young posted but I was better pleased that it was so much higher than W.R.'s. To give you some idea of the lamentable deficiency in the education of the teachers—in this county—those gentlemen told me that out of the seventy-six teachers examined in this county, about three were as high as I. None did better. I do not wish you to say anything about this before Calvin or anyone who may ever see Winneconne because it might come back [to] her. Remember don't let anyone know what is in this unless Morris.

I am going to spend all my spare time in study this summer. Next fall, the 2nd grade certificates will be issued to those who can get them. Beside the common branches, Physical Geography, Physiology-U.S. History, natured Philosophy and Algebra. That will be something worth striving for. Out of the seventy six teachers inspected at . . . [remainder of letter missing].

EMILY

April 21, 1862, Monday: We all felt a shock of deep sorrow this morning when news came through that Gov. Harvey had been drowned in the Tennessee River as he was going from one boat to another. His loss was a terrible blow to his wife. She was on the street when the report came getting subscriptions for the relief of a poor family in town. She inquired why the Capital and Court House flags were at half-mast and they would not tell her, she then told them to tell her if he was dead and reading it on their faces, dropped senseless to the ground, as soon as she was sufficiently composed she took the cars for Chicago, where their friends reside. The stores and places of business were all closed and draped in mourning as also the State House. The deepest sorrow is felt by all for the untimely death of so good a man. His place cannot be easily filled. There was a meeting of citizens at the Capitol tonight to [indecipherable] resolutions in regard to the loss sustained by the State and his personal friends. He died in the discharge of a noble duty, and as duty in the service of his beloved country as though pierced by a rebel bullet and his name will be forever associated with this crisis of his affairs as one which [crossed out] whose honor never shrank from duty, who honestly and conscientiously did all in his power to aid the cause of freedom & right. He was a member of the Congregational Church, a good Governor, an able man a kind friend and warm-hearted Christian. Peace to his ashes.

As the first year of the war drew to a close, General Henry Halleck reorganized the Army of the Mississippi and named General Grant second in command as the Union Army began its advance on the strategically important railroad junction at Corinth, Mississippi.[73] In Virginia, Stonewall Jackson began the Shenandoah Valley Campaign.[74] The Union victories at Pittsburg Landing; New Orleans; Savannah Harbor; Island No. Ten; and Fort Macon, North Carolina, had heightened expectations that the war would be a short one. In an overoptimistic response, the federal government closed all recruiting stations.[75]

CHAPTER 2

May 1862 to April 1863

As the war entered its second year, Wisconsin was deep in mourning for Governor Harvey, who had perished while providing for Wisconsin's soldiers.[1] Although Emily had taken enthusiastic interest in public events in the spring of 1861, her comments on this event were rather cursory. Although she did refer to the Confederate prisoners at Camp Randall, her thoughts centered on her domestic responsibilities and on another trip to Mazomanie, this time to complete papers as she hoped to find a teaching position, a quest she continued to follow throughout the summer. In August, Emily began working for her Pa, compiling scrapbooks of letters sent home by Wisconsin soldiers and working on Wisconsin's Civil War military history.

At the end of the month, many Wisconsin troops participated in the Battle of Seven Pines, the largest conflict in the Eastern Theater to date. Wisconsin troops included the 4th Light Artillery and the 5th, 6th, 7th, 19th, 36th, 37th, and 38th Infantry.[2] Concerned about the large number of Wisconsin wounded, Governor Edward Salomon urged the Wisconsin legislature to provide funds to bring wounded Wisconsin soldiers back home to recover. This practice was not initially supported by Lincoln and the Union generals, who feared that it would lead to increased desertions.[3]

Faced with losses in battle and a realization that victory was not imminent, the federal government reopened recruiting offices on June 6.[4] In early July Lincoln issued a call for an additional three hundred thousand troops, who were promised an advance of a month's pay if they enlisted for three years.[5] In yet another effort to encourage enlistment, Lincoln signed the first national pension act, which provided lifetime benefits to those wounded in war and to the families of those who were killed.⁶ On July 17 Lincoln signed the Second Confiscation Act, which granted freedom to slaves on lands taken by the Union Army, a complement to the Emancipation Proclamation.⁷

EMILY

May 1, 1862, Thursday: At home this forenoon. This was the day set apart by Gov. Solomon [*sic*: Salomon] for the funeral ceremonies of Gov. Harvey, but it rained incessantly all day. I did not go but heard that the Hall was quite full, Mr. McKenney came to tea. He and Mr. Gillett staid in the evening. We played chess and backgammon.

May 4, 1862, Sunday: Went to the Methodist Church this morning. There was quite a number of soldiers present belonging to the nineteenth Regiment, which is now guarding the Rebel prisoners in Camp. Read in the afternoon. Went to Church in the evening.

May 5, 1862, Monday: Rose at five this morning. Got ready and Pa accompanied me to the cars. Started at 7 o'clock for Black Earth, found Dr. & Mrs. Hooker waiting for me at the depot. Went to the hotel another young lady was there with her father. We commenced dining the forenoon. I finished my papers about two o'clock then went to see Mrs. High. Spent about an hour there. Dr. Hooker came for me, said if I was going to Mazo Manie I must hurry cars only stopped a moment, paid my bill at the hotel and got ready in time to see the cars go without me. Staid in Black Earth until six and then started on foot for Mazo about three miles distant, arrived there I went to see Mr. Brown one of the school board told me that the school was engaged, but hoped I would apply for it in the fall as he would like to have me teach. Went to the hotel with intention of going home in the 11½ night train concluded to remain all night.

May 6, 1862, Tuesday: Rose, breakfasted took a walk around the village and at nine o'clock the cars for Madison arriving here at twelve. Mr. Craig was waiting for me at the depot, but I missed him and came up town. Went to my German lesson and to the Lodge in the evening. Mr. Craig came to board here today.

May 12, 1862, Monday: Cleaned house all the forenoon. Went out on a Soliciting Committee for our festival in the afternoon. Spent the evening at Mr. Bradley's.

May 13, 1862, Tuesday: Went up town this morning. Finished papering the dining room. Went to my German lesson without knowing it. Went to the Lodge in the evening, Mr. Campbell not being there in season and the report of the Festival Committee being called for I was obliged to make the report. Mr. Campbell came afterwards. The arrangements for the Festival were made and it will come off tomorrow night. I was elected chairman of the Publishing Committee.

May 14, 1862, Wednesday: Rose early this morning. Committed to memory half a dozen pages of Widow Ristoff [?] for performance tonight at ten. Mr. Campbell came for me with the buggy to go up to the Hall. We looked at two or three rooms and then concluded to have the supper in the Lodge Room setting our tables there. We had quite a nice supper and a very pleasant evening. Mrs. Allen sang "Kingdom Coming" and "Old Southern Gentleman" beside several others pieces and we had recitations and readings. There were a number of people from the Sun Prairie Lodge and they seemed to enjoy it much. Some of the young ones got up a dance in a lower room and we adjourned at about half past twelve.[8]

May 15, 1862, Thursday: Went up to the Hall this morning. Arranged and assorted the dishes and tablecloths for the owners and then went up town. Got my German lesson, recited it. Played Chess. Went boat riding tonight for the first time this summer. We went to McBride's Point, got some flowers I sat by Mr. Gillett and rowed with one oar all the way home. We all enjoyed it much.

May 17, 1862, Saturday: Went up town with Ma this morning. We got a new carpet for the sitting room. Maria & I made and put it down today. Did not have a word of my German. Received a letter from the Clerk of Schools at Cross Plains saying I could have the school think Maria will take it.

May 18, 1862, Sunday: Did not go to Church. Attended the funeral of Rev. J. C. Russell this afternoon at his home. There was a large number of persons present. We went to the grave, Rev. Russell was respected and esteemed by all who knew him and his loss is deeply felt. Went to church in the evening.

May 19, 1862, Monday: Commenced teaching in the First Ward Grammar School today in Fannie's place she being to ill to teach. Like it very well.

May 28, 1862, Wednesday: Went up to the University this evening with the intention of going upon the Dome of the new building. Found that the workmen had the keys, and they had gone. We were obliged to content ourselves with visiting the Museum & then went to Sarah Turner's to spend the evening.[9]

June 7, 1862, Saturday: Sewed until nine o'clock went to teacher's meeting. Mrs. Wise and Kate Kavenaugh came to tea and remained until dark. Maria came home this noon. She has been gone almost three weeks. It is her first assay at school teaching. We went up town after dark.

June 8, 1862, Sunday: Went to church this morning. A Mr. Johnson from Michigan preached at the Baptist Church. A beautiful day. Came home and wrote two letters and read The Antiquary. Went to Church in the evening.

June 9, 1862, Monday: School very thinly settled today a great many of the scholars gone to the Business Picnic. Edward Everitt [sic] lectured this evening to a full house at the Baptist Church subject Origin & Progress of the War. A very good lecture. Everitt is a fine looking man about sixty-five years of age, and a good speaker.[10]

June 10, 1862, Tuesday: School as usual. Went to my German lesson. Sarah Turner came home with me. Went to the Lodge. Two of the members charged with violating their obligation yesterday at the picnic, one of them confessed it and was re-obligated.

June 14, 1862, Saturday: Dr. Reed remained all night and we rose at six o'clock with the intention of going on a fishing excursion immediately after breakfast. Arrived at the lake and found it so rough there was no possibility of doing anything in the fishing line that time. We fished off from shore a little way and found that the water came over the boat, conceded we wouldn't go and came home quite disappointed. I went to Teacher's Meeting then up town. Celia came in today to stay a short time. At home all the afternoon and evening.

∽

By mid-June, Ann Waldo was back in Winneconne, and Morris Waldo was at Cape Girardeau, Missouri, where the 1st Cavalry was "surrounded by many dangers." Ann shared news about their daughter's lonesomeness for her Papa as well as news of soldiers from the area. Her financial worries seemed to have eased although she did inquire when she would receive allotment money for Morris's service in the war. Ann's report of death, illness, and responsibilities at home as well as her concern for Morris stand in contrast to Emily's accounting of her lessons and social activities.

ANN

From Ann Waldo at Winneconne to Morris Waldo in the Union Army in Missouri, June 15, 1862, "Sunday Afternoon"

My Dear Husband,

As usual I have seated myself for my regular Sunday afternoon employment of inflicting a long scrawl upon you for perusal, you see how partial I am to you as I use a small sheet of paper in writing to all my other correspondents, and methinks I hear you say, <u>I wish you would to me</u>. But if I write more than you care about reading at one time, you can lay it by, for employment when you have nothing else to do. I rec'd a letter from you last Monday in the midst of washing, written two weeks ago today, and I feel very anxious to hear from you again, as you seem to be surrounded by many dangers, both seen & unseen. You seem liable to be fired upon at any moment, and do be on your guard & not expose yourself unnecessarily. Dr. Johnson's escape was truly providential. I think he would not care about employing the same barber, to take off another lock of his hair in the same manner. What has become of those men that you left with a rope around their necks two weeks ago? I hope they are not standing there yet. How is Dr. Gregory getting along with his wound? I thought he had been discharged, how does he happen to be there? It does not seem safe for the Reg. to be so scattered in the midst of [illegible], neither does it seem right to remove them to any other locality, after they have encouraged the Union people to return and put in their crops & promised them their protection. It would be too bad to leave them now to the tender mercies of the Rebels. Do get one of those Vests by all means, won't you?[11]

Della has gone to Sabbath-school alone, she is very devotional. I think she takes after her father. Joseph Brewer passed in a wagon the other day. Della saw him & clapped her hands and called out, "Oh, There's Papa! There's Papa!" the poor child looked quite disappointed when she took a second look & saw her mistake. She says she wonders if Papa wouldn't like to have a little girl to comb his hair & kiss him. I hope it may not be many months before Papa will be at liberty to come home, before "No war, nor battles' sound, will be heard the world around."

Oren [sic: Orrin] Rice was buried yesterday he died Thursday night quite suddenly, he was in town last Monday, report says. We don't know how true it is that Dolphis [Adolphus] said to him the night before he died, "Well, Oren, do you want a Dr. or don't you? Got to go clear to Oshkosh after one, you're getting old and have to die sometime, might as well die now as at any time." Poor old Oren was too sick to make any reply. They were sawing wood with the machine out in the yard. Dolphis says, "Well if Oren dies, we shan't have to burn so much wood another winter, had to keep three fires all winter." The next morning after Oren died, Dolphis went & rummaged in his trunk & got his watch, & tried to sell it to young Prime that worked there.

Julius Stevens got home on the boat Friday morning, he has been sick in the hospital at St. Louis for six weeks & he's just got able to come home. He is on furlough they say he looks very feeble. The body of Joseph Post of Wayauwega (the one that had his house burned there a year or two ago) was carried home on the boat about two weeks ago, he was a Lieut. & was wounded at the battle of Pittsburgh [sic] Landing & died from the effects of his wounds. It seems to have been a mistake about young Thompson being paroled & sent home, as he is among the missing.[12]

Willis rec'd a letter from home the other day containing the death of Mrs. Marcellis Monroe (Janette Rudd) of consumption, Arasminta (Mrs. Stillman Andrews) died in Feb. of the same disease & Mary is said to be nearly gone with it. Susan went to Oshkosh on the boat Wednesday and staid until Friday at Mr. Hamlins. We mean to go to Ripon some time this week if the cars can get to running to Omro. So you may venture to send your next letter after you get this to R. Appleton, Fairweather [Susan and

Ann's father]. I shall not stay a great while as Susan wants me to keep house for her so she can go out when the currants are ripe. Della has been having a very hard cold on her lungs for a week & has coughed very badly, it is a little better. As for myself, I cannot say I have felt well this summer. I have not much appetite, nor strength, & feel so tired all of the time. Why don't you say something about your health, you don't say whether you are well or not, <u>where is Mrs. Beckwith</u>? I saw Mrs. McCloe the other day, she wanted I should ask you when I wrote again, if you knew anything about her husband, she has not heard from him since they left St. Louis. How am to get that allotment money? I don't know where to apply for it. Have you rec'd. a half dozen papers that I send you. I sent one to Mr. Jackson the other day. You are not <u>jealous are you</u>? You see I have managed to fill this big sheet of paper. Write often.

Accept much love from Ann

I will send you a piece of some dress I got for Susan & I went to Oshkosh. 20 cts. Per yard (the gray) the calico is a piece of Susan's dress she got the other day.

Emily

June 21, 1862, Saturday: Fannie & I & Mr. Craig went down to the lake after breakfast this morning and caught some worms to fish with this afternoon. Went to teacher's meeting at nine and then went fishing, staid until three o'clock and caught three fish, came home with a terrible headache.

June 22, 1862, Sunday: Did not go to church this morning. In the afternoon went with Mr. Craig to the University to hear the Baccalaureate Address. It was cool and pleasant. Went to the Methodist Church in the evening.

June 23, 1862, Monday: Went to school as usual this morning. After school went up town. At home in the evening. Went fishing in the afternoon, did not catch anything.

June 24, 1862, Tuesday: Visited Mr. Allen's school today. Some of the scholars went with us. Went to the City Hall in the evening to the first of the Commencement exercises. The poem by Hebbel was very good. Anna Main sang.

June 25, 1862, Wednesday: Went to the City Hall at nine o'clock to the Commencement exercises. They closed at twelve. We had a picnic in the afternoon at McBride's Point. Sarah & Mary Turner and Campbell and McKenny were with us. Had a pleasant time. Went to Prof. Lathrop's lecture in the evening.

June 28, 1862, Saturday: Went to teacher's meeting this morning. Exercise on the elementary grounds. Fannie & I and Mr. Craig went fishing this afternoon. Took our supper with us, landed at six and ate it under a large tree on the point. It was very pleasant. We caught about fifteen fish and enjoyed ourselves wonderfully.

July 4, 1862, Friday: Was awakened this morning at sunrise by the ringing of bells and firing of cannon, a pleasant day somewhat cloudy and not at all warm. Miss Crocker, Fannie & I wishing to escape the noise and dust, walked three miles to the cemetery, staid all day, had a very pleasant time. Went home by the lakeshore took off our shoes and stockings and amused ourselves by wading in the water, had a splendid time, came home. Found Mrs. Hayes and Artie Mills there, spent a pleasant afternoon, went to see the fire works in the evening. Tired enough to last me three weeks.

July 20, 1862, Sunday: I have not written in my diary for two weeks, have been very busy of late preparing to go to Janesville to the Teacher's Association. Went to church this morning. We all went this afternoon to the University Guards and staid until teatime. Went to church in the evening.

July 23, 1862, Wednesday: School as usual. Preparing for examination tomorrow. Went up town after school.

July 24, 1862, Thursday: Went to school at eight o'clock. Examined six classes in the forenoon. We had quite a number of visitors. Kept until nearly five in the afternoon. The scholars presented Mr. Potter with a book at the close of the exercises. I was very tired tonight. Went to hear the Hutchinsons sing tonight. They had a large audience and gave entire satisfaction. They sang the poem by John P. Whittier which they were prohibited from singing on the Potomac.[13]

July 25, 1862, Friday: Miss Crocker & I went up to the Third Ward School today. Met Mr. Allen who accompanied us. Went to Mrs. Wise's to dinner. Spent the day in the school and came home at night tired enough.

July 26, 1862, Saturday: Went to Teacher's meeting this morning. Drew my quarter's salary, paid my debts, spent most all my money. Went to see Hannah Chapman and afterward to Mrs. Olney's. I had not been to see Nettie since she died, she looked very peaceful and happy, the pain had all gone out of her face. She has suffered so long, that I was glad to see her at rest at last. The funeral is to be on Sunday. Went up town again in the afternoon. Fannie & I and Mr. Craig went over to picnic point. Mr. C. was sick, and we coaxed him to let us row, which he did all the way there and back. We took luncheon with and staid until nearly dark.

July 27, 1862, Sunday: Warm this morning. Did not go to church. Went to the funeral this afternoon. There were a large number of people present. We went out to the cemetery.

July 28, 1862, Monday: At home today getting ready to attend the Teacher's Association at Janesville tomorrow. Mr. Craig is going today and promised to find us a good boarding place.

July 29, 1862, Tuesday: Rose early this morning. Packed my satchel and was with my sister all ready when the Omnibus came for us. Had a very pleasant ride to Janesville. There was quite a large number of teachers and others who went from here. Arrived in Janesville at half past three, found Mr. Craig there, who accompanied us to the boarding place he had selected, we were tired and rested ourselves until tea time when we went down we found Mr. & Mrs. Covell and a young lady daughter in the supper room. We're very much pleased with the family. Mr. Craig came for us to take a walk after tea. We went up to the High School Building, and through several pleasant streets after which we went to the Hall where we heard the opening address by _____ of Michigan. It was very good indeed. Tired enough to sleep soundly I think tonight.

July 30, 1862, Wednesday: Rose early this morning dressed and waited quite a long time for breakfast. Met Miss Sarah Covell at the breakfast table this morning. Very pleasant. Went to the Association morning, afternoon and evening. Tired enough at. The day was warm and the room close and uncomfortable. 325 teachers reported themselves today.

July 31, 1862, Thursday: Cool and pleasant this morning. Saw Mr. Wilcox up town as were going to the Association, he gave us some peaches. When the afternoon session of the Association was over, we, that is a number of us went to visit the High School Building. Climbed up several hundred steps into the Observatory where we had a fine view for our pains. I enjoyed the walk too much. Went home to tea and then to the lecture in the evening.

August 1, 1862, Friday: Mrs. Lee from Milwaukee has been here, she is quite a pleasant lady. I liked her much. This is the last day of the Association. Fannie & Mr. Craig and I went to see Mr. Comstock yesterday in regard to the schools here and I applied for a place. The examination takes place tomorrow. The Association adjourned at noon, and they all left on the cars. I was quite lonely after they went away. A young gentleman Frank Whittier called in the evening.

August 2, 1862, Saturday: Went to the examination this morning, came away with little hope of getting a school, as Mr. Lockwood said there were only two vacancies, and there were 10 teachers present. Miss Sarah and I called on Mr. & Mrs. East this afternoon, I liked them very much. We also called on Mrs. Anderson. Went to see a neighbor in the evening.

August 3, 1862, Sunday: Went to church this morning. I had no bonnet with me, but Sarah persuaded me to go and wear my hat. We went to the Methodist Church, as I thought they might think me extremely outré at the more fashionable Trinity though after a good deal of persuasion I went there in the evening.

August 4, 1862, Monday: The girls and myself went up town this morning. I had my picture taken at two different galleries this morning, remained up town longer than I intended and after a hasty dinner, ran to the depot to find that I had missed the regular Madison train but that by waiting an hour I could take a train which connected with it at Milton. Bade the girls good bye and settled myself to enjoy my ride. It commenced raining in a few moments and continued to do so until we reached Madison. To my great joy I found Gus waiting for me at the depot. He came last Friday morning. Found Kate Kavenaugh at home when I arrived.

August 7, 1862, Thursday: Commenced working for Pa today. Played chess in the evening.

Emily's next entry describes the "great excitement" in response to the Militia Act, which authorized the implementation of a draft if states did not meet their quotas. Even in Dane County, where Madison is located, the response to Lincoln's call to provide 11,904 men for three years was slow, for "the easy gallantry and bravado of 1861 had given way to a much more calculating attitude among Madison's young men."[14] When the War Department issued General Order 99, requesting a draft of three hundred thousand additional troops, Wisconsin citizens were so opposed that its implementation was delayed until after the November elections. This order was seen as unfair because it exempted people in specific occupations, including members of Congress.[15] A Wisconsin citizen, James Longerman, explained the opposition to the draft in a letter to Governor Salomon : "Nobody talks of resisting the Draft; they merely desire that the rich man be placed on equal footing with the poor man."[16] In an effort to free more individuals to recruit soldiers for the cause, Madison businesses closed earlier than usual on August 12, 13, and 14 so that groups could go door to door persuading men to enlist.[17] The renewed emphasis on recruiting elicited comments from Emily on the bereavement that the war had brought, a stance that stands in stark contrast to her, and the nation's, enthusiasm in April 1861, when the first soldiers willingly volunteered to put down the rebellion. In response to this renewed emphasis, Emily refocused her thoughts, if not her efforts, on supporting soldiers at the front.

August 12, 1862, Tuesday: Went to the office. There is great excitement in town in regard to the prospective draft of soldiers to make up an additional six hundred thousand men for our army. There is to be a war meeting tonight and a great many of our men have already enlisted McHenry and Leonard Bradley enlisted today.[18] My heart aches for the thousands that must be bereaved ere this cruel war ever end. Went to the Lodge tonight but few present, all gone to the War meeting.

August 14, 1862, Thursday: Went to the office as usual this morning. Mrs. Benedict visited us to meet the Misses Farnham at her home this afternoon. Had a very pleasant visit. Came home and went to the War Meeting in the evening. There was great excitement and noble men came forward by scores to give their money and lives to their country's service. Over ten thousand dollars have been raised within the last three days as bounty for volunteers. So the work goes bravely on.

August 15, 1862, Friday: Maria came last night when we were gone. Went to the office this morning. Maria is going back in about two weeks. All went to the War Meeting again tonight. It was so crowded that we were obliged to stand. Heard some good speeches and music, came away at ten, though the meeting did not adjourn until nearly midnight.

August 17, 1862, Sunday: Went to church this morning. Mr. Johnson preached a very good sermon. Mr. Craig spent the afternoon here. We did not go to church in the evening. Mr. Gillett who returned yesterday, spent the evening here. He is going into camp tomorrow with the 20th Regiment.

August 18, 1862, Monday: Concluded to have our famous lake voyage today. Rose early. Got our things ready, and started about eight o'clock. It was a beautiful day. We enjoyed it exceedingly. Took our dinner about four miles from town, stayed there about three hours, rowed to the opposite shore and thence around the Lake, to McBride's Point by which time it was quite dark of a moonless night. We landed however, and spread our cloth for supper on the grass beneath the stars. Then we had any quantity of fun resulting from our efforts to spread our bread with pie and eat our honey with butter, concluded as the repast was entirely by the sense of feeling. I think I shall never forget the mistakes we made or the laughter caused by jokes at each other's expense. After supper we rested awhile and then started for home, where we arrived twenty minutes before one and found Ma in a terrible state of mind. I presume she never expected to see us again and she gave us a sound scolding for staying so late.

Once again, Ann Waldo went to join her beloved Morris. Leaving their daughter, Della, with Susan Brown and her family, Ann traveled to Cape Girardeau, Missouri, to care for Morris, who had fallen ill. Her travel to Missouri exposed her to the dangers of warfare, for on August 3 Morris Waldo's 1st Cavalry had fought the Confederates at Jonesboro and at Languelle Ferry and sustained losses of twenty-one killed, forty wounded, and twenty missing.[19] In her letter to Ann, Susan provided a detailed description of a ball held to honor the volunteers.

SUSAN

From Susan Brown at Winneconne to M. A. Waldo, Sgn. E, 2nd Battalion, 1st Wisconsin Cavalry, at Cape Girardeau, Missouri, August 26, 1862, "P.M. 5 o'clock"

Dear Ann,

I commence at the top of a formidable sheet of paper, as if I had something to say, but I have not much. I am sure that I sometimes have the faculty for covering much paper with little matter.

I rec'd yours from Cape Girardeau yesterday while I was washing. I had expected it for several days. This is a very warm afternoon. I am sitting in the south piazza writing by the stand there. Eddie and Della are over to Mr. Rowley's a little while. Willie is somewhere and Waldo is out on the prairie helping thresh.

Della is very much such a girl as she is when her momma is at home. Sometimes very good and sometimes not very good. She has been very well. Attends church and Sunday School regularly and last Sunday went alone. She sleeps on the lounge with Fanny and wishes me to be sure and tell you not to forget to tell her father about Fanny. She usually inquires once, sometimes twice, a day when you will be home and sometimes what I think her mother will bring her.

Everything is as quiet or quieter than usual in Winneconne but I do not feel at all lonely. I was busy the remainder of the week and a portion of the next putting things to rights.

Last Thursday afternoon, Mrs. McIntyre came up here and spent the afternoon. Brought a 'housewife' she making for Willard on which I assisted her. Toward night Mrs. Harrington came here, intending to go away the next day but Friday night a ball was to be given to the Volunteers for which she staid.

The village people did the baking. The tables were all set in Mr. McIntyre's back parlor and dining room. Tea, coffee, honey, etc. all of which was contributed. About one hundred took supper there. The dancing was in Mr. White's hall. I was there two or three hours. Mrs. Kilborne, Mrs. Williams, and Mrs. Tennyson were there. Mr. Hamlin came in a short time to see the dancing. Mrs. Webster, Lake and Rush's consciences were in the way of their assisting. (The children have come, clamorous for some supper so I must stop.)

After tea

The Volunteers have not much increased in town and there is another call to fill up old regiments and it is feared that after all drafting will have to be resorted to here. William Ball & Thomas Heicox were refused. Elick Scott has since enlisted but has been thrown out. Thomas Roche has enlisted. All the volunteers from here went down yesterday to Oshkosh where the 21st Reg. is to go into camp. One of the volunteers gave me his picture in a handsome case yesterday which I prize very highly. (The picture not—the case.)

Silas Clark wished Waldo to be sure and inquire after Messrs. Bracy (Brasy?), Stacy, and McClo(?) as no one here has heard from them since they left St. Louis (Mrs. Wood is just passing the gate and says give my love to him.)

Abel Livermore is dead. Died on board a boat which was conveying him to New York to the hospital. I enclose a letter from Caroline to you but cannot send the poetry in this letter (tho' perhaps I can). On the eighth of September Mr. Munger opens a normal school at Omro to continue four weeks. Board can be obtained for $1.25 per week. Tuition is nothing. Inspection to be delayed until after that time. Mrs. Harrington, Sarah Brown, and Delia Spies are going.

Report says here that Col. Daniels is dead. I suppose you have heard of the casualties which occurred in that skirmish in Arkansas. Mr. Bushnell of Omro was killed. Miss Alin's brother is among the missing. Mr. Dunmore was killed.[20]

(It is now sundown. Waldo sits on the bench. Eddie sits astride the fence holding the clothesline for a bridle and Della is riding behind him. Waldo is expostulating with her because she sits astride. He tells her women don't ride so. Well, she said then she was a man.) She is wondering now if she couldn't ride the clothesline.

Wednesday morning

While the rest of the family are finishing their breakfast, I will finish this letter. I have such a cold this morning I can scarcely speak.

There was a Cape Girardeau paper come here the other day and on the outside was Morris' writing so I supposed he was better before I received your letter. I presume your care will help to cure him. Was he not surprised to see you? What accommodations has he? When you write again give some description of the hospital life.

We shall probably make an effort to get up an Aid Society here again I would like know something of the accommodations, what is the care and food which they have. You must know something of the Cape Girardeau Hospital, too.

Alice Murphy started yesterday to see her husband who is very low in a hospital in Alexandria. Is Hiram Baker there? Answer all my questions when you write. Della want me to tell you "When are your coming home?" Write immediately when you get this. Our love to Morris and yourself. Take care that you don't stay long enough to be taken prisoner. The whole rebel army is making a northward move. In Virginia, Kentucky, and Tennessee. I don't know about Arkansas. Your's affectionately. Look out for your self or you will be sick there going at this season of the year.[21]

Susan

E M I L Y

August 23, 1862, Saturday: Went to the Office this morning, finished the names of the Thirteenth Volunteer Regiment. Fannie and I got the key of Mr. B's boat and took half a dozen of ours and the neighbors' little folks out riding. Went over to picnic point two miles and back. We thought we were rather smart to row four miles alone. Went to Mrs. Cleary in the evening.

August 24, 1862, Sunday: Went to church this morning. Mr. Johnson organized his Bible class. Rev. Mr. Blohm, hospital chaplain at St. Louis preached or rather lectured this evening to a crowded house at our church. He made an earnest appeal to the Ladies, and others for aid for the sick and wounded.

August 27, 1862, Wednesday: Started at 8 o'clock to go out to Kate Kavenaugh's in the boat. When we reached the Lake Shore, found it very rough but we wanted to go very much and after a great deal of difficulty and getting quite set, we got the boat launched. The wind was very high and we soon began to wish ourselves on shore. There was a good deal of water in the boat and when there came an extra large wave it was pretty close to go over the prow. I did not feel at all afraid and after about two hours hard rowing we landed at picnic point. There we remained until the wind went down which was about five in the afternoon and then came home. We were in a sorry plight when we landed, Fannie, Maria, and Gus being about as wet as they could be, I alone being in a presentable condition. They took off their shoes and stockings and hung them up to dry and Gus boiled his hands in the attempt to dry his shirtsleeves. We had not thought to carry anything in the way of lunch with us and were quite ravenous by the time we arrived at home.

August 28, 1862, Thursday: It was quite pleasant this morning and we thought we would try it again. Gus and I went over to the Lake Shore to see what the prospect was. The water was quite calm and unruffled and getting ready we started again. Fannie would not go this time and so we convinced Ma to go with us. Took luncheon this time and stopped about three o'clock and remained an hour. Reached Mr. Kavenaugh's about a walk of a mile and a half after leaving the boat. Found Kate <u>not at home.</u> Had a very pleasant visit with Annie and after partaking of a good cup of tea and other refreshments started for home about five o'clock. Had a very pleasant ride home where we arrived about nine.

September 1, 1862, Monday: Did not feel or look very well this morning, found my face more swollen than yesterday. Worked around the house all the forenoon, and in the afternoon Maria went back to her school at Cross Plains today.

September 2, 1862, Tuesday: Nothing of importance occurred today. The swelling in my face having nearly subsided, and having a paper to read, I went to the Lodge.

September 3, 1862, Wednesday: Fannie went to the office. We concluded to go boat riding at eleven o'clock. Got started about twelve. Went to McBride's Point, remained there all the afternoon came home by the light of the moon.

September 4, 1862, Thursday: Found Celia Easton at home when we arrived last night, was very glad to see her. She remained all night. We went up town this morning, were going to have a boat ride this afternoon but it unfortunately rained before, during and after the time appointed.

September 5, 1862, Friday: Raining this morning as though it would never stop. We had made a great many plans for today but found ourselves at home, weather bound very much against our wills.

September 6, 1862, Saturday: Still raining. At home all day until four o'clock, when in sheer desperation Celia & I put on our hats and sallied out despite the rain. Went to the office and helped Mr. Campbell mail the Farmer. Staid about two hours and came home quite contented with the weather.

September 7, 1862, Sunday: Went to church this morning. Mr. McHenry came to dinner and Celia, Mr. Campbell, McH and myself went out to the Camp. Staid two hours were invited to tea. Went to the Mess House and ate at the Captain's table. Had a very pleasant time. Went to church in the evening.[22]

~

September 10, 1862, Wednesday: Sewed at home all day. Legislature convened for an extra session under call of the Governor.[23]

September 11, 1862, Thursday: Rained again today. Maria came home to make a cake for a soldier's picnic to be given at Cross Plains. Went back tonight.

September 12, 1862, Friday: At home all day, the forenoon. Went up to the office. Gus extracted three teeth for me.

September 13, 1862, Saturday: Mr. Campbell came this morning with Captain Ryard [?] of the 29th Regiment. They proposed going over to Camp after breakfast to see the 23d Regiment leave and invited Gus and myself to accompany them. We started but found before reaching the Camp that they were not going until Monday. Stayed to witness Battalion drill, came home about eleven. Regiment came up town in the afternoon, we went up to see them. Mr. Campbell and I played chess in the evening.

September 14, 1862, Sunday: Went to church this forenoon. Mr. McKinney stayed to dinner and spent the afternoon. I bade him "good-bye" as I suppose I shall not see him again if the Regiment goes tomorrow. One more of the thousands of brave boys going to face danger perhaps death in his country's service. God bless them all. Went to Church in the evening.

September 15, 1862, Monday: Went to the office this morning in the rain. Wrote until noon and remained at home in the afternoon. Mr. Campbell, Gus & I spent the evening at Sarah Turner's.

September 16, 1862, Tuesday: Wrote this morning, went to my German lesson. Sarah took tea at our house and went to the Lodge with me. Mr. Scofield read a paper which was very good. It commenced raining violently about nine and Gus came home after rubbers and umbrellas for us. Sarah staid with me. We were quite wet when we arrived at home.

September 17, 1862, Wednesday: Wrote all day at the office. Staid at home in the evening.[24]

September 18, 1862, Thursday: Wrote this morning and until four in the afternoon. Went to German and to a lecture delivered by Prof. Reed before Athenaean and Hesperian Societies of the University, this evening. Fannie & Gus went to spend the evening at Hannah Chapman's.

September 19, 1862, Friday: Wrote this forenoon. Fannie & I went to make some calls up in the Third Ward. Called on Mr. Johnson's people, were quite pleased with them. Mr. Smith came in the evening quite unexpectedly. Miss Crocker also came for me to go to the lecture. George C. remained only a short time as he expected to leave on the evening train.

September 20, 1862, Saturday: Maria came last night after we had all retired. We were going boat riding but after a long time spent in arrangements for it found that Mr. Pickard was going to use the boat. Maria & I went up town in the afternoon. She had her Photograph taken. At home in the evening.

∽

Emily made no entries in her diary from Monday, September 22, through Saturday, November 1.

For a time after the September 13 attack on Bloomfield, Missouri, Susan Brown was not aware of the whereabouts of her sister, Ann, or of her brother-in-law, Morris. A letter from Maggie Swem, a cousin in Koro, may have helped to set her mind at ease when she reported, "Waldo is getting well, thanks to his noble wife." Maggie also provided an amusing perspective on the timing of the Emancipation Proclamation, which Lincoln had announced on September 22, although it would not become effective until January 1, 1863.[25] "The chief excitement, political, is the President's Proclamation, which many say 'Amen' to, but that characteristic three months time spoils it for me, giving the rebels abundant opportunity to liberate the slaves themselves. Surely eighteen months time and warning is enough to extend to traitors without adding on more for them to employ in slaughtering our brave men. Abraham Lincoln must have been born three months too late."[26]

Susan Brown, having learned that her sister was ill at Greenville, Missouri, wrote in October with hopes for her improved health. Susan continued to provide news from home, including the results of her own teacher's examination, before she returned her thoughts to the war and reported on casualties from their area. She also intimated that Ann's absence from Wisconsin to be with her husband had affected Susan's ability to teach during the winter.

Susan

From Susan Brown at Winneconne to Ann Waldo at Greenville, Missouri, October 20, 1862

My dear Ann,

I was much relieved to receive a letter from Mr. Gable this morning as I could not conjecture after receiving Mr. Calkin's letter why you did not come. Mr. C's letter was ten days reaching here, so I of course supposed I had not time to answer it before you left. I hope this may find you and Morris much improved in health. No one mentioned the disease with which you are afflicted. I was very much concerned after reading the capture of Bloomfield concerning your fate, but I wrote you nevertheless and I presume you have received the letter.

I received a letter from Orange [their brother] Saturday inquiring concerning you which I replied to yesterday. We are all well here, Della included of course, she has not been unwell a day since you left, and is very well contented and getting a little wild. Maggie spent last week with me, coming

Tuesday on the boat from Oshkosh where Mr. V. left her, and going to Omro on the boat Saturday to Eureka. I spent two days at Teacher's Institute at Omro and enjoyed it very much. Mr. Munger was here last Monday and Tuesday only 11 teachers were inspected, 8 of which received certificates. Namely, Mr. Arnold, Mr.Bell, Mrs. Brown, Miss Sarah, Miss Della Spies, Miss Hamilton from Omro, Miss McFale. I was the only one who applied for a second grade certificate, and I was quite astonished myself. My certificate contained 12 branches each of which was marked 10. Natural Philosophy belonged to the 1st grade instead of the second so that all I lacked of receiving a 1st grade was Geometry. So that still leaves me dissatisfied that I did not review Geometry as there was but one lady in the county who rec'd a 1st grade (Mrs. Beech of Menasha) a graduate of Oberlin and one besides myself who rec'd a second in Menasha also so far. I wish you could have been with and would have kept house for me this winter. I think I should have taught. I was offered the school across the line but should not have taught that. Everything moves on its usual course here. No news. The 21st Reg. have been in one battle in Kentucky. They were quite unfortunate to their officers. Col. and Major and 2 Capt. killed or have since died of their wounds. Two men from Company B (William's company) was Mr. Shower's brother. Maggie says Charles Swen died in the hospital sometime since.[27]

 A distressing casualty occurred in Col. Hamlin's family last week. Willie and Lizzie were playing in a room alone when Willie lighted some matches setting Lizzie's clothes on fire and before anyone could come to the rescue, the front portion of them was burned off her. The burns outwardly were as high as the nose, but it was supposed she inhaled the heated air. She lingered about twelve hours and expired. Her mother was away from the home at the time the accident occurred.

 I received a letter from Caroline today—enclosed in it is part of the sheet from Mr. R. on politics as I expressed a wish to Caroline in my last that Mr. R might "return from the error of his ways" he has taken up the glove. I have received two letters from Willard since he left. I had a letter from Juliette also the other day in which she says George's colts ran away with him—threw him from the wagon, he was picked up insensible with one of his ribs broken and otherwise injured. It is evening I sit here by the table under the clock. Willie sits here reading; Waldo downtown as usual. Della gone to bed on the lounge. Eddie also retired. Willie has been in and gone again since I began this.

The wind is howling dismally as it has all day. How I wish you were here and I think you must echo it. Write as soon as you receive this, as I wish to know how your health is particularly. For three weeks I have watched the boat, I shall look no more immediately. Accept our love, be sure and get someone to write if you cannot yourself.

Susan

Ann Waldo died of her illness four days after Susan wrote her letter and was buried in Missouri.

EMILY

November 2, 1862, Sunday: A long time has elapsed since last scribbled on your pages old diary and I come back to you with something like the pleasure of greeting an old friend. I went to Cross Plains on the 24th. Left to visit Maria, Gus accompanied me. We remained all the week met Mr. Toyell [?] there, had a pleasant time. On the 12th of Oct. went to Oakland to visit at Mr. Smith's, went to visit Mr. Purdy's school at Fort Atkinson, to

In later years Ann's daughter Della would say that she hated to hear the crickets in the evening for that was the sound she listened to as she sat waiting for her mother to return on the train. (Wisconsin Historical Society, WHS 142061)

Lake Mills to visit at Dr. Williards and to Jefferson, remained nearly two weeks and enjoyed myself very much. Came home and found Sarah & Mary Covell whose visit I had anticipated so long had been here nearly a week, and were going the next morning, they had expected me every day and so had not written. I persuaded them to stay two days longer and we had a very pleasant visit.

On the 29th of Oct. I received a letter from Jefferson requesting me to take the school in that place for the winter. Pa did not want me to go and I wrote to them that I had made different arrangements. Went to the Sociable at Mrs. Reddens in the evening had a very pleasant time. Yesterday, went up town in the forenoon and sewed in the afternoon. Cold and snowy this morning. Did not go to church. It is real November weather, dreariest of all months, I think November is. We have been having glorious Indian summer and this change is not of the pleasantest. I am going to write for Pa next week and perhaps the week after and then I am going to Janesville to spend three or four weeks. I think I shall learn Photograph painting and perhaps remain in Janesville all winter.

November 6, 1862, Thursday: Went up to the University this morning with Miss Crocker to her recitation. It was a very pleasant walk, and I enjoyed it. I like Dr. French very much. Went to the office, to the Historical rooms in the afternoon, and also shopping with Ma. Got me a set of jars. Went to a Sociable at Mr. Miller's in the evening. There were a large number present, and it was very pleasant.

November 7, 1862, Friday: Went to the office, staid in the forenoon. Worked for myself a little in the afternoon. Got my German lesson and went to the Historical Rooms a while commenced reading Macaulay's History of England, like it much. Went to my German lesson. Mr. Smith here to tea, said they were much disappointed out in Jefferson because I did not come.[28]

November 8, 1862, Saturday: Went up to the office this morning did not stay. Sewed all day until three o'clock. Hattie Benedict & Cassie Farnham called, also Mrs. Carpenter. Went to the Historical Rooms at four, read an hour and a half. Sarah Turner came, staid to tea and spent the evening, translated a part of Schiller's Song of the Bells.

November 10, 1862, Monday: Went to Gus's office to have my teeth filled remained all day. Went to the Sunday School Convention in the evening. German lesson in the afternoon.

November 11, 1862, Tuesday: Went to the office commenced pasting my scrapbook. Went to Lodge in the evening. Fannie joined again tonight. I was appointed on a committee for lectures and also on one for editorials this term. Had a very pleasant time.[29]

November 17, 1862, Monday: Went to the office this morning, remained until three o'clock finished my book. Went to the Historical Rooms at four and to my German recitation at five. Sarah Turner came home with me and we went to the Sabbath School Convention in the evening.

November 25, 1862, Tuesday: Up to town all the forenoon. At home in the afternoon. Went to the Exhibition of the University Societies in the evening. It was very good. The best orations were by Messrs. High and Spooner. We intended to go to the Lodge afterwards, but it too late.

November 26, 1862, Wednesday: Busy today preparing for Thanksgiving up town in the forenoon. Went to German in the afternoon. At home in the evening.

November 27, 1862, Thursday: Snowing this morning. A veritable Thanksgiving Day. Gus & Maria & I went to church. Came home Mr. Craig came at two spent a pleasant afternoon. Dined at five. Played chess in the evening.[30]

November 28, 1862, Friday: Had intended going to Janesville today, but not feeling well postponed it until tomorrow. Went up town to German in the afternoon. Sociable this evening, all went but myself.

November 29, 1862, Saturday: All ready for a start at 10 o'clock. Waited until half past ten for the Bus, it did not come and having my trunk to be sent I walked to the Depot. Had a pleasant trip to J. Nettie Danning & Martha Winne were on board bound for Milwaukee. Arrived in Janesville at half past one. Found the folks all well and glad to see me.

Emily again stopped writing in her diary from November 30, 1862, through March 21, 1863.

In his State of the Union Address, delivered on December 1, President Lincoln reaffirmed his commitment to the Emancipation Proclamation, despite the negative impact that the proclamation, announced the previous September, had had on Republican candidates in the November elections. He also discussed several proposed constitutional amendments on slavery, including amendments to free the slaves, prepare for colonization in Africa, and pay reparations to their owners. He declared, "In giving freedom to the slave, we assure freedom for the free."[31]

As December ended, preparations began for the Vicksburg Campaign as Union soldiers, including the 1st artillery, embarked south from Memphis by steamboats. They participated in the first assault on Vicksburg on December 27.[32]

The valor of Wisconsin's soldiers continued as the New Year dawned at Stones River, Tennessee, where forty-one thousand Union soldiers battled thirty-eight thousand Confederates on a cold and rainy day. The bravery of the 10th Infantry led one general to comment, "They would have suffered extermination rather than have yielded their ground without order." The battle concluded on January 2, with the Union in control of this disputed land and occupying Murfreesboro, Tennessee. One-third of Union forces were killed, wounded, or missing. During the rest of the month, Wisconsin troops also saw action in Arkansas, where the Union finally repelled the Confederates at Springfield.[33] Despite the pride Wisconsin took in the contributions of its soldiers to the Union cause, conditions for those training at Camp Randall were deteriorating. On January 27, Governor Salomon sent a letter to the State Senate and Assembly reporting on the actions he had taken to call the attention of federal authorities to the conditions at the camp.[34]

President Lincoln signed the Emancipation Proclamation on January 1. Reaction in the Northern states was mixed; even the Illinois legislature, in which Lincoln had served, criticized the Proclamation as "unwarranted in military and civil law." In Wisconsin the issuance of the Proclamation was seen as proof that the "war for the Union" was, in reality, "a war of abolition, of violation of the Constitution, a war by the Eastern oligarchy."[35] In contrast, free African Americans in Pennsylvania hailed the Proclamation as the beginning of "a new era in our country's history."[36] Eleven days later, in a message to the Confederate Congress, Jefferson Davis called the Proclamation "the most execrable measure in the history of guilty man." He further vowed to release captured Union officers to state governments for punishment by death for the crime of "inciting servile insurrection."[37]

Annie Cox carried on a lively correspondence with Gideon Winans Allen, a student of law at the University of Michigan. Annie's statements are particularly bold since she knew that her dear "Winans" was a staunch Copperhead. She asserted her right to discuss politics but asked that if he disagreed with her he "neither hang me nor threaten to."[38] Gideon had previously been a student at the University of Wisconsin and resided in Madison from 1857 to 1862. Annie addressed Gideon as Winans in her letters; his early letters were signed G. W. Allen. Gideon suffered from an eye infliction that impacted his ability to write Annie as often as she wished.

Annie

From Annie Cox at Madison to Gideon Winans Allen at Ann Arbor, Michigan, January 25, 1863

Seated in a flood of sunshine, I am thinking of and writing to you. The day is warm and sunny. When I build my house I'll have every room facing south. Who would not live on the sunny side of life? . . .

. . . Your letter came to me on a cold evening, right after closing school. I had looked anxiously for it and excused its delay by considering your affliction. Winans, I do wait impatiently for your letters and count the days intervening between any letter mailed and the forthcoming answer and imagine some evening when unemployed what Winans is doing or of what he is thinking and then Annie hopes that he is seriously thinking of the next life to come, and will, mid the bustling and jostling of this, prepare for it for what are all the acquirements and honors without real happiness and you know my brother that these will not gain it or sustain it alone. You will not think one too importune in thus [enjoining] this matter. For I cannot expose my friendship for you more emphatically than thus [enjoining] you. So you will not feel offended or disgusted will you? I know you will not. . . .

Mrs. Lamb and Tichnor received a letter from Mr. Clawson last week. He has been wounded and promoted—two very useful acquirements in war.[39]

Yesterday while passing a soldier I heard these words which have rung in my ears ever since, "My wife is at the point of death—perhaps will be a corpse ere I reach her—I must go." Sad, sad world! The muffled drum counted some breaking heartbeats yesterday as it tolled three funeral knells of a dead comrade being taken home. Sad greeting will it give to the marching and wailing. He was shot by one of the Ozaukee rioters—The democrats held a real "Secesh" meeting last night. Is it wicked to call down God's curse upon them? They are cursing our land, our homes, our nation.⁴⁰

From Annie Cox at Madison to Gideon Winans Allen at Ann Arbor, Michigan, February 1, 1863

... I had a dream last night, I'll give it to you with its interpretation. I was in the Insane Asylum with a number of my companions, men and women. With it was connected the idea of a prison for me were there for the crime and insanity of <u>Anti-Slavery ideas.</u> G you were not. There I "was" with the poet "not mad" but thought I "soon should be." I thought I could never hear again the birds warble, or the streams ripple, never see the green fields, nor the faces of friends. All communication was cut-off, therefore could never hear from you again as were of the force. I finally entered into an agreement with the keeper's daughter to release me and conduct me to Madison. We gained the road, drew a breath of fresh air, but we met her father. I fled again into the woods, came again into the road, and encountering an old woman in a wagon, jumped in, came to M[adison]. Convinced my friends and my entire family, gained my papers of proof, went with them back to the asylum, got an honorable release.

Interpretation: The insane were the Republicans, the keeper and outsiders were the democrats. Our imprisonment in an insane asylum showed the triumph of the democrats and the insanity of theirs on the "emancipation question." The little girl who released me was youth. She lead me to collision with party spirit at first—yet—"Youth crushed to earth will rise again." So when far enough advanced in the right road and without difficulty, she left me to work out my own destiny. I gained [illegible], obtained my papers. The final Proclamation returned to the oppressed Republicans. I gained my own exemption from the appearance of intrigue or dishonor and came out with my companions, free, exultant as a party, professing and possessing peace and good will to all men of all parties and professions. Well, Winans, what do you think of my dream? Am I not a prophetess?

Nary a word about politics. But you know women who be housekeepers at home, darners of stockings, with a little womanly indulgence, now and then, of scandal and scolding, yet I'll transgress upon Adam's domain a little. I do not wish, Winan, to be foolishly prejudiced on [illegible]. But I cannot help but think that democrats support or countenance [of] slavery, thereby crush free speech, thought, and action. We never could espouse an honest opinion in the south if contrary to this peculiar institution. And why? Slavery oppresses the white even more than the black. Intelligence, refinement, progress of every stamp done in an evil direction in this before this. Now do not the majority of your party encourage its existence and extension? What is the cause of the superiority of our intelligence over the South—you must say—Slavery in one case and its non-existence in the other. Another disagreeable phase of the parties is dump the [illegible] with it. That is ignorance and vice and, of course, if triumphant, overrides higher and noble principles. Individuals of this class, one of our nation's true noblemen, taken as a party, I cannot respect their principles as seen in results. What else can one judge them by? Every democratic [illegible] we have had here, has espoused the great cause of freedom. If I speak in too unqualified a manner, correct me. I will read those speeches and give you my opinion further. All I hope is that we be restored to unity and peace." . . .

From Annie Cox at Madison to Gideon Winans Allen at Ann Arbor, Michigan, February 15, 1863

. . . How peaceful Nature's bounty today in her year-end darkness. How I love her in the grandeur of this month or the year-end peace. My "friend home" was with you Sunday last but it attended blindly for it knew not where you were. You are with me in imagination today but I don't think imagination a very good substitute for the reality, do you Winans? I'd like to change with the reality for company to church this evening. What pleasant walks we have taken together but we are better acquainted now. I think they would be still pleasant. . . .

I think a woman's place is in home's sweet retreat. She may sympathetically encourage, make home a green pasture and still attend to the business man's sick companion but it is his place to meet the stress of outside cause. And yet, there is this to consider—all men are not fit to take that responsibility.

. . . Now for the politics. Your politics was good and if arguments [was] the process to turn republicans to democrats I should be one but one this point ignored I shall have to agree to disagree. I think Harvey's vision possible with union freedoms on [illegible] therefore should be removed. If God foredains everything that comes "to pass" this was created for a good purpose. Man with all his buried hatchets and peace pipes could not have predicted it—therefore we could not have predicted the revealing of his will. I think there is an infallible guide to right. The Bible, else why do we sustain today by its instructions, a vision and better people then when conspicuously without it. Why does Seneca Lodge want a Protestant King? But that she sees the influence of our religion upon advancement of intelligence and liberty. If one takes Christ's teaching for an example, slavery will not exist longer. The great cause of our suffering is the want of virtue and religion and the love of gold. Therefore we need to suffer as did our forefathers to be like them united and peaceful. Yet God grant our punishment is most ended. I cannot feel as some do about the war for have no very new friend in it, yet I must wish myself rest from the very sound of the name.

'Tis very sickly here, averaging about a funeral a day—my school is almost broken up by it. Mr. Allen's school go up to the university next time. I mean is going up on the hill as cover [?] three times when they are there....

From Annie Cox at Madison to Gideon Winans Allen at Ann Arbor, Michigan, March 1, 1863

... And here let one say a word to you, Winans. Go into society, into your good polished society, gain of the customs and etiquette all you can—it will be of great value to you hereafter. For trifles sometimes mark in us. You cannot learn those in your room, in books, or in a courtroom. You will not misunderstand one in this. I do not mean that you are rude or coarse but perhaps do not understand some of the quirks of customs. But of this enough.

Winans, they are going to draft soon, I suppose you are going to be one of the fated? That would be worse than me going to California, don't you think so? I will not think of it.

Henry and I went to the Congregation Festival this week, promenade, ate oysters and ice cream, met with many friends, witnessed some very fine tableaux, came home at twelve. Wrote twelve letters the eve before for him. I've got a new dress, Winans, it is fawn colored trimmed with blue. I think it is pretty—come and see it.

Faced with the demands of running a farm and taking care of her large family, Margaret MacNish Patchin's letters to her husband, Augustus, a member of the 10th Infantry, were decidedly less spritely than Annie's. She

described her family's need for him and her disappointment that she had not been able to persuade him not to enlist, and she encouraged him to resign. Margaret's lament that her husband should come home stood in contrast to the continuing need for soldiers. The US Congress passed a national conscription act on March 3, 1863, calling for 121,202 draftees between the ages of twenty and forty-five. The number of soldiers drafted was reduced by those who volunteered, those who hired a substitute, those who did not pass the physical, and those who paid $300 to excuse themselves from service. In the end only 628 draftees from Wisconsin actually served.[41]

Margaret

From Margaret Patchin at Wyocena to Augustus Patchin, March 3, 1863

My Dear Husband

We received three letters from you last week one each mail and was glad to hear that you was gitting better but I want you to try to come home if you are lame perhaps they will accept of your resignation do try it for your Boys need so much and I am so unwell all the time that they are running right over me and it is growing worse all the time yours of the 11 found me on the bed very sick not able to read it for two days I am very glad that you got Herbert's picture it looks like him but I wish that mine had been rubbed off as you dont appear to like the looks of it baby wouldn't set still long enough dont look smiling much of the time yet I think that I am not cross at least I do not feel so but I feel so lonesome so much as if I wasn't any longer loved by the Father of my Children.

Oh it is hard to think that I hadn't influence enough over you to keep you at home but may God keep you my much loved Husband from all dangers and permit you to soon come to me so that I can see you and hear you talk and pray for Oh I miss you so much forgive me if I write to plain for I don't wish to hurt your feelings and I do so wish that you would come home.

Annie

From Annie Cox at Madison to Gideon Winans Allen at Ann Arbor, Michigan, March 18, 1863

... Please, Winans, I don't want to be managed for I shall have to wear a sweet saint-like smile, both of which I have an aversion to as a necessity. Let me be a mortal with hopes and expectations common to all, your sympathizer in joy and disappointment. Might I? ...

... You speak of your experience in society-seeking as it having been thoroughly made and the matter all summed up and laid upon the shelf forever. Look among the violets and the dahlias of society. Mrs. C. represents a large class of community whose positions are their salvation in society. They know nothing of real nobility which receives its education from the heart. The medium is the safest ground. I would go to the middle ground for real gentility and refinement. Try again, Winans, these rebuffs are a part of our education. Speaking of education and experience, I must tell you of a schoolteacher boarding at Vernie's. He makes pretentions of great discernment of character of which he is ignorant. We have talked upon different subjects. I always taking the opposite side. And when I thought he read me, I would fly off in another direction which would blind him again. I enjoyed it hugely. He asked Vernie the other day if I was not rather a peculiar person. V. asked why? He wished to know if all the young ladies of M. were as sharp as me. She purposely misunderstood him. He said he thought I must have seen a great deal of the world for he could not speak of any phase of human character but I was perfectly familiar upon it. He did not know it was his ignorance displayed instead of my wisdom....

... I am not going to teach this summer. Pa and Ma have vetoed the matter. Pa says he will sing joyful when this one closes which will be tomorrow....

After time away from Madison, Emily welcomed the opportunity to again write in her diary and compared her recent activities to her usual routine. She lamented the lack of gaiety in Madison this social season because of the shortage of young men. Although she had described her church attendance in many earlier entries, Emily now expressed her deep feelings of faith for the first time in her diary and in mid-month was baptized. Even this spiritual gift did not fill the hole in her heart, and she ceased writing in her diary until June 1863.

The University of Wisconsin faced a crisis of enrollment as young men, in the words of Governor Salomon, "exchanged the musket and sword for books and studies."[42] In response, the university decided to reinstitute the normal school program for women. Emily and her sister Maria were among the seventy-five young women enrolled in the normal school program in 1862, and all had access to the other lectures at the university with their principal's (professor's) approval. Emily expressed enjoyment in her studies, whereas Annie Cox, who was not allowed to attend classes, expressed the opinion that the women students did not like attending the university. By fall 1863 more women than men were in attendance at the university, and a portion of the earliest campus building, South Hall, was set aside as a dormitory for them.[43]

EMILY

March 22, 1863, Sunday: Here am I again, my long neglected diary, sitting down after so long an interval to scribble once more upon your pages. When I last visited you the cold and frosts of winter were around me and we were preparing ourselves to spend its cold comfortless days and long bright evenings to the best advantage. Now as I write here by my window a drizzling March rain is pattering outside and my eyes meet as they gaze out, only a monotonous expanse of spring mud. The interval between these two points of time has been as eventful as the routine of my usually is that is I have read and worked, visited and received visits, eaten and slept and in short done everything [that] goes to make up what we call life.

My visit at Janesville was a very pleasant one. I remained four weeks during which we walked and talked and shopped and visited to our heart's content. We visited the Blind Institute and the Woolen Factory which are the principal points of interest in Jv. I became acquainted with many pleasant people during my stay and like Janesville very much. Spent Christmas at Miss Kavenaugh's and enjoyed it very much. Came on Saturday. Mother was preparing to go East. She and Charly were going. Maria & I went out to Celia Garton's the day before New Year's. Gus took us out in the buggy. When we arrived found that Celia had gone to Sun Prairie. They sent for her and she got home about three o'clock. We spent a very pleasant afternoon and evening. The next day it rained almost incessantly so that it was impossible for us to get home, we remained another night and the rain having cleared, came home in the mud the next day. Mother started for the East the Wednesday after New Year's, leaving me installed as housekeeper. I liked it very much. Madison is not very gay this winter as many of our young men have gone that our society is rather thin. The winter has been warm and pleasant, with very little snow. Celia Easton came here to board and brought her fiancé. Mother & Charley came home on the fourth of March. Pa went after them, they remained in Washington a week. Mr. Campbell has gone to Ohio and Fannie to Milwaukee. Maria & I commenced attending school at the Normal School last week, we like it very much. I am to study German & French, Household Science and

Philosophy of Teaching. The University session commences tomorrow. Today is Sunday, I attended church this forenoon and remained to Bible Class. There was quite a large number present. It is rainy and disagreeable and I fear we shall not be able to go this evening. We have been having some very interesting meetings during the evenings of the past weeks and it is hoped that some have been converted to God. I have resolved that henceforth I will live for him, and hope that God will forgive my sins and help [me] to do right for the remainder of my life.

March 26, 1863, Thursday: We all met with the University students in the chapel this morning. I came home at noon and went back again in the afternoon. Went to meeting in the evening.

March 27, 1863, Friday: First recitation to Prof. Finch's in German this morning. I like him very much. Came home to dinner this noon. Staid to hear Prof. Carr's lecture tonight. Went to meeting.

March 28, 1863, Saturday: At home this forenoon sewing. Went with Mother to the Ladies Union League this afternoon. We had a very nice meeting. Afterwards went up town and then home. Went down to Miss Crocker's in the evening.[44]

ANNIE

From Annie Cox at Madison to Gideon Winans Allen at Ann Arbor, Michigan, March 27, 1863

... I've seated myself in the sunshine like a cat with my claws shielded and I look as amiable as possible. Soon after writing your last letter I was taken sick, yesterday I was out for the first time. Feel pretty well today but should feel better if I had a decent pen and could paint some. Well, when I arrive at the age of plain linen collars, knitting, and "Aunt Annie," I shall have time. My nose shall be at the right angle and my fingers bony enough then and I shall be so rude no one will trouble me.

... I want very much to see you but I do not want to be selfish. I wish that you could obtain the desirable employment here and come at once. But if you cannot, find it where you can and come when you can. I should like so much to have you here at commencement. We shall then be settled in our new home as we move next week. ...

... Mr. Allen is nicely settled in the south building on the hill with his school. There are some hundred scholars. The students don't like it very well, I guess. How I wish I could go to but I want to do my little all to help father get a home of his own—if it is a possible thing then I shall attend more directly to myself. If I had obeyed my own father I should have been at school long since and every thing at my command yet how much happier I am.[45] A great many thoughts—it was my duty to go and live with him but I thought my duty was with those who had cared for me from babyhood up to now and my mother would have been brokenhearted and I homesick. Always deserve the esteem and honor of all, my brother. Your sister will always be on your side. . . .

All send their kind remembrances to you and would like to see you. The older daughter in particular.

EMILY

March 29, 1863, Sunday: A beautiful Sabbath morning. Went to church. Mr. Johnson preached a very fine sermon, from the text, "While I was at work, here and there, he was gone." Staid to Bible Class, which was very large today. Did not go to the Third Ward Sabbath School today as I had a headache.

March 30, 1863, Monday: Went to school. Commenced reciting today in all my classes, like the school very much. Went to meeting this evening, had a very interesting meeting indeed.

March 31, 1863, Tuesday: School as usual. Came home to dinner. Remained to the lecture in Prof. Carr's room, a very interesting & instructive one. Went to meeting in the evening and afterwards to Lodge. Appointed a sociable for tomorrow evening.

April 1, 1863, Wednesday: Very pleasant today, went to school. Expected to go to the sociable in the evening. Got ready and about eight o'clock Mr. Scofield came to tell us that the room was occupied by the Masons. Quite a number came down to find out the reason and remained during the evening.

April 4, 1863, Saturday: At home today. Sewed all the forenoon, went to the Union League in the afternoon. Afterwards went up town. At home in the evening. Mrs. Eaton & Fannie came to pay a farewell visit, they go to Chicago Monday. Mr. & Mrs. Currier were also here & Ella Fox and Professors Donaldson & Howell. We spent a very pleasant evening.

Margaret

From Margaret Patchin at Wyocena to Augustus Patchin, April 5, 1863

My Dear Husband,

We received yours of the 22nd on Thursday, and yesterday we got yours of 26th, and we are always glad to hear from you; and when we get a letter it is dated so far back that I always think that perhaps you are sick now.

Oh, Augustus! This anxious waiting is hard, and how much longer shall I have to wait. It is 18 months today since you left home to go into camp, and I can't see as there is any more prospect of the war being closed than at that time. Do you calculate if you live, to stay till it closes? I should like to know for it seems to me that you haven't tried very much to come. You are gitting to be quite a mystery to us. You write strange, we think, for you was coming home in the spring, then in the summer and so on. Now, Augustus, I am quite anxious to know what is the reason that you can't git your pay. I thought that you was in the same company with Murry, and his money got home the 21st of March; and I heard that some others came with it. Have you got into trouble, or what? If you have got into trouble, I would rather that you tell me what it is than to have anyone else send home word; for I hear so many stories that I am kept quite uneasy. James thinks that they are agoing to cheat you out of all your pay.

The children and me have to work very hard to git along, for we made up our minds to try to support ourselves and save your wages; for to us everything that comes from you is thankfully received. I don't want you to deprive yourself of things that you need; but tell me what the matter is and how you manage to git along without money; for you know that I can't git along without thinking about it. I want to know about everything that you do, for I think of you all the time and you never look kindly at me when I am asleep. How do you look? Are you growing old fast, or how is it?

Monday evening

The children are all abed and asleep and I will try and finish this, hoping that you will come home so that I won't have to scribble to you.

Oh, Augustus! I can't help urging you to come home, for I love you and I love your children. You had aught to be with them; time with them is precious. They are on the stir all the time, and I lack both wisdom and patience to guide them aright.

Oh! That you would come home is the constant talk here in our home, and this baby will have a great many kisses for you, and he is very sweet; but I must stop and remain your lonesome, but loving wife.

M. A. Patchin

Home is a lonesome place without you. What is the reason you can't come to me, your own wife?

Emily

April 12, 1863, Sunday: A beautiful Sabbath morning. Went to church. Had a large congregation and a very good sermon. Returned home immediately after church to prepare for baptism. About two o'clock on the margin of Third Lake [Lake Monona], fourteen young persons were baptized, myself among the number. This is the most blessed day of my life. May God grant that I may ever be faithful in the course which I have commenced. There was a very large crowd collected upon the banks of the lake, and everything passed off well. Went to church in the evening.

Margaret

From Margaret Patchin at Wyocena to Augustus Patchin, April 12, 1863

My Dear Husband,

Yours of the first came to hand on Thursday. We was very glad to hear that you was well. I do not wish to hurt your feelings when I write to you— for I think of you with a yearning desire to see you safe home. In your last you said that you wished that I would inform you how you could get home. Now, you told me before you went away that a commissioned officer could resign and that if you could get a commission you would resign, if you could not get a furlough. Well, you had to work a year before you got a commission, and I thought that perhaps you had seen enough of the war, and I thought that you would do as you told me even though the babe was a year old and a boy at that. He is smart. Dear Augustus, he reminds me of Nancy very much in his ways for you know how quick she was to learn things. His nose is like Amelia, other ways he looks like Horatio.[46]

The children are all abed except James—he went to church this forenoon and Elbert and John went with him; they came home but he has not come, and it is bedtime—he has just come and I will go to bed with baby. He is nicely weaned and is doing finely. I think his health will be better, but I hated to wean him for he think so much of me; but he kisses me just as much as he did before I took it away from him. He makes Orlo feed him a good deal at the table; he has a high chair but he will get down and go to him or some of the rest—they all fuss with him Elbert, Orlo or John can dress him, and they like to.

Monday evening [April 13, 1863]

I am very tired tonight as I have been washing. We are all very busy now, there is so much to do; and how are you my dear husband? I am so 'fraid that you will have another battle there; may God protect you from all harm and permit you to return to us in safety. Oh, how terrible it is to think of you exposed to so much as you are!

Do you remember that this is Elbert's birthday? He is about as tall as I am. I must stop—so good night, dearest.

From Margaret Patchin at Wyocena to Augustus Patchin, April 16, 1863, 10 p.m.

My Dear Husband

We received yours of the 5 to day and was glad to hear that you was well I feel afraid that you are a going to be disapointed about the war closing this year I cant see any thing to encourage me to think so still I hope it will and that you will be permitted to come home to take care of your children I think this being in the army is a good deal like being in State prison for if a man keeps well he cant come home till his time is out if he lives that long and I am afraid that but few will live to come but you will say that I have got the blues I have them all the time Augustus if I have them now for I dont very often get a kind word or look from any one So many tell me that I have such reason for thankfulness because I have a plenty to do with I feel so vexed to hear them talk so when we have worked so hard to get a home and you away suffering so much and their Husbands at home to great courage to do any thing but make remark about what they call the war widows as they call me one of them you know that I dont like the title I am setting up in the bed writing and I cant see a line on the paper so I scratch away the baby is snoring away by my side he runs all around out doors and the boys are all asleep they are working very hard so they are driving team and huring up in their sleep good night Dearest

Sabbath afternoon

How are you today my, dear husband? Are you well? Will I ever have the privilege of talking to you again?

It is quite a task for me to write and spell, and I know that I make a great many mistakes; but you know that I must talk to you. It is almost 9 o'clock now, and I have just got your baby to sleep, so that I can write. The boys are all abed, and asleep.

James, Elbert, and Orlo have been to church today. The last time that I went I took Herbert, and he acted so bad, and I was so tired that I thought that he would have to stay at home till you come to take care of him, or he gets old enough to behave himself. He is so full of fun that he cuts up all the time. John and him has regular play jump.

You wanted me to tell you about Mrs. Dickson. I don't tell you much about the folks because you said before you went that you wouldn't mind much what I said about the folks, I was so set in my own way. I have found that I was not mistaken in the way that I told you people would do, and I have tried to do as you told me; to but I will try to tell you about Mrs. Dickson. I had heard that they were very hard up; and as I have been sick so much this winter, and tied with the baby, I hadn't seen her for some time, only as she went past, and that is quite often.

The boys have cut and dragged a good deal of wood to town this winter, and I thought that with what they raised last summer they could get along; so when I heard the story of their being in a suffering condition, I didn't believe it; but I went up there to see, and she complained more than I ever heard her before. The children was very ragged, but no worse than I have seen them often before when their father was at home. They have more things in their house than they used to have—looked more comfortable. She was all in rags, though the dress that she had on was new when the news of his death came; and another that she got since is worn out, but you know how they string things. The folks have brought them some provision, but I think that they had enough, for they have killed 9 hogs this winter; they are all very healthy. Walter is to work for William Edger, Maggie is with her grandmother, and Jimmy is putting in their greens. Mrs. Dickson thinks that she needs them at home. She has so much to do, but

I think that they can be spared. They don't have to work near as hard as our boys do, but you know that folks think it isn't anything for us to work; they act so any way. Her papers wasn't made out right, so she will have to wait some time for her money. I wish she could get the back pay. She was making a new dress for one of the girls. She said that they had enough to eat, but complained about the clothes. She has laid out more than double, I presume, since you went away, than I have on dress; yet, we are comfortable for things, but we all want you.

Monday evening [April 20, 1863]

Another hard days work is done and Elbert and Orlo and John is a bed and James and Herbert is on the lounge it is rain quite fast the boys is putting in a bunch of wheat they are calculating on your keeping your word with them that is that you will come home to help them harvest it they talk about it a good deal try and not disappoint them for you of all others had aught to keep your word with them. They have got tired of your promising to come and when the time comes then you set another time they say that if you want them to believe you must keep your word with them you have laid out a large summers work for your boys and I hope you will come and help them harvest I have just put my little bedfellow in bed and he gave me a kiss for you from your loveing wife

M A Patchin

Both the federal and Confederate governments continued to develop legislation and policy to deal with the ongoing conflict. On February 24 the Confederates imposed a comprehensive tax bill that included a 10 percent tax on agricultural products, an action that was seen as an affront by Southern farmers who were already losing income because of the practice of both Southern and Northern troops of taking farmers' produce for their own needs. Also on this day, Lincoln issued General Order No. 100, the first attempt to codify international laws regarding war.[47]

The second year of the war ended with a day of fasting and prayer called by President Lincoln. On the war front General Hooker established headquarters near Chancellorsville, Virginia; Grant's forces crossed the Mississippi as they advanced on Vicksburg; and Colonel Streight's forces in Alabama were engaged in battle with troops led by General Nathan B. Forrest.[48]

CHAPTER 3

May 1863 to April 1864

The third year of the war was a turning point both on the warfront and on the home front. In the West, Grant moved closer to the capture of Vicksburg and Union control of the Mississippi.[1] In the East, Union soldiers, including Wisconsin's 2nd, 3rd, 5th, 6th, and 7th Infantries and the predominantly German 26th Infantry, were defeated by a smaller Confederate army at Chancellorsville, Virginia. This defeat set the stage for Lee's invasion of Pennsylvania and their fateful meeting at Gettysburg.[2]

In the third year of the war, Annie Cox became engaged to Gideon Allen and, in accordance with her fiancé's wishes, agreed to honor his thoughts on the war and to stop discussing politics. Annie found this a difficult vow to keep, but she finally succeeded in stopping her discussion of politics in February 1864. Margaret Patchin faced new fears and uncertainty when Augustus was taken prisoner at Chickamauga in September and she no longer received mail from him. Augustus survived his imprisonment at Libby Prison in Virginia and was mustered out of service on December 19, 1864.[3] Emily Quiner found a new way to contribute to the war and to fulfill her longing to make a difference in the world.

Annie

From Annie Cox at Madison to Gideon Winans Allen at Ann Arbor, Michigan, May 3, 1863

... Winans, I am sorry you have got the name of copperhead—don't deserve it, brother, will you? The "Union League" in Madison is taking the city by storm. Everyone who doesn't belong is a copperheadess. Is your humble sister one of that sly class of animals? Well I always liked snakes. I am not particular of that color, however. They carry the matter to ridiculous lengths. Mrs. Carr (the president) had better see to the signs of secession in her husband's coat-sleeves and her boys' pants. There's anything but a spirit of union there! I do dislike that woman, Winans. I love the cause of freedom and our country but choose to explore it in a different way and am glad that there is a higher power to judge me than M. Union League. All wish to be remembered to you and by you. Write soon, Winans, maybe you will feel more like it next time. Now good-bye.

Annie

From Annie Cox at Madison to Gideon Winans Allen at Ann Arbor, Michigan, May 15, 1863

... I shall not write very joyfully tonight, Winans, for I am a little low spirited because a little sick and miserable toothache prevents me from sleeping so I am now going to write a while. I am going to scold a while too because my brother expresses an inclination to tardiness of duty. Be punctual, Winans, to the minute in business and pleasure if you will succeed in life and do this because it is right and [not] for my sake alone for if you would lose your sister where would be your reason for doing right if it were based upon her.

I do not know how far I may have influenced your course in life, my brother. I do not know what your past life has been, only as I may have surmised from your having been homeless and things you have said, but this I know, Winans, there has been an even exchange of pleasure for any ray of pleasure I may have sent through the gloom of your countenance one equally bright has returned. My life has not been all sunshine, 'tis less obscured now than ever before. This is a part of our education I am not inclined to murmur....

... I am glad the faculty [at the University of Wisconsin] have given you an invitation to graduate and thought I would not accept it. Though I would be careful in what manner I expressed my mind to them.

You are going to change your business. What do you propose to do, Winans? I was sorry to learn you had been sick—you must take grand care of yourself....

Margaret

From Margaret Patchin at Wyocena to Augustus Patchin, May 24, 1863

My Dear Husband,

How are you tonight? Hoping that you are well, I will try to write a few lines.

We received yours of the 9th and 11th on Tuesday, and was glad to hear that you was well. Oh, that I could have the privilege of seeing you and talking to you! It is such hard work for me to write. You know that I would not try to write to anyone else; and I do to you.

My much loved Husband, my daily prayer is that God will protect you, and hasten your return; and that you will love me more, and then you can get along with my faults. I try to mind you in everything; but in thinking that it was your duty to go and leave me to take care of myself and children, that I never can think was right; but you will say that I have said enough about that.

James, and Orlo, and John went to church today. I did not feel able to go, and Elbert stayed with me; and a few days ago, he went and had Henry shingle his hair, and he cut it so short all over that Elbert is ashamed to have anyone see him; so, he stays at home, but he has gone with James this evening to the village. Orlo and John is abed, and I am in bed sitting up writing. Herbert is snoring by my side. Oh, you don't know what a smart boy he is knocking around into everything! I do wish that you could see him! I know that you would be proud of him, for your looks is plain to be seen in him.

Mrs. Hodges has another girl; that is the two since you went away; smart, ain't they? But, I shall have to lay down and try to sleep. So, good night, from your lonesome wife. May you soon be here with me and the children God has given us.

Monday evening.

I am very tired as I have been washing and baking today. My hand trembles so that I don't know as I can write much.

James has been to Pardeeville with wheat today. I am going to let Uncle Jonathan have the money to pay for a colt. I will let him have 66 dollars; and Curt is to send the money to pay me or to pay you, there, just as you think best. You never told me whether you had paid Curt that ten dollars that you sent to me last summer, or not. If you have not, straighten it now; don't owe anybody; for, I should feel quite comfortable, now we are out of debt.[4]

If you was only here to help me take care of the children, and fix up things; and then I could talk to you. I don't have anyone now to tell my feelings to; for, I don't feel free with anyone but my children and you. You are my world, and I want to live with you.

Tuesday morning.

This is mail day again. John is going to the village in hopes to get a letter from you, for it is a week since we had one; and we are so glad to hear from you. We are dreading to hear of another battle where you are; but I trust you with God, feeling that he is able to take care of you, and restore you to me.

Oh, that the time would come that you could come home to stay with us, Dear Augustus! Is there not some way that you can git away honorably? I mean, for as much as I wish to see you, I don't want you to do a dishonorable thing to git away; but, I think that you have done your share in putting down this rebellion, and we do want you so much here at home. Your boys all need you, and the baby takes someone to look for him all the time, and you are just the one that he wants; but I must stop and remain your loving wife,

M. A. Patchin

From Margaret Patchin at Wyocena to Augustus Patchin, May 31, 1863

My Dear Husband,

We received yours of the 17th on Tuesday and was glad to hear that you was well and that there is some prospect of your coming home.

I want that you should tender your resignation and urge to have it accepted so that you can come home a free man, for the thought of parting with you again is terrible to me; for I think that I have the best right to you of any one save God—his I know that you are.

You have been there so long and they have let others come home that could have stayed away just as well as not, and yet they keep you; and all of the commissioned officers that belong around here have been home on furloughs of one or two months at a time. I don't know what the reason is that you can't have some privileges as well as others, for I am sure that your family loves you as much as any other man's does him.

You ask if I would hate to go to church all day as bad as I used to. Augustus, I am not able to go all day—you don't think how unwell I am all the time. Do you know how old I am today? Ask any doctor that you are a mind to and see if a woman of my age don't need care and kindness shown to her. Yet I get neither. I have to be busy at all times and at all hours—no one ever thinks that I get tired. My back and hips is so lame all the time I can hardly move. I think it is weakness that causes it.[5]

It is evening now and the children are all abed and asleep and I am in bed too, lying on my side writing to you. Oh, that I could talk to you! Herbert was sick all last night and I did not get much sleep. I think it was worms that ailed him; and his teeth has not got through. Yet he is a good bedfellow; kisses me a great many times every night—ain't you jealous of him? He asks for "Pa" a great deal. I think that he would know you if he could see you.

Good night.

ANNIE

From Annie Cox at Madison to Gideon Winans Allen at Ann Arbor, Michigan, May 31, 1863

... You wish to know my name. I wish you did not for it has painful associations made up. Not that there is any dishonor connected with it. But here it is: Annie M. Poad. Put a T. where old P stands and you have a subtropic name. But, Winans, please do not ever write or speak this name to me.

What do I think of immersion? Well, I would not call it a humbug but have no faith in it as a saving power and it often does more harm than good. A Madison lady says she has known seven confirmed invalids to be cured by this means. So far so good, I have known several healthy persons to be killed by this same means. There are several to be immersed today. Miss Quinn was dipped awhile ago. She was too large and heavy—the minister too small and light. He came nearly going over with her into the lake. Would that have been very solemn? ...

... Ask the widow if she can find a clear case of immersion in the bible. She may be inferring it but not by direct statement. ...

Margaret

From Margaret Patchin at Wyocena to Augustus Patchin, June 7, 1863

My Dear Husband,

We received yours of the 23rd on Tuesday and was glad to hear that you was well; and I do wish that you would try some way to git your resignation accepted. Can't you git away as well as the Captain did? I am sure that his wife and children does not need him any more than yours does. I have been to church today and am so tired that I can't write. The minister that has been preaching is going away; he preached his farewell sermon today.

Monday evening [June 8, 1863]

I am not very well; have had to keep very still today. I have overdone and it has bought on that old [weakness?] that I used to be troubled with. I have got Permelia Elles to work for me; she came today and I have to give her ten shillings a week; she is to stay with me all summer for I can't git along alone. Oh, that you would come home and take this burden of care off of me! Mary is here now, but she expects to go back to Portage next week. My hand trembles so that I make worse work than usual I believe.

If I don't write much it isn't because that I haven't got anything to tell you if I could see you, but I have so many things to see to and git tired-out so quick.

James and Elbert has been to Pardeeville today with wheat; they got a dollar and 5 cents a bushel. Orlo and John went a strawburyin' this afternoon and they got about three quarts. We don't eat anything that is nice without thinking of you and wishing that you had some of it.

The boys is crazy almost for your old clothes; this coat that they have fits James and Elbert both; it is a great deal better than they think because that you wore it so long.

I don't know what to do with the wool. We expect Cross to come and shear tomorrow.

Tuesday [June 9, 1863]

Morning breakfast is redy we are waiting for Mary to git up and Herbert is asleep so I will tell you about him he is so mischevious but he is so plesant with it that he is a regular play thing he will go whare the Boys is and bothers them he is so fond of the horses that I am afreaid that he will git hurt he is up and dressd and out doors cutting around Oh that I could see him in your armes my Dear Augustus and hear you say that you loved him and the rest of us you stay away so long that it looks strange to every one for all the officers has ben home two or three times since you went away but I must stop and remain as ever

your loveing wife Margaret A Patchin

June 14, [1863]

My Dear Husband,

    We received yours of the 4th of this month on Tuesday, and that of the 31st on Thursday, and was glad to hear that you was well; but, I was very much disappointed that you should send to have things sent to you, instead of your coming home to get them. I have got the best I could find, and I will make them for you, and I am sorry that I didn't get a handkerchief for you, but I don't know what you need nor what you have.

    Oh, Augustus, it is a hard life that I have! I am afraid that you are a going to disappoint us again by not coming. You had not aught to tell us that you are a coming, and than make no effort to get here.

    I have been very unwell for a few weeks, and I thought at first that I couldn't go to Portage to see that doctor; but, after a hearty cry over it, I plucked up courage and went. I didn't go to find fault with you, nor your children, nor to complain of my health; but, I went to see a man that had just seen my husband, and knew how he was; and to see-if he would take the things that you wanted. Would you go as far to make inquiries about me if I had gone away and left you as you did me?

    Oh, how I do want to see you and tell you how things go here! You have often told me that I must be indulgent to the children if I was left to take care of them alone. Well, I think that I have been too much so with some of them. James is no longer willing to be guided by me. He thinks that I am getting too old to know what young folks want; and, it hurts my feelings very much to have disrespectful words from my children. It makes me feel worse than it did when you was here; for then I thought that you loved me, and would make them mind me. I don't know what I have done to forfeit the respect of my family, without it is that I have loved them with too selfish a love. I know that James is better than the most of boys to mind (he is no longer a boy; he is a man in years and judgment); but, I think so much of him that I can't bare the thought of anyone having more influence than I have over him.

Margaret: "I plucked up courage and went [to Portage]." (Wisconsin Historical Society, WHS 23562)

Wednesday morning

We are as well as usual. There is some prospect of rain today, and we need it very much; but, James has got to go to Portage with this, and I don't want him to get wet I could not get the colored flannel that you said, but I got the best I could; and I have made them hoping that you will live to wear them out, and a good others besides them.

James is ready to go; so, goodbye for this time, from your lonesome, but loving wife

Margaret A Patchin

June 15 nine oclock in the evening

My Dear Augustus we received yours of the 7 this forenoon and was very glad to hear that you was well and I hope that this will find you comfortable you seen to think that I mite write as often as you can dont you know that I have to work all the time and that I have a very fussy baby to look after as well as the rest of your boys and your farm and a great many other things to tend to and I dont go from home very often and there is hardly aney one that comes here so that I dont hear much news onely some things that is not fit to put on paper and I have to take time when the rest is abed to write to you I have made you two shirts this week with Mary help and she sends you a nedlebook I have fixed a few things in it that I think you will nead if you dont come home we shall be very much disappointed if you dont come home soon for I want to have it so that I can put confidence in what you say so you must come for you have promised it so much you did not tell me whither you had paid [Cart?] or not I want you should for his folks is in such awory all the time because that I have monney and aint willing to let it all out to them I wrote to you that I had let Uncle Jonathan have 65 dollers for to pay for a colt for Cart with and Cart is to save his monney to pay it you will have to see to it for his folks is very hard up as usuel it is ten oclock and the musquetues is very thick around the candle and me so I must go to bed.

we shall send this by the Docter good night Dearest

Annie

From Annie Cox at Madison to Gideon Winans Allen at Ann Arbor, Michigan, June 14, 1863

... Still no letter, I looked for you yesterday till the time past for your coming. Thus my conclusion. You are either sick or offended. I would rather have you comfortably sick than offended, Winans. I say and write too many ungentle things that I wonder my friends are not of time displease. But, Winans, you must tell me of any fault and I'll try and improve. Don't be offended till you are addressed[,] an offense wasn't meant. If you are sick my sympathies and wishes for a speedy recovery are with you. You must not get sick away from home. I hope you will answer this letter in person. The commencement is a week from Wednesday. Try to be here the last of this week if you're not too mad. We have had a Sabbath School convention here during this last week. Some four hundred persons from different states were here. It was such a long cheering how these things turn Madison near [illegible]. How I wish you could have been here.[6]

June 16

... No it is not expected one woman should know everything for she would have all the Adams of creation to care for. She has the large share now for some have only one idea and that leads to the dinner table.

You know my opinion of the war. I cannot call that an abomination which frees one, gives me liberty to speak my mind, North and South. I cannot call that sentiment an abomination which called out many of our bravest and best and kept them cheerful and unwavering (some have striven to make them unhappy or tentative) in the most intense suffering. I cannot call that war a humbug in which thousands hitherto, in wicked careless ways, are now seeking that course of higher and noble warfare, even against sin and moral degradation. God never would have thus visited the bloody field in mercy and love if displeased or dishonored. And if all had been united, there would never be a need of draft. The Southerners themselves, admire the most those of the north who are whole hearted in this cause. God speed the right and enable us to leave a pure, <u>free</u> union to the coming generation that they may not have to fight for their freedom. If our forefathers had done this they would not have forced upon us this dreaded war. Well I am getting pretty earnest. But, my brother, if you don't want me to get earnest don't make any such speech, so unworthy of your otherwise noble nature. I should feel the trial if you should be drafted but could never say and write to any with such sentiments. But enough of this. Forgive that which may be ungentle.

I wish you would have stated definitely when you would be here whether the last of this week or the first of next. I am like yourself waiting with much pleasure the time of walks and talks with my brother—and hope he may arrive in health and happiness.

There is still one recourse if you are drafted. Buy yourself off. A quieter and better way I think for you are not strong enough for army life.[7]

Norman Powers, from Fox Lake, left his wife, Sarah, and three young children when he enlisted in Company 3 of the 29th Infantry of the Wisconsin Volunteers, a regiment that was distinguished by the large number of foreign-born members. Of the original 882 members, 562 were born in foreign countries, with only 28 members having been born in Wisconsin.[8] In June Sarah learned from neighbors that Norman was among those wounded at the Battle of Port Gibson, and she wrote a letter to him. Norman complained of not receiving letters from Sarah while in the hospital—on June 4 he reported that the last mail he had received was from April 10.[9]

SARAH

From Sarah Powers at Fond du Lac to Norman Powers, June 18, 1863

Father had just returned from town and brought me four letters one from you the first to read of all and how much it does relieve my anxious mind you better believe that I have had much anxiety about you since the first time you landed, and your letter I received last night was the first one I had receive since you left Helena but your letter kindly explains all since you went into the battle of Port Gibson. Kendall folks received Charley and Mrs. Lawrance got letters from her husband that lives in town and it was a great wonder to me and us all whey we could not hear from you. Charley Kendall was wounded in his left leg in the battle at Champion Hill as soon as the battle was over the wounded were taken and put aboard transport and sent up the river or a good many of them so Charley is at Memphis the battle was on the 22nd of May. Mrs. Lawrance have wrote to her husband to inquire after you. I had also wrote to Charley to [k]now if you was in the battle or of he [k]new anything about you and had wrote three letters to Fox Lake but strange to state Mrs Tyrell had wrote to me the 25 of May a few lines to let me [k]now of your being wounded a day or two after it she received one of my letters then she immediately wrote again the 28th of May giving me the full particulars of all the killed and wounded and those that died and those that had fingers thumbs and limbs amputated, and I never received her letters until last Saturday evening mail over two weeks since she mailed them. I also received a letter from Mrs. Wiliams and one from Marie and another from Mrs. Tyrell. Norman I have wrote this in a great hurry this morning while Beck getting ready to go to town. I will write again Sunday we are all well but mother and overjoyed to hear from you write just as soon as you can and often have you paper stamp envelope.[10]

From Sarah Powers at Fond du Lac to Norman Powers, June 21, 1863

I received yours of June 7th yesterday, the 20th, and was highly pleased to hear from you again and yours of June 3rd, we received last Wednesday, 18th. They were both on the way a long time coming, but we were overjoyed very much to hear from you . . . glad to hear that your wound was so slight, and that is healing up so hope that it will not be long before your fingers will be restored to being limber though I am a little fearful that they will not, but is [sic] they are to remain stiff it will be better than as though they had to be amputated, but your slight wound pictures to me that it has been the means of saving your life during those three heavey battle that the 29th has been and I hope that before you are called to join your Regt that all fighting will be accomplish in that army and that you was in your first and last battle and the time is not far off when you can return home to your family and we can to our pleasant home, Fox Lake. . . . I must patiently wait for the interesting hours we shall have when you do return, hope that the time will never be that you will be placed where you cant mail a letter to us, you had believe it is not a desirable suspense to live in expect every hour to hear of your being killed or severely wounded and suffering for the want of care I dare say that you went hungry many days before you got to Millikin Bend again. I wrote three letters to Fox Lake to hear if I could if anything had happen to you and then when I heard that Charley Kendall was in the hospital in Memphis with a flesh wound in his left leg I wrote right to him to know if he knew whether you was in the battle at Champion Hill or the one at Jackson also to George if the friends at Fox Lake write there, the friends of the army there to write to it to me for any anxiety had got to be treat and it was through him that I first heard of your being hurt as the news came from there first he heard that you were killed then slightly wounded . . .[11]

MARGARET

From Margaret Patchin at Wyocena to Augustus Patchin, June 28, 1863

My Dear Husband,

How are you today? Do you think of me, and how long it is since we have seen each other? Twenty months this morning since you went away. Oh, it is like an age to me, and no prospect of the war being closed! Every thing is dark and gloomy about it. Don't your faith fail, or do you still think that it is all for the best? We haven't had any letter from you this past week and I am feeling very anxious about it for fear that something is the matter; or are you coming home?

James and Elbert has gone to church today. Orlo and John has just brought in currants for dinner; they are getting quite ripe. Herbert is sitting in the door playing with the whip. I think that he is smart enough to suit you. or any one else that loves babies.

Five o'clock in the afternoon—We have had a fine shower, and everything looks refreshed; and I think that I would be too if you was here by my side, or on the lounge with your sleeping baby. Oh, he is so nice, Augustus! I don't know but I am in danger because that I pity him because that you wasn't willing to stay and take care of him; but he has a very loving disposition and thinks more of me than he does of anyone else, and my heart asks for love. So he suits me, but I want your love. Oh, it is so hard to think of things past and present that I don't know what to do with myself! Will I ever have rest or will you never come to take the burden off of me? For, I can't be happy without you are here; I can't get used to doing without you; my heart is sad all the time. I think of you all the time. I am told by them that have seen you since I have that you are cheerful and happy, so I suppose that you have better company than me where you are; but I ain't willing to give you up, for you promised to be mine as long as you lived if I lived that long, and I hold you to your promise. Now don't feel hurt at my writing this to you, for I am in earnest; but I trust you with God, feeling that you are His even more than you are mine.

I wish that I could send you some currants; we have such a bunch of them. I have preserved some strawberries for you and I shall try to keep them for you. We didn't have many in our bed for the dry weather parched the vines all up.

When do you think that we had better sell the wool. It is bringing a pretty good price, but I don't know but it will be higher, and I don't know what to do with the money; for I have all that package that you sent home and nearly fifty besides that in the house, and I think that it is hardly right to let it lie idle when we have paid interest so long; but I have had such strong hopes that you would come home and fix up the things here, and I haven't had any good chance to let it. Money is plentier than it used to be, I guess.

The family is all abed and I must go, but I thought that I would tell you about Herbert. Just about sundown he was in my lap playing and I asked him if he hadn't got a kiss to send to Pa. He said yes, in his way, and he went to work and kissed me. Oh, so many times; I think as many as fifty times, and he would say "Pa," "Pa," then he would smack away and then he would stick his tongue in my mouth. He learnt that of you, I think, don't you? Have you forgot how to kiss? I kiss him for you everyday a number of times.

Good night, Dearest Husband.

Monday afternoon. [June 29, 1863?]

It is raining nicely, and I will try to finish this letter. Oh, how I wish that you would come home so that I could talk to you and hear your voice again! James is lying on the floor asleep and Elbert is tending Herbert; he thinks there never was such a nice baby; and Orlo and John is at school, they haven't been much for there is so much to do all the time. Mary is fixin a bonnet for Ellen.

Seley Bull came here to see if he couldn't get one of them company rolls, and I told him that I supposed that there wasn't any had them but those that paid for gitting them printed. He is very anxious to get one. He said that if you could git one for him he would pay any reasonable price for it and wanted I should tell you so.

The children is all at home and they are so noisy that I can't write nor think of anything to tell you. If you think that you can't come home so as to build this fall, had I not better put the money in the bank, or what shall I do with it? You see that James is rattle-headed about gitting married, but I guess he ain't in much of a hurry about it—he is calculating to go away to keep the Fourth of July. Oh, I wish that you was here so that I wouldn't have to stay alone on that day. We shouldn't dare to go away for fear some of the meddlers would take our currants, you know. I want to make some wine if I can get something to put it in, and I shall have to get it this week. Elbert has just been out and got a nice basin full for supper; they have ripened very fast this year, it has been so dry. I think of you every time that I look at the bushes.

I shall have to stop, and remain, as ever, your loving wife.

M. A. Patchin

From Margaret Patchin at Wyocena to Augustus Patchin, June 30, 1863

Dear Augustus,

We are as well as usual this morning. Write more about yourself for we are so anxious about you all the time, and you are suffering so much all the time that everything is so dreary to me.

Your lonesome wife,
M. A. P.

Emily

June 28, 1863, Sunday: Another long gap in my diary, and I promised myself at the last that that there should not be another if it was in my power to prevent it, but such are human resolves. The last two months I have been very busy, between attending school and the meetings and getting my lessons, my time has been fully occupied. I never enjoyed a mission better in my life and deeply regret that I am not able to go on with my studies, when

I think of what I might do and what I might be if I only had an opportunity of continuing my studies for two or three years. I can hardly reconcile myself to the necessity which exists for me to do something else, but it is so and I must be content. I am going to commence taking painting lessons next week which I shall enjoy very much. We have had a very busy and pleasant time during the past week. The University Examinations and Commencement was fast over and the long summer recreations commenced. I want to accomplish a great deal during the summer, which I hope I may. We have had a very dry time this month of June. It has not rained this month and it seemed as if the very earth would turn to dust and be shifted away in the first gale, but today there is a change. This morning was the most sultry of the season. I did not go out until time for Sabbath School and on coming home got a sprinkling and now it is raining quite hard and the air is deliciously cool. Thank God for rain! Mr. Craig is down and I must go down but not until I renew my resolve not to neglect you again old diary as long as I have power to chronicle my daily thought and the events of my life for your pages. It is a long time since hand took my pen for the first stroke upon your fair pages, over two years. In those two years though apparently the same in circumstances I feel that there has been a change in me. I [am] not the same woman who sat here this day two years ago and wrote of her life. God grant that the change may have been for the better, I think it has. Sitting here today I hope that I have higher views of life, wider and broader comprehensions of its duties and responsibilities than then, and now looking back through those two years, their experiences, their trials and their sorrows, for there have been all of these, many known only to my God and myself, I thank him that he has given me them to teach me the life lessons which without their aid might have been unlearned, and looking into my own head today I believe that I am willing to hear shattering bad news and fulfill whatever obligation he may impose. May he give me strength which I so much need to do all this. Looking around upon the life that I lead from the daily duties of my position, I often think it a barren field and long for something that shall more fairly fill and occupy my mind and heart than that monotonous routine of every day duties and cares. Life seems very bleak to me sometimes and looking forward I see nothing but gloom and darkness. A great hope has gone out of my life in the last few months, and for a time it took all its sweetness and joy but with God's help I will confess my weakness, and bear bravely the yoke of life. I believe that God sends us trials to try our spirit and temper and refine us as gold in the fire, and I thank him that he has thought me worthy to suffer, may it do me good.

June 29, 1863, Monday: At home today. Went up town in the afternoon. To meeting in the evening. When I got home Mr. [George C.] Smith was there. He is going to Memphis tomorrow. He wanted us to go with him to take care of sick and wounded soldiers in the hospital. I told him I would go. I think Fannie will too. We sat up very late laying our plans. Mr. S. is going to remain another day. Pa did not like the idea of our going at all, but finally gave his consent. Went to bed with my mind very unsettled tonight.

June 30, 1863, Tuesday: Up early this morning, having a great deal to do, getting ready for so long a journey. We are to stay two months before coming home. Jennie Chapman & Lou Richardson are going also. There is quite an excitement in town about our going. We have been receiving calls all day. Mr. Craig has been here all the afternoon. He feels very badly about our going. I went to Mr. Johnson's to a party tonight and leaving early visited the Lodge. My friends all seemed to feel sorry that I was going to leave them though all thought it a noble work. They gave me their best wishes. After Lodge we went to Waltzinger for ice cream, found the store closed, disappointed. Went to bed very tired. We are to start at eleven tomorrow.

July 1, 1863, Wednesday: Rose early, ironed, packed trunks, dressed myself, went up town and did a great many other things. We went up and had our pictures taken. Found that the omnibus had left, when I got home, quite a number of friends waiting to walk to the depot with me. Fanny went in the bus. The sitting room at the depot was crowded with friends, waiting to see us off, bade them good bye, and soon found ourselves under full steam for Janesville, discovered soon after starting that about half our baggage was missing. Mr. Campbell who accompanied us to J[anesville]—said he would go back and get it, if we would stay over one train at J. We went to Sarah Covell's and stayed until about 7 o'clock Thursday morning, went to the depot, found Mr. C and the missing baggage, and started for Chicago. Mr. Campbell brought letters from home and a paper with a very complimentary notice of our departure for the sunny south. Rode all night.[12]

July 2, 1863, Thursday: Came into Chicago at 6 o'clock & I took breakfast at the hotel, stopped about two hours and then started for Centralia. We had a very long, warm, tedious ride, and arrived at Centralia at 8 o'clock. I am tired, hungry and almost out of spirits. An excellent supper and a rest of two hours made us all right however, and then we took sleeping cars for Cairo, we were in the best spirits in the world.

July 3, 1863, Friday: Passed the night comfortably. The stopping of the cars early this morning awakened us. Found ourselves standing still in an apparently interminable swamp with two or three feet of water as far as you could see on either side of the track, with rank grass and trees and weeds. The cars were very close, and I very imprudently opened a window near me repenting of it immediately, however, for the first breath of the air was like pestilence, I came near fainting and did not recover from the effect of this for some time. After stopping here for something like half an hour owing to some derangement in the machinery, we moved on and soon entered the city of Cairo. The most miserable, desolate-looking place on the face of the earth is this same Cairo. We only stayed long enough to go down to the wharf and get aboard the steamer, but that was as long as we cared about staying. We hardly got a glimpse of any body but negroes, and poor white folks. Went on board the steamer Hope, got our breakfast, and soon had made ourselves comfortable for the day. The captain took us up to the pilothouse where it was cool, and enjoyed the prospect very much. The Mississippi River was quite a disappointment to me, instead of the majestic stream of which so much has been said and sung, I saw only a comparatively narrow and a superlatively muddy stream, that looked anything but majestic, as the steamer moved down, however, it widened and seemed more like my preconceived notions of old Mississippi. We reached Columbus [Kentucky] early in the forenoon, stopped about two hours. It looks like a strong military post, the cannon flanked on the heights and the white tents of the garrison in the distance give it quite an aire militaire, while the mule teams and contrabands which throng the streets give one quite an idea of a Kentucky town. We stayed in the pilothouse until dinnertime. On the opposite shore from Columbus is the site of the famous battle of Belmont, so disastrous to us. It is an innocent looking spot enough, being a level piece of ground, partially covered with timber. It is hard to realize that these places have ever been the scene of such terrible conflicts. Met a brother-in-law of Gov. Solomon [*sic*: Salomon] on the boat, he is a very pleasant man, said he would send us transportation to Vicksburg He offered us wine before we had been acquainted fifteen minutes, which owing to our temperance principles we were obliged to refuse. Went to bed tonight very tired.[13]

July 4, 1863, Saturday: Independence Day! And we floating down the Mississippi! Who would have thought it, on such an errand too? It was very warm this morning. I sat down immediately after breakfast and wrote a long letter home to be mailed at Memphis. After this we went up to the pilothouse and had a good view of Fort Pillow which we passed about ten o'clock. It looks like a very strong point indeed. Very high banks surrounded by a high board railings with one or two guns visible from the river, is all that meets the eye now. Hardly a vestige remains of what must have been a formidable looking place. We passed Island No. 10 in the afternoon. It is garrisoned by Negro troops. New Madrid is also quite a large place on the river, which has been the scene of a hard fought battle. A lady who came down from Cairo with us, and who is commandant at New Madrid, got off here. In a short time after this, we got a view of Memphis from a point in the river which is about four miles from the city, where the Mississippi bends in an abrupt curve. It looked beautiful in the light of the setting sun, and was quite a welcome sight to us, when a few moments after we found ourselves approaching the scene of our future labors. It is situated on high banks overlooking the river, and has many fine public buildings. We went immediately to a boarding house on our arrival, and retired to rest, or rather to try to rest for the house being nearly full, four of us had only a single room with a bed and a lounge as sleeping accommodations. We had quite a celebration on board the steamer today. The gentlemen got a flag and unfurled it in the cabin and then drew up resolutions, sang songs, and had a general good time. Jenny & I were appointed as committee with these gentlemen to draw up resolutions. We had quite a celebration. Met Paulus Adams & Rebels on the boat today. They are going to Lake Providence.

July 5, 1863, Sunday: A terribly warm day. We went up to the office after breakfast and staid two or three hours. Had a splendid shower while there, a regular tropical deluge, which passed leaving the air apparently as hot as before. Met Mr. Wayne tonight, a Madison man whom I remembered having seen in Madison but do not think I should have recognized without an introduction. He is quite pleasant.

July 6, 1863, Monday: Another warm day. We went up town this morning, visited the park, which is an exquisite little bit of greenery, teaming with squirrels which are so tame that they will eat from your hand here. I saw a magnolia blossom for the first time. They are splendid and grow in almost every garden here. There are also a great variety of evergreens, and beautiful flowering shrubs and trees meet the eye on every hand. Here is the monument of Jackson, famous for having suffered mutilation at the hand of a rebel colonel, who would have blotted out the motto it bears "The Union it must and shall be preserved." We went up this evening with some gentlemen at the house where we board and Mr. Smith to get ice cream. A beautiful cool evening. We enjoyed it much. Did not visit any of the hospitals today.[14]

SARAH

From Sarah Powers at Fond du Lac to Norman Powers, July 6, 1863

. . . inform me whether you can get a furlough to come home do Norman come if possible try hard to persuade them to let you come tell them that it is necessary that you should come to see to your business and an improvement to your health O, I have wanted you to come so bad ever since I heard that you was wounded (not saying anything about the time before when you was wounded) for it will be as much better for you are liable to be attacked with fevers diarrhea or what not then and as to the ague I hope you will be spared from having it any more I shall look for you until the middle of next month then if you are not hear by that time I shall think the surgeons are cruel that they don't let you come for they may as well let you be at home as there living in the Hospital.

. . . we have had no news by the papers from the Potomac but still better telegraphic news from Chicago confirming the victory of the army there still more & more encouraging instead of 12,000 prisoners we have 30,000 and some 10,000 dead and wounded rebels and rebel Gen. Lee perfectly surrounded so that he can't possible get away and it seems that he sent a messenger to Jeff Davis at Richmond, Va, to send him reinforcements and on the messengers return he was captured with the dispatch it was impossible for his troops were but few and they were liable to be taken any day for we have 50,000 on their way to Richmond and right about there and Lee had offered to surrender if they let him have some kind of post but that will be impossible for as now they have got him and all his forces surrounded I hope that they will not have it over to do over again it is generally believed that Johnston troop are poor articles Lee has also asked for two hours to buried [sic] his dead but it is not granted so they do not play that old trick upon Gen Meadows as he is not the commander in chief of the Potomac army as Hooker has resigned I should think that the Tennessee rebel is quite weak for Roscranse is in full pursuit after them it is rebel Gen Bragg that is in that part of the country. . . .[15]

EMILY

July 7, 1863, Tuesday: Excessively warm. We had a nice shower, however, in the forenoon, which cooled the air somewhat. Louise & I started out this P.M. to go up town. We were going to the Union Hospital. It looked very much like rain and before we had gone two blocks down it came. We took refuge in a grocery, the only available shelter, and spent about an hour and a half in the agreeable society of codfish and potatoes. It cleared up after a time and we went on, did not visit the Hospital however. Went up to the Park this evening.

July 8, 1863, Wednesday: Started immediately after breakfast to see Dr. Irwin Surgeon General of Hospitals here, he immediately engaged us for hospital duty and gave us our papers. We visited the Jackson Hospital and afterward the Gayoso[16] where we were engaged. We found Mrs. Wemple, a Wisconsin lady and Mrs. Green a sort of under matron here, very pleasant. They told us some very discouraging things and for some time I felt rather blue over the prospect. The surgeon in charge, Dr. Hartshorn came in and assigned us our wards. Fannie's is next to mine on the same floor. The wards are long rooms containing from fifty to seventy beds. Each one has a surgeon, a ward master and four nurses besides a female nurse. Dr. Nelson the surgeon of my ward seems to be a very pleasant man. There are some very sick men in my ward and being an entirely new business to me I went at it rather awkwardly, I expect that I shall soon learn how to work I hope. Mr. Smith and another gentleman came to take us to walk in the evening. We had ice cream, sat a while in the park, and then came back, and I went to bed feeling sensibly the oddity of our situation on our first night in the hospital.[17]

July 9, 1863, Thursday: Rose this morning at the sound of the bugle at five, dressed and went down to my ward. Went around and said good morning to all my men, attended to the giving out of the breakfast, fed one man, there are some who are very sick. One man was having fits when I entered

Harriet Douglas Whetten (pictured) was another "female nurse" from Wisconsin. (Wisconsin Historical Society, WHS 1882)

the ward yesterday, he had them at intervals all through the night, and they think that he will not live through the day. After breakfast the surgeon came and I made out the diet list for the day under his directions. I staid in my ward nearly all day, at night I was so tired and my feet were so swelled that I could not sleep. There is a great deal of noise in the street, and sleeping in strange rooms is not just the thing for nervous people.

July 10, 1863, Friday: Dreaded to go to my ward this morning, the air is so bad there. There are some very sick men here and they require my constant attention. I already feel very much interested in some of them, some who are very sick. Wm. Clark a boy of about 19 who has chronic diarrhea, I am afraid will never get well. I feel very badly about him and shall do all in my power to help him, he is very low however and there is but a bare possibility of his recovery.[18] There are several other cases of the same disease, all doubtful. One man, Alfred Kent, about twenty, I should think, and from Ohio, is very low with fever & debility, I am afraid that he cannot recover. I was very tired tonight. A young man died in Fannie's ward. I felt very sorry about it. His name was Martin.

July 11, 1863, Saturday: In my ward early. Clark better today. I talked to him a long time about his home and friends, told him I thought the doctor would give him a furlough and send him home as soon as he was able to go, he seems to feel discouraged, and, though he listens to my plans for him and acquiesces in them, yet he seems to think that he shall never see home again. I am afraid he won't, poor fellow! Went out with Mr. Smith this evening. Went to the Park, sat awhile, got some lemonade and ice cream, saw any number of ladies, and contrabands. Tired out when we got home.

July 12, 1863, Sunday: My first Sabbath here. When I went down this morning, found the boys in some cleaning the floor, and after breakfast they changed the clothing of the men and also the beds. This is always done Sunday because this is inspection day. The Surgeon General comes around to inspect every thing and it must be in prime order. But not so well today. A man died in Fannie's ward today of chronic diarrhea. It does not seem like Sunday at home. I should not know it by any such actions here. Some of the men are worse today. I have been in my ward most of the day. Mr. Smith came this afternoon with a Wisconsin Captain who was very pleasant, said they would call and go to church in the evening.

MARGARET

From Margaret Patchin at Wyocena to Augustus Patchin, July 12, 1863, "6 o'clock in the eve"

My Dear Husband,

I have just got up from the bed where I have been trying to rest; for this forenoon, just as I was ready to begin to write to you, Eliza sent for me to come up there; for she was very sick. Our children had gone to church with the team, all except Orlo and baby I left them and went up there and found her in great distress. She had the colic very hard. I fussed awhile, sent for my gun and my bottle of painkillers and after a little she got easy; then I came home and had to start the dinner and get it ready for the family; and it is the first time that I have walked so far since you went away.

I am very lame in my shoulders, but I am feeling so anxious about you that I can't think of much. It is so long since we heard from you—the 23rd of last month was the date of your last. Oh, for one line to say that you live and are well—this suspense is terrible! Dear Augustus, it is dark and the children is all asleep but James. He is reading with Mary; he has been to prayer meeting, and Elbert and Orlo went with him. He has heard a rumor that there was four Wisconsin regiments in a skirmish and that the Tenth was one of them and that there was 89 killed, wounded, and missing out of the four. Oh, what is it—is there any truth to it, and where are you, my husband. The promises are strong in my mind. I still seem to hear you say, "God's protecting care is still over me, and I am not hurt." Oh, that I could feel to trust you in His Care knowing that He is able to take care of you.

I don't know what to write to you, only about how much we need you and how very lonesome I am. The children do not miss you as they did at first—you have been gone so long that they have got over their loneliness a good deal. Not so with me. Oh, I can't give you up! Nothing cheers me—only the thoughts of your soon coming home. My heart is sad all the time; even the baby can't cheer me, and he is a very lively little fellow—the greatest mimic that you ever saw of his age. He is beginning to call his brothers by name; he says "Orlo" quite plain, and, "Elbert," and "John." He don't try "James," yet.

I must quit and go to bed; so good night, and may God grant me the privilege of soon seeing you and hearing you talk.

SARAH

From Sarah Powers at Fond du Lac to Norman Powers, July 12, 1863

. . . Today Aaron is busy putting the reaper together for mowing he will help father do his haying and harvesting father thinks that his clad wheat will be ready to harvest in two weeks the crops about hear never look so promising but many under quite an excitement of feelings about the wheat for fear of the fly and weevil now there is some kind of an insect to work on it the weather has been very hot for the last three weeks and dry till Friday night two o'clock it change blew very hard and cold, a cold wind yesterday, mother for the last few days has not been as strong as the fore part of the week and fare to be quite feeble for all summer she get feel the overdoing of taken care of tem all when they had so much sickness father has to have a good nerves shake every few night.

... there has been a great deal of fighting in Pennsylvania for the last two weeks every body is crying out with the hopes of our taken rebel Gen. Lee, our forces have captured a great number of prisoners and they have lost three Gen. we two, and 1st and 2nd July Phineas was in battle all day mother & father are anxiously waiting to hear the result of Phineas, it was quite a rejoicing through the country to hear of the fall of Vicksburg....[19]

EMILY

July 13, 1863, Monday: Rained the forenoon, made it very cool. Went to my ward as usual. Men getting along very well. Did not go out tonight. One of my men very sick. He cannot live, he is an Ohio boy, he is a very fine fellow about 20 years old. I would almost give the world if he could live. I wrote a letter to a cousin of his in the army at Vicksburg telling him how he was and asking him to write home, and inform his friends. He is very grateful for anything I do for him and though he never says much, his eyes follow me everywhere. He is very homesick. How my heart aches when I think that this is the way that the flower of our country's youth are perishing in this cruel contest. I am thankful that God has given me the opportunity to do some good, and pray that he will give me strength to do my duty faithfully in the fear of His Holy Name. Tired out tonight, went to bed with a heavy heart, almost expect to find Kent dead tomorrow morning.

July 14, 1863, Tuesday: Pleasant & cool this morning. Men about as usual. Kent is better this morning, ate quite a breakfast. I do wish he could get well. Clark is getting better slowly. I think he may get well, he seems to be in better spirits. Jennie & Lou went up town this morning. Mr. Smith & Mr. Wayne called in the evening. Tired tonight. Today as I was sitting by Kent, Dr. Nelson came in with a passion flower, which he got at the Jewish cemetery. I pressed it.

July 15, 1863, Wednesday: Warm today. In my ward all day. Mr. Smith & Mr. Sweetland of the Adams Hospital came this afternoon to have us go up to the Officer's Hospital to see a Wisconsin Captain. I did not go, the rest of the girls did. I feel too anxious about my men to go anywhere, there are three or four that may die any time. Kent is very low tonight. I have sat by him all the afternoon, he is very quiet. It seems as if I could not bear to see him die. The doctor will not let me tell him that he must die, for there possibly may be a chance for his recovery, he says. I have no hopes of it. God pity his poor old mother and God pity all the mothers whose hearts will ache through the terrible consequences of this unnatural war. Went to bed tired enough.

July 16, 1863, Thursday: A warm day, it rained about noon and cooled the air somewhat, a real tropical shower it was, the rain coming down in sheets. I enjoyed it, but I guess some of the boys who lay under the ventilator didn't, for the rain came right through. In my ward all day. Kent has been stupid all day. Had no appetite for food, could hardly rouse him to take his wine. I feel very bad about him, he will not live through the night I fear. God have mercy upon him, poor fellow. I would do anything in my power to give him back the lost life power, but alas human arms are too short and human effort too weak to help in such cases. There is another man in my ward whom I fear will die today. I wrote to his wife yesterday.

9 o'clock P.M. Kent is dead. He breathed his last a half hour ago. I closed his eyes, they prepared him for the grave and took him away. I shall never forget the sorrow I felt for his death, he was so young, so patient, so lonely and homesick and so grateful for everything I did for him. I shed as bitter tears over his dying bed as I ever wept in my life, it is so hard to see our noble boys die here alone, so far from friends who would give their lives almost to have been with them in their last moments. I shall write to his mother. The saddest duty of our position is this breaking the tidings to anxious loving hearts at home. God give you strength to bear it, poor loving mother. My ward will seem lonely after this. I have watched him and fed and cared for him so long that the sight of his poor pale face on the bed seemed a part of my life. Poor fellows, so they die.

SARAH

From Sarah Powers at Fond du Lac to Norman Powers, undated fragmented letter

... that this rebellion will be crushed before late in the fall for as soon as Charleston is captured we shall succeed in capturing Richmond. Rosencranse is progressing well with his part of the army our last letter from

Phineas was wrote and mailed the 9th we are in fear that some accident has happened to him....[20]

... the draft has been postponed for a while in this state, the riots in New York City and Boston are all quiet now. New York they thought they were going to quell they by firing blank cartridges among them but now the President has issued a proclamation to fire no blank cartridges to quell [the] riot....[21]

EMILY

July 17, 1863, Friday: Went to my ward as usual. Did not feel very well today. A little blue. I shall have to go out more. Fanny, Louise & I went up to Mr. Smith's office this morning. It rained after we got home. In my ward the rest of the day. Tired tonight, glad to get to my room.

July 18, 1863, Saturday: Louise & I took a long walk this morning, went as far as the Soldier's Home, a very pretty place. We had a great deal of fun going out & back. There are so many comical things in Memphis. Wrote a letter home today, and also one to a cousin of Kent's at Vicksburg. Went to bed early. Very tired.

July 19, 1863, Sunday: Warm today, men in my ward about as usual. In my ward all the forenoon. Sunday is Inspection Day here and a general cleaning up has to take place in the morning. This afternoon Mr. Smith came with a captain of the 17th Regiment, a very pleasant man. They said they would come and go to church with us in the evening, but did not come, we did not go out.

July 20, 1863, Monday: Fanny, Louise & I went to market this morning at five o'clock. There is a very nice market here and we see a great many green things. I enjoy it very much. This morning I saw an old market woman coming in on a mule with a straw hat upon her head, the brim of which was at least half a yard in width and her face was so browned and sun burned that she would have safely passed muster among the Winnebagoes.[22] Lou & I went up town after breakfast. In my ward all this afternoon. Dr. Nelson brought me scale from a large fish which was caught in the Mississippi at this point called the Elephant. Mrs. More and the rest of us went up to Mr. Smith's office this morning. Met Dr. McGaryhay of the Indiana Agency, a very pleasant man, looks like Dr. Williard of Lake Mills.

July 21, 1863, Tuesday: In my ward all day. Cool and pleasant, men doing well generally. I wrote a letter for one man to his wife. He is a Virginian dying of chronic diarrhea. He says his wife is only 17 years of age. They have been married only about a year. He must die. Mr. Smith and Dr. Sweetland of the Adams Hospital came to see me, said the Hope was lying at the wharf. The girls went down to see the captain. I was too busy to go.

July 22, 1863, Wednesday: Warm today. Rose early. Went to my ward this morning, found that my poor Virginian had died during the night. The nurses were with him when he died. They said that he died easy. I am sorry for his wife. I must write to her. I have been in my ward all day. This afternoon the Ward Master brought me an order from the Surgeon in Charge to the effect that the ladies employed as nurses in the Hospital should not enter the kitchen, as they have been accustomed to, for the purposes of cooking for the sick men, neither leave their wards on any account unless by permission of the Surgeon in Charge of the ward. This was sent as a general order to all the nurses in the Hospital. It created quite an excitement but we had a good deal of fun about it, as when we asked our surgeons to let us go out in the afternoon they gave us permission to go out at any time we pleased. A man died in Fannie's ward last night. We all had an invitation to go to the theatre in the evening, it was a Soldier's Benefit night and we went. It was crowded to excess and so very warm that it was almost impossible to breathe, and I had not been there five minutes before I heartily wished myself back at the Gayoso. The acting was the most miserable I ever saw and if anybody ever catches me at that place again, I hope that I shall have as miserable a time as I had then.

July 23, 1863, Thursday: Mr. Smith came up this morning and said that if Fanny wanted to go home, she could go up with Mr. Hicks and Lieut. Cantwell today. They were going directly to Madison. She has been talking of going for some time. She concluded to go. I was almost angry with her. I do not think she ought to go off and leave me here. She left here about 12 N. I did not go to the boat. I felt very lonely all day, and would have had a real good cry if I had not been too provoked about her going. About four o'clock this afternoon, Col. Howe of the 32d Wisconsin sent the ambulance for us and about five we started for the camp. It was my first experience in the ambulance riding. We enjoyed the novelty immensely. I don't see how so much jolt ever got such one vehicle as that ambulance contained, we had

May 1863 to April 1864   147

a great deal of fun about. When we arrived at the Colonel's headquarters we alighted and were conducted through a nice yard. The colonel lives in a very pretty house which used to be the property of a Secesh lady and was confiscated. We were very agreeably surprised at meeting a sister of Col. Howe whom we liked very much indeed, she has been here about a week. Col. Howe is splendid. We enjoyed our visit very much indeed. I was sorry that Fanny could not be there. We met a Miss Ballou of Green Bay, she is taking care of the sick in the Regimental Hospital. We went home tonight having spent the pleasantest evening we have had for a long time.[23]

July 24, 1863, Friday: In my ward most of the day. We all went up to Mr. Smith's office. He had just been down to see the boat off, which Fanny went in. She had been there waiting for the boat to go ever since she started yesterday. Lieut. Cantwell went with her. A friend of Fanny's, a Ms. Judson of Beaver Dam, came to see us this afternoon. Wrote three letters today for the boys in the ward. A boy about 16 years of age died in Fannie's ward today. His brother was with him, has been here for some weeks. He was a fine little fellow, has been sick for a long time of Typhoid fever.

July 25, 1863, Saturday: At home all day. Clark is getting along well now, I think he will recover. I have two Wisconsin boys in my ward, one of whom was wounded in the foot, he is from Manitowoc. His name is John Barnard. The other James Farrell is suffering from a bad finger, the result of running a sliver into it while rolling pins in a ball [bowling] alley. We did not go out tonight. We have been suffering terribly from mosquitoes until today. Mr. Cotton brought us some fixtures for our beds and we shall sleep under the protection of nets tonight.[24]

July 26, 1863, Sunday: Sunday morning again, it does not seem much like it here. I have not been to church since I have been in Memphis. I am so busy during the morning that I cannot get ready by church time and in the evening I am very tired. Today was time for General Inspection. Somers from Washington came through the Hospital today. He complained very much of the bad bread, said we should not have any more such. One of my men is very low, I do not expect him to live more than a day or two. I wrote to his mother on Tuesday telling her that she had better come to him as he was very anxious to see her. I expected her yesterday. I fear she will not reach here before his death. We went out to Col. Howe's again today in the ambulance. They were very glad to see us and we spent a very pleasant evening. Col. & Miss Howe made a great deal of sport about their commissary arrangements and we had a great deal of pleasantry at the supper table about the viands, came home about 9 o'clock.

SARAH

From Sarah Powers at Fond du Lac to Norman Powers, July 26, 1863

My dear husband

Again I will write to you to see if this letter will not be more successful than the others and be received, I am real sorry Norman that you do not get my letters for I have never failed of writing to you every week and sometimes twice a week and I cant see no earthly reason why your mail cant be sent to you so you are right in thinking it cant be that I have not wrote for I have ever been punctual in writing to you I am sorry to hear that you are trouble so bad with the ague, and fear that it will hang on to you for sometime it is such a plagueful disease where it gets on to a person it seems to be for ever getting out of there system again. . . .

. . . I do want to see you so bad and it will be so pleasant for the children they talk about you very much and were wholly delighted with the letter you wrote them in your letter of June 3rd and Milton treasure up his $20 bill that you sent him very much says write papa that he can spell Milton and Powers to and lot, lots & lots of others he does very well at spelling words of four letters and often gives me a kiss for there papa Adelaide goes every day when it aint rain she learn very easy say her papa must send her a present but I suppose you are where cant get a little card or nothing. . . .

[Mrs. Tyrell] had not received but one letter from Truman since the surrender of Vicksburg she thought by there writing they were all the happiest set that ever were at its fall but were ordered to march that afternoon of 4th and was sorely disappointed at not having the privilege of seeing the inside of the City after there hard labor around it and in the rifle pits Mr. Burchard is back to the lake on a furlough say the 29th Regt did not go from Vicksburg that afternoon but thought they would be likely to be sent wherever there was work to be done Truman writes that the 29th were one of the company selected if it had been necessary on Vicksburg and its is now surely true that we have got the Miss river clear and it is expected that we shall have Charleston in a few day, for we already to of the island that were heavy fortified, our forces have 180 siege guns besides all other kinds of gun that be imagine I dare say you have heard of rebel Lee crossing the Potomac and of the battle at Gettysburg which was on the 1st, 2nd, 3rd of July it is well known that the rebels in that move lost 50,000 in wounded, killed, and prisoners.[25]

Emily

July 27, 1863, Monday: In my ward all day. Went out in the evening to get ice cream. Very warm.

July 28, 1863, Tuesday: A warm day. We went up to Mr. Smith's office to get some things from a box which came from Wis. The man whose mother I wrote to last week died today, he was not quite sensible when he died. He asked very much to see his mother. I expect she will be here soon.

July 29, 1863, Wednesday: In my ward early. Immediately after breakfast the Ward Master came to tell me that there was a lady below who wished to see me. I went down and found it to be the mother of the man who died yesterday, she was almost inconsolable when she found that he was dead. I had to undertake the task of comforting her, with poor success, I fear, for who can comfort or console such broken hearts, he had died without a word for his friends and she an old lady had come this long distance to see her only son and found him dead. I could not find words of comfort for her only begging her to look to God for consolation in her hour of bitterest need.

July 30, 1863, Thursday: In my ward all day. That old lady went home last night. Mrs. Brown, wife of one of our sick men in my ward, is here taking care of her husband. Billy, our medicine man, was sent to his Regiment this morning and another one appointed in his place. We went out for a walk tonight. Got some flowers & leaves of the mimosa, a large and beautiful tree of the same species as the sensitive plant.

July 31, 1863, Friday: In my ward early. A warm day. Lou & I went to the office this morning. Mr. Smith was not there. We waited a long time for him, as Ms. Davenport said that he had letters for us, did not get them as we were obliged to leave before he came. Ms. Davenport brought the letters in the afternoon. One of them contained very sad news for Lou. Her youngest brother, one of the 11th Regt., was killed on the 10th of June, near

Jackson, Mississippi. She felt almost broken hearted. Miss Howe and Mrs. Bedlow called this afternoon and staid two or three hours. They went through our wards. We spent a very pleasant afternoon. At home in the evening.[26]

August 1, 1863, Saturday: Capt. Pitman of the 23d called to see us this morning. He is going to Madison on furlough, we were very glad to see him. In my ward most of the day. The men are all getting along well. Sent several letters home by Pitman.[27]

August 2, 1863, Sunday: In my ward all the morning. Dr. Nelson asked me why I did not go to church. I plead want of time, but fear that want of inclination might also have formed a good part of my excuse. I have lost all my energy of late, have not the least ambition seemingly to do anything which is out of old routine of ward duty. I can neither read, write nor talk as I used to do. I have almost despised Southerners heretofore for their want of energy, but shall never do so again. This southern air is depressing beyond belief, and I do not wonder that sick men do not recover for many months in this climate. Col. Howe sent the ambulance for us today, and we spent the afternoon and evening at his residence. Enjoyed it very much. I was very near sick, however, and was glad when I got home. I was sick all night and did not go down in the morning until after breakfast.

Margaret

From Margaret Patchin at Wyocena to Augustus Patchin, August 2, 1863

My Dear Husband,

We received yours of the 17th and the 19th on Tuesday; and was very glad to hear that you was well; and as the money had got through before the letters did that was to tell us about it, we did not have any worry about it this time.

We received yours of the 22nd on Thursday. You said that you wasn't very well that day. Oh, I do hope that you ain't sick, my much loved husband, away there so far from me; and, I should consider it such a privilege to take care of you if anything is the matter with you; but I am bid to cast all my care on Jesus and am told that His protecting care is still over you! Hoping that you are well now, I will trust you with our covenant God, hoping that he will soon restore you to us for this separation seems so cruel to me.

We are disappointed in you not being appointed captain of your company, but not so much as we was last year when they put one from another company in as first lieutenant; but why is it you are jumpt again, and one holding the same rank as you should be put in over you, when you have had to act as captain so long? It seems unjust to you, if you are kept away from home, and do as much as others, why do they jump others over you? James says that I am over-ambitious about you, but we are all very much disappointed, seeing that you will stay away. I did want to think that I was a captain's wife, not that I should love you any more for it; but because that I like to think of your being looked up to by others instead of being jumpt over, as you have been this time, unless they jump you to some other company, or let you <u>come home</u>; that will suit me the best of anything. So, do try hard to come to me. You have been away so long, and suffered so much hardship; and, as long as you stay and are well, you will have a hard time; and, Oh, how hard it is for me to get along without you; and I am so afraid that you will get hurt, or be sick!

They have all gone to church, but Orlo and the baby; they are fixen some string beans for dinner. I say "they," for baby helps, in his way. He has just been to me for a piece of bread, and butter, and sugar on it; that is the way that he will have it fixed. He will take hold of me, and pull me into the buttery, and point to what he wants; and when he gets, it he goes away to his play.

I think that he is as smart as any 16-month-old baby that ever called me "Ma." I do so want to see him in your arms, and to hear you say that you love him, as you did the rest of your children; and, I want to know how you look, if you ain't coming home. Do send your picture; have it taken large, so that I can have it put in a frame, and hung up; but if you can come home, we will have it taken here, and you hold the baby.

About that land that Roblier bought of Bull: the trade was made the forepart of June, when I was expecting you home. I did not know that it was for sale till I heard that he had bought it; then I said that I would have bought it if I had known about it; but I thought, that as you was coming home, you could see to it; but you did not come, and I have such a large family to see to, and such poor help, that I don't very often go from home; and it is always on business most that I go; but he has sold half of it to Mr. English; and the railroad runs on the other side of it; and he asks twenty dollars, or twenty-five, an acre for it; and the house is about as large as we will want to have ours ell, if we ever get it isn't lathed so as to build.

Dear Augustus, if anything should happen to you so that you cannot come home to live with me, I don't want to have to live in Wyocena! I have always told you so; and I should rather live on our farm, than go to there with our boys without you for to look after them. I think that Mr. Hedge offers his farm as cheap as the Bull place. According to what there is on it, he offered it to me for two thousand last winter; so you see, things is up here on account of the prospect of the railroad; it is going to feed them all. If you can come home, then we will fix on a place; if you don't want to live on the farm, we had better sell it, and buy a nice place than to go to Wyocena. That is my mind, and you wou[ld] think so too, if you was here I think, for it grows no better.

The boys all went to the caravan, and were very much pleased with it. They all send love to Pa.

M. A. Patchin

Emily

August 3, 1863, Monday: In my ward all day feeling miserably. The men are doing well. They will probably get furloughs, at least a large number of them very soon. I shall be glad to have them go as I think it will be so much better for them. We went out this evening.

August 4, 1863, Tuesday: In my usual routine of duty today. Men are doing well. Did not go out today. Some of the gentlemen connected with the Hospital called this evening.

August 5, 1863, Wednesday: In my ward all day. A man who is in Ward D, Lou's ward, died this morning immediately after having an arm amputated. His father and mother have been here for some time. Went up to the Officer's Hospital today with Mr. Smith. Sat in upon Rusk of the 25th who has been very sick, is getting better, alas Adjt. Shopiere and Capt. Henry also were there, very sick. There are quite a good many Rebel officers in this Hospital and we met a large number of ladies from the city with baskets and I presume all manner of good things, bent on deeds of charity to the secesh. It made my blood boil when I thought that it was such as these who had caused and were still causing all the misery that we were encountering daily in our life in the Hospitals.[28]

August 6, 1863, Thursday: Mr. Smith left for Vicksburg today, Lieut. Billings & Lieut. Townsend called upon us this morning. The former is on General Solomon's [*sic*: Salomon's] staff and will go up the river with him on furlough in a few days. He promised to call upon us when he went though. Townsend is one of Gen. Prentis's staff and remained here so that we shall probably see him often. I had a very polite invitation to take a life partnership with a gentleman in ward B today. Very tempting inducements held out, and if all that was promised could have proved true I should indeed have "lived in clover," but not having any inclination to walk so flowery a pathway, I very respectably declined.[29]

August 7, 1863, Friday: A very warm day. I went into my ward before breakfast but was obliged to leave it soon after and lie down. I did not get up until afternoon. At home this evening.

August 8, 1863, Saturday: In my ward most of the day. Walt Judson came today at five o'clock with a hack and took us out to Elmwood Cemetery, a beautiful place. I never enjoyed anything in my life more than I did that ride. There are the most beautiful evergreen hedges around the lots that I ever saw in my life, and very large evergreen trees of many varieties fill the grounds. There is a great variety of trees here with a predominance of elms, which give the place its name. There are some very fine monuments and vaults, and in one place a large number of Union soldiers are sleeping side by side in their last slumber. It is a beautiful spot and a worthy resting place for noble hearts who have laid their all a sacrifice on their country's altar. At home in the evening.[30]

Sarah

From Sarah Powers at Fond du Lac to Norman Powers, August 8, 1863

... harvest is going on as well and as fast as it can for it is a very wet time. This forenoon the men have had to work hard to set up the shack that blew down in the night as our rains are mostly nights and are accompany with heavy winds. I must finish getting dinner. I presume you can imagine many thing that will be cook. well today we are going to have chicken pot pie how I wish we could have you here with us, hope we shall before long.

Last Tuesday there was a Mr. Oscar Larance came of Co. H (or the Waupan company) on a furlough of twenty days tells Parish that the Regt. was returned back to Vicksburg, he tell Parish that he has never as yet became acquainted with you I should like to see very well but shall not have an opportunity [indecipherable] as the Regt as got back to Vg [Vicksburg] I should think that they would let you go down to your regt if not to return for good when you feel able which I hope you are gaining as fast as possible and will not take any of those diseases that is there in the hospital. . . .

. . . My last I wrote you that Adelaide and Georgie had been exposed to the whooping cough and just coming down with I think they do not hoop as yet cough night and breath bad I am in hope I shall get along with them as well as one can though I am dreading it some. Milton has had quite a sore throat but getting over it. . . .

. . . well Norman I must close for this time hoping to hear that you have got a letter from me this and it will you growing in health receive this from your wife with love.[31]

MARGARET

From Margaret Patchin at Wyocena to Augustus Patchin, August 9, 1863

My Dear Husband,

I will try to write you a few lines today. I am feeling very anxious about you as we have not had any letter this past week; yours of the 22nd was the last that we have heard, and you was not very well then.

Oh, are you sick away so far from me; my heart yearns so for you all the time! If you are sick do git some one to write to me, for my mind is on you all the time. I think that I will go to you if you are sick, if they will let me; but you know that I don't know anything about traveling, and I should have to leave the children all at home; but you are dearer than life to me, my Husband. Oh, that I knew how you are so that my mind could rest! Me thinks I hear you saying, "God's protecting care is still over me." In His hands I trust you, feeling that He is able to shield and keep you; and that He will soon restore you to us is my sincere prayer; and that we may live together in His fear, and train up the children that is committed to our care to honor and obey the Saviour. They love you so much that you can do better for them than I can. They have all been good boys to work this summer; harvesting is done and each one tried to do their part well. They are all gone to church today except baby, of course, he is with me; he is in the cradle sleeping. He is so busy all the time when he is awake that it keeps me on the jump to look after him!

This is very bad weather for securing the grain for it hasn't been dry more than three days at a time for two weeks, and yesterday we had the hardest shower that we have had for three years, I think; the grain is very wet.

It seems strange to me that from all the other armies that is in the field that they grant furloughs but the one where you are. Is it because you ain't bragged enough about, or don't they think that you do as much as the rest, or what is the reason; for there is a good many home on furloughs that haven't been gone near as long as you have; it makes me feel very bad to think how it is and to hear other folks say that you could come if you was a mind to.

Mrs. Dickson hasn't got any money from the pension office, nor any of his back pay. I don't think that it is right for them to keep it from her, and make the excuse that it is because that she hasn't a marriage certificate, when there is so many that knows that he always acknowledged her as his wife. She is about discouraged trying for it. Her boys are doing the best that they can to git along. I let them have things, and they work and pay for them; and they have worked enough in harvesting here to come to twelve dollars in money. Mrs. Dickson has been taking care of a little babe that it's Mother died when it was born; it's father is some relation of theirs; the child died yesterday at William Edgers and is to be buried this afternoon. I think I will go down there. Mrs. D's boys have the best-looking crops on their place that they have ever had we think.

Half past six

When James came home from church today he brought a letter from you Wheton had carelessly overlooked; it is dated the 29th. Orlo and John went after the mail yesterday. We never miss agoing, for we are so anxious about you and I am so glad to hear that you are well. That your precious life and health will be spared is my earnest prayer, and that you will soon be home to live with the children and me, for we need you very much. I am so lonesome I feel as though I hadn't any company, but I am afraid that you won't think that I am good enough company for you if you live to come home; for your letters, some of them, read as though you don't feel very pleasant towards me; for I do try to be kind to your children and I do want you to come home God knows I do, I think, if I know my own heart. He knows all about me, and I do feel thankful to Him for His care of me and of you. It is hard to think that I am an unloved wife, and I didn't think that I was till you went and enlisted; and now to have you say that if you live to come home you shall do different than you ever did, so much so that you think that I will wish you away again. Oh, tell me if you have lost all love for me, if you have changed as this last letter seems to say you have. You thought that you could stand temptation, and I thought that you didn't go in your own strength; and I have trusted you in His care, feeling that He is able to help all that put their trust in Him. My husband, my heart is almost breaking; and to have you tell me about having the blues, is it right? I know that I am very different from you in disposition. I feel it my duty to take care of my children and my husband too if he is sick and I could get near to him. You did not think it your duty to take care of me, although you was the cause of my sickness; that is a very bitter pill for me to swallow, it is the bitterest of anything that ever happened to me, but if I could only see you—perhaps after I had a good talk with you I would feel better, yes, I *know* I should if you ain't changed too much.

It is a great while since you went away, almost two years. Everything has changed here; the children are gitting to be as large as men, the two oldest I mean; for Elbert is as tall as I am and Orlo and John is a great deal larger than they was when you went; and the one that you never saw is no longer a little baby; he runs all over the yard into the lane and to the barn, and when he is in the wagon he will have hold of the lines and cluck to the horses; he is always on the stir; and people say that I look ten years older than I did before you went away, so you must think of me as an old woman; very sad all the time, not very talkative, longing for my husband.

It is ten o'clock; the family is all abed and asleep and I must go to bed; so good night, Dear Augustus.

Monday afternoon.

James and me have been to Portage today, and I am very tired but I will try to finish this so as to mail it.

I don't know what to do with the money that I have on hand, for money is so plenty that they refuse to give any interest at the bank for it; so that I don't know what to do with it. There is a great many things that I need, but I want a house so bad that I want the money used for that first, and then git other things; but I can't enjoy anything without you so, do come home and fix things; and let us love one another as we had aught to, and see if we can't take comfort together; for we have enough to be very comfortable if you was only here to help me to fix things.

The children is all playing around as happy as ever; they want you to come home and help them to eat some honey.

I must stop, and remain as ever your loving wife.

M.A. Patchin

EMILY

August 9, 1863, Sunday: Today passed as usual. In my ward most of the time. James Farrell, a Wis. boy, had his finger amputated the other day, and his hand is very much swelled and inflamed, he has been up stairs. They brought him down today and he is very sick. I got him something nice to eat, bathed his head, and have sat by him most of the day. He suffers a great deal with his hand. Did not go out at all today.

August 10, 1863, Monday: In my ward and Ward B all day. There was a boy about 19 in Ward B who has been under the influence of opium for two days so that he was perfectly stupid and could not be roused. The Dr. told me to give him strong coffee every half hour, all day. I did so but it did no good and about 8 o'clock in the evening he died. I felt very badly about it as I believe he died from an overdose of the drug.

Sarah Powers's statement "if we ever meet again" in her July 26 letter proved to be a premonition when Norman Powers died of congestive fever (malaria) on July 30, 1863, one of twelve thousand Union deaths attributed to this disease.[32] Norman's letters to Sarah from February through his injury in May often included complaints of feeling ill, sometimes describing symptoms typical of malaria. In mid-August Sarah received a letter from J. G. Dunning, a member of Norman's regiment, telling her that Norman had died without receiving even one of the letters Sarah had written to him since he was hospitalized, which had prompted Norman to write on July 14: "I feel quite lonesome without my mail."[33] She sent a letter of thanks to J. G. Dunning, who had assured her that Norman "had been put in a coffin and decently buried."[34] In her letter she asked whether her letters that Norman had never received could be returned to his family. Dunning had also been wounded on May 1, 1863, at the Battle of Port Gibson but recovered from his wounds and returned to his regiment. He was mustered out of service on June 22, 1865.[35]

Sarah

From Sarah Powers at Fond du Lac to J. G. Dunning, August 11, 1863

... I write to acknowledge the receipt of your letter, which reach me last evening to inform me of the painful intelligence of the death of my husband. I am very grateful for your kindness and would like to have you write to me again, and give me the full particulars of his sickness. Write me if he was delirious or not, and what words he said about his family, the last kind letter I received from him was dated July 23rd. I received his letters regular, and every one informed me that he had never recv a letter from me since he went into the Hospital ... poor husband how lonely, lonely he must been, not able to get one word from his wife and to hear of his children, did he talk much about his family, he often would write that he felt certain that I wrote to him and it is hard and severe that he could not be favored with his mail when he tore himself away his home and relatives, for his country's call, do you no if he received any letters from me after the 23rd of July up to the time of his death and if he was able to peruse them or have read to him, ... I am unacquainted with the rules of a hospital as to the mail that comes for a deceased one whether they are returned to the author or not, ...

... greatly obliged to you for your kindness bestowed upon him in his last hours of sickness and suffering, and for his burial I feel thankful for the respect shown him and fervently hope that his grave will be marked so that if ever, should wish to visit it there will be no difficult in searching it out. I was much in hopes he would get a furlough to come home and the third of July he wrote me that after the fall of Vicksburg that he thought he could, how eagerly I watched for his coming but quite different now I am sorely afflicted and many relatives to mourn his absence.

P. S. Knowing how trouble friends as to procure stamps, I enclose one.[36]

Emily

August 11, 1863, Tuesday: Lou & I went to market this morning. Mr. Smith went with us. After breakfast went up to the office to see if Mr. D. had any letters for us. I got two from home. In my ward the rest of the day. Our box which we have been expecting so long came yesterday. Mr. Cotton said that he would have it brought up for us, which he did this forenoon. We had a regular jubilee over it and acted just as children would act with a lot of new toys. Everything in it was nice and we shall live in style after this while our box continues to dispense its stores.

August 12, 1863, Wednesday: Warm today. In my ward all the forenoon. Some of the boys are expecting to go home on furlough soon. We had a little party this afternoon of Wis. boys, Johnny Reed, John Bausard, Homer Jones, Wm. Welch and Persy _____ I have forgotten his name, and James Hodges were invited up to our room, we distributed some papers for plates, Jenny & I went down into the kitchen and made some lemonade and then we passed around cake and lemonade and did the honors in grand style.³⁷

Mr. Hayne came in just in time to be treated. We had quite a pleasant time, somewhat marred at the last however by the fact that Mr. Cohen came in after a time and said that we would be under the necessity of moving this afternoon, as the rooms we occupied were to be fitted up for a library. The boys helped us move and fix up our room. We do not like it at all. It is an inner room and very warm and close. I expect that we shall all be sick if we stay long. Very tired at night after our exertions in party giving, moving, etc.

August 13, 1863, Thursday: In my ward all day. Louise & Jenny went out walking tonight. I did not go, went to my room and went to bed. I had just got into a comfortable doze when Lou came in and said there were a couple of gentlemen intending to favor us with their company for the evening. Here was a nice fix, we had no other room and it was too hot to live in the clothes press [their small interior room]. I could not make up my mind to lie still and say I was sick, so there was no help for it and I got up and dressed, in very good humor, of course, and after a little while Mr. Casey made his appearance accompanied by Mr. Wardrobe whose acquaintance we had not made before. I like him very much, he is a Wisconsin man, from Waukesha. Mr. Casey had been taking a wee drop of beer and was very talkative indeed. I got thoroughly disgusted with him, the more so, that he seemed determined to stay forever. They did go after awhile.³⁸

August 14, 1863, Friday: A warm day. In my ward all day. Men are getting ready for home, they were paid off today. We were intending to go out tonight, I had an invitation to go and get ice cream, the other girls were also going but it looked so much [like] rain that we concluded not to go. Went to bed early.

August 15, 1863, Saturday: Spent the day as usual in my ward. Fannie [*sic*: Jennie] & I went to market this afternoon. There were a large number of people present. It was very warm indeed. These Saturday afternoon markets are a great curiosity to me, there are so many things to be seen which are wholly characteristic of the South. After we had made our purchases, we met one of the boys in Lou's ward, who invited us to have some ice cream. This conveyed an idea of coolness and we consented, standing and eating our cream in one corner of the market where every moment we were jostled by the crowd. It was delicious and I think I never enjoyed anything more in my life. We went home and past this side of the market met my ward master and one of the nurses, who wanted us to go back and have something. We assured them that we did not need anything, but they seemed so much hurt and disappointed that we told them they might get us anything they chose. On our arrival at home, we found awaiting us two huge melons which they had brought from market. I had four invitations to go and get ice cream tonight. I could not accept them all so went with the first one who invited me. We had a grand time altogether. Got some ice cream, peaches and ice water and came home rather late and very tired.

August 16, 1863, Sunday: Very warm indeed today. Went to church this evening for the first time in my stay in Memphis, went to the Union Church, it seemed to be a Methodist Church, unfortunately with Southern principles, so that Uncle Sam thought it should be about the right thing to confiscate it, which was done accordingly. It looked rather queer to see a church decorated with pictures of Washington and Clay and festooned with flags, but I am getting used to almost anything.

August 17, 1863, Monday: Today has been a very busy day with us, a large number of the boys went home on furlough. We went down to the boat to see them off. It made me homesick to see them start. We staid on the boat two hours. About 1 hundred and forty went from our Hospital today. The wards look desolate. There are only about fourteen men left in my ward, and some of them go tomorrow. I feel very anxious about some of my boys, for fear they will get sick in going up. At home this evening.

August 18, 1863, Tuesday: More of the boys went today. The house looks very lonesome. I have been at home all day.

August 20, 1863, Wednesday: We went out to the Small Pox Hospital today with Cordy Reynolds. Went all over it, also to the Catholic Cemetery where we rambled around an hour or two, accompanied by the sexton, an old Irishman and quite a curiosity in his way. He told us a great many stories about the occupants of the graves and of their families.

Met Dr. Worthington, the Surgeon in Charge, a Wisconsin man, and Drs Pegan & Bowen. The former is from Indiana. We liked him very much. We took supper in a tent under the trees. It was perfectly delightful there and we had a nice supper. After, we had a very pressing invitation to a dance on the green ward. The boys had a fiddle which gave forth melodious sounds under the magic touch of one of the [indecipherable], and we danced one quadrille to the entire satisfaction of all concerned and then went home, having spent a very pleasant afternoon. Found them all doing well at home. Did not go out in the evening.

August 21, 1863, Thursday: To my great surprise and also very much to theirs, five of our convalescents received furloughs and started home today, this leaves us only 7 men in the ward beside the nurses. I am glad to see them go home because it is so much better for them, but I do not expect ever to see them again and it makes me feel sad to say good-bye to those who have been with me so long.

Mrs. Brake, Dr. Nelson and I went to walk after tea. We started to see a cotton field, but it got so late before we came to it that we concluded to defer seeing it to some other time and start earlier. Stopped at the Church Hospital when we came back.

August 22, 1863, Friday: Received an invitation today in common with the other girls to a picnic at the Orphan Asylum. In my ward most of the day. Did not go out in the evening.

August 23, 1863, Saturday: It looked like rain this morning, but cleared up before noon. I staid in my ward all day until noon. We started for the [Orphan] Asylum about two, a couple of gentlemen from the Small Pox Hospital came with hacks and took Jennie and I, also Lou & Cordy. The gentlemen with whom Jennie & I went did not know anything about the direction of the Asylum, as unfortunately did not the driver. We however, took the road which seemed the most likely to be the right one, and started, after going a mile or so out of our way in two or three different directions, exploring a cotton field, being stopped by the pickets and inquiring our way several times, we managed to get into the grounds of the Asylum by the back way. We found Lou & Cordy who had started before us, they had been there some time and they tried to rally us on having been lost, which we would by no means admit. After resting a little while we went down into the woods at the back of the house, where they had put up a capital swing and enjoyed ourselves for an hour or so, and then came back to the house to supper. All the ladies in the Hospital were there and Drs. Nelson, Fearing & Watts. We had a grand supper in the dining room, after which we enjoyed ourselves, according to our tastes. Dr. Nelson & I walked through the grounds. He told me the names of all the trees with which I was not familiar, and we collected quite a bouquet of rose leaves and grasses and flowers.

There was a cotton field near the grounds, which we visited and I saw for the first time a cotton boll and the cotton plant growing with its flowers. I had some to bring home with me. I enjoy the society of the Doctor very much, he takes such an interest in every thing that I like, and I believe him to be a noble minded honorable man. I would like an opportunity of being better acquainted with him, but he is going away in a week or two and I presume we shall never meet again. About six o'clock all the people from our house except we young folks went home, and we danced under the trees by the light of the moon until we were tired, and then returning to the house, sang songs and talked nonsense until ten o'clock, when we concluded that it was time to go home. We met a Captain Pierce & wife from our 32d Reg't, who were very pleasant people. Mrs. P's is going up at the same time we do. We had a pleasant ride home and altogether enjoyed the day very much. I pressed my flowers as soon as I got home.[39]

Mr. Smith returned from Vicksburg today. We shall probably start for home Tuesday next.

August 23, 1863, Sunday: At home all day. The girls went to church this evening. I remained at home. Mr. Casey spent the evening with me. Dr. Nelson called this afternoon and we analyzed a flower which we found yesterday, which was very singular. It was Indian paint or Spiderwort. He showed me a picture of his sister, a girl of thirteen, a nice looking little girl.

August 24, 1863, Monday: At home all day making wreaths of evergreens for my ward. A young sergeant of the Guard by the name of Andrews helped me. He is quite a fine fellow and I liked him very much. I have seen him a good many times before, he made two or three large wreaths for me and helped the boys put them up. I worked all day and with the assistance of the

Ward Master and the boys, the ward was trimmed beautifully, everybody said it was the prettiest in the building. We had some flags, and mottoes and I think it was a perfect success. Lou & Jennie went out riding with Mr. Cotton & Mr. Twill and I having company remained at home, George Wicks [sic: Wick] spent the evening with me, and also Mr. Wardrobe. Dr. Nelson came in and staid an hour or so. I spent a very pleasant evening.[40]

Margaret

From Margaret Patchin at Wyocena to Augustus Patchin, August 25, 1863

Dear Augustus,

We are all as well as usual this morning. James and Elbert have gone to help Colten thrash; Orlo and John is tendin Baby and doing chores; Herbert thinks he helps.

I have bought a patent beehive, and yesterday Elbert and me drove the bees from our hive into it; we have but one hive as one of ours killed out last winter and the bees haven't swarmed this summer. I don't know but it is too late, but I thought that I would run the risk. It is called the self-protecting beehive. I think I have as much as 80 pounds (I don't know but there is 90) of honey; some of it belongs to Bealy, for I took some out of a hive. We had twelve pounds in a box and there is another box most full on another hive. Oh, how I wish you could come and help us to eat it!

Last night was quite cold, but no frost here. I was cold in bed and wondered if you was warm or if you sleep cold. Oh, I think of you all the time; do you of me? Tell me all about what you do. Orlo is going for the mail and I shall be very much disappointed if we don't get letter from you today for it is a week since we had one, and I am so anxious about you all the time; write just as often as you can.

I must stop for this time, so goodbye my much-loved Husband, and may our covenant-keeping God shield and protect you from dangers and temptations and send you safely to me soon is the sincere prayer of your own loving wife,

Margaret Patchin

Emily

August 25, 1863, Tuesday: We went up to the office immediately after breakfast to see what the prospects were for going home. Mrs. Burke went with us, Mr. Smith said that it was very probable that we would go tonight. We made a few purchases in town and then returned to prepare for our journey. I packed my trunks and dressed myself after dinner and then went to bid the boys good-bye. Went through Ward 1 first. Poor boys, some of them cried at parting with me, I have been up there a good deal and it seemed very hard to go away and leave them so sick. I went through Ward B and also the kitchen and shook hands with all the boys, before going into my own ward. I felt as bad at leaving my boys that it took away all the pleasure I had felt in the prospect of going home, some seemed to feel sad at the thought that I was going to leave them poor fellows they are so grateful for any kindness shown them. I was glad when I had got around, I shall miss my ward, and my poor sick boys, whether they do me or not.

I had not much time to spare, I had a long talk with Dr. Nelson in which he very kindly advised me in matters affecting my interests, and whether I take the advice or not I shall always be grateful to him for the interest he has taken in my welfare. He has been very kind to me and I shall always remember him as a true-hearted gentleman. He gave me some cotton flowers to bring home and also another rose flower whose name he did not know, and also a book which he had lent me. He asked me for my address and gave me his, promising to call upon me in Madison on his way home if he possibly could.

We bade all our friends good bye and started for the boat about half past four. Mr. Watt, Mr. Cotton & Dr. Jackson accompanied us. The boat was almost ready to start and we bade them good bye, and shortly after starting on the guards saw the domes and spires of Memphis receding from our view. I stood on deck until the city was lost to my view behind the winding banks of the river and then went into the cabin.

I felt sad tonight and for several reasons, the principal one was leaving the boys sick in the Hospital. Most of them I shall never see again, if any, I felt a sort of presentiment when I came away that I should never return, however that may be, the God who careth for us all keep them in His kind guardianship. We took passage on the Platte Valley, not a very large boat but a good sailor. Went out upon deck after supper but could not remain long on account of the chilliness of the atmosphere. Retired early.

August 26, 1863, Wednesday: Rose early after a good night's rest and after dressing, finding no one in the cabin, went out upon the guard. It was very cold. We passed Fort Pillow in the night. After breakfast I read a short time and then took my diary, which I had not had an opportunity to write up from my notes before. I wrote all the forenoon. The girls and Mrs. Brake went to sleep. In the afternoon we went out on deck and staid for some time. I read some, and wrote some. Mrs. Brake, Charley and I went on deck after supper and saw them take on a load of bags, it was beautiful moonlight but very cold. Retired early. Major Rusk and Captain Berry of the 25th are going up with us. There are two or three very sick soldiers on board, whom we went to see.[41]

August 27, 1863, Thursday: We had quite a fright early this morning. I think between two and three o'clock I was awakened by a loud crash, and afterwards we heard screams and the boat stopped suddenly. We rose immediately, hastened on our clothing and went out to inquire the cause of the stoppage. Found all the ladies up but could get no definite idea of what was the matter, one lady said "God knows I believe we are sinking." Some thought we had been fired into. At last a gentleman told that a snag had run through the wheelhouse on one side, smashing the wheel. This was not very pleasant news, as we lay near Columbus, [Kentucky] nearly twenty miles from Cairo, however they assured us that there was no immediate danger and we felt better.

After a while, when the real extent of the injury became known, it was found that the wheel was not injured but that a very large rupture had been made entirely through the boat to the upper deck just back of the wheel house, and within two feet of a state room door. It seemed very singular that it should strike just there, almost any where else it might have done a great deal of injury and caused loss of life. We stopped here about four hours.

About 6 o'clock the boat was ready to start and went off in fine style. It was very misty, and before we had got three miles from Columbus the fog closed around us so densely that nothing could be seen beyond the space of a few feet from the boat. The river is very low and the consequence was that we were very soon fast on a sand bar within 10 feet of a low sandy shore. The fog was so dense that there was no use in trying to start again, so we lay still waiting for it to clear up. Went to breakfast and after about an hour the boat was again in motion. We passed the Desuse which passed us yesterday morning, she was fast on a sand bar and had probably lain there for some hours. She got off a little after us and we had quite a race for a little ways, when we distanced her and she running into the fog got fast on another sand bar. She came into Cairo about a half a mile behind us. We reached

Cairo about eight o'clock, disembarked and went to the hotel where I am writing. We are expecting to leave here about 1 ½ o'clock this P.M. and in the meantime prepare to find out whether there is anything good about this miserable city.

Later. We have taken a long walk around Cairo, went into several stores, bought some knick-knacks to take home with me of a soldier who was pedaling them at the depot. Cairo is a miserable place, that is a fact. There is only one street in the city which is passable in wet weather, unless it is those which are back up on piles five or six feet in height. The principal street runs parallel with the river and is much higher than the rest of the city. We did not see any one but soldiers and military and several officers. The streets are thronged with them. There are many gunboats and steamers lying here. We returned from our walk just in time for dinner. Major Rusk and Mr. Smith went down with us. The St. Charles Hotel is a very good house and seemed to be well patronized.

Took the cars [railroad] at 1 ½ o'clock, and left Cairo with very little regret. The scenery and vegetation along the route from Cairo to Centralia is more tropical than any that I have seen since I left home. The forest on each side was a perfect jungle, trees, limbs and vines seemed mingled together in inexplicable confusion. Near Cairo, and extending for some distance from it is a swamp, which is called (and very properly I think) by the 'natives,' the gangrene swamp. It is the most desolate, horrible looking place I ever saw. We had a very comfortable ride from Cairo to Centralia, arriving at the latter place about 8 o'clock. Took supper here in a great hurry and then took berths in a sleeping car for the night.

August 28, 1863, Friday: Rose early this morning after a passable night's rest, dressed as well as the motion of the cars would allow and went into the other car. It is very cold indeed, not much like the weather we have been having in Memphis. Got into Chicago behind time so much so as to be obliged to take our seats in the cars immediately, could not wait for breakfast, but Mr. & Mrs. Fuller at Chicago coming to M., also several other Madison men, Pvt. Dean among them. Did not feel very well today, owing somewhat to not having had my regular breakfast and somewhat to fatigue.

Arrived at Madison at three o'clock P.M., not having stopped since we left Chicago. It rained heavily, but this was the best looking place I had seen for some time. Folks all glad to see me of course. Alice & Charley were in the country so that I did not see them. Pa was very much relieved and I guess a little surprised to see me at home safe again. They are all unwilling to have me go back. Several friends came in to see me tonight. I was very tired and went to bed early.

August 29, 1863, Saturday: Rose this morning with a strange feeling at finding myself at home, not very well, did not eat any breakfast, unpacked my trunk, made me a white apron, and wiped the dishes, then dressed and went up town. Went down to Lou's, found the girls all right. They got ready and went with me to call on the Governor. We went into the Treasurer's Office and Mr. Scofield went up with us. Our friends there were very glad to see us. The Governor was very kind, complimented us upon our perseverance and said he was glad we were going back. Went up to Bartel's Store and afterwards left the girls, went to Gus's office and came home with him. Sewed a little in the afternoon. Fannie & I went up town, made some purchases, went to see Lou & Fannie found them at Ms. Weaver's. At home in the evening.

August 30, 1863, Sunday: Went to church this morning. Mr. Goodspeed of Janesville preached for us. He gave us a very good sermon. Staid to Bible Class. It seemed good to be in our old church once more. Mr. Campbell came to see me in the afternoon, remained to tea, and accompanied us to church in the evening.

August 31, 1863, Monday: Did not feel very well this morning. Went up town. Saw Joe Curtis, an old friend, at home on furlough. He goes back in a few days. Got a new calico dress. Several friends called upon me today. It seems very pleasant to be at home again. I am a little undecided about going back. I would like to attend school this semester and finish German & French and take painting lessons, but I am afraid I could not content myself to settle back into the old routine again. I should be so glad to feel that I had done something, however little, for my country in this, her hour of need. I have always wanted to do something and now that a way is opened for me, I feel as if it were my duty to walk in it. Father & Mother would rather I should stay at home but will offer no objection to my going. I did not feel well enough to go to meeting this evening.[42]

September 1, 1863, Tuesday: A cool day though pleasant. Mrs. Easton came to dinner and Celia went home with her. I sewed all day, although not feeling well. Went to the Lodge in the evening. There were very few present owing I suppose to the fact that so many had gone to the Grand Lodge. It seemed natural to be in the Lodge Room once more. I returned early. Mr. Johnson called this afternoon and also Seba Bodwell. Seba wanted to go to church.

September 2, 1863, Wednesday: Quite uncomfortably cold. I have been shivering all day. Went up town this morning. Sewed all day. Some friends called in the afternoon. Went boatriding with Fannie, Gus & Mr. Craig. The lake was splendid, I enjoyed it very much. We went to Picnic Point. The lake flies were altogether too thick to be agreeable, and after resting a little we ate our luncheon and then came home.

September 3, 1863, Thursday: Had intended to go up to the German class with Mary this morning, but found on rising that I had over slept myself, so that it was too late. Sewed until about four in the afternoon and then dressed myself and called on Addie Purple whom I had not seen since her return, she is looking miserably. Also went to see the Miss Turners a few moments and then came home. Company in the evening.

September 4, 1863, Friday: Went to the University this morning. Dr. Finch seemed pleased to see me. The class is very small this term, I translated a part of the lesson. They were reading William Tell, which we commenced last term. Dr. Finch was very sorry that I was not to be present this term. Went into the schoolroom to prayers. The school is very full this term and I saw a great many friends both from Madison and the surrounding country. Mr. Allen and Miss Moody looked as pleasant as ever and I felt as if I must go to school. Agnes Reid begged me to come and study Rhetoric with her, she recites to her father. I would like it very much. At home all day. Attended covenant meeting in the evening. A large number present.

September 5, 1863, Saturday: Mr. Scofield returned last night, I saw him this morning. He says Mr. Smith will not be well enough to go back next week so that we shall have plenty of time to get ready for one stopped at Columbus. I have had calls almost all day and have answered the same questions in the same way so many times that I am heartily sick of it and have about made up my mind that I prefer being a humble private individual to so much celebrity. Company in the evening.

September 6, 1863, Sunday: Went to church. Staid to Bible Class. Wrote several letters this afternoon one in answer to one received from Henry Fisher. I was glad to hear that he arrived at home safe and was doing well. Mr. Craig came down in the afternoon and remained to tea. Went to church in the evening. I am beginning to feel as though I would like to visit the Hospital again.

September 7, 1863, Monday: Had some teeth filled and also two extracted, they pained me a good deal. Sewed this afternoon. Fannie, Lou & Bertha came in a little while this evening. The girls are both well and anxious to go back.

September 8, 1863, Tuesday: Went up town this morning. Sewing all day. Went to the Lodge in the evening. All our old friends present. Reports were heard from several who had attended the Grand Lodge. The evening passed pleasantly. Gus read his article on Tobacco which was well written and well received by the members.

September 9, 1863, Wednesday: Went up to the office again to have my teeth operated on. Sewed in the afternoon. Mr. Turner called to ask Ma & I to come out tomorrow and spend the day. We promised to go.

September 10, 1863, Thursday: We were reminded this morning of the variety of human expectations immediately upon opening our eyes. It was raining heavily and Ma & I reluctantly confessed that our visit to the country was out of the question. The sun shone out once or twice in the forenoon, but it finally settled into a steady rain and signals being useless, we settled ourselves to work with what grace we might. Mr. Craig came in the evening.

September 11, 1863, Friday: Bright & pleasant today concluded we would make our visit and ten o'clock A.M. found us on our way. Spent a very pleasant day. It rained a little on our way home. Found a Mr. Bond from Camp in the garden. He was very agreeable, and we all spent a pleasant evening.[43]

September 12, 1863, Saturday: I was almost discouraged about ever getting ready this morning. I have so much to do. I sewed steadily all day. Fannie helped me some on the machine. Pauline Drakely called this afternoon. I sat up until twelve tonight.

September 13, 1863, Sunday: Rose with a severe headache, went to church, however, did not stay to Bible Class. A most beautiful day. I wonder if we shall have any such splendid weather in Memphis. At home in the afternoon. Went to church in the evening.

September 14, 1863, Monday: Busy all day making preparations for leaving. Went up town in the afternoon. Kate Kavenaugh and Mrs. Wries spent the afternoon here. Mrs. Emmons & Pollie & Alice Weatherly called, also Ella Casey and Hattie Mann, Jennie & Louise came a few moments in the evening. We expect to start tomorrow night.

September 15, 1863, Tuesday: A very busy day with me. Sewed until ten o'clock and then went up to the office to have some teeth filled. In the afternoon Pauline Drakely called saying they would like to [go] South with us if she could make arrangements to do so. I would like to have her go, Nellie, Gus & I went to Walzingers to get some ice cream after tea, and then I went to the Lodge. Spent a pleasant evening. Mr. Campbell was there, he returned this morning. We were much disappointed at not seeing Mr. Smith today, and much surprised at not hearing from him. I am afraid that he is sick, we expected to go tonight.

The correspondence between Annie Cox and Gideon Winans Allen resumed when he left Madison to earn money to fund his return to the University of Michigan Law School.

ANNIE

From Annie Cox at Madison to Gideon Winans Allen at Waukesha, Wisconsin, September 15, 1863

... What a glorious Autumn morning, one ought to be happy with such beauty and joyousness all around. Yet we are always searching out after the dim future almost unheeding the present and when that future becomes present, shall we rest for a morrow. My future is your companionship am I wrong in searching forward to it with such intense desire and to regard the present as something to be endured and redeeming all that happiness for that future.

... I am glad you are enjoying yourself so much. I would like to join you in some of your merry making but I am going to scold you cause while you were here 'twas all I could do to get your to Vernie's to spend a quick evening much less to a party or excursion. What do you think of that? Since I was sorry to know that the machine had not come for I am interested in that matter you know. It will put you back too much but do you think you will succeed in that business any way. I suppose you can tell nothing about it however till you try. You must tell Mr. Stewart if he does not enable you to gain means sufficient for my departure this fall I will haunt him all the days of his life.

... I am glad you are going around so much. It will initiate you in the art of being communicative and sociable. Don't forget it when you come back but I am beginning to think seriously of having you insured.

One thing I think of is the uncertain affairs of the nation which contain such individual affairs. So anyone is liable to have his prospects and happiness immediately and effectively crushed out. I sometimes think 'tis best to sometimes grasp all the happiness in the present or can be, that is, to concentrate all possible in the present time for in a few months 'twill all be beyond our grasp. Good morning, dear Winans. What a pleasant shower we have had. Pa and I went to hear a Seventh Adventist surgeon last night. He thinks Christ is coming in 1868, will rule on Earth those who have died will rise and be judged with the living. The wicked will be condemned to everlasting death and the living to everlasting life. One of his proof texts was "Behold I prepare a place for you and I will come again" [John 14:3]. I had [illegible] you to myself, that where I am ye may be also. He says he can't find a text in the Bible where we are told we shall go to heaven or away from earth. Well I have learned one more creed. It will make but little difference where I shall be if I can only insure my future happiness and the happiness of those I love.

Emily

September 16, 1863, Wednesday: Up early this morning, a very pleasant day. Ironed some this morning. Went up town. Ma, Pa, Gus & I went across the lake to Mr. Turville's this afternoon. They have a nice place, and are very pleasant people. We had a splendid boatride. At home in the evening.

September 17, 1863, Thursday: We have not heard from Mr. Smith yet, and I am beginning to be extremely anxious. We cannot go this week unless we go today. Jennie says we must go alone, if Mr. Smith is not able to go next week.

September 18, 1863, Friday: I went up to have my teeth finished this morning everyone who meets me wonders at seeing me and says, "Why I thought you were in Memphis!" Fannie, Celia, Gus and I went to the Hesperian Society at the University this evening, it was quite cold, but we had a pleasant time. The debate was on the question of the legality of the suppression of the Chicago Times, the jury decided it to have been illegal.[44]

September 19, 1863, Saturday: Up town in the morning. Sewed all day. Jennie & Lou came to spend the afternoon. Mr. Craig came in the evening.

September 20, 1863, Sunday: Did not go to church this morning. Wrote and read all day. Ma & Fannie attended the Second Advent preaching at the City Hall this afternoon and came home quite full of it. Mr. Craig came before tea, remained and we all went to the City Hall in the evening.

ANNIE

From Annie Cox at Madison to Gideon Winans Allen at Waukesha, Wisconsin, September 20, 1863

... How I would love to be in a quiet home of my own this calm, beautiful, Sabbath evening with my noble other self. What a sweet companionship! No jarring words or rude intruders but kind, intelligent expression of thought making the review of the day a pleasant task. May such be our future, dear companion. But I have much self-culture to accomplish before I am fitted thus to fulfill my future place in life. God grant we may both realize this great happiness—just beyond our present grasp apparently. But I must say goodnight as it is now church time and will wait the arrival of your next before finishing. And now goodnight, dearest and best.

... Your machine has gone to sleep somewhere on the road I guess. Never mind my business about coming, all will end for the best. I have been taking some lessons in life and can say, at the present time anyway, I am content while in possession of the affection and the promise of future companionship of one ever so good. Heaven bless you, Winans, and present you perfect earthly happiness. Almost any home on the day a prayer is breathed for your protection and prosperity and a future on my part to be a Christian counselor and companion.

EMILY

September 21, 1863, Monday: Very cool this morning, went up to the office to have a tooth filled found it very sore indeed, did not have it done. Spent the evening at Lou Richardson's.

September 22, 1863, Tuesday: Jennie & Lou came this morning to tell me that they had received a letter from Mrs. Smith saying that her husband was very ill indeed, that he had been delirious since Monday last and that we had better go back without him. We were all very sorry to learn this, but have concluded to go tomorrow. We went to see the Governor, who received us kindly, and told us that he would do all in his powers to help us to get through safely. We then accompanied by Lieut. Taft visited the Hospital at Camp Randall a long walk and we found ourselves at home at one o'clock very tired, as well as very hungry. Sewed all the afternoon. Went to Lodge in the evening.[45]

September 23, 1863, Wednesday: Went with the girls to see the Governor. He took our order for transportation and sent it to Gen. Pope and we shall probably hear from them in two or three days. We are very anxious to go at once if at all. I finished my preparations today, and am all ready to start. Went to prayer meeting in the evening.

ANNIE

From Annie Cox at Madison to Gideon Winans Allen at Waukesha, Wisconsin, September 23, 1863

... The new Catholic Church caught fire last night and burned all the tools inside. Did not injure the building, I believe.

... Mr. Vilas has resigned and returned under the plea of "pressing business." If I had staid in the army until I had expended my patriotism and filled my pockets, I would not offer such a ghastly excuse as "pressing business" for leaving.[46] I'd leave boldly and honorably. His father fell a few days ago and sprained his ankle. They say he will never recover the use of it again.

... It will be an autumn scene thus highly colored. Please suggest any improvements. The water will be calm and the trees clearly reflected upon its surface.[47]

Annie's sketch of the Madison lakeshore. (Allen Family Papers, Newberry Library)

EMILY

September 24, 1863, Thursday: Cold this morning. Went to see if our transportation papers had come were very much disappointed to find that they had not been heard from.

September 25, 1863, Friday: At home all day until afternoon, when we went up to the Governor's office. Mr. Watson told us that our papers might be at the Quartermaster's. Pa went for us and found that they had not heard from them. We are getting very tired of the suspense not knowing what we are to do. I went to see Cora Williams she came home with us to tea. Went up town with her in the evening.

September 26, 1863, Saturday: At home until four o'clock, then went up to see the Governor. I wished to find out whether or not he would give us transportation if we should not obtain it of Gen. Pope. He told me that as soon as he received an answer from Pope, yes or no, he would consider the matter. I am very much disappointed but I am afraid we shall be obliged to make up our minds to stay at home. Pa does not wish me to go and all the family unite in hoping that we shall not get transportation. I am going to commence going to school Monday, that is in the forenoon and am going to write upon Pa's History in the afternoon. If anything happens to make it convenient for me to go to Memphis, I shall go, however. I went up to Sarah Tanner's found Addie Purple there, staid to tea. The girls came down to choir meeting in the evening.

ANNIE

From Annie Cox at Madison to Gideon Winans Allen at Waukesha, Wisconsin, September 26, 1863

. . . I was sorry to hear that Winans was engaged in any such contemptible business as a "n—r hunting," under any consideration, it was beneath an intelligent man, but perhaps there was something in it, however I cannot tell as you wrote none of the particulars. I am afraid you are in a poor neighborhood for your political principles.

From Annie Cox at Madison to Gideon Winans Allen at Waukesha, Wisconsin, September 27, 1863

I am sitting in our bedroom this afternoon. Is there anything in this time and place suggestive? I hoped to read but thoughts and images of Winans blurred the words. I tried to sleep but could not keep from thinking what I had to tell him when I write. So I am seated to do what my heart most desires. Three weeks ago today we were out in the old cemetery sitting under the shade sometimes soberly and sometimes lively. Soberly as the occurrence of the previous evening came to mind but our resolves were noble and we were both made better and happier by then. Winans, we will keep them. Experience has taught us this best. About which I will talk with you when we meet. But back to our walk, was such a day as this, less comely by far. The evening will be the same but I sit alone on the lounge this afternoon, my paper and pen tell why. This evening I will go to church alone and wish the absent one there, shall come home, and avoiding the old rocking chair, stretching its arms out in the moonlight. I shall go to bed to dream of pleasant chats and walks after dinner.

I have been reading Libscomb on "Home" today. He says "a man without a home or prospects of one is a ruined man."[48] I thought of you, not as a ruined man, but as one looking forward to all of the pleasures and comforts of home yet in one sense homeless. To be sure you have a home here and are welcome and loved as one of its own. Yet it is not your home nor your settled place as regards the future, neither is it mine, dear Winans. Therefore, Winans, I wish for your sake and for mine, that you had a home now at this time of life when you can best love it and must need it. And, Winans, I can go with childlike faith to the Great Father and ask this blessing for us both with full faith of receiving it if we both do our duty in that service which we are doing. This faith in a special Providence is the brightest side of religion to me. In fact it would be a worthless name without it. I can feel that God senses for our every tear and smile and the miniscule affairs of life. All the philosophy could not wrest this from me. Indeed I think it is the true philosophy that God who cares for every blade of grass who formed it, will also care for his noblest creation, man. My greatest wish is that—the dearest object on earth to one, would relinquish his ever unhappy belief that he is tossed through life's story unthought of, uncared for, his sorrow unknown, his joy uncared for, yet hastening to the presence of that unfeeling god. Some of these days I feel absorbed by this same faith that he will and wait patiently. I wonder if Winans is talking to his little girl at this hour. I shall know tomorrow.

EMILY

September 27, 1863, Sunday: It was a glorious morning, warm as summer. I went to church. We had a good sermon from a Mr. Smith of New York, who is to preach for us again this evening. Wrote and read in the afternoon. Went to church with Celia in the evening.

September 28, 1863, Monday: Rose early this morning. Got ready and went to the German recitation this morning. They were reading William Tell. Commenced French or rather a review of my French Grammar with the class this morning. When I came home at noon, Nellie met me at the gate telling me that Pa had received our transportation papers. I was very glad to hear it at first, and went to work immediately to get my trunk packed ready to start. Pa was very unwilling that I should go, however, and after getting my things all ready and the time nearly at hand to start, I yielded to the persuasions of my friends and concluded to remain at home. Pa wants me to write for him on his history, and though it is very hard for me to give up going when I have thought and planned so much about it. I do not know but my duty lies in this direction. I could not go away to be gone so long, possibly never to return, and leave such hard feelings, as I felt he would have behind me. I went down at about nine o'clock in the evening after I had decided not to go, to tell the girls of my determination. Fannie & Ma went with me, we met them a little way from home, and went back with them. Fannie & Lou went to see if Miss Boardman would go in my place, she willingly consented, and said she would be ready at the time. Saw the girls finish packing, get ready and start in the omnibus for the depot. I felt so badly all the time that I could hardly keep the tears back and when they were really gone it seemed as if I could not bear it.

I cried all the way home and I would have given worlds almost to have been with them. I did not sleep much that night. It seemed as though I had almost committed a crime in not going. I shall never forgive myself, if it should prove that I was needed there, for not going. I am so miserable about it, I have always longed so much to be able to do something in this great struggle for the life of the nation and now that an opportunity offers, I have thrown it away. Yet God knows it was not for myself, I would willingly bear any amount of inconvenience or hardship knowing that it was in a good cause, and that it was worthy some pangs caused by this war, and I never knew so much real happiness in my life as I have experienced in the few weeks which I spent by the bedsides and ministering to the wants of the sick and dying in the Hospital. It is being deprived of this happiness, perhaps more than anything else, and the feeling that I was at last able to do something of actual good to my fellow men, that made the disappointment so keen, and now thinking of it when it is past and impossible for me to go it seems as though I could not bear it.

There is another thing which also adds to my sorrow which I must record in you faithful old friend, as being a part of my life and which I may wish to remember in the future, that is that the old sorrow pressing so sorely on my spirit for so long a time, seemed almost light when I was away, my mind being so fully occupied, and my sympathies so fully excited for others, I had little time or opportunity to think of myself. At home now in the comparative quiet of the life I lead, it comes back upon me with all the old pain and like the opening of an old wound, bleeds afresh. This more than any thing else makes me sad and heartsick now, and I think of it and of my disappointment so much that it seems sometimes as if should go mad. I cannot help thinking of it, and tonight I believe I can say truly is the most miserable of my life. I am sad when I think that the last page of my diary should be made to chronicle such a fact.

It is time soon I shall bid you adieu, faithful friend, after having gone in your company for nearly two years and a half, laying you away among the relics of my dead past, no more to look upon your pages, save as reminders of what I have been as chronicled in you and what I shall be no more forever. Thirty months seems a short time, looking back upon them, but when I think of what I was then and what I have been in them and what I am now, they are not to be counted by days or months. God has prospered us greatly in these months. His blessings have not been few nor small, and although looking back on myself at that time I see a lighter heart, a more youthful face, lit with far more hope for the future and joy for the person than it would be possible to find in the one now bending over these pages, yet I am sure that were it possible I would not exchange the one for the other.

The discipline which contact with the world, rough though it may be, together with that chastening of the heart which sorrow gives, has I hope not been lost upon me, and now writing these last words of my life record as far as this book is concerned, I feel that if a sadder, I am also a wiser woman than when I began. I feel now that although it is a thing sad and terrible to be robbed of the homes and promises which early youth holds out for the future, and to be made to feel that life instead of being a flowering path, down which we can go with winged feet and joyful hearts, it is oftener strewn with thorns which piercing our feet leave stains of our own blood to crimson the pathway, yet the pain and heart weariness, if it be borne bravely, will prove a greater blessing in the end, and lead our lives to higher walks and plain aims than mere pleasure and happiness in the present could do. I began this record in April when the young leaves were springing, and the infant year was first girding himself with the green robes of festal gladness, eager to run the golden sound of the seasons. Today as I write, the leaves touched by the white fingers of the frost, have turned to gorgeous tints of gold and scarlet, of purple and crimson assayed for the last time in State robe, 'ere he parts on that last white garment, which will cover the sunken boughs, and wrap them for the sleep of winter.

Farewell my diary, thou hast chronicled many pleasant times, thou bearest on thy pages the names of many friends dear to me in the past. Keep them sacredly. I give thee them in trust.

Annie

From Annie Cox at Madison to Gideon Winans Allen at Waukesha, Wisconsin, September 29, 1863

... I was disappointed in not receiving your letter yesterday but was just as glad to receive it today. It contained matter for serious thought of which I am hardly capable today. That is to say serious thought for I am sick but any judgment may receive the color of my feelings. However, you shall have my thoughts upon the matter. In the first place I want to ask you if Mr. Stewart lends you the money if you will start by the first of October or what I think the better way wait as long as the Prof. will allow thereby perhaps earning enough for your own expenses and perhaps partly enough for mine if Mr. Stewart could supply the rest. If you should not go til the last of November—a hundred and fifty should cover the whole, I should think. But if you would have to borrow the whole amount for yourself it seems a pretty hard risk to commence our life $100 in debt without any immediate business in which to engage to say nothing of our prospects of getting a home or even being married. You say you will abide by my decision. My dear, I do not wish you to. I wish as far as possible to lay aside all personal desires or selfish feelings in the matter. Of course I cannot help but feel badly that our engagement must be prolonged indefinitely and are separated meanwhile.

I have been thinking over the matter today and the more I think of it the more I think the more unfavorably I am impressed with the idea of you borrowing the money to go to Ann Arbor this fall. For you will not only have that in the Spring but will have other debts for you owe Stewart for the money lost last winter, for your money to go to Waukesha with, and the expenses of sending for the machine. Then what you have in Ann Arbor will make all together some $140 or $148. I have seen so much trouble from getting in debt. I would hate to see you thus involved at the commencement of life. I know it will be a sacrifice to give up the idea of going back and such a loss to you. You can study and thus gain all the central knowledge therefore lose nothing but the honor that you really have anyway for it has already been bestowed. If by any means you can earn the means to go back I shall be glad to have you go whether I go or not. That should not trouble you though I wrote rather discouragingly yesterday for which I am sorry but I felt very badly that things did not proceed any better for you. Poor dear boy you did not want a discouraging word but rather all the cheer possible. Forgive me for being that selfish. I'll be more aware hereafter a helper in sympathy and a counsel in times of need. Therefore do not worry about me hereafter nor take me into consideration with regards to your expenses in Ann Arbor. But do not, dear Winans, for your own sake get into debt. You will never rid yourself of it if you do for I have seen the system tried faithfully and always faithfully failed. I hope time will be afforded you to sufficiently to earn the amount required. If you can stay out eight weeks the expenses there will be small for you alone if you went yourself and I never would support Mrs. Buckland's family again as you did last winter. . . .

From Annie Cox at Madison to Gideon Winans Allen at Waukesha, Wisconsin, October 1, 1863

. . . I was in the historical room this afternoon reading. I go there almost every day. It is still and pleasant until some country man and woman come in with squeaking boots and cross going ones as they did today.

. . . I have one consolation in your going to Ann Arbor this time. I shall see you some for a little while. I shall have your dear presence. Then a long winter of sorrow and of cold winds and of wailing winds of fitful sunshine and lingering gloom. I'll shut my eyes to other scenes, then opening them again I shall see melting snow, laughing loving sunshine, twittering birds, and then a coming home of the dear absent. Will I see all this, Winans?

. . . I have just finished reading your letter, kind and good as ever. Dear Winans is it possible that the old rocking chair will soon receive its old occupant? I can hardly realize it—indeed I do not, I only look at it as a pleasant romance—but not to be believed. I am afraid what Stewart says of the machine is too true but why should it have fallen to your fault lot? 'Tis best, I suppose that it should be thus if you cannot see it.

The only objection I have now, my dear one is involving you in debt to that degree with our settled business in vain in the spring but even this business seems to be obviated by Prof. Corly's letter. You can certainly remain out long enough to earn your expenses there this winter thus leaving you free in the spring to earn money for another and important purpose, important to us both, but perhaps more so to me. . . . I have entirely given up the idea of going to Ann Arbor with you yet I cannot say how cheerfully. You know how tenacious I am of anything upon which I have set my desire.

The Historical Rooms that Annie visited were housed in the Baptist church across from the capitol. (Wisconsin Historical Society, WHS 23184)

From Annie Cox at Madison to Gideon Winans Allen at Ann Arbor, Michigan, October 17, 1863

... They are going in draft today, suppose they draft you. You may not know it until you are one selected unless you deposit your subscription fee to be delivered as soon as your name appears.

... At supper had one of the Southern aristocracy to visit before us in the full glory of the red bandana and gold earrings.

... I have made an agreement to take lessons in [illegible] coloring of the originator of that and he is a splendid artist. I commence tomorrow. I am glad enough to turn the world over. Are you not glad with same? He is in Fuller's gallery.

... I took my first lesson this morning, must go again this afternoon. If I learn you may see my heart jogging toward Ann Arbor. I'll send you one for a sample. He charges from $8 to $10 apiece for them. Zounds, I be rich if I succeed.

Rosabella (Belle) Augusta Arnold, from Berlin, Wisconsin, wrote sprightly, news-filled letters to her friend Charles Palmer. She signed some of her letters as Belle, some as Bella, and others with her middle name, Augusta. Charles had worked at the *Berlin Courant*, where Belle worked as a typesetter, before enlisting in the First Heavy Artillery on August 14, 1863. The Milwaukee Typographical Union went on strike when women began to be hired as typesetters at half wages. The strike was unsuccessful, and the women kept their jobs until the male typesetters returned at the end of the war.[49]

BELLE

From Belle Arnold Sleeper at Berlin to Charles Palmer at Mumfordsville, Kentucky, November 12, 1863

My Friend:

I don't wonder that you are out of patience with me for neglecting you for so long. And I shall not blame you much if you think a few hard things concerning one Belle. And now, Charley, I am not going to offer one single excuse: I am just going to tell you a few plain facts, and then if you will not overlook and forgive my past neglect, why I must suffer the consequences I suppose. But Charley, if you will just forgive and forget the past, this once-why I promise I will promise most anything you can possibly ask.

But I suppose you are very anxious to hear what I have to say for myself, and for fear you are real angry at me and will throw this letter aside with out taking the trouble to read it through, I will tell you right straight, I am going to tell the truth if by doing so I lose your friendship and one of my best correspondences.

    I did get the letter you wrote me while you were at Louisville but Mother was quite ill-not able to do the housework so a good deal dissolved on me while out of the Office and when I went into the Office I still had a good many home duties to see to, and there were about four weeks when I did not even write to Wiley [Arnold, Belle's brother], finally he wrote one such a letter and told I had "got to do differently." This awoke me to a sense of my duties and I wrote to him and then got your letter and reread and said I would write to you and before I got the first line written in came Mr. H, and writing materials had to be thrown aside and so evening after evening passed and I kept thinking that each mail would bring the promised letter from you. Since I received your last letter I have not had time to write to anyone. Clarence was preparing to leave us and there was good deal that I could do for him that I felt I must do and it has occupied all my time out of Office hours. But he is gone now and we are all alone—just Mother and I, and I can't tell you how lonely it is. Wiley and Clarence are both gone now. I hardly know which is the dearest to me or which I shall miss the most. Clarence has gone to Nebraska Territory. I don't know how long he will remain there.[50]

    You surely will not think I have forgotten you when I tell you that the "Skirmish" that H speaks of, was occasioned by my saying something in Courant not being sent to you when George flew into a passion and then Roxy said that Charley Palmer was a true gentleman and had more manners about him that he (George) even thought of having. You had better believe that there were some hard words passed between those two. (Roxy and George). T.L. came in just in season to stop the fight that was sure to come off. George threatened to put her downstairs, and she declared that if he swung at her again, she would "slap him in his mouth." I knew from past experience that it would not do for me to say anything so kept quiet and let them have it all to themselves. No, Charley, I do not blame you for feeling as you do toward him. He has done you great injustices. But, Charley, he doesn't know any better.[51]

    Roxy is in the Office again. I don't know how long she will remain there. She and George <u>seem</u> to be on excellent terms. I speak to him in the Office and treat him with <u>due respect</u> but out of the Office I do as I please and I seldom please to speak to him.

We had a "Surprise" up to Roxy's last Friday night. All met at Tripps's at 8 o'clock and went from there together. There were nearly twenty-five if not quite, so you see we have an addition to our "Clique." We had a good time. Apples, cider, and cakes of all descriptions were in attendance. How I wish you had been here, I think you would have enjoyed it. Clarence and I came home about 11 o'clock, but the rest did not leave for sometime afterwards. This is the only party of the kind there has been since you left. There is a series of dances already imminent. Manager-Gavitt and Cameron. The second one was held last night at Beckwith's Hall. I have not attended, though I did have a very <u>pressing</u> invitation. Some how I do not care for Partying this winter. Roxy has attended and told me they had a "splendid" time. The last dance I attended you were there also. I wonder when we shall both meet at such a place. There is a little fellow by the name of Wilson who has lately come into town and is to work at the "grave stone" business who is paying his attention to Miss Nettie and she seems to be well pleased with the attention.

Lizzie Palmer has gone up to Plover, Portage Co., to teach school this winter. She went last Monday. I don't know how George will get along, though I think he is trying hard to console himself in the society of Miss Leticia Jenkins—Nellie is to work at Mrs. Tripps' yet. She can take pictures famously. Nettie is in the Spectator Office setting type at 12 cts per thousand emms.[52] Roxy and I get 15cts per thousand and that is little enough. I can't think of any news to write you, but will try to make my next letter more interesting to you—I most forgot that I don't know whether I am to have the privilege of writing to you again. But, my friend, if you can find it in your heart to forgive the past and allow me still to be your friend, I will take care that you will not have a chance to complain of my negligence again.

I am glad that your health is good and you must take care and keep it good—you have seen something of Army life before, so you can profit by what experience you have had.

I see Hi occasionally, I saw him a few moments last evening and I told him I was going to write to you and he told me to remember him in my letter. He is not in town much of the time—but there is no use of my trying to post you in regard to him.[53]

I have not found the <u>Courant</u> you spoke of yet and will send one if I can find one. —Roxy is wondering why Griff does not answer her long after

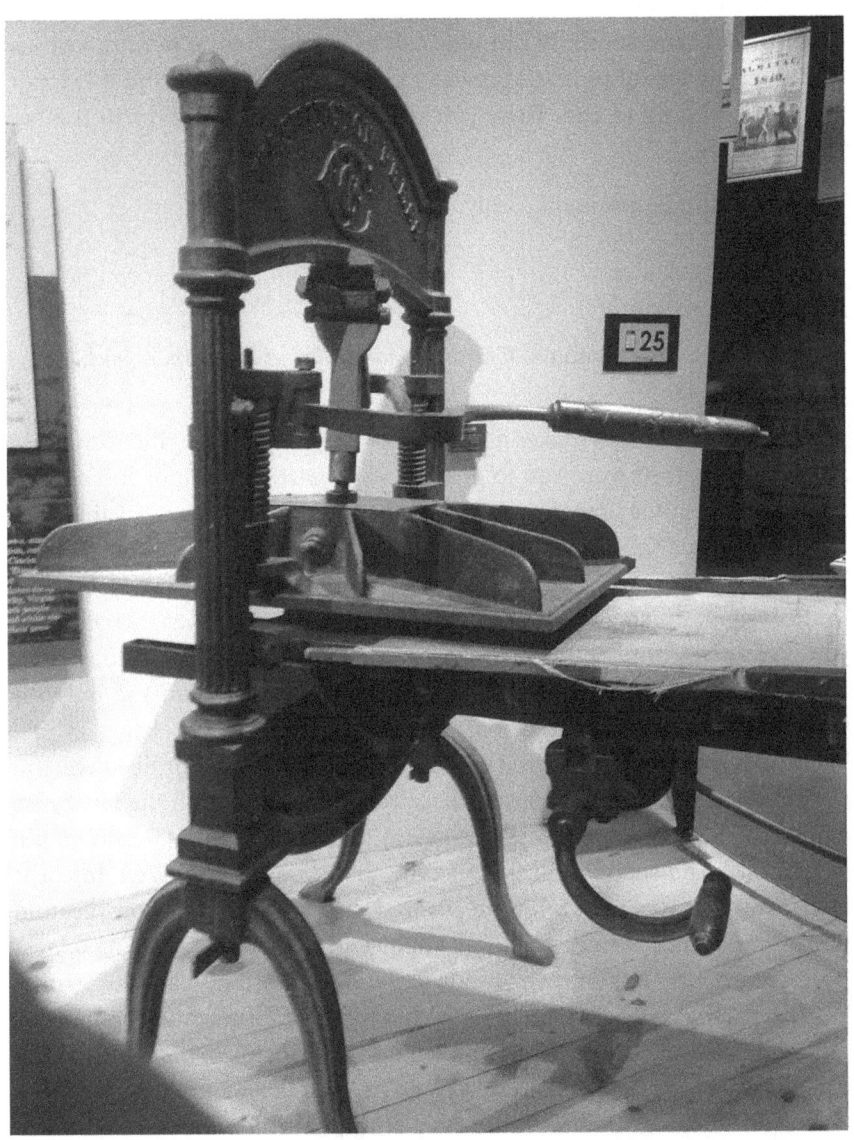

The printing press on which Belle and her friends set type was probably similar to this one. (https://upload.wikimedia.org/wikipedia/commons/2/27/Printing_press_1850.jpeg User:quadell [CC BY-SA 3.0 (https://creativecommons.org/licenses/by-sa/3.0)]).

she writes him. She directed to Mumfordsville, Ky. Won't you speak to the young man about it?

Give my best respects to him and tell him I shall write to him soon as to answer the letters received previous to this. I must now bring this letter to a close, hoping to hear from you ere many weeks roll away in the big wheel of time.

Yours in Faith, Hope, and Charity.
"Augusta"

Annie

From Annie Cox at Madison to Gideon Winans Allen at Ann Arbor, Michigan, November 15, 1863

... I think your sister takes a wrong view of your politics. She would not respect you herself were you to give up an honest opinion for the sake of another, no matter how dear.[54] You have misunderstood me in thinking I ever suggested this. It would be no additional proof of your love for me. I believe you to be honest in your convictions and much as I may deem you in the wrong, much as I may wish you of different mind, yet I would have you stand firm until convinced of your errors, always open to conviction and in no unnecessary haste to express your opinion. I am sad only for your own sake. In this age when politics influences every relation in life. When one is allowed the freedom of speech if he speaks in obedience to the authority of the ruling party, when friendships and even the tender tie of sisterhood is governed by it, I am sorry that my Winans is found on the wrong side. You seem to think, however, that you are right. Well, my dear boy, if you are right God will protect you. If you are wrong, my prayers and hope in God will convince you of that wrong. That there are some dishonest Republicans I do not deny for it our party is made up of fallen humanity. Yet the party you picture out is not composed of either fine republicans or democrats but only of those who would sell principles, honor, anything else for the all mighty dollars sake. I do not call that republican anymore than I call those of George B. Smith's stump tour democrats.[55] Who will change opinions and principles to suit his command. To the rich he talks "parties" and whiskey. To the ignorant of every regard the grand idea of power and wealth if they be comfortable, willing party. But know this my Winans, wherever and whatever you are, my affections are with you however much my judgment may differ. It would be pleasant that we agree in this matter, but I did not give my hand and promise my heart to your politics. I chose another object, they are given to the man, not to his politics. They are Winans's dear and whole as ever. If he should be influenced to dishonorable acts by them <u>then</u> my duty might be different. Now my duty's pleasure is to stand by his side through good and evil report. And should I talk, as a sister, to win you from error, 'twould not be by calling you a traitor.

On November 19, 1863, at the dedication of the cemetery at Gettysburg, Lincoln made a two-minute speech that received a tepid reception from the fifteen thousand people gathered there. The main speaker for the occasion, Edward Everett, astutely assured Lincoln that he had said more in his two minutes than Everett had in his two-hour-long oration. By the time of the dedication the cemetery was only one-fourth completed because the local contractor hired to bury the bodies could move only one hundred a day. Two days later Lincoln came down with smallpox and commented, "At last I have something I can give everybody."[56]

Reflecting on both the blessings enjoyed by Wisconsinites and the terrible toll the war had taken on so many in the deadly battles of 1863, Governor Salomon issued his annual proclamation for Thanksgiving Day on November 26, 1863, asking the people of Wisconsin to "offer their gratitude to God for the blessings and favors we have been permitted to enjoy during the past year . . . in that gratitude . . . remember the many noble and departed heroes . . . and their weeping widows, orphans, relatives, and friends . . . those who have sacrificed health and limbs in this great national struggle. . . . In offering our Thanks, let them be mingled with Prayers for a speedy and permanent restoration of peace, unity, and happiness to our distracted country."[57]

From Annie Cox at Madison to Gideon Winans Allen at Ann Arbor, Michigan, November 26, 1863

. . . Enlistments are increasing every day, they think they shall not draft here in January because the quota will be supplied before that time. That does not meet Mr. Stewart's views as expressed in one of your letters. Winans, he is a regular secessionist, even to the favoring of disunion and the success of the south. I do not wonder the republicans are bitter against the Copperheads when they express such intense hatred to the government that has protected and prospered them all these years and when they favor and sympathize with a government and policy that if carried into effect when once established would grind just such a one as Stewart into powder, then they would have a taste of slavery themselves. And when I see slams and ridicule cast upon a common effort to aid suffering humanity—as in the case of the fair at Chicago, ridiculed simply because its professed object was the Soldiers and the relief of their families, I cannot respect them as a party.[58]

Acceding to this says that no one is unselfish nor one humane but them. God pity the country if it is so. I heard a lady say they were not going to help at the dinner next week. They had got tired of helping soldiers. Tired helping those who are guarding their homes. Winans, I am often told that you advocate such a cause. I hope and trust that you do not go to the same length that Stewart does. Well I did not intend to allude to this subject—ere will agree to disagree. You are a dear noble boy and have a generous noble heart. I love you even if you are a Copperhead.

From Annie Cox at Madison to Gideon Winans Allen at Ann Arbor, Michigan, December 1, 1863

... Have you heard anything of my property in Trempeleau yet? I am interested in the settlement of that affair. Friend and Campbell are indicted for perjury. ... Good democrats. Mr. Screen's church is asking a fine because he would not have the President's hymn sung Thanksgiving Day. Winans, once again I caution you to be careful.[59]

From Annie Cox at Madison to Gideon Winans Allen at Ann Arbor, Michigan, December 9, 1863

... the wife has the privilege of salting her husband's coffee, of putting pebbles in his slippers, slandering him, casting loving glances to his neighbor in shoulder straps.[60]

Annie continued to be concerned about the impact that Winan's politics would have on their future, particularly after his actions of December 12, when, the University of Michigan reported, "Gideon Allen, 'an outspoken Copperhead student in the Law Department,' defended a visit to the Copperhead leader Clement L. Vanlandingham [sic] and led a march of 300 students defending Vanlandingham and the Union." Winans may have felt that his environs provided him some protection as the University of Michigan attracted many Copperheads during the war. In contrast to the situation at most universities, Michigan's enrollment increased during the war. The medical school's enrollment increased from 164 to 415 and the law school's from 90 to 260 during the course of the war.⁶¹ Clement Vallandigham was the most prominent of the Northern individuals whose right of habeas corpus had been suspended on the basis of a May 26, 1861, ruling by the US Supreme Court. Annie may have feared that Winans would be imprisoned for his views.⁶²

From Annie Cox at Madison to Gideon Winans Allen at Ann Arbor, Michigan, December 19, 1863

. . . But my Winans, I often wish you had chosen some other avocation than that of a politician, for I see you prefer that to the law, as far as my understanding goes, it is a life of constant excitement and wrangling. It leaves but little time for domestic happiness and gives not solid enjoyment in return. God protect my Winans from the perils of the path he has chosen and enable me to lend him all peace and happiness in my power.

. . . Of your proceedings in the Vanlandingham [sic] affair, I shall say but little. You know I cannot approve it. The whole affair seems to me too much like a common mob proceeding above the attention of one so good and noble as my Winans. Besides it is setting up naught the laws of our country and beating its soul with contempt which is a sin in the sights of God. Yet you and [I] cannot agree there so I will drop the subject. Only hoping my Winans will do nothing unworthy [of] the name and honor of a good and wise man.

. . . I see by the paper that the copperhead or democrat portion of the Congress has adopted the war platform. That speaks better things for them. Anything to be in fashion, you know. I expect the Patriot will follow in the [illegible] before long. Little dogs do as big ones do, generally. Did you ever notice of what two words the Patriot was composed: Pat-riot. That means Irish mob. Quite appropriate, do you not think so? Dear Winans, do not feel hurt at my stirrings. When anyone speaks of Copperheads, I am silent and troubled because I do not like to hear of principles or opinions that W. has embraced, slandered. Not slandered, but spoken harshly of. I could wish we were united in this matter but as we are not, we must avoid any unpleasant feelings in the matter. I do not think it well for women to meddle in politics anyway for they are more [illegible], more excitable and more governed in their contact by their opinions. Therefore they could not meet an opponent as the men do after a hot argument as pleasantly as before, they would carry the matter into their social relations.

As 1863 drew to a close, Northerners and Southerners had markedly different views of what it had brought. Secretary of the Navy Gideon Welles wrote,

"The year closes more satisfactorily than it commenced.... The heart of the nation is sounder and its hopes brighter." In contrast, the *Richmond Examiner* editorialized, "To-day closes the gloomiest year of our struggle."⁶³

From Annie Cox at Madison to Gideon Winans Allen at Ann Arbor, Michigan, January 4, 1864

... When I spoke of you siding with cruelty, crime, and so on, I meant you favoring those politics and that people that advocated all these. Winans may desire peace. That is what we all desire and we are aiming at permanent peace which we have not had for many years. Peace cannot be where those millions of <u>human beings</u> are groaning under oppression and crimes of which they are innocent. The world is more enlightened at this moment than ever before. Look at the progress of the colored people since their emancipation, and the acknowledgements of the Southern people. See how they are flocking to the protection of the old flag. You will say this is the slant of abolition papers. What then are we to believe if the testimony of thousands of eyewitnesses is of no account? We have given the South ample opportunity to come back without slavery and not impoverished, but they choose to return to their wallowing in the mire of sin. The present aspect of our country is full proof that God is smiling upon us and punishing the South. You say you hate crime and ask me if I will believe it. Winans, it is consistent with all I have said to you, to ask this question. As I have been sincere in my multiple expressions of affection for you I either love the criminal or believe you good and pure. I do not wish to misunderstand Winans, but I have heard you express yourself very strongly to others upon this matter, and I understood it as a decided sympathy with the actions of the South. You sweet darling, I never meant to cause one pang in your heart but I have met just retribution for my heart aches while I write and even alone a tear blistered letter would testify to it. Yet sigh nor tear cannot be written. We will not talk politics any more for I see in them a cloud no bigger than a man's hand, but dark and cold. My own Winans, our love must let it aglow and build it into a beautiful sunset golden cloud, only beautifying the land.

From Annie Cox at Madison to Gideon Winans Allen at Ann Arbor, Michigan, January 6, 1864

... Don't write me such a cold letter again. When you call (as you have often done) the Republicans cowards, office seekers, despotic, and call those of the East as you did a few letters back, a mean, contemptible and I don't know what else kind of profile, I did not think you meant me, Winans, although you know I sympathize with them. I did not get angry with you when you could hardly find bad enough names for them I knew what you meant and let it pass although I could not agree with you. For I think we might, with thorough search, find good sensible people in the East and North and those of moral quality as good as the South. They differ from you, that is all, Winans, and when you condemn them so thoroughly you do just what you blame them so much for doing. It is hard for us to love our conquerors but it is a sign of a noble spirit to do so. But, Winans, whatever you may do in the world as a politician do not let this subject be the cause of bitter feelings between us.

From Annie Cox at Madison to Gideon Winans Allen at Ann Arbor, Michigan, January 7, 1864

... Madison is a scene of life. There are 2,800 soldiers in the camp and 200 more in Harvey Hospital. I am going out there as soon as it gets a little pleasanter.

From Annie Cox at Madison to Gideon Winans Allen at Ann Arbor, Michigan, January 13, 1864

... I wish you could see Madison now. The Legislature has opened. The 7th Regiment is in town, have come to reenlist. Nearly three regiments in camp and hundreds of volunteers coming in every day. They have more than they can tend to. There will be no draft here now. And I guess not anywhere in this state. The streets are a perfect zoo all the time, the boardinghouses full, and all the hotels more than they can accommodate. We have had several applications. One a young lady, she was determined to come but we could not take her. They are charging four and five dollars for day boarders.

From Annie Cox at Madison to Gideon Winans Allen at Ann Arbor, Michigan, January 24, 1864

... One of the city guard was stabbed last night by a citizen. It is said to get his money as he had just been paid. Yes, he is living yet. I do not know whether the assassin has been arrested or not. A poor soldier boy has been to Dr. Morse this morning to get relief. He is sick and maybe to become a cripple for life if he is not immediately cared for. Dr. gave him a paper to get his dismissal.⁶⁴ [Yesterday I] visited the Assembly, heard a discussion about supporting Abe Lincoln.

BELLE

From Belle Arnold Sleeper at Berlin to Charles Palmer, January 27, 1864

Well, Charlie, I will try once more to get a letter to you, though I must confess that I have but small hopes of success. I am discouraged, so there. You are not going to give it up easily I see, and if you, away down there, have so much courage and perseverance, I ought to exhibit a little more. I think perhaps you did judge me a little harshly, but under the circumstance you were very pardonable. I see you were a little surprised at what I wrote Griff, but I tell you I believed it all and even more at the time I wrote. You seemed to wish to correspond with me although I did at first propose it. I well knew that I was not a good little sister and that I could not make any letters very interesting to you, and yet you thought I would try to enliven some of your hours of camp life, and there was pleasure in the thought. I cant' imagine why you have not received any letters from me. I have not been very particular about who got or carried my mail. George most always brought my mail to me till within the last two or three weeks. I have politely requested him to let it remain in the Post Office in the future. Oh, how I hate him! He is the smallest, the most contemptible specimen of mankind I ever saw or heard of. You can scarcely imagine how unpleasant his presence makes the Office. I some times think I will give up trying to work there. Because I will not accept his intentions—will not allow him to pay me any attention under any circumstances, he takes every advantage of me he possibly can. He is so overbearing—so insulting in his language. He is certainly beneath any ones notice, and yet one can't help but be annoyed by him, when he is constantly around.

Charley perhaps you will be just a little surprised to learn that Mother and I are living in Mr. Beckwith's stylish residence. We have been here for weeks, and shall stay about a week longer, when his Sister, who has lately arrived from California, will assume the responsibility of his household affairs. Everything has passed off very pleasantly since we have been here. Mr. Beckwith has tried in curious ways to make the time pass pleasantly. But, Charlie, he is a <u>Copperhead</u>.⁶⁵

I received a letter from Wiley this morning; he had just heard of the death of his little boy, who died some two weeks since. Wiley feels his loss deeply, as he almost idolized his little Georgie. I cannot grieve for the child. Wiley was at Memphis when he wrote, though he expected soon to go from there. The Regiment has been dismounted, he didn't quite know the particulars, but said he had frozen his toes which excused him from active duty.

I was surprised by the sudden entrance of Miss Lizzie yesterday afternoon, when I thought her safe in Plover where she has been teaching this past season. I tell you, I was glad to see her! She had been here but a short time when Dan called. Some how, they always manage to come to town about the same time, though each declares they did not know the whereabouts of the other, and of course I feel in duty bound to believe them (!). Lizzie came home with a certain soldier from the 5th, VanNorman by name, who is home on furlough. He has reenlisted. Lizzie will return to Plover in a few days; and without seeing George for that young man is taking care of John Woodehull who has the real small pox. Won't he curse the flowers that be. And I am just wicked enough to be glad of it.[66]

I can't write you any more news, Charley, as I am confined to the house on the "sick list" and it is with a good deal of exertion that I write at all. I will try and make my next more interesting. Hi called in a few moments last Saturday evening; he told me he had received a letter from you and should answer it, soon as he could. He started, or was to start, the next morning from Wausau.

I am very tired, Charlie, and you must excuse me from writing more now. I hope this will reach you and that I will soon receive a reply. Remember me to Griff, tell him I will write him soon.[67]

Think often and kindly of Belle. (I forgot and signed the wrong name.)

ANNIE

From Annie Cox at Madison to Gideon Winans Allen at Ann Arbor, Michigan, February 3, 1864

... I think you do wrong to cast soldiers as a whole among the impure and degraded base set as you do. They are from the best and worst of society—the worst perhaps in majority but some come from refined, religious homes and must they because they have chosen the soldiers' lot, hard at best, be thrust forever from society or at least while they are away from home? What saner way to complete their ruin. That is just what makes them bad and wicked. Winans, if you were a soldier, would you wish to be discarded by all your friends? I think they are no worse than the company of our city boys and we know just as much of their character. There are a great many of our citizens, young men, who are away from their homes. Shall we treat them so mean who have no innate principles of honor? Will, when we think of society or home is summoned, show not their character? Do not think I am trying to excuse myself for going with soldiers for I have never been with one except Clawson nor with any young man since our engagement. The gentlemen boarding at Hattie's I have met there and found as utter gentlemen. One a quiet, smiling country boy in spite of his shoulder straps. He leaves tomorrow, perhaps will be here this evening with Hattie and some of the others boarded. I do not approve of running around with different ones, especially soldiers, for it would attract unpleasant notice. . . .[68]

BELLE

From Belle Arnold Sleeper at Plover to Charles Palmer, March 6, 1864, "No. 4"

Dear Ben,[69]

If you will pardon me for writing to you with a pencil I will send you a few lines to let you know that I have not forgotten you, and that I do intend to answer your letters just as soon as I am placed in a position where I can do justice to said letter. I received your good letter in due season but was too unwell to answer it. I must say that I was very much surprised when I found that you had actually got my letter. I can hardly make up my mind to accuse anyone of intercepting letters between us, but I must confess things <u>do</u> look rather suspicious. How <u>could</u> he have done such a thing! Among all the many <u>mean</u>, hateful, things that he has been guilty of, this has been the worst, if it is true. But I will mail my own letters after this and take any mail from the office, so there will be no chance of any one to take such liberties.

You will see by the Courant, if you have learned it in no other way, that this evil genius of ours is at last married! I am just as glad as ever can be. And now I hope he will let me alone. He'd <u>better</u> any ways. <u>How I do hate him!!</u>

You will wonder where Belle is that she cannot write to you in a decent style. Well, I will tell you. I left Berlin some three weeks ago and between you and I, Ben, I really do believe that I had no business coming from home so soon, but there were several reasons I felt like leaving when I did. I have paid for it I can tell you. (Private) By the way, Miss Roxy has taken it upon herself to inform people why I left. Oh, Ben, if there is one thing I do despise it is two-sided folks. She has made trouble between me and every one she could, and now she is trying to make trouble between me and the world at large. Hang such actions! She is always so good to my face—then to make such stunning remarks it makes me feel anything but comfortable. I am now stopping at Mr. Strosses [illegible]. Shall return to Berlin in two or three weeks at the furthest and I think before that time. I have no chance to write here—so many children that I can't think, even if I wanted to. Lizzie has returned to Berlin—went back with Hi and I couldn't help myself!! I hear that Will Harnish and Roxy have fell out; and it is no child's play either. I can't give you any news that will interest you. But I will make a big effort to write you a good long letter when I return home. And I shall expect to find a letter from you, too, when I return home, though I must confess that I don't deserve it. But please don't disappoint. And now, Ben, I know you will be only too glad to excuse me from writing any more. I will write you as soon as possible.

Yours with many kind wishes
Augusta

As the third year of the war drew to a close, the Union Army had all but destroyed any opportunity for a successful Confederate invasion of the North, General Grant was coordinating attacks by four armies, the Mississippi River was fully under control of the Union, Sherman was beginning his march to the sea, and 146,634 Confederate soldiers were held in Union prisons. Jefferson Davis had sent a delegation to Canada to begin negotiations for a truce with the federal government.[70]

CHAPTER 4

May 1864 to April 1865

As the fourth year of the war dawned, ten Wisconsin regiments were among the 150,000 soldiers fighting on the outskirts of Atlanta, a prize that was second only to Richmond, Virginia, for its strategic importance. Atlanta was the center of Southern railroads and a major industrial center, with factories that built gunboats and railroads. Atlanta also housed extensive warehouses that supplied food to the Confederate troops.[1] In the east, eight Wisconsin regiments participated in the Wilderness Campaign in Virginia. Between May 5 and June 12, they suffered extreme losses in numerous battles. In the initial two-day battle, thirty thousand Union and Confederate troops were lost, with neither side emerging victorious. Wisconsin troops were once again recognized for their contributions. Colonel Lysander Cutler of the 6th Infantry took command of Union troops when their general was lost in battle. Union troops were repulsed at the Battle of North Anna River and were forced to seek a new crossing downstream. Conflict in the east also included the Spotsylvania Campaign, another series of bloody battles with no clear winner at which eleven thousand Union soldiers were killed or wounded. Wisconsin regiments among the hundred thousand Union soldiers involved in this campaign included the 2nd, 5th, 6th, 7th, and 36th Infantries. The deadliest day of this campaign, dubbed "Bloody Angle," was May 12, which ended with the trenches built by each side filled with wounded and dead soldiers. Almost 10 percent of the casualties for the entire Civil War were victims of the Wilderness and Spotsylvania Campaigns, with a loss of 59,800 men.[2]

Despite the carnage at the war front, Rosabella (Belle) Augusta Arnold, of Berlin Wisconsin, joyfully shared the news of her marriage to Hiram Sleeper. However, her joy was tempered by Hiram's enlistment. These two events would result in substantial changes to Belle's life and happiness.

BELLE

From Belle Arnold Sleeper at Berlin to Charles Palmer at Fort Clay, Lexington, Kentucky, June 19, 1864

Friend Charley:

I am just going to write to you without asking you if it will be agreeable to receive a letter from a married lady. I know that you have many correspondents, and perhaps I am intruding, nevertheless I shall presume our past friendship enough to ask of you a reply to this poorly written scrawl.

I have before me your last letter to me March 20 and to Hi of April 7th. Now Charlie I am going to make a clean breast of this, and tell you what a bad girl I have been. The morning before Hi left for Madison he received your letter and knowing he would have no time to answer it he passed it over to me saying, "Bell will you write to Charley and tell him just how it is; and tell him to write to me?" I told him that I would do so, and this is the way I have kept my promise. To say that I am ashamed of it would be too tame an expression. Perhaps there is some excuse for me, but I will not attempt to excuse myself in the least. I have done wrong, and I am sorry for it. Now, Charley, won't you write to that husband of mine? He will be so glad to hear from you. Being Orderly and not understanding his position well, his duties must necessary be laborious. He complains most bitterly about his friends forgetting him. You know what a letter to a soldier is. Do write to him, Charley, for I know he is wondering at your long silence, never dreaming that his wife is the only one to blame. His address is C. C, 38th Regiment, Wisconsin Volunteers, Washington, D.C.

As for myself, I have only this to say. I did get a letter from you when I returned from the North, and I was glad to know that I was still remembered by my absent friend Charley. I fully intended to answer the letter immediately and tell you of the approaching event, but found no time to write to my own mother. I was very ill after I wrote you at Stanton for several weeks and it was with the utmost difficulty that I succeeded in getting home. And I had been home but little over a week when I was married; and one week from the day we were married my husband left me to raise his good right arm in defense of our glorious "Old Union," since which time I have not looked on his face. Furlough not being granted from Madison. But not knowing this I was looking and waiting his return 'til he wrote me from Washington. His last letter, dated June 4th, was written at "White House," twenty-one miles from Richmond. They had been run on through to the "Point" to guard a supply train through. They were expecting order to march to the point when he wrote, in fact, the "remove" which generally precedes such an order had been present in camp for a day or two. Hi seems to be in excellent spirits—says he likes soldiering.

Griff starts for Madison tomorrow morning from thence he expects to return to the Army, so I shall not attempt to give you the news and gossip of town. Now Charley if you will be a real good boy and forgive this naughty girl—why Charley I'll do most anything—submit to almost any punishment you see fit to inflict. I assure that Mrs. Sleeper will be just as glad to hear from her friend Ben as ever. Write soon.

Ever the same—Bell

James Patchin of Wyocena, Wisconsin, the eldest son of Augustus and Margaret Patchin, enlisted in the 47th Infantry on May 27, 1864, for a three-month enlistment and was mustered out of service on September 16, 1864. Despite her May 24, 1863, statement to Augustus that "You know that I would not try to write to anyone else," his mother, Margaret Patchin, wrote him frequently during his brief enlistment in 1864, sharing concerns about the farm and encouraging him to keep faith in God. James's father, Augustus, was still a prisoner of war when James enlisted.[3]

Margaret

From Margaret Patchin at Wyocena to James Patchin, July 12, 1864

My Dear James,

How are you, and where are you is the thoughts that is in my mind all the time that my mind is off from your Father. We haven't heard a word from him since you went away, and my health is giving way under it. I am no worse than I was last week. I am able to go around the house some and to see to the things, but when I begin to think about any business that there is to be done, or to think that I have got to go from home to see about things, it takes all my strength from me; indeed at times my memory goes with, it but I never forget that you and your Father is away from home and that you are suffering many privations.

Wednesday forenoon.

My dear child,

I hope that you are well and that you will continue to be so, and that you will not have to get very near the Rebels; for I am so afraid that you will be venturesome or that something will happen to you and that you will get hurt. My sad heart thinks of a great many things, but in the midst of all comes the comforting thought that you are in God's hands and that He will never leave nor forsake those that put their trust in Him; and I do feel to thank Him for His goodness in bringing you to feel your need of Him. Oh, be faithful, and do not neglect secret prayer. Never be ashamed of the cross of Christ, but be an active living Christian. Strive to grow in grace all the time. I feel that I have made so little progress in Holy things that I am not fit to teach; but I have a duty to attend to towards my children and I hope that I may be enabled to do it in the fear of the Lord. I feel that I have lived beneath my privilege and perhaps that is the reason why I have so many things to trouble me; perhaps the Lord saw that my mind was too much given up to the things of this world, and that I loved my husband and children more than I did Him; and that it was best that I should be brought to see how I stood. I have felt afraid that it was on account of my unfaithfulness that you was so unconcerned about your salvation when others have been awakened and have given their hearts to the Saviour; but now, as you have become reconciled to Him, I feel like saying thou hast been angry with me but now thou comfortest me. Oh, that I could have the privilege of telling this glad news to your Dear Father; it would gladden his heart even in prison to hear it!

It is six o'clock in the afternoon, and Herbert is very busy all the time and he don't like it to have me take a pen in my hand; he wants that I should give up time to him. He improves very fast in talking, and he understands everything that we tell him, and he clings closer than ever to me, and he isn't willing that Mary should go away and stay overnight. Poor child, he is so lonesome without his Brother Jimmy and your other brothers; and I am afraid that they will work too hard and hurt themselves; for part of the corn did not come till after it rained, and then John's eyes was so sore that he could not do anything and they ain't well yet, but he is to work Orlo is quite feeble part of the time and don't look as if he was able to work. It makes me feel bad to have to call on him.

The corn has got very weedy but they are adoing the best that they can to clean it. Elbert is trying the best that he can to git along and I am afraid that he will hurt himself as he is so young to cradle. The chinch bug is to work very bad in the wheat; I don't know as they are in all of ours, but they are in part of it. That piece beside the winter wheat is quite bad. They say the rye across the road will have to be cut the last of this week the other is cut. We haven't engaged any hay as I have been so unwell that I can't go away from home very well; and the boys has to keep a horse in the corn all the time that they can; but I must stop.

Take as good care of yourself as you can, and write often to your loving Mother. I will send you a few stamps and some money; the reason that I will send so little at a time is that I haven't any greenbacks that is small, and I have forgotten to get any when I was away.

Eliza was here last week and Mary was with her; she coughed a good deal; but they make her work all the time, and she says that her health is good. I guess that Hugh is pretty bad off from what she said.

Thursday morning.

All as well as usual.

I left a spot here and thought that I should not be able to write much, but we are countin the time that you are to be gone. Oh, that you won't have to stay any longer, but come to us, is the sincere prayer of your loving mother,

Margaret A. Patchin

From Margaret Patchin at Wyocena to James Patchin, July 18, 1864

My Dear James,

I will try to write a few lines to you this evening, for it is now seven o'clock and you know that it isn't very still here at that time.

It is quite wet here now though it hasn't rained any today, but it did yesterday and the day before. We haven't got our winter wheat in the barn yet and I hope it won't rain any more till we get that secured.

We received yours of the tenth on Saturday and was very glad to hear from you that you was better and that you was more contented; for I love you so much my Dear Child that I want to have you happy, and it will be for your health to be contented. I am counting the days that you will have to stay away and praying that you will come then to take your place at home and to take a place in the Church. Oh, what a happy time that will be to me if I am permitted to live to see it and if your Dear Father is allowed to come home to us and mingle his prayers with ours!

Oh, won't we be happy; my heart says, "bless the Lord" for His great goodness unto me and mine, and may his loving kindness ever be around us; and, at last, may I be permitted to say here, "Lord, and the Children that though hast given me."

Tuesday morning

We are all as well as usuel this morning I am able to go around the house and attend to the things but it is hard work John eyes is quite sore yet though not quite as bad as they have ben but worse than aney of you ever had before Orlo is rather better than he was but if I could get help he should not work in the harvest field at all for he looks so feeble Elbert is working very hard and is pleasant most of the time him and Orlo is cutting the rye acrost the road today the wind blew so yesterday that they could not work there and Elbert went and got the two bulls shod so that we could draw the wheat into the barn as soon as it gets dry it thunders this morning and I am afraid our wheat will hurt if it is wet much longer you know that one extreme generly follows another we have the strangest weather this year that I ever remember of seeing the chinch bug has distroyed a great deal of the grain some of the folks is cutting theirs wheat as it is all turned yellow by the bug ours is some hurt but not near as bad as some of the folks is we will cut the wheat in the woods this week for they are in that the worst we shall have enough for our own use and some to spare if we can get it taken care of I dont knew where our help is to come from but we will do the best that we can John is planting corn in spots where it did not come for fodder we shall keep rite on in our harvest and I shall try and get help if posible but help is scerse and a good meny is sick Herbert is very buisy all the time he says that he dose want to see his brother Jimmy so bad and then he will kiss us for you very often every day.

we all send love and kisses to you be as careful as you possibly of yourself and may God shield and protect you and restore you to me soon is the sincere wish of your loveing Mother

No news from your Father yet.

I will send some stamps and a little change I forgot to get green backs but will the first chance.

BELLE

Belle Arnold Sleeper at Berlin to Charles Palmer at Lexington, Kentucky, August 13, 1864

Friend Ben:[4]

Well really I don't know as I ought to commence this letter quite so familiarly. I forgot the fact that I now addressing a Lieut. But however I shall now proceed. Lieut. Palmer, allow me to congratulate you on your promotion. Right glad was I to hear that Charley has got the "Stripes" And as he has glided quietly from King to Saint, may be 'ere long have a "bar" laid upon his shoulders. He has served his country well and as I trust he will be rewarded. You have my best wishes for your onward and upward progress. I know you are not and never will be content until gaining but a round or two up the ladder of promotion of Military fame. I expect to hear of you "high up" one of these bright days.

And so you thought my letter "decidedly cool." Now, Charley, either you or I labored under a great mistake. Why, guess I thought it was your place to write to me first. I know that you wrote me last, but you know, with the all the fixing and excitement of getting married, I didn't have much time to think of my many correspondents, even my only brother suffered the same plight. And then the thousand and one little things a wife can find to do for a "Soldier Husband" kept my hands and my heart busy for some time. This with my poor health made me seem to many of my friends careless and negligent. I sent you a "Courant" containing a notice of the event, and I really expected to 'ere long hear from you. But in that I am disappointed. I met Dora one day, and enquired after you, and during the conversation I asked her what you would think to receive a letter from Mrs. Sleeper, she thought it was about time I wrote and found out, and the first opportunity I did write. I began to think I should never find out by writing, but I was intending to try once more before giving up entirely, when lo and behold yours of the 23rd of July arrives. I was away from home when it came, visiting among Hi's sisters in the Prairie, so it was some time before I got it after it arrived in Berlin. Many thanks, Charley, for your generosity in overlooking my neglect, also for your kind wishes. You say I need not presume in past friendship, but in present friendship; the truth was when I sat down to write that letter to you, I had been thinking of our acquaintances after your return from the "Cavalry"; of how much we had each had to annoy and vex. I wondered if after all you would not think hard of me for I had promised so faithfully to write often, and I well know that I had come far short of making that promise good. But you have generously overlooked all this, I shall say no more about it.

I presume Griff has told you all about Roxy and Will Macnish. You must bear in mind that it is the Carleton side he tells and there are always two sides to every story. The truth is, Charley, Miss Roxy is about played out. Her gentleman company is not of the most refined character, and she must expect that good society will shun her when she seems to prefer bad or low society. But this could be expected from a girl who would stoop to tell a falsehood just for her own selfish purposes. Charley, I haven't got one particle of sympathy for her. I could have overlooked her treatment of me when I was in the office if she had stopped there, but she did not. No sooner was I gone from town then she cast out the blackest of insinuations against me, and fortunately for me a friend of mine was present to put [an end] on her insinuations, telling her if she knew any thing concerning me it was best for her to tell what it was and not insinuate. She backed out of it the best way she could, and all this time she was writing me long friendly letters. Charley, I despise her!

Nell and George have had trouble, and Nell has left the office. He screams at her too many times. I don't know what they will do now. I tell Nell if George will only scream at T.L. now, I shall be satisfied. He swears about him but never to him. Geo. has lost all the friends he ever had in Berlin— no one speaks well of him. I guess that he has found out that Bell is not the only one who won't be sworn at. He has regular quarrels in the office with his wife. Oh they are a happy couple.

The last I received from Wiley was July 27th. He was then in Decatur, Ala, was well and in fine spirits. The Cap't had got the gold leaves on his shoulders. Wiley will soon get his commission I suppose. I shall tell him to write you.

Hi is still in front of Petersburg. His last letter, August 2nd was written in great haste, just to let me know that he was alive and well. He has been transferred to the command of an Ambulance Train so he is not in so much danger from rebel balls nor is his labor so heavy, he has a horse to ride all the time. How long he will remain in command I do not know. He has witnessed some terrible sights as well as terrible fighting since he left home. Captain Woodworth is still in town. How easy for some officers to keep in a safe position.[5]

Osier Wheelocks' brother was killed in the battle of the 30th. He belonged to the 39th [sic: 37th] Wisc. Reg't Vol, and a noble fellow he was. Osier feels it keenly. How many more hearts must bleed. Oh, it is terrible to think of.[6]

Write soon as convenient and oblige.

Yours truly
Augusta

Margaret

From Margaret Patchin at Wyocena to James Patchin, September 2, 1864

My Dear James,

I will try to write a few lines to you today as Mary has got one letter ready, but I don't know as I can make any sense to it; for Bertie has a pen and paper and he is writing to his dear Jimmy. He has to put his pen in the ink very often; now it is Pa that he is writing to. He sends a kiss to you and is very busy.

Elbert, Orlo, and John is fixin' the cistern. We came very near losing Kit in it; she broke thru and just saved herself; that was some six weeks ago, but we could not git anyone to help to fix it, so the boys is fixin' it themselves. They have got the thing all off with out gitting hurt, and are fixin' the lid to put on. It is all clean, so I think they will get along with it. It is very dry still, and I think that our chance is not very good for large potatoes this year; and there is a very great scarcity of vegetables of all kinds. You never saw anything like it, but I think that we can git along if you and Father only come home; for we have got wheat, and we have got cattle to kill for beef; and when you come I think that we can git along.

This has been a very hard year for the farmers and it has been a very sad one to me, still I am thankful that I have the hope that my dear ones still live and, of course, I am in hopes to have the privilege of seeing you and your dear Father soon. Oh, that I won't have to wait much longer for his coming! For, I am so lonesome, and the boys are gitting the upper hands of me; for I can't stand it to have them or anyone else speak cross to me. It makes me sick and that is the reason that I am so feeble this summer. Oh, my dear boy, I hope that you will soon come to help me! There is no chance to plow, for it is so dry. You must be very careful of yourself, for we are making calculations about your coming that sometimes I think of how often I have been disappointed in your Father not coming; but all things work together for good for them that love the Lord, and perhaps it is for the best, though we can't see it; and trusting you with the Lord I will stop and remain as ever your loving mother,

M. A. Patchin

As casualties mounted, the Union continued to recruit additional soldiers, among them Andrew Burwell, a corporal in the 5th Infantry, Company H, who was mustered in on August 24, 1864. His twenty-three-year-old wife, Mary, wrote frequent letters over the next nine months that were filled with loving support and news of their young daughter, Lucy.

MARY

From Mary Burwell at Packwaukee to Andrew Burwell, September 12, 1864

Dearest Husband

I now sit down to answer your letters. I was glad to see the letters come but was so sorry to hear you have such hard times, it makes me feel so uneasy I can't hardly contain myself. I felt as if I would leave all and take my baby and fly to you, how I do wish I [was] near you where I would make you a good soft bed to lay in and a good meal of victuals to eat. Oh how I do wish my dear one you was close of it I don't believe there will be any draft, but I would not have you do anything to cause them to punish you, like them men you wrote about there, may something turn up before long, but it is hard to bear but you have it the hardest. I hope you have your clothes by this time or you must suffer for the want of clean ones. I hope you will not let your self want for anything that you can get for money, and do be careful and not sleep when you stand guard. I shall be so glad to see you and your help will be very acceptable to me and father we won't be done haying until the last of the week and then he will cut up the corn, and I don't know what I am going to do, for someone to stay with me. Till and Leroy [Mary's sister and brother-in-law] is going to leave this week they have taken Lindsley's place over the river and he wants to go to ploughing. I can't leave on account of the grain and I can't stay alone very well. The old cow gets out once in a while and never thinks to come home. I have had one letter from mother and Emma. They are well, their cow bothers them about laying out.

Oh dear husband it seems to me there is no one missed so much as you are. I hope you will not leave Madison before election, and then I do hope and trust there will be something done to stop the war and reprieve you the dearest darling of my heart, our dear little Lucy is so winning she calls her papa, she creeps all over as fast as can go, she will get up by the lounge or chair or anything she can get a hold of. You wrote about sending some things home. I don't know what the price of delaine is there. I have inquired the price here and there's nothing short of 60 cents a yard if they are more than .50 there don't get them we can't afford it I will get along with something else that is cheaper. Your potatoes are going to turn out good they is large and a good many in a hill. The further piece of corn is not good for anything but the stalks. I shall be so glad when I am free of this place. I have a great deal of sewing to do for myself and baby and the Indians are here every day or two so I can't settle down to sew at all. I wished I had to sew for you this fall, Oh how it makes my heart ache when I think I have no work to do for you. I can pray for you and I do my dear one every day and night of my life. The baby is worrying and I must stop.

When your money comes will the five dollars come too or won't it come yet, when you send your clothes send me your picture if you ain't going to get a furlough but try and come if you can get one possibly. I can't write any more at present.

Do the best you can for yourself and take care of yourself. I have lots to tell you but can't write it. Good-bye for the present accept these few words from your own affectionate Wife and baby.

Mary E. Burwell

Mrs. Gage told me to tell you she wished she could see you running into her pantry for something to eat.

From Mary Burwell at Packwaukee to Andrew Burwell, September 15, 1864

My Dearest Husband,

I am very sorry that you had not received any of my letters when you wrote last, but do not think for a minute, dear one, that I would neglect to write to you, but I think by the time this reaches you, you will have three. I have answered your letters as soon as I got them. Mattilda and Leroy and myself have been up to Harrisville to mill today. He was going up with a grist for himself, and some for father, so I thought I would have some go too, and in fact I was out of flour, so tonight, Till and I are alone. Leroy has gone to town with the team that he hired. They intend to go to housekeeping next Monday, and then I expect father will be here cutting corn, and I shall either have to go down house and stay while he is here, or mother will have to stay alone nights, or father go home and I stay alone, and it is so far he can't stand it to travel back and forth and work all day too and I don't know what is best, for me to do. They think it would be best for me to go down home and stay two or three days and leave enough cooked to last him that long, and he would milk the cow and feed, and I don't know how I am to do that. I do wished you could come home long enough to get the grain moved and me settled, but dearest husband, don' t let these things trouble you. I will get along the best way I can, but the hardest of it all is to think my dear loving husband is so far away from me, it is as you say, it don't seem possible that we can be separated so long. It seems when I am setting up late as I am tonight, all alone, that I am waiting for you to come home to sleep with me and dear little Lucy, but I don't hear your voice nor your footstep coming. O, Darling, it seems sometime as if my heart must burst. I have never felt so grieved before, but darling one, we must both cheer up and comfort each all we can by writing letters and trust in God that we may be reading them both together before long. I am sorry you have such bad company around you, but oh, I am so thankful that you do not take pattern by them. I hope my dear husband that you will continue to resist all evil that may come in your way. You have my prayers, dear one, and many others. I think sometimes how happy we shall be if you live to come back and Lucy and I live to see you. What comfort we will take talking of things that happened while we were apart, but oh dear, what shall I do when you leave the state. They tell me here that your year don't begin until you are mustered. Do tell me if that is so. I will believe it when I hear from you.

From Mary Burwell at Packwaukee to Andrew Burwell, September 20, 1864

Dear husband,

Another day of this lonesome time has passed and it is night and all is still and quiet so I thought I would write a few lines to let you know that we are all well and I hope you are the same. I am down home now staying with mother while father cuts up the corn. I went to town yesterday to get that money but Mr. Gaylord said the certificate had not come yet and for that reason I will not get the money. He was intending to start for Fox Lake the same day.

The 22nd

You see I did not finish writing this the same night that I began it. I thought I would have that money business all settled by this time so that I could tell you all about it but I can't this time. I don't see the reason why they was not sent right along. I expect Leroy will be going with you. Mr. Gage said he would send the five dollars with Leroy. Mr. James Jones was here today as he was on his way to Madison. I saw Mr. Hubble and he said he was going to get up a box of stuff to take back with him and I thought I would send you a roll of butter and I will take some cake of some kind. I have written to mother and sent for those boots and if they get down in time I will send them out if I can get another pair that is at home toed and heeled. I would like to have you find Leroy and I in the box. I was very glad to see your dear face when I opened that letter and that little curl of mine that I thought so much of. I will send you mine and baby's as soon as I can get them. If you thought I might have made a mistake about the grain. I might have done it but I took it off from the book where Richard wrote it all down. He might have made a mistake in writing down the figures but I will send you the leaf that it is on when I write again. The book is not with me now. I got along very well with the Threshers. Father and Richard and Till and Leroy stayed with me that night. I will have you think how I felt about you. I can't write it in words to you I have no time but dearest husband we will talk lots when we meet again. Andrew do be careful about being out where there is danger of being shot if you are not obliged to be. How hard it must be for that poor woman to see her man die so. When you get your picture taken again I would get it on a plate. You look some lonesome but it looks very much like you. It is bedtime and I must bid you goodnight with a heavy heart.

From your ever affectionate and loving wife, Mary.

Please excuse the grease that is on this letter, it went against the lamp. Mr. Stowe is dead and Mr. Weaver's little boy was not expected to live one minute from the other on Wednesday. I have not heard from it since. Our little Lucy has got one tooth on the under gums.

I would write two inch sheets as this full if I had the time but you will excuse me dear one as it is very late.

I suppose you are not going to have any office. If you need another blanket let me know.

From Mary Burwell at Montello to Andrew Burwell, September 25, 1864

Dearest Husband

    It is Sunday and the baby has gone to sleep, so I thought I would spend the time I have writing to you. I have not much more to tell you this time, but still I have got plenty to say to you. The weather is quite pleasant here now we have had some frost that killed the vines all down, it is very warm to day. I should like very much to come and see you if I could, but it is impossible for me to come with the baby I would have so much to do to get ready and then you might be gone the time I got there. I should have liked to been there when the 42nd Regiment left, how pretty they must have looked, but dear Andrew, it does make my heart ache some when I think you are gone to the army.[7]

    I can't hardly contain myself it seems so hard to direct your letters as I do sometimes. I think how can I write that direction. I feel so sorry for you, not to get my letters often. I think the reason they was so long they went by the way of Kilbourne, and I will mail my letters in Montello until I move and they will go to Pardeeville and right on to Madison quicker than the other way. I hope when you leave where you are you go to Minnesota so you will not be in so much danger there I hope, but I hear the Indians is troubling there again. I shall worry some about you if you go there but not so much as I would if you went south but my dear husband you know that I have great faith praying to God and I know that he does answer my prayers. Now dear one I hope you are striving to do as you promised me when you went away, you know you said you would stop swearing. I think a great deal of that promise and the little book you took away with you and pray to God every night you have the chance to and then we will both be doing the same thing at the same time.

    I have had a bad cold since I came down here but am getting better now, the baby is very cross just now she is cutting her teeth though now she has got one. She is in my arms the most of the time and I can't get much time to do anything. I write your letter in such a hurry that I am ashamed of the writing but will excuse it all, you know how it is. Father has hired Jacob Shibely for three days to finish cutting the corn. He has got to cut his buckwheat and sell his hogs this week so I shall have to go back home in the morning and live with Jacob for three or four days and tomorrow I will bake something for my dearest husband to eat if it is not so nice as some of the other parcels will be it will be some of your Mary's cooking and butter, and

Mother sends you a roll of her butter too. I showed little Lucy your picture today and she acted as if she knew who it was, she would hold it up over her head and kiss it. And lay it down on her lap and look at it as if she knew it was her dear papa. Jane says she wished you was here to bother her again, she was very pleased with your hair. I will send you some of mine and the baby's if you don't come home before you go off. I do hope they will let you. I can't bear to think of not seeing you for a year.

My dear husband I have met with a disappointment this morning. Mr. Rood came down here to buy father's hog and told me that Hubble had gone back, so I can't send you anything more. I may have another chance before long I feel so bad about it I don't know what to do. Rood tells me you are to leave right off. Hubble promised to let me know but because I am so far from town and can't go after them, they will go and I wont' know anything about it until they are gone but good bye dear one for the present from your dear loving Wife,

Mary.

From Mary Burwell at Packwaukee to Andrew Burwell, September 27, 1864

Dear Husband

It is night again my little charge has gone to sleep. I am left alone to think of you're the dearest on earth to me. I have fretted considerable to day, on account of your leaving the State, and going to a different place from where I expect you would go, meeting one disappointment after another here at home it just about fills my heart full, you must think it hard of me not to send you some things out by some of the men being back and forth but my dear husband they come and go and I won't know anything about it until after they are gone, I did see Hubble and he said he would let me know if he took a box time enough to send you some the things the first I know he was gone, you can't think how grieved I did feel. I would have sent the socks anyway if I had them, but I should think mother would have sent them to you by this time if she had the chance.

About our pictures my dear one I did not get the letter until after the men had gone and I can get them taken short of Portage but I will send you the ones I have here the next time I write. I thought I would not send them this time because I am not sure whether you will be home or not, but the time I write my next I expect to know but dear love, you shall have them, but oh how hard to have you leave without seeing me but don't yourself into trouble for the sake of coming it is hard enough to put up with what you are obliged to, without making it any harder think one month has gone what a long time it does seem since I have seen you. I dream of you almost every night. I pass a great many sleepless nights.

I have sold my hog and got 18 dollars for him. I have found out the mistake that I made in the amount of grain. I took the one dollar & 6 cents for the bushel instead of what it is. It is plain enough when I come to look at it but I will send you the leaf and then you can see yourself, don't worry about me not going to live with mother. I am going up there just as soon as I set everything straight. I have a good deal to see to and it is hard me to write with the baby she is very cross these times and I have to catch my time to write to you but I will do that if I don't sleep. You know the baby don't sleep long to a time in the day, she don't give me much chance to work. I will send her some money to get the paper with and will write to her but it will be long before I will be there. I can't do much sewing till I get there, I am at home now until father gets his buckwheat cut. The poor man I do pity him so much for he can't get a day's help from anyone. I wrote to you that he had hired Jacob Shibley but he did not come. I will have to hire someone to help him draw the grain to Oxford he dreads that worse than all. He has so much on hand he don't know what to do first. I could get up there sooner if he had not got so much to do, but I can't leave the place until my things are all off, I suppose mother and Em has nothing to do more than usual so that makes the time seem longer to them. But if they both was here and see what I have to get along with they would think they had their hearts and hands full but trouble will pass along with if my dear husband is only spared to come home to live with me again. I can put up with everything else. Don't worry about me, my own dear one, but trust in God and if he should see fit to take you to that home above, first I will strive to train our dear little girl up for heaven and live so as to come there myself we will dwell there together forever never to be parted again, but will hope to meet again here. It is very late and I must close with my best love to you my dear.

From Mary Burwell at Packwaukee to Andrew Burwell, October 2, 1864

Dearest Husband,

I received your much welcome letters of the 24th and 28th yesterday and was very glad to hear you are well and in such good spirits and I hope this will find you enjoying the same blessing still as it leaves me well as usual but little Lucy has got some cold but nothing serious. I have had some trouble lately with the Cattle and horses getting in the field they have destroyed the most of it in spite all I could do we shut up what we could get in the stable one morning and sent word to the owner to come and pay the damages and get their horses, but that night some one came and let the horse out it was not the owner for he was to Portage it was Mr. Booth that owned them and I sent word to Sam Stimpson and I hired Marvin Busseck to come and get rest of the corn and last night they finished it and Sam is coming tomorrow to husk it and with all the misfortune Father has hurt his hand so I have hired Mr. Russell to take a load of grain up to Portage and Marvin to dig my potatoes. I could not do any other way it is coming cold and I can't stay here any longer than I am obliged to on account of my dear baby it is hard for me to get along with her. Mornings she wakes up as soon as I do and wont stay in bed till I build a fire, and the house is too cold for her to get up unless there is a fire, but all these little troubles will be over this week and then I will go to Mother's and do some trading and when father gets able to move me I will go to Oxford. I have sold the cow to Mr. Hovey as you agreed to but now I don't see what we want with so much hay. The heifer and Cherry will not eat all of what the cows fetches and what we have too, I don't know how much you have got to Kingsley's please tell me, but if we have more than we want, we can sell it. I have got your bounty money and let Gage have it and got the note and mortgage all right and when I go to Montello I will record it. About our pictures hardly know what to do for I was afraid to send them to Madison for fear you would be gone and they get lost when you get settled again I will send them to you without fail, my dearest one. I have given up coming to see you but my darling husband, don't think that I blame you for I don't. I know you would come if you could it seems awful hard to have you go away off down there. I hope you will not have to go into battle. I am glad Em sent you that little work pocket I was going to send you one but that will do just as well if I would like to send you a great many things if I could ever get the chance. I am looking for you every night now but when I hear you have left Madison I shall have to give it up for so long. I tell you dearest husband it looks dreary and lonesome here. No hog to feed, no cow to milk, and Till and Leroy is going to leave me when I got my letter wrote and then I shall be all alone. They are in a hurry to go and the baby is crying so I must draw this to a close. I will take good care of the baby and will try to live in hopes of seeing you again. Receive this from your ever affectionate and loving Wife.

From Mary Burwell at Packwaukee to Andrew Burwell, October 5, 1864

My Dearest Husband,

Once again I sit down to write to you to let you know how I prosper in this world of trouble. I am well and Lucy is getting along nicely. I hope you are well and enjoying yourself as well as you was when you wrote last week. I felt better reading them letters than any I have had yet. I am glad you have so little to do. It must seem funny to you to have so little work to do. I hope you won't have any more to do than you have now, while you stay. We are all overrun with work here. How glad I should be if you could happen to be as lucky as Christopher Cook has been. He found a little fault with something, I forget what, and they gave him his discharge and told him to leave, but did not pay him a cent. He is home now and is going to work his own place, but I would not care for your wages if you could only come home and be free once more. The Packwaukee folks are trying to raise money to clear the town. They have got the men ready. I do not know who they were. Mr. Russell took a load of grain to Oxford for me on Monday, and mother came back with him. I was very glad to see her. Till and Leroy had left me on Sunday, but they sent Laura up to stay with me, so I was not entirely alone. The corn is all off, but not husked. Marvin Russell has got my potatoes dug, but they are out in the field yet. He fenced around them good and high and covered them up good so they will not hurt for a day or two until father comes and gets them in. I don't know exactly how many there is, but he said he guessed there was forty bushels. They are nice and large. I had to pay him a dollar a day and his brother twenty shillings for going to Oxford. I tell you, dearest husband, it comes hard for me to hire such things done, it ain't like it was when you was here to look to everything yourself, but I will do the best I can with it all. I am willing to put up with all the troubles I have to go through with, if you are only spared to come home to cheer up this lonely heart that is wishing and praying with all earnestness for your safe return.

My own dear one, it seems as if you had been gone long enough now to be gone a year, but dear me, it only five weeks. It does seem so hard to have you gone so long from me. I have lived in some hopes of seeing you before you left Madison (for I expect you are gone by this time), but now I shall have to give it up, with the hope that you will come for good before the year is up. But oh how hard it is my darling one, to have you go away off down there where I can't get to you if you are sick, but be sure to take the best kind of care of yourself, and I will do the same, and your dear little girl will be taken care of and clothed warm and good. She is a dear little creature. She mocks me setting the dog on the cattle and shakes her little fist at them. If I ask her where her papa is, she looks over in the field for you. I believe she would know you if she could see you. I have not received your letter this week yet, so I don't know whether you have left Madison or not, but I think I will wait until I write next time before I send my pictures. I will send the ones I have at home now, and will send the baby's after I get her winter dress made, but I will send the ones I have now. She will look different to you than when you seen her last. I will send you a lock of her hair and mine this time. This will help you wait for the pictures. I think of the ones you sent me. My dearest Andrew, have you applied for the five dollars that I draw, or must I apply for it myself? Your mother tells me I must go before a Justice. Nancy said that she had to go, and it cost her 50 cents to get the first papers made out. Now, dear one, let me know if you have said anything about it, or if I must. I sent mother some money to subscribe for the paper, and I think we will get another one this week. I hope you have got your clothes by this time. How you must need them. I am so sorry you did not take more with you, seeing I have not had the chance to send you any. I think of you every minute of the time. When we have something to eat that you like so well, how I do wish you was here to eat with me. You sent me some pretty little verses, but my own dear love, it made my heart ache and the tears run in spite of me when I read them. I hope you don't think that I have forgotten to write to you, the one that I love dearest of all on earth, the baby included, it says, what can the matter be, why don't I write? My dear one, I do write two letters every week to you. But don't think I take it to heart and think you mean it, because I don't trust to me dear one, and I will trust to you. But let us both put our trusts in God and he will bring us safe through all our troubles. It is bedtime, and I must close with love to my dear husband from your loving wife.

Mary E. Burwell

From Mary Burwell at Montello to Andrew Burwell, October 18, 1864

My Dear Husband

I received three letters from you this morning and was very glad to hear from you, I have spent some very uneasy moments since you left Madison until I heard from you, but dear one what anxious hours I shall spend now you are so far away from home amongst the dangers and so many accidents happening all the times. But all I can do is trust in God to keep you safe from harm, I should like to have been travelling with you to see the beautiful sights that you have seen but I should not like to see you sleeping on the sidewalks and eating such poor victuals. Oh how hard it is to know that you have to put up with such hardships, when we used to have, what little we did have, so comfortable at home, but I do hope we shall live together again. I am trying to keep up my spirits as well as I can but when I think where you are it sets me to worrying so I can't hardly keep my mind and reason together.

Little Lucy is growing very much like her father in her ways. She seems to understand most all we say. She is very cross all the time she has not got any more teeth but will have soon. She is not out of my arms twenty minutes all day and sleeps so little at night to get my sewing done and I feel very much tired but dear husband don't worry about me, I will take care of the dear little creature for you to love when you get home. I suppose you have our pictures by this time. They was taken on the 13th but don't think I look quite as bad as my likeness looks for I don't. We started for Portage before daylight and by the time we got our trading done we were very tired and not having any dinner either made me look worse and the baby was so cross I could not do hardly anything with her. Mrs. Jolly said I could not have her taken any other way, she did not care how I looked so long as the baby's was good. Jason Daniels took Mother and I out for twelve shillings apiece. I bought the baby a blue cloak that was a yard long, 5 bib aprons, and three dresses, hood and pink apron and white and two dresses for myself and some flannel for some undershirts. I send you some pieces of our dresses that red one the baby had on when her picture was taken. I was sorry I could not get a new one to have mine taken in but I could not get time to make if I had it, it paid me well for going down. I got delaine 6° and I had mother get her likeness taken it is a very good one.

I tell you my dear husband I am very glad you sent me your pictures in your soldier clothes. It looks like very good but oh how it makes my heart ache to see you dressed in such clothes. I hope you never will have to use that awful looking gun you have hold of. I like the one that is alone the best your face looks so sweet to me. I would like to know what you meant by going into the field. I hope they wont set you to fighting the first thing but I suppose your Camp is in the fields. What pretty verses you sent me. I could not read them all at one time, it made me feel so bad when I rec'd the letters hear how many accidents happen. I hope you will keep out of danger so far as is in your power, my dear one. I had no idea we were so far apart, dear one, it does seem as if I could not have it so. I dream of you most every night sometimes wake up very disappointed. Oh how I do hope and pray you will not have to go into any battle. Do let me know all the particulars about yourself, my dear one. Don't keep anything from me, if you get sick do be careful and get things that you need and take care in time don't go into the hospital for fear of catching disease. I don't know how I should live if I heard you was in the hospital sick and I can't come and take care of you with my baby it is a hard thing to think of, I think and wonder I am alone will you ever come back or not. Then something seems to tell me he will be coming back then I cheer up. Oh dear Andrew, won't we be happy when we go to housekeeping again we will have so much to tell each other and I hope a dear little girl to chatter with us. I have got your satchel and clothes. I will wash them and keep them until you come home. Father has been writing too and told you about his affairs on the place so I have no need to write about it. I don't know of any news. They have not drafted here yet and some think they won't. It is eleven o'clock and I must stop and go to bed. I think of going to Oxford next week if nothing happens my dear husband. I want you to keep a paper with your name and where you live and then if anything happens to you they will know who you are.

From Mary Burwell at Packwaukee to Andrew Burwell, October 23, 1864

My Dear Husband,

It is Sunday evening and I thought I would spend it writing to you. I and baby is well as usual. I came up to Packwaukee yesterday to make Mrs. Gage a visit, and Matillda and Leroy one also, but did not get any letter from you, but suppose I must not expect so many now you are so far away, but I am so anxious to hear from you that I would be glad to hear every day if it was a possible thing, but it is not, so I must be satisfied with what I can get, but my own dear Andrew, I do feel so lonely for you. Wherever I am, I am thinking of you every minute. Oh, how it does worry me that you are so near the fighting. I am so afraid they will put you into battle, I cannot rest a minute. I just tremble and shake all the time since you wrote to me and sent your pictures. I look at dear little Lucy and see her play so cunning, and then I wonder if her dear papa will be here this time next year to see her play, and then the tears will roll and the dear little creature will look at me as if she would ask me what the matter was if she could. But oh my dearest husband, it does seem as if my heart must break sometimes when I think what a dangerous place you are in and so liable to get sick, and I was telling mother the other night, whilst I might be sitting here sewing and trying to think what you are doing, you might be suffering in great misery or you might be dead. Oh what awful thoughts that my dear little man should ever suffer such things. God forbid it my darling one, it almost makes me crazy at times to think of it I do really trust and pray to the Lord of heaven, that you never will be called to fight and I hope the war will be closed in a short time after election. It is coming near now. I am here with Mattilda and Leroy tonight. I tell you dear one, it makes me think us when living alone at first. They have new dishes and a very pleasant house and place as far as I can see tonight. Oh what comforts we would all take together if you was only here to go with me, but my darling one, I feel like one alone wherever I am since you have been gone, but I suppose I had not ought to complain as long as I am well cared for. Folks ain't as they was before you went away. I do as I am a mind to and have what I have a mind to when I am at home, and as long as you are well, I had not ought to worry so, I know, but you think of everything I fret and worry it will be so, but my own dear husband, let us pray earnestly and believe faithfully in God and we will live together again. We will hope for it anyway. Oh, I hope we will not be disappointed. I am going to Oxford next Saturday with the stage. There will be such a load and I should have to stay there overnight on the place and baby might take cold being without a fire. I could not do that. Father is going up with the goods on Friday and come back the next day. I shall be so glad when I get settled where I shall stop until you come back, and then I hope we shall have a nice little home of our own, I hope sooner than we expect it. I was up to see Mr. Weaver's child today. It is alive yet, but that is about all. It is an awful looking sight, it is so poor. The report is around that ____ Clark and Sarah ____ is getting married. They may be now for what I know. I have not heard. I hear they are going to commence drafting here the 1st of next month. I am afraid Leroy will have to go after all. That will be too bad, after reenlisting him, I should feel worse about you if you were the drafted man. My dear one, your pictures brings tears to my eyes every time I look at them, and I look at them every chance I get. The one that is alone does look so sweet, the face I mean, not the clothes. But most every one that has seen them say that you are the best looking soldier they have seen, and your mate looks enough like you to be your brother. Give my respects to him and I hope you will both take care of each other as well as you can. Till and Leroy has gone to bed _____ and I must bring this to a close. Let me know your situations and all you hear that is going to be done with you. Pray for me and Lucy, when you pray. May the Lord bless you while striving to be a Christian and bring you safe home to _____ is the prayer of your ever affectionate wife,

Mary.

From Mary Burwell at Oxford to Andrew Burwell, October 30, 1864

My Dear Husband

Once again I set down to write a few lines to you to let you know that I and the baby is well as usual, and I hope and trust that this will find you enjoying better health than when you wrote the letter dated 19th. I am so afraid you will get so that you can't stand it to lay out at night, in all kinds of weather, I can't help but worry about you, dear one. I know just how much care you need when you are sick and I know you won't get much care down there, but I want you to take all the care you possibly can take of yourself. I wish I could be with you to help you bear your hardships or I rather wish you could be here with me free from the war, I did feel quite encouraged when you wrote about doing Cook for the officers and not having guard duty to do, but the next letter you had been doing such a hard time of it that I could not bear to think of it. It does seem as if the ground would not hold me. My feet feel as if they would leave the ground and fly to you if it was possible. I do hope they will station you all to one place or the other before long. I do wish I could see you here tonight. It don't seem as if it could be so that I am not to see you all winter.

I arrived here at Oxford safe and sound last night and was glad to get here for I was very tired and it was dark before we got here. Little Lucy has been very busy creeping all around in her new home today. Poor little thing, she has been from one place to the other so much lately that she don't know what it means. She has not forgot to call her papa. She thinks a great deal of Father and it pleases him very much, she took right to him when you left. I have twenty-five bushels of corn left for my share. It is more than I expected to have, it has been an awful sight of trouble to me and might have been more if I did not have any other trouble. But my own dear Andrew, I can put up with almost anything if you can only be spared to come home to cheer your little woman's heart again.

Oh what a joyous time that will be, my dear one, when we can be together again. I often think of it. What comfort we will take in reading the letters and talking of what has happened while we have been apart. I have lots to tell you, and I know you have got lots to tell me, how I do hope and pray that we may be favored so much as to see one another once more.

I would like to know if you have got my picture yet. I am afraid they will not come to you. I hope you will keep the situation of being cook as long as you can, anything to keep out of battle. Leroy is very much afraid he will have to go to. Till says she will live there on the place if he does go. Have you heard from Richard yet? Our folks have not heard from but once since he left. He is to the same place that he was when he was away before. When you write to him if you do before he writes to you direct to Poynette, Columbia Co.

I have just been up to the Post Office and got a letter from you dated 23rd. I feel some better about you to day, since I got your letter. You see I did not finish my letter last night. I thought I would wait until the mail comes in today. I am so glad that you are Cook and that you are well. I really do hope that you will keep the place. I have made application for my five dollars. The baby does not walk yet but she tries to talk, and will walk by the side of the bed or chair.

I don't see the reason why you have been so long without a letter from me. It may be because you move around so much. I feel very anxious to know if you have received our likeness or not. I would like to know if you have a stove to cook by or do you have a fire on the ground. How do you bake bread? When you have chicken you can cut them up and wash them clean and put them in your kettle to boil and put some salt in when you part them over, and skim scum and when they are done stir up a little flour and make a gravy. That will be nice on bread or whatever you have, and Mother says if you can get some Williams baking powder it would be handy for you. You take two tablespoons of the powder and stir it good in your flour and take a pint of water and a little salt and a little butter, if you have it and mix your dough and bake it. I don't know how you manage to bake. If you have beef to fry, don' put water in it. You like the way I cook beef. I just fry it in fat or butter and pepper and salt it and fry it fast and not too much. When you write again tell me what you would like to know about the cooking. I could tell you a great deal more if I know whether you could get the materials or have the convenience to cook them with. I should think you would have plenty of fruit to use, my own dear husband. I shall be so thankful if you can keep this berth. I hope you will pray to the Lord to keep you safe, go to meeting when you can, and I will do the same.

Dear one, you keep telling me to tell you all the news. There is not much news to tell, only such sorrowful news of poor men losing their lives and leaving their poor families to mourn for them. George Stafford is dead. He was drafted and went to Madison, and lived there two or three weeks after he went there, his wife is almost crazy about him, and Theodore Stalkers is dead.

If you was here, my dearest one, I could tell you more than I can write. I would have give worlds if you could have been here with me this last week. My heart has been almost broke, but never mind my darling keep all to yourself, don't worry about me. I will put up with everything for your sake. I only hope and trust you will be spared to come to me again, accept these lines from your ever true and loving Wife

Mary E. Burwell.

From Mary Burwell at Oxford to Andrew Burwell, November 6, 1864

My Dear Husband,

I received a letter from you last Monday date Oct. 23rd and have not had any since, but expect one tomorrow. We are all well as usual with the exception of a little cold that I have taken in my head someway, and it is settled in my teeth. They trouble me considerable. I hope you are in good health that is such a good thing, how I would like to see your village of dog tents as you called them. I think they must be very cold to sleep in, some of these awful cold nights, but I suppose you wont see such cold weather there as we had here last winter at least I hope not. I don't want to either.

I hope you are cook yet, dear husband you remember what a fret I was in this time last year for fear you would be drafted. I did not think then that we should be as far apart now. I was in hopes the wretched war would be closed before this time but my dear Andrew it is hard as it is but how much harder it would be to have you drafted, and you surely would be if you was here. I shall hear who is drafted so as to tell you the next time I write. Oh my beloved husband, it does seem so hard for you to be away from you all this long time. How glad and rejoiced I should be if you could come home in the spring. I do miss you so much to talk with, there is not a minute passes without my thinking of you, and I dream about you most every night.

Our dear little girl is growing so nicely, she tries to talk. She will say "see there" plain and just begins to call her mam mam, she almost stands alone. I think, if she does well, she will run alone by the time she is a year old, but how I do want you here to see her perform, for she is just as cunning as she can be. I am going to make her cloak this week if nothing happens. Next Saturday and Sunday is quarterly meeting, and I want to go if I can get ready. I wish you was here to go with me, the old place looks so natural to me whenever you and I used to go, but my dear one you can't think how lonely it makes me feel when I look around where we have been together so much, and now you are away off so far from me, but we can't help it. Put your whole trust in God, my dearest husband, and we will try and think it is all for the best. I only hope and pray that you may come home safe to join our family circle once more.

I went down to the place last Thursday to get the remainder of my things that Father could not bring. I had to hire a team a boy to fetch them and then I had to get Mr. Russell to help lead them, the boy was too small and had a sore finger, too, but it was all I could get. Men are very scarce here, and I could not take the heifer that night, so I went over to Mr. Pitt and got his two boys to bring her up the next day. Well they brought her us the next day and she is very contented, they charged me twelve shillings. Mr. Russell did not charge me anything for leading but wanted I should tell you he sends his best respect to you and wants you to take good care of yourself. Mother bought a little Suffolk pig and wanted I should buy one like it so I did and give 50 cents for him, they are . . .[8]

Lincoln was reelected on November 8, 1864, with Andrew Johnson, the federal military governor of Tennessee, as his running mate. His Democratic opponent, the still popular George McClellan, received 45 percent of the vote but won only three states (New Jersey, Kentucky, and Delaware).[9] The vote at home in Wisconsin was close, with 68,887 voting for Lincoln and 65,598 voting for the Democrats; however, the soldiers at the war front voted overwhelmingly for Lincoln, with Wisconsin soldiers voting for Lincoln 11,372 to 2,428.[10] Although Lincoln was the overwhelming choice of soldiers throughout the Union, winning 116,877 to 33,748 votes for McClellan, the soldiers' votes did not change the election results in any state.[11]

From Mary Burwell at Oxford to Andrew Burwell, November 13, 1864

Dear Husband

Once more I have the opportunity of writing to you, we are all well as usual, and I hope you are enjoying the same blessing. I am glad to hear that you are in good spirits, sometimes I am in good spirits but they are soon gone. I hear of someone that is snatched away from a dear family, no more to return in the world, or I hear of some awful affair or other that has happened, and I can't help but worry and fear and tremble for you, the one that is so dear to me. I and Emma and Lucy has just got home from quarterly meeting we heard a very good sermon and little Lucy was very good; how I wish you was here to go to meeting with me once more, it is my daily prayer to God, my dear husband, that your life may be spared to cheer this lonely heart of mine, and not mine alone but a mother's and Sister and a dear little girl that I know misses her dear papa. I was glad to hear that you had received my picture. I felt I looked bad but I don't look quite so bad as that looks. I was very tired and worn out with the trouble and care of the place that it made quite an alteration in my looks. I begin to recruit up again now my appetite is very good and I think I shall get along pretty well. I don't intend to wean the baby until spring. We have no milk only what we buy, you write in every letter to take good care of her, I will dear one. She is not neglected a minute. It takes me thus about all the time to do our chores and house work and take care of her.

It is too bad that you don't get our letters faster. I feel very bad for you, we had been most two weeks without getting a letter from you, until last Thursday. I got me that one that was written the 27th of October. We were all very uneasy about you, but you had better believe I was glad when I found out you was all right, my dearest husband. I want you to write on a piece of paper your name and residence and your family's name and then if anything should happen to you, they would write to me and I would know all about you.[12] But dearest one, I hope there will be no reason for such a thing, and another thing I want of you. Your mother says that the Southerners poison the oyster beds and then they are put up and sold to the Soldiers, and a great many has lost their life in this way, and now dear Andrew for the sake of your dear wife and baby, and all that is dear, be on your guard for such things as these, don't eat any more oysters for fear that they are poisoned.

They say that the guerillas are going to burn Milwaukee and Chicago and are doing great disasters on the railroad.[13] I am afraid they will make trouble out this way if that is the case, the men is scarce in these parts, that we should fare pretty hard. I am afraid that the men that was drafted in Packwaukee was Columbus Cook, Ed Muffrey, John Palmer, Winegardner, John Kelsey, Sid Gifford, James Jones, and some others that I have not found out who they were but Leroy was not drafted. Mitchell Ramsey is dead and was brought home to be buried and they don't know whether Henry Conger is living or not. They can't find out. Charley Allen is dead.[14]

Oh my dear husband, I earnestly pray and trust to the Lord that you may be spared to come back home again. I can't think of anything else but you, and where you are, and what you are doing is my thought when I get to bed at night. I am alone then with my dear baby and can think where is my absent one tonight. What thoughts run through my mind but we will hope for the best. Three months have almost passed away.

Aunt Eliza is here now is going to stay a few days. She is looking for Avery home on furlough but don't know for certain. It is bedtime and I must draw this to a close they all gone to bed and I must bid my dearly beloved husband good night with the hopes of having you to sleep with little Lucy and I before long.

Write as often as you can and let me know if you want anything that I can send to you and I will do so.

Good night dear Andrew.

From your Mary

From Mary Burwell at Packwaukee to Andrew Burwell, November 24, 1863

You see by this letter that I am in Packwaukee tonight and I have a chance to send a letter to Portage to be mailed so I thought I [would] write a few lines to you, and hope they will find you as well as it leaves me and Lucy both well as usual. Mattilda has been sick and Leroy sent word for me to come down, so I came last Saturday on the stage and am here yet but she is better. I am going back tomorrow, on account of me being down here I have not got any letters from you this week but have heard that you are all right.

My dear darling one, it is Thanksgiving to day. You and I were together a year ago tonight we did not think then that would be so far apart at this time, but dear one, three months of this long dreaded time has passed I can feel thankful that you have been spared so far. I think by the appearance of things are far as I can understand, the war will soon be closed, at least it is my daily prayer that it may be, before spring.

Oh, my darling husband, I hope you won't have to go into battle. What an awful thought that is to me, dear one when I think of it I want to come where you are and hold your aching head in my lap once more. How good it will seem to have you come home and love little Lucy and I again. I miss you so much to talk with. I have so many little privacies to tell you, that I dare not write, but can't hardly wait to tell you but my dear love won't we have a grand time talking when you do come if the Lord sees fit to spare your life. I wish you will be home to spend Christmas with us but I don't expect you can.

Our little Fanny had a lamb last Sunday night. I haven't seen father since I left home but Leroy seen him and he says she is doing well. Zekiel Chapels wife had a pair of twins two or three weeks ago and both died. One was a boy, I think they will do. Mrs. Freeland had another little girl and Stephen Chapels wife has a baby, Remely has yet another but I think I have told enough about the babies.

Richard is coming home next month and is going back again to stay a year. I expect he has got him a wife picked out down there but don't know. I have not had any money from the State yet nor any of your money but I suppose it will come by and by. It is getting late, dearest one and I must close. Excuse this poor paper its something Leroy gave me. Receive these few lines from your loving and affectionate wife.

Mary Burwell to her Andrew—a kiss for you

I would write more if I was not afraid the baby would wake up but I will write more next time.

From Mary Burwell at Oxford to Andrew Burwell, November 27, 1864

My Dear Husband,

Once more I am permitted to write to a loved one that is far from me. I am glad to hear that you feel so well as you do. I am well, as usual. I have been down to see Mattilda for the week past, and last night, they brought me home. The weather has been very cold and stormy here last week, and it rains today. I would like to know what kind of weather you have where you are, and how you are off for stockings. If you need some, I will send you a pair and pair of mittens too if you need them, and I think they would be very good for you when it is cold weather. I am very much relieved when you wrote that election passed off still and peaceable. I was so afraid there would be a great fight.[15] I really do hope you won't have to do any fighting. I had rather you would do the cooking. I hope the fighting is about done. They seem to think so up this way. The copperheads are all very still up this way since the Election. I am very happy to hear from you, my dearest husband that you have taken the course you have since we have been separated. Improve all you can, dear one, and ask God to help you, and I will do the same, and do every day of my life, and I hope He will spare your dear life to help me bring up this dear little girl. She is such a dear little creature. You said you did not think she would know you. I don't know about it; she might. She thinks a good deal of your pictures, and will kiss them and say, papa. I tell her that is papa. I wish you could come home, my dear husband, for a little while. It would seem so good to see you here again. Lucy will stand alone and walk a few steps from one to the other alone, but don't go entirely alone yet. She cuts her teeth very slow. I think maybe it is better for her. She is great hand to eat meat. If she sees meat on anyone's plate, she gets down off my lap and creeps to them, and will eat apples as long as well feed them to her. Mr. Gage takes her behind the counter and lets her help herself, and that pleases her very much. She always aims for the biggest, if they give her a little one, she throws it down and points to the big ones. We all think she is about right. I am going to send to Portage for a highchair for her the first good chance I get. You wanted I should tell you all the news of importance. I don't know as there is any more than I wrote in my last letter, the one dated the 26th. I have sold what hay was down on Kingsley's marsh to Leroy for four dollars a ton, and I am going to take when we want of Hovey. He has brought us on one load. I thought that would be better than to hire a team to draw the hay so far. I shan't take any more hay of Hovey than we want for the two cows, and the rest he must pay in money. Dear Andrew, don't you think we had better keep the calves if we have good luck with them. They will come [in] handy if they are both steers. They will be so near of an age, and we can get something for them, if we don't want them. But my dearest one, I hope that you will come home to keep house with me again.

    I am sorry you have to carry such a load, but I suppose it is all needed. When you get to your stopping place, I should think they would let you put your knapsack in one of the wagons. Leroy said you ain't obliged to carry it, seeing that you are an officers' cook. If you will carry it, he says you may.

"The weather has been very cold and stormy here last week." An American farmyard in winter. (Wisconsin Historical Society, WHS 2382)

They won't hinder you, but if you are a mind to stand out about it, they would let you put it in the wagons. I shall be glad when you are put into winter quarters. I would like to have you here to spend Christmas and New Year with us. If you can't, why, I must be contented to think it is as well with us as it is, dearest one, as you say. The Lord does all things for the best. I would give a good deal to see you tonight. It would seem so good to talk with you once more, and I have lots to tell you that I can't write in a letter. I received Mr. Kribb's picture in one of your letters. He looks very natural.[16]

Give my regards to Mr. Thompson and tell him I hope he will go through this tedious year safe for the sake of his aged parents, and hope you will both take comfort together, after you get home. My dearly beloved husband, it's getting very late, and I must close this. Receive this letter from an ever true and loving wife, to an affectionate Husband.

Mary E. Burwell

From Mary Burwell at Oxford to Andrew W. Burwell, December 4, 1864

My Dear Husband,

It is Sunday evening and I have just got my dear little girl to sleep, so I thought I would spend the remainder of the evening in writing to a beloved husband, that is far from me tonight, my dear one. I miss your company so much on Sunday. Living here so close by Mr. Bell's brings to mind the many happy Sunday evenings you and I have spent there together. Only think, dearest Andrew, how many changes has taken place since then. We did not dream of being separated from each other so long as this, but dear husband, let us be thankful that it is as well with as it is. Many are worse off than we are. I feel as if I had not ought to complain, when you are in such a good place. It makes my heart ache when I think of poor Nancy Wright. We got a letter from her last week, and she writes as if she thought she would not live long. She said in her letter, if it was not for her two children, this would be of no consequence to her, since Ebb is gone.[17]

I would feel just so myself my dearest husband if you was taken from me. My dear little girl would be all that tied me to this world, but I hope we shall live to see one another once more and enjoy each other's society again. I do wish you could be here this winter and see our dear little Lucy play. I know you would laugh to see her. She trys to do everything she sees us do. When she gets to the table, she call for tea as plain as I would say it, only she has such a cunning way with her. She understands almost everything we say to her. She is getting quite fat. She is like her father, a great hand for apples, and she wants us to take a knife and scrape them for her. She almost runs alone. I tell you, when she does go, she is going to travel fast. Her movements are as quick as ever. We have to keep our eyes open when she is around. Do you have any fruit of any kind or any cider? Mr. Gage has three barrels of cider and barrel of boiled cider. I have not had any of it yet. Does the Guerillas go trouble any down where you are? We read about them in the papers. I am afraid they will come along when you are alone in camp sometime, and then if they should, you would have a poor chance. Tell me if there is other men left in camps around you. I suppose there is some about. You ain't left all alone, are you? I suppose you think I am a good hand to find something to worry about, but my dearest husband, I can't help but think of all these things. There are so many dangers where you are, to what there are here at home. O dear, won't I be a thankful creature if you arrived home safe of your year or sooner. I had rather it be in the spring and then you would not have the hot weather to go through. I am afraid you can't stand the heat, but we won't borrow trouble so far ahead as that.

I have no news to tell you that I can think of. I bought me pair of shoes the other day. I am busy making my new dress that I sent you a piece off, and mother is spinning. I have been trying my hand at it and done very well for the first. I think by next fall, if I live, I can spin my own wool. What kind of weather do you have down where you are? It is quite comfortable here now. We had a little fall of snow last night. Do you have a better bed than you did a while ago?

I have not had a letter from you since last Tuesday, but I hope tomorrow night will bring one. I can't think of any more at present that I can write. Good bye dear husband for this time.

> Do not droop my dearest love
> Though grief may burden some
> Look up to God, for he hath love
> And comfort in great store
> And oft times moveth human hearts
> To bless us oer and oer

From your true and
Affectionate Wife, Mary Burwell
And a good kiss to you

From Mary Burwell at Oxford to Andrew Burwell, December 7, 1864

My Dear Husband,

I received a letter from you last night that was written the 26th of November was glad to hear that you was well and in good spirits. We are all well as usual, but we all feel very bad on account of you not getting our letters more regular, I don't see what the reason the mail can't go that way as well as coming this way. We get your letters a great deal more regular that you get ours. We get one every week and sometimes two, I think it is really too bad, it is hard enough to be away from home, without being deprived of the privilege of hearing from home, but, my dearest husband, don't think for a minute that I neglect writing to you for I don't. I send out two letters every week, I would write to you instead of sleeping rather than you should be without letters on my account, dearest one. I know how bad and disappointed you feel when you don't get a letter. There was a spell here, that we didn't get any letters from you. I tell you, my dearest Andrew, it seemed as if I should fall to the ground when Abbot [the postmaster] would say, no. But I get a letter every week now some weeks two, but when you don't get letters don't worry about us, it is the fault within the postmasters as they get delayed in some way, but we get along with our chores and with our business first rate. Our papers come regular every week, would you like to have us send you one now and then or do you get some there. Dear husband don't worry about me having a hard time doing chores, there is nothing too hard for me to do, as long as you are safe, you have it the hardest. I do it all for you, dear one. I get groceries and things that I want from Gage on the heifer account. I have not had any money at all yet. I don't see the reason of it. I am afraid they are neglecting to tend to it. I can't have time to write any more because the Stage has come and I must mail this letter so as to have it go right out.

Keep up great courage, little Lucy is well and begins to walk alone, she is a dear little girl. I hope and trust that peace will be declared before spring, so that you can come home [and] see your dear baby play. You would take so much comfort playing with her.

I must stop, we can't send this one out until Friday. It is hard to leave so much paper, I hope you will get this, right along.

Receive these few lines from an ever affectionate and loving Wife

Mary to her dear husband
A kiss to you love

From Mary Burwell at Oxford to Andrew Burwell, December 9, 1864

My Dearest Husband,

I received a letter from you yesterday and now hasten to answer it. It leaves us in good health and I hope it will find you enjoying the same blessing. I feel somewhat downhearted about you leaving to go on the boat. I am so much afraid that you be sick. I have felt quite encouraged about lately, but dear me, it was for so short a time, my dearest Andrew. It does seem so wicked and cruel to have you disappointed in getting my letters, when I write so many to you. It made my heart ache to read in your letter that you felt so bad because you had no letters. My dearest husband, I do not blame you for feeling bad, but it is not my fault. I write as I have said before, twice every week, and this letter makes the third for this week. It makes me feel bad when I am writing to you to think that it will be so long before you get it, and maybe not get it at all.

Oh my dear husband, what hard times these are. How I long to hear from you again so that I can know where you are going to be sent to now. How I do wish they were going to send you home. It is my daily prayer to God, my dear Andrew, that He will spare your dear life, to come home before the year is out, as you say, never to leave my side again until death separates us. I am afraid you will see some sick days if you are going on the water. I hope it is nothing but a rumor. Our dear little girl runs alone considerable, and she understands about all we say. She knows that when we get a letter, it is from you.

We have told her that it was papa's letter so many times that she can say, papa's, and is as pleased as we are to see one come. She can't wait until we read it, she is in such a hurry to have it, but I can't let her have them long, for she would destroy them. I save every one so as we can have them to read when you get back, if we all live to that long looked for time. Our little darling tries to talk, and some words she can say quite plain. She has got four teeth, and tries to do everything she sees us do. O dear how I do wish this cruel war would end before spring, so that you and many others could come home and enjoy the society of loved ones that are so dear. It does seem, sometimes as if I could not have it that you are away off with the army. Only think, dear Andrew, how long I have been fearing this, and now to think I have come to it, after all, it makes me want to fly away to you. It seems sometimes I could not stand it another day, but what can I do? I must put up with it, and pass away the time as well as I can. If you only keep well and could get my letters more regularly, I would feel better. I go to my bed at night with my dear little girl thinking, where is my dear loved one tonight, and will lay half the night thinking of times that is passed, and while (as you wrote in your letter) we will be together a year from now, and the Lord only knows my prayer is that we may be permitted to see each other again and live together as we did before you went away, only I think we shall live more like Christians than we did then. May God grant it, my only loved one, if I could only see you here again, I would be satisfied. It would be all I would ask. Such a load of anxious hopes and fears would be gone, but I must stop talking this way or you will be impatient and homesick. Keep up your courage as well as you can, dearest. When I think you are in good spirits, it makes me feel better. The wheels of time will soon roll this year away. If we try to keep a light heart, that will help time to pass off faster. I was glad to hear you had that goose. How did you cook it? On the evening of Thanksgiving you was writing to me, and I was writing to you, and mother was writing to you too. I think your Sgt Farr is very good looking.[18] It is a nice picture. I will take good care of all you send home. Old Mr. Farnham is come to town. I seen him around the streets, but have not seen him to speak to him, nor don't want to. It has been awful cold weather here for a few days, but is warmer tonight. There is not much snow on the ground. It is getting to be bedtime, and I must close with my best love to you, my dearest husband, from your ever true and affectionate wife,

Mary E. Burwell
My heart to you.

From Mary Burwell at Oxford to Andrew Burwell, December 11, 1864

My Dear Husband,

Sunday evening has come again and finds me writing to a beloved husband that is far from me. I am well, and straining my best to keep up my spirits for the sake of those around me. Many times when I appear to be in pretty good spirits, it puts me in mind of the sun trying to shine through the clouds. Sometimes I can laugh and talk, but beneath is a heavy heart, but dearest husband, I hope I shan't have to carry such a heavy heart long. I hope you will be relieved of your burdensome life before long. I hope you are well, wherever you be, and I hope you keep up good courage. I think that is a great thing to help you pass away time, not to be downhearted. It will soon be four months of the time gone. It passes away very fast for me. The days are short and I have a good deal of sewing to do for myself and Lucy.

I have not got any knitting done yet. Emma has knit the baby some striped stockings. The little thing takes up a good deal of my time when she is awake, and she is just as she always was, a regular little wide awake, but she is getting to sleep better night now, than she did. It would make you laugh if you was here to see her hold up her little hands and go from one to the other, alone. She is so pleased to have a letter from papa. She will go from one to the other as if she knew all about it. I don't know whether the little creature would know you or not. I almost think she would. I hope and trust, my dear Andrew, that she may have the chance to know her dear papa again. What lots of comfort we might have took with her this winter if you was only here, but we will trust in God and hope for the best. By the time you get home she will be so that she will talks some to you, if she lives, she will walk and you will take lots of comfort with her. I hope, if the Lord sees fit to spare your lives. The time looks long to look ahead, but when it is passed, a year seems but a short time. It don't seem but a very little while since last winter at this time. It has been one of the old fashioned blustering days today. The wind blew and drifted the snow and it was very cold, but we got along doing chores first rate. We bundled up warm. Emma and I are chore boys. We don't let mother go out in the cold any more than we can help. But my dear husband, the thought of you being out in the cold with so little clothes to keep you warm is harder to me than being out in it myself, because I know I have enough clothes to keep me warm, and I don't know that about you. But I hope you have enough to keep you comfortable. If you have money, you can buy what you want. Have you been mustered to pay yet? I have not received any money yet. I can't imagine what is the reason, but I ain't the only one. The rest of the women has not had any money either. I hope it will come out all right. I have money to use, but I am anxious to have what you send and what is coming to me all come right, for we won't have any to lose. I know you will find a place for every cent, if you are spared to come home. I do think that Till and Leroy might write to you. It might be they have, and you have not received them. When I was down there, I got acquainted with Mark Mielz's wife. He is in your company.[19] She is a real nice woman. I had a good talk with her. She is coming to see us when you and her man gets home. She worrys and frets about him for fear he never will come back. I suppose they don't mean to give any furloughs to you while you stay. I do get so impatient sometimes that I do not know what to do with myself. Only think I have not seen you in almost four months, and I dare not think how much longer it will be, but my dearest darling, I hope it won't be much longer. We can love each other if we be far apart. My love, is the same for you as ever, I know yours is the same for me, my only loved one.

> I love but in dying, for long have I known
> The spell which thy loveliness around me has thrown.
> I change but in dying, and while life shall last
> I am ever the same as in days that are past.

From your ever true and loving wife, Mary, to her Andrew dear.

I wished I knew where you was tonight. I wish you was here to sleep with me and your little Lucy. I write in haste to have it come faster. That is all.

From Mary Burwell at Oxford to Andrew Burwell, December 16, 1864

My Dearest Husband

Once more I seat myself to write to you. I have just been up to the office, but did not get any letter from you. I got a letter last Tuesday from you that was written the 24th of Nov. It looked as if it had been carried in some one's pocket a long time. It was dirty and worn through on the edge, but is one week yesterday since I got a late letter from you that was written Dec. 2nd. You wrote that you was going on board the boat. I hope you won't have to stay there long. We are all well and doing well and I hope you are the same. I am very anxious to hear from you. I suppose your Regt will be put in the field to fight when you get where Sherman is. I hope you will not have to go out with them, you can't think how close we watch the papers. Oh my dearest husband how I do hope that this winter will end this cruel war, so that you can come home in the spring. I did have some hopes of you coming home on a furlough so as to spend Christmas and New Years with us. But I have give it up now.

I shall have to wish you a happy Christmas and New Year, far from you, with the hope of being with you before many months shall pass away. Almost four months has gone, eight months more, providing you have to stay the year out, but my dear Andrew. I do hope you can come home in the spring, it does seem so long since I have seen you. It seems as if you have been gone a year already. We have had some from here tonight, George Bell & his wife, and Perry Miller & his wife, and Seirr Miller and our new doctor that came in Waterhouse place, all got out into the road to slide down the hill they got a bob sled and all the women could get on that and the men would start it agoing and then they would get on and sometimes they would run off into the ditch and tumble off into the snow. We wanted to play some game with them but did not get the chance to. I suppose Seirr thinks she is got a man now, she has chased him close to his heels ever since he came to town, but I guess you have heard enough of this fun. We are not going anywhere Christmas. I don't think Mattilda has asked me to go down there they going to have company but I don't know whether or not the weather has been very cold along back and unless it gets warmer, I can't take the baby out. My dearest Andrew, our dear little girl is getting to be so cunning, she learns so many funny tricks. One morning I was shelling corn for the hens and she was crazy to get her hands in the pan, so I let her work and she would take out a handful of corn and throw it on the floor and called the kickies (as she calls them). She has learned to bow when we go out or come in. She does a great many things that I would give all the world almost if you could see her. Lately when she wakes up in the morning har (for hark) papa. She seems to know all about you, but I don't suppose she does. Next Monday the little thing is a year old she has only four teeth and does not go entirely alone but she could if she was not afraid of falling but she will get over that after awhile.

I sent ten bushels of wheat to mill this week by Mr. Dunn and he got three hundred and thirty-five pounds of flour out of it and two bags of bran. He says that wheat don't yield very good this year because it is shrunk up so much on account of the dry weather but I did not think yours looked scrunch much. It looked real nice plump wheat. He charged a dollar for taking it up to Lawrence.

I tell you, my dear husband, we miss you in everything we undertake to do. When I want to go anywhere it seems so odd to have someone else take me, or I have to stay at home. My dear one your place can't be filled while you are away, there is no one like you for me. My dearest husband, whenever I am alone, I am whispering a prayer to God for you that he may shield you from danger while you are away and bring you safe to my arms again. Don't lose your hope in God, my dear one. Trust in him and he will carry you safe through at last.

I must close now for it is getting very late. I send you a lock of baby's hair so that you can how it looks now. I was going to have her picture taken when she was a year old but there is no artist here now.

Receive this from you loving Wife Mary to her Andrew

From Mary Burwell at Oxford to Andrew Burwell, December 22, 1864

My Dear Husband,

As I have few moments to spare while your stockings are drying, I thought I would set down and write a few lines to you and let you know we are all well as usual, and I hope this will find you enjoying good health and spirits. I try to keep up my spirits the best I can, considering all things. I send you a couple of handkerchiefs for a Christmas present. I could not think of anything else that would be of more use to you, that I could get here. They don't have much of a choice. I send you some corn to pop when you get a good chance. If you want another pair of socks, let me know and you shall have them, or anything else that I can send you. The other day when I went to the office, Jane Fish was getting a paper of tobacco done up to send to her Andrew.[20] He is at City Point, but I am glad dear Andrew that you don't use tobacco. I had rather send you a pound of tea, but you say you have plenty to eat and drink, so I won't send you any eatables, but dearest one, how I wish you could come home and stay, not to go away from me again until death shall separate us. But dearest husband, it would seem a little better to be together if one of us should be taken away, but I trust the Lord will bring you safe back to me again. I can't think you ain't coming home. Whenever I get to worrying and fretting about you, something seems to whisper to me, he will come home, you will see him again, so then I calm down and seem to feel so easy about you for a little while. According to the old saying, you will live to wear out these socks, for mother and I both had to rip the toes before they were right. It is awful cold here today, but we get along first rate, so far. It don't take us long to do what little chores we have to do. We do a little to a time when it is so cold. The baby is getting so she understands about all we say, and can say quite a number of words herself. She knows I am writing to you or she acts as if she knew. She stands by me, stretching up to see on to the table and cries, papa. Now dear one, it is getting late, and I want to take these things to the office and get them done up before dark—so you must excuse my short letter this time. Dear one, I have plenty to say, but have not the time, so good bye for the present, from your dear wife.

Mary, to her loving husband, Andrew
A kiss to you, love.

From Mary Burwell at Oxford to Andrew Burwell, December 27, 1864

My Dear Husband,

Again I am seated to write a few lines to you to let you know that we are all well, and I hope this finds you the same. I am thankful that your health is as good as it is. If you was sickly, I should worry so much more about you. I don't want you to think that I think you neglect me when you don't get time to write. For I don't think so. That is the last of my thoughts. When I don't get your letters regular, I think you have been moving, or something has happened to you. I can't tell you all the thoughts that run through my mind, but I never think you neglect me. But my dear husband, I must say that I worry more about you lately than I have done, but it is as you say, if God does not protect you there, he won't anywhere. It is my daily prayer, my dearest Andrew, that he will protect you wherever you are. Don't worry about us doing our chores. We get along first rate. We have had some cold weather, and last night, I should [say] there was sixteen inches of snow fell, but I put them boots on that you sent home, and they keep the snow off good and make good tracks. You wrote about having some words with Kribbs. What was it about? I hope he won't make any fuss that will cause you to lose your place, dear one, I think, it is a good place for you. I should hate to have you lose it. I suppose it is true that three hundred thousand more men has got to be raised. I was in hopes they would not draft again, but they will have to order to get so many as that. Leroy did not pay me for the bay, but said he would as soon as he could get to chopping for Gaylord. I told him I thought you said there was two ton of it, but he said he did not think there was more than a ton and a half. He went and got a load while I was there, but I will tell him you said there was two ton. I do keep account of every thing I get to Mr. Gage's. I traded the heifer account all up and owe 44cts, but intend to keep him paid up and not let any debt collect there at all. Yesterday, I received fifteen dollars of my state money They keep one month pay back for some reason or other, but I will get it at the end of the year. I have got eight dollars and half by me, besides my fifteen that I got yesterday, and all that I have got coming to me is what Leroy owes me for the hay, that was four dollars a ton. I don't intend to lend any more money, but I could not help lending Mr. Gage what I did, because he knew I had it with me, but he has paid it all up now. I paid Mrs. Warehouse our bill that was three dollars and 25 cts. That is not as much as I expected it would be. Dearest one, money goes very fast. When I break a dollar, it don't last long,

I have to spend a good deal for postage stamps, but we must write. We don't write much to anyone besides you.

Once in a while, I write down home, but don't think I spend any in waste. I am too anxious to save it until you come home, if you live to see the time, dear husband. I know that you think I am saving as I can be of our money, and get what Lucy and I want. I guess by what we read in the paper that there is a good deal of fighting going on. I hope that will get done by spring. It seems as if they might be a conclusion before long. How anxiously I do watch the weeks as they pass away. You are in your fifth month now. Dear Andrew, the time flies by, for all it seems so long. You say you can't have a furlough no how, but I hardly expected you would, but still I hoped you would. So I suppose I must make up my mind that I can't see you until your time is out. I can't think for a minute of not seeing you again, dear one. I hope it will be our happy lot to meet again in this world and take comfort as we used to. We can take so much comfort with our dear little girl if we are all spared. May God hear and answer our prayers and guard you through all the dangers you may have to encounter with. Accept these few lines from an ever affectionate and loving wife. Excuse this poor writing. I will try and write better next time.

Mary to Andrew

From Mary Burwell at Oxford to Andrew Burwell, December 30, 1864

My Dear Husband

I received your letter written the 19th yesterday, and was very glad to have you in such good spirits and more than all to enjoy such good health. It is a great thing to be thankful for, dearest Andrew. When I hear you are in such good spirits it makes me feel better. The weather has been very blustering here today, it looked like one of the old-fashioned days of last winter. The snow drifted in large drifts, filling in the tracks. I am glad you have such mild weather where you are, but dear one don't worry about us, we get along doing our chores very nicely and we get along first rate everyway. The most of our trouble is about you away off there alone, as you might say, with no one to speak a kind loving word to you, but my dear husband, I hope and trust that you may be spared to come home again. Oh how good that will seem to see you and talk with you once more and I think we shall. I can't think any other way, dear husband, it seems all the time as if you was going to come home, at least I hope you will.

I hope they will get through drafting men before you come home. That would seem worse than all to have you go again after your year was up. I do hope this spring will end up the war.

Lucy gets along very nicely. She has got four nice big teeth and is about cutting two more. She bites me sometimes when she is nursing and when I make a fuss about it she will look up so roguish and laugh. She does not run alone yet but she might if she only thought to. She is afraid of falling. She is a noisy little thing. I tell you if things do not go to suit her, she makes them fly. I thinks when she talks she will talk very plain. What few words she says now are quite plain, we take the best kind of care of her.

I am just as busy as I can be all the time sewing and knitting. I have something to make for her all the time. I am going to make her white apron this week and another pair of shoes for her. I tell you dear Andrew, I do wish you could see her when she is dressed to go out with her nice blue cloak and cape, and little red and white bonnet on, she looks very comfortable.

There is a donation party here this next Thursday for the Methodist minister and mother and I are going if we can and the weather is fit for us to go out. You can't think how I do miss you when I want to go anywhere. But dearest one, I hope it won't long be so.

I got a letter from father yesterday and he is very anxious to have you write to him, he says that Fanny and her lamb are doing well. The little thing eats hay and oats and bran and grows nice.

Richard had been home and stayed one day and night. He had the team with him and had to be back the next day so I did not see him. I suppose he has got a girl down there or he would not stay there so steady. They did not write whether he brought her with him or not. I am afraid he will have to go to war now.

You want some tobacco, well I will get you some but you must not chew. I am glad you smoke. I think it will be good for you, dear Andrew. I know you won't chew, it is only my fun saying you must learn. I sent you some candles I thought they would come in handy, and a piece of soap. I thought I must send something besides the tobacco and I could not send anything you could eat because it would taste bad by the time it gets to you. You sent back the little envelope that I sent you. We all looked at it and wished we could go and come back with as little trouble as that did, but I think I should want to stay with you longer than that did and when I come home to bring you with me never to go to war again.

My dearest husband, how I do hope you can come home in the spring. We must trust in the Lord for all things he knows what is best for us better than we do ourselves. Do you have any meetings where you are, what do you do Sunday?

I must draw this to a close for this time. I hope it will find you well, I have not felt very well today. I have had the sick headache all day, other ways we are all well, good-bye for this time.

From your ever affectionate wife
Mary E. Burwell to her Andrew

As 1864 drew to a close, Savannah fell to Sherman's troops, while 110,000 Union troops continued the siege of Petersburg and Richmond, Virginia, where 66,000 Confederate troops continued to suffer from the cold, low rations, and disease.[21]

From Mary Burwell at Oxford to Andrew Burwell, January 3, 1865

My Dear Husband

Once again I am seated to write a few lines to you to let you that we are all well as usual, and I hope you are the same. I have not received any letters from you since last Thursday, but it is only Tuesday aft. I hope to get one next Thursday, my dear husband. If I don't get one letter a week from you then I think there must be something the matter, but I am thankful dearest one that you have got along so well so far. How I do hope you will continue to do well. Oh dear one I do get so anxious about you once in a while that I can't hardly contain myself. I get to thinking about you sometimes and think I must come and see you, but dear husband, I know I can't so I have to bury such thoughts away out of my mind, and ask God to spare your dear life to come back home to live with me again. Oh my darling husband dark and desolate indeed would this world be to me if it was not for you. My dear little girl is a great comfort to me and I think she always will be, at least I hope so and I do earnestly pray for you to come back and enjoy the comfort with me.

Mrs. Waterhouse is going to start for Washington in a short time. Mother is there helping her get ready. William Pierson has got home but he is crazy as he can. It takes three men to guard him all the time now and they say they don't think he will get well again. Dear husband I hope you will come home alright and agreed as you went away.[22]

William Olden has written home that every man that would go and dig in Butlers' canal, can have their discharge by working two hours there. Now my dearest husband I don't want you to go there. If you do you will surely get killed. They say they are but there two hours before they are killed. I want you to come home bad enough, but you had better stay longer than not come at all. I suppose it is all true, but dear one don't run any such risk for your life.[23]

There was an oyster supper and dance down to Packwaukee last night and there was a good many went from here, but I did not go. I heard that Mattilda and Leroy were there, there is a donation party this next Thursday for the Methodist preacher—his name is Atwater. I don't know whether I shall go or not, when you was at home I would go any place I wanted too, but now I don't care so much as going as I did when you was here to go with me. But my dear Andrew, I hope we may have the chance to go together again.

I dreamt last night that you had come home and we was talking just as natural as if you was here. I thought you had gone to bed and I was getting ready to come too, and I asked you when you was going back and you said at one o'clock in the morning, and I told you, you should not go as soon as that and you said you was not going back so soon, you would stay two or three days, they told you that you might stay as long as you was a mind to. Dearest one when I dream such things it makes me feel disappointed all day.

Last Saturday, the last day of the year, I mailed a pound of tobacco for you, it cost 40cts a pound. Have you got your stockings yet? I think it is about time you got them.

My dearest husband this letter is not very interesting but I have written two to you since I received any from you so I have answered all your questions I believe and there is not much news to tell. It is all about the draft here now, but my loved one I don't have that to worry about this winter. It is something else now—they have got you but I hope not for long.

The baby is getting uneasy and wants me to go to bed with her so I must bid you good night for the present.

From your own loving Wife Mary Burwell to her Andrew dear

I wish you a happy new year and may God grant His blessing on you that you may live to see the end of it, and that here at home with your dear Wife and baby

From Mary Burwell at Oxford to Andrew Burwell, January 6, 1865

My Dearest Husband

I received a letter from you yesterday dated 28th and was very glad to hear you was well, we are all were as common, my dear husband. I am glad you are as comfortable as you are, some of the [indecipherable] men from this area has written home that they had to lay in the bare ground in the mud and snow, and only a slice of bread a day to eat. But dear husband, Emma has just come back from the office and brought me a letter from you stating that you have gone back with the Company again. That is bad now I suppose you won't fare as well, but I hope you will. I have felt easier about you since you have been cook, than I should if you were in the Company. But now I can't rest so easy. I am well aware the Lord is able to save you, that you believe he will, and I hope and pray that he will, but dearest Andrew, what hopes and doubts and fears I am in now about you. But my dearest I will try and keep up the best courage I can.

Tell me what you have to do, and whether you have got your gun returned to you or not and tell me if your living is as good as it was when you was cook. Don't you tell me not to worry now because I do but I can't help it a little to think that you had to be taken from such a good place. Now I suppose if the Regiment is called out to fight you will have to go with them. But my dearest husband I will try and let my doubts and fears go and cling to the hope I have in the Lord that he will hear and answer my prayers as he has done before, that he may spare your dear life for me.

I am glad that I sent you something that was so useful. I could not think of anything that I could get. I do have to send you anything that will comfort you away off there alone (as you might say). Oh how I wish you was here with me!

You spoke about a dollar a cord being too much for cutting wood. They don't do the least thing for nothing. When I moved the last load of my goods here, I had to pay ten cents to get a man to help unload. That was when I got Smiths little boy and team to go, they all think that the women are alone, and what they can't do themselves they have to pay dear for. Our nearest neighbor has not even asked us if he could do a chore or shovel snow, or do a single turn for us and now I don't want them to. We can do our own chores as long as we have our health. When I go out to clean the steps there is most always two or three men on the tavern steps a gawking at me but I don't care it is a honest trade. One day I was out cleaning out the stable and Seira Miller's young Peter stood looking at me. I had a mind to throw him a fork full, he feels so very nice.

I think Hovey is not doing what he should do about weighing the hay as long as I have wished him to weigh it. I have not had any from him since that time that I wrote you about him refusing to weigh it but I have sent him word that I was most out so I am expecting some every day now. You said you did not see into it, about him charging 7 dollars a ton, and Leroy only gave me 4. I will tell you, the market price was 7 dollars delivered, and 4 dollars and fetch it themselves so you see Leroy went and got his and Hovey brings mine and puts it in the barn. It looks a big price to give but I have to do as others do in that respect.

You wanted to know how much money I have got in the house. I have got ten dollars and 60 cents now. I let mother have 8 dollars yesterday to pay her taxes with. She has wrote to David Ormsby for some money, but has not got an answer yet, she expects one every mail. But dear Andrew, she shall not want for anything while I have got money. I think too much of her to let her or Emma want for anything, we get along first rate with one another not the least hardship between us that I know of.

I must draw this to a close for it is getting late and I must [tell] you good night for the present. Pray to God for me, my own dear husband, and I will pray for you at home, and let us have faith that he will hear and answer our prayers.

From your ever true and loving Wife Mary

Accept this in the white envelope [it] is a letter for you to read alone.

From Mary Burwell at Oxford to Andrew Burwell, January 10, 1865

Dear Husband,

I received your much welcomed letter of the 5th, stating that you was out of writing paper and envelopes and money, so I thought I would send you some, and then it would last you quite a while. I send you 60 cents in money. I thought a little would be better than none. If you don't get your pay before you answer this, I will send you some more. My dear husband, I don't want you to do without anything that I can send you. Here are some linen rags for you to do up your fingers with, if they get sore. I am glad you continue to keep well. We are all well. Little Lucy is cutting more teeth and is very cross. It takes about all my time to tend her. Other ways, she is well. You spoke about them giving you a furlough. I hope it will fall to your lot to come home. I would give 20 dollars to see you. I am glad you are in the same camp as you was when you was cook. That was awful enough about that man that was shot. Dearest Andrew, I am glad you are not in a deserter's shoes. Do what is right, dear one, and all will go well with you I hope. I must close, for it is almost time for the stage to come. Excuse this short letter, for I have no time to write any more just now. Accept all I send you, and let me know if you want anything that I can send, and I will do so.

From your ever affectionate wife, Mary, to her Andrew

On January 12, Governor Lewis presented the last Governor's Annual Message of the war. He announced that the state had debts of "Two million and five thousand dollars," all but $100,000 of which was funds owed by the federal government to Wisconsin for costs of the war. He proudly recounted Wisconsin's contributions to the war: "44 regiments of Infantry, four regiments and one company of cavalry, one regiment of heavy artillery, thirteen batteries of light artillery, and one company of sharp shooters, making an aggregate of 75,133 men." He also acknowledged the contributions of Wisconsin's women in caring for sick and wounded soldiers: "To the Ladies' Aid Societies especially is great credit due for the assistance they have rendered. . . . [They] have doubtless been the means of saving some valuable lives. The thanks of a grateful people, the gratitude of the brave soldier, the destitute orphan, wife and mother, are their rewards."[24]

From Mary Burwell at Oxford to Andrew Burwell, January 22, 1865

My Dear Husband

Once again I am seated to write to you and I hope this will find you enjoying good health and also in good spirits for I am always glad to hear that your spirits are good. We are all well at present.

I have worried a good deal about you lately for you are so near to the rebels, and they have so many strikes at the Pickets lately that I could not help being uneasy about you. I read a piece in the paper about the Rebels making an attack on a Picket line on the right of the 2nd division of the 6 corps, capturing a few pickets and they were dressed in our men's uniforms so that our men did not fire on them as soon as they would have done if they knew, and it was between daylight and dark, so they could not see very well. They took nine of our men away with them. Dear Andrew you can't think how it sent me to worrying about you when I know that you are in the same situation that those men were in. That happened on the 9th of this month, and the last letter I got from you was written the 8th, and I got it the 11th and I answered it the next day and sent you some writing paper and envelopes and 60 cents in money and some linen rags and string to do up your fingers with if they be sore.

My dearest husband what hopes and fears I am in about you all the time, when I do try to cheer up and feel encouraged, there will be something come along to discourage me and darken my mind for it is a dark and gloomy time with little sunshine. But my dear Andrew, I still have hope if you are in such a dangerous place, the Lord is able to save you, if your every man was taken from your side it would not be impossible for the Lord to save you if you live his will. It is my earnest prayer by might and by day, that God may be with you every hour and keep you from the hands of the enemy, and to spare your dear life to come home and make me happy once more.

Since you spoke about your men having furloughs, I have thought so much about it that it seems as if you was coming home pretty soon. How I would like to see your dear sweet face. When I look at your pictures it seems as if they might speak to me but they won't. I don't expect to see you until your time is out but I hope if you live to see that time you won't be kept two or three months after it is up, as some have been. The time does seem so long to look ahead, but I will be thankful if I can see you home safe and well. The day after tomorrow is five months of the time you will be gone.

Do you want me to sell any oats? They aint fetching much now as they have been. The are 70cts now in Portage but if they should come up had I better sell them. I want to keep some.

Our dear little girl runs all over the house and begins to talk like everything. Her hair curls real easy. She has got a nice head of hair. She will drink tea as strong as I can, and eat beef like a pig. She loves apples as much as you do. I get her some every week. I wish you could be here with me when I wean her. I shan't wean her till May and then the nights will be shorter and it will be warm, and we will have milk, and it will be better every way. Mother went to Portage last week and I sent by her to get a high chair for Lucy, and she did. She sits up to the table in it, but the greatest trouble is, she wants to have a spoon and feed herself, but that won't do, she has to be fed yet awhile. But my dear husband, I hope the time is near when you will be here with the dear little creature.

When Mother went to Portage, I sent and got me a blue dress like the piece enclosed. Dear one you know I was very bare of clothes, and now if I get a few things ahead, I shan't have to get anymore for two or three years if I live so long and I think I can make them last me a good while. I have got Lucy clothed up so that she won't need much more until next winter if she lives. I want to get a pink calico dress for her in the spring. I don't buy her shoes. I make them myself, the cost is six shilling and a dollar and it won't pay to buy them, for she wears them out so fast.

I must close for now for I see my paper is giving out, my loved one I would give lots to see you tonight. I do hope I shall get a letter tomorrow from you, to ease my aching heart. But dearest Andrew, as long as I know you are all right, don't worry about me because I feel so uneasy about you, but I can't help it when I hear such work going on, but I will try and not worry about anymore than I can help and pray that it will end soon.

Your dear Mary to her Andrew

From Mary Burwell at Oxford to Andrew Burwell, January 27, 1865

My dearest husband,

It is now evening and all is quiet so I thought I would spend an hour or two writing to a loved one far away. We are all well as usual and I hope this will find you enjoying the same blessing. The weather has been snapping cold here all the week but just begun to moderate a little today. If you should have such cold weather as this where you are, I guess you would suffer some, but I don't think you do. I am glad you keep your gun looking so nice and bright. I am taking good care of your little gun that is here with me, I suppose it is nothing like the one you have with you. I am thankful, dearest husband, that you have enough to eat and that you fare as well as you do. I don't see the use in anyone sending such hard stories that aint true home to their folks. It's hard enough to know the best of the Soldiers' fare without hearing such hard news. I did not believe it when I heard it so I won't worry anymore about you. I am glad you take as good care of yourself as you do, how do you manage when you wash your pants? Have you got two pairs? How I do wish you was at home where I could wash and mend your clothes once more. Dear Andrew, don't let yourself get bare of clothes or stockings.

Let me know if you want anything [with] time enough to get them to you before you get clear out. Will they let you have more than one suit of clothes or do they calculate one suit to last you a year? I hope they have paid you by this time for your sake. I am not out of money nor shan't be if we keep well. I want you to keep enough money with you to get what you need, don't wait to get word from me if you should get things or not. My own dear husband, you know best what you can afford and you know that I am willing that you should have everything you need while you are away to make you comfortable, for it is but little comfort you can have there, I am sure. Oh how thankful I will be if you live to come home so that I can make you comfortable myself and know where you are and how you are; while I think of it, I would like to know if you have some of that Belmoncy [?] yet? If you had not, I'd better send you some.

Poor Mattilda, she is feeling very bad now about Leroy being drafted. He went to Green Bay to get clear but he did not so he has got to go. She went as far as Oshkosh with him, she wrote a letter to me after they had got back and said he had got to go this week. I do not know where she is going to live nor did she not know herself. I am going down to see her as soon as the weather gets warmer, and then make a visit down home the next news I hear. I expect it will be that Richard is drafted, for there is not much danger of him enlisting. I suppose it will about use mother up to have Leroy go to war and if Dick goes I think it will quite.[25]

It is too bad that this cruel war cannot be ended, how many hearts has got to ache again now for this call for men. Terry Miller, Bill Smith, Tom Black are all going to York State to enlist this next week and many others talk of going, Our small town will be cleaned out pretty clean this time. I don't know what we should do if a fire or anything should take place. We would have to go for it I guess, but I do hope there will be peace made before a great while.

Dear one, five months have gone, you are now on the sixth. It don't seem possible that you have been away all this time but I do hope you can come home before six more shall pass away but if you can't I will be thankful to see you home well and hearty at the end of the year if the Lord sees fit. How I do wish you could see your dear little Lucy for one week just now. She runs all over into everything and through every door and she gabbles away all day such a string of talk that no one can understand except a word once in a while. She keeps us from being lonesome a good deal. I am busy doing something for her the most of the time. I have sent out for another payment of my state money this week for Black was going to send out a lot of orders before he went away, and so I thought I would send with the rest. My dear one, I must draw this to a close for I have the sick headache tonight and want to go to bed. Take good care of yourself and write all the news that you think I would care about and I will do the same. And let us both trust in God and He will carry us safely over life's rough seas, we will trust in him to see each other in this world and dwell forever in the world above. I must bid you goodnight for this time.

From your loving wife, Mary, to her dear husband, Andrew.

From Mary Burwell at camp at Oxford to Andrew Burwell, February 3, 1865

My dear husband,

Again I take my pen in hand to write to you, to let you know that we are all alive and well, and hope that this will find you the same. I received your letter of the 25th and was glad to have such a good long letter to read, I am sorry you didn't get mine right along as fast you had ought to, for dear Andrew, I just know how disappointed you feel if you don't get one every time you expect it, but I mail two and sometimes three every week. I won't neglect writing to you once, dear one, while you are away. I would sat up till morning rather than do that, the weather is very rainy and unpleasant here just now but it is just what we want to fill up the wells and cisterns, for they are all about dry.

I was thinking of going down home this week but can't on account of the rain. I shall wait until it comes pleasant again, we are going to lose our snow now, so I will have to give up having a sleigh ride this winter unless we have more snow.

I should think you must have been scared when you heard such cannonading as that, dear me, it made me tremble to read about it. I do hope they will keep their distance from where you are. Every letter or paper I get I expect to hear that your Regiment has been ordered somewhere. I fairly tremble every line I read, but my dearest husband, I am thankful that you have got along so well as you have so far and I hope and pray that the remainder of the time will pass as well with you as the first part. Yes, dear Andrew, I well remember the day you agreed to work for Uncle Sam, and I hope he will pay you before long, it must be hard for you to be without money if I knew you was so near out, I would have sent more with the writing paper, but I thought maybe you would be paid by the time that got to you, but I will enclose two dollars in this letter for you, that will help you along a little, don't worry about me. I have some money left yet, when I go to Packwaukee I guess likely Matillda will pay me for the hay. I wrote for it before he left but had no answer, I had not heard that Leroy had run away, until you wrote about it. Till wrote that he had been to Green Bay the week before and could not get clear, and was going that week. I hope that he has not run away for his own sake, dear Andrew. I would rather have you go as you did, and come home honorably than to do any thing that was wrong. That would be double trouble for me, but dearest one, that is the last of my thoughts, that you would do anything to disgrace yourself and family. My only trouble is that you will have to go into battle, or that you will get sick when the hot weather comes but dear Andrew, all these fears that I have about you, I ask the Lord every day to keep you from ever having to experience them.

You wanted to know what Mr. Gage was doing. I have not heard anything from them for quite awhile, but when I go down there I will find out all I can. I hope they won't go away before you come back if you live to come. I should not want that property to go through any one else's hands until you get your three hundred.

I do not know what they intend to do now [that] Leroy is gone. I will write and let you know the particulars about it when I go down there. Packwaukee men knows anything about what we write back and forth about Leroy and his folks so they will write everything right now to his folks, and it will go right to them. Vene Russell got clear again. I would think they would not enroll him again. I had not heard about Kingsley being drafted until you wrote it.

Wednesday morning Tom Black, and Perry Miller, and Mr. Dunn started for York State to enlist and the talk is that Abbot is going but I don't know for certain, as for Richard I have not heard from him since he was at home. You must not resent it if he don't write to you for you know he don't write to anyone, but I should think he might write oftener than he does, but never mind, dear one.

I will write as long as I am able to hold a pen but I would rather have you here with me where I could talk to you now. I could write another sheet full and not begin to tell you half what I want to but I shall have to lay it away until you come here, dear one. What a nice time we have visiting if you only live to come home and we will all live to see you well, dear one. It is time to stop, my paper has run out from your Mary.

From Mary Burwell at Oxford to Andrew Burwell, February 6, 1865

My Dear Husband.

Once more I have the privilege of writing to you, we are all well as usual, except Mother, she is troubled a great deal lately with the nervous headache. She and Emma has just gone up to the doctor's office to get something to help her. I hope this will find you enjoying the blessings of good health and good spirits, dear Andrew. I am always glad to hear that you are in good spirits, it helps to cheer me up a great deal.

We went to meeting last night and heard what they call the world's preacher preach, how I do wish you was here dear Andrew to carry your little girl to meeting for she is getting much too heavy for me to carry. It would please you to see her act. When she is there, last night she got down and run around a little for the first time in meeting. She loves to go out doors. She will get a bonnet and put on her head and her cradle quilt and wrap around her then tease to go. To night I was sitting down holding her and I was talking to her about you, and told her, papa has gone away off, and she got down from my lap went into my bedroom and pointed to a box that was on the stand, with your likeness in and said papa two or three times, so I took one out and give it to her and she was so pleased with it she kissed it, and wanted mother and I to kiss it too. My dear husband, you can't imagine how much comfort the dear little one is to me, if you only live to come home and can stay with me as long as we live. What a happy creature I shall be, it makes me feel so lonesome when I go to meeting where we have been together so much, and not see your dear face there. I can't hardly make it seem possible that you are so far away, but dearest Andrew, I hope and pray that you won't be far away long if you have to stay the year. I do hope they will let you go then, and not keep you a month or two longer, if your life is spared until then. I shall be so impatient for you to come, I won't know how to wait any longer than your time is out.

I have got a chance to get to Packwaukee tomorrow so I think I shall go, and from there down home, and make a visit there. I shall try and get back again as soon as I can, on account of getting your letters. I shan't get them while I am away so fast as I do here. But Mother will send them to me after they have read them.

William Rood died this morning is to be buried tomorrow. This must be quite a blow to his family; he will be missed in Packwaukee if he was not liked very well. I think I shall get down there time enough to go to the funeral, but my dear one, how I do miss you everywhere. We used to be together so much. Oh my darling husband, this world would be of no consequence if you were gone out of it. But as long as you and my dear little girl is living it holds a dear tie that binds me to this world. Dear one I feel like one left with one little comfort. But still I have the hope of seeing and enjoying your company again. But if you was gone forever, it seems to me that the world would be dark indeed, but we will trust in God for our help. It is my daily prayer that He will be with you at all times and wherever you may be called to go, and keep you from the hands of the enemy, and bring you safe back to my arms again.

Dear one, I can't bear to think that I can't see you till next fall but I will wait patiently if I can see you then. I must close, dear one, for it is very late and I have got lots to do in the morning. Before I start take good care of yourself and I will do the same, and when you come home we both take care of one another. If you hear anything you think I would like to hear just write it to me in your private letters. No one ever sees them, not mother don't feel jealous nor think we write anything about anybody. She says we can write all we are a mind to and she won't care. Dearest one, you had better burn up mine for fear any one might find them some time.

Accept this from your dear Wife to her darling husband. A kiss and hug.

Belle Arnold Sleeper's husband, Hiram, had been captured on September 2 during a skirmish, part of the Siege of Petersburg, and sent to Salisbury Prison in Florence, South Carolina.[26] Hiram was one of the 8,740 prisoners crowded into the prison, which had a capacity of 2,500. The week of October 5, 1864, brought a record number of prisoners to Salisbury. Because of this overcrowding, no interior shelter was provided for prisoners.[27]

BELLE

From Belle Arnold Sleeper at Brooklyn to Charles Palmer, February 6, 1865, "Monday morn 1 o'clock"

My Dear Brother,

The old clock has just rung out the hour of 1. But methinks you are wondering why I am up this early in the morning. Mother Sleeper is again ill. I took care of her all night last night, or rather the night before last, but retired last evening, leaving her to the care of others till 12 o'clock and now

I shall care for her until morning. When I mailed my last letter to you, I thought to stay in town for some time, but Mother grew worse so rapidly that Henry (my brother-in-law) came after me once again before I had time to answer your No. 7 which came to hand in due time. How long I shall remain here I cannot tell. It doesn't look to me as I shall be able to leave for a long time. Some days it hardly seems possible that mother can live through the day. She has suffered extremely. For the last three days we have kept her under the effect of Laudanum, enough can't keep her free from harm. She has been near death and we do not think her out of danger yet. Poor Hiram, how he would suffer if he knew how ill his Mother is. I am glad he cannot know, as he cannot come to her.[28]

Nellie and Mr. Nolan came out to see me yesterday bringing with them your No. 8. Brother mine do you believe it possible that she will marry him? Just between you and me, sometimes I fear she will. I fear she will marry him, not because he will not be kind to her for I believe he will; and that he loves her no one can doubt who sees him gaze at her once. But I should fear to trust my future happiness to one who was so indifferent to his Country's need or woe, as not to take time from fixing a stable for his horse, to go and cast a vote in behalf of his Country's honor. Yes, sir, he told me with his own lips, that he was fixing a stable for his horse that day and didn't care enough about voting to go down town. Though if he had cast a vote it would have been for Lincoln. I had understood from Nell that he did vote for Lincoln. And I believe at one time she thought he did. I couldn't trust a man with my happiness, who cared nothing for the happiness of his country. And so I told Nell. Perhaps she still thinks she can redeem him, but I should consider him past redemption. But it would be a noble work to redeem a soul so near low.

Nell tells me that Osier [Gene?] really is going to enlist. I confess I am disappointed. I did not think he would do so, but I am glad on many accounts. He has experienced religion they tell me. Enlisted under the banner of Christ, then under the banner of our fine Yankee Nation. Lucky we may hope for great results to follow.

Al Sleeper has enlisted again going into the 49th Wis. Reg't. He was not here today. Some one has been telling him a quantity of trash purported to come from one—that I turned him out of Father's home and shut the door in his face. As near as I can tell it came from George C. Will he never let one alone! He has been my evil genius for the last two years, and now haunts my footsteps. Of course Al was very angry.[29]

Has anyone told you of the little stranger that is domesticated at Clayton's residence? Hear that George has an heir. I hope he will pay attention to that, and home, let other affairs alone. George Leansbury talks largely of enlisting. I think it very doubtful though.

I wonder if anyone has told you of the gossip concerning Mr. Beckwith and Wife Sarah Keyes—how he cuts around with this span of spirited bloods and takes her out riding now and then, and declared, "Mr. Beckwith is so intelligent." I can't say that I think either one display very excellent taste.

I received a letter from Wiley while I was in Berlin. Your Brother's letter shows plainly the state of his feelings. He made no complaints but his letter was so sad, almost dispirited. He didn't seem to care to come home, he has no home to come to.

I must not neglect to tell you of the three letters I have received from Hiram although they were of so ancient a date. Nearly four months since the last one written. The first two were written in Libby Prison and dated Sept. 7th and 18th, the last was written Oct. 13th and he was then at Danville, VA, but was to leave the next day for Salisbury, N.C. He said he was not wounded or hurt in any way, that his health was good and he was well treated and fed; his letters were in good spirits. He says prison life is very irksome but his courage is equal to all imagined, his greatest trouble being the knowledge how others are suffering on his account. He tells one to trust in God and be courageous even as he is, that he believes "God doeth all things well," that he will return to me when God sees fit that it shall be so. He writes that he was captured the 2nd of September but that he had no room to give me the particulars. These letters are a prize coming as they did, the three together, but if they had been permitted to come when they were written they would have saved me some heart pangs.

A.D. Richardson, Correspondent of the N.Y. Tribune has lately escaped from Salisbury and I have written him to learn, if possible, some thing concerning my husband.[30] I mean to write to Abe Lincoln pretty soon, if he don't hurry up the exchange of Prisoners, and I'll tell him to, that so many thousand brave heroes cannot languish in Southern dungeons and he be blameless—that a just God will not permit it. Do you know that I feel very rebellious sometimes—that I almost wish that I had used my influence to keep Hiram at home. Yes, it would have been wrong, but—oh my brother, it is very hard to feel every hour that the one who is dearer to me than life is suffering from cold and hunger, is slowly starving to death. O, God! Give me strength to endure this.[31]

It is now nearly 4 o'clock. I did not think I would ever write this much when I commenced. Mother needs such constant care. You'll excuse my writing with a pencil, I have to keep near Mother's bed and have not conveniences for pen and ink. I think I will lay this aside now and finish another time. Good night and pleasant dreams, My Brother.

Tuesday morning, 8 o'clock

I was "off-duty" from 7 last evening to midnight, and didn't I sleep through, and didn't my brain whirl when I lifted my head from my pillows; but since partaking of a cup of excellent tea, I feel quite like myself, and now I will try to finish this letter. I cannot answer No. 7 or 8, in full. Each letter I receive from you strengthens the hand of friendship—teaches me more of my brother—how to prize his brotherly love and interest in my welfare. Will the time ever come when there shall be discord between us. God forbid! We are wiser and know each other better than in days of yore and I will not allow a thought to trouble me. If ever I offend by word or deed, you will tell me plainly, that I may correct any errors forever it will surely be. Never willingly will I pain my Brother's heart—I have no fears in that regard to you.

With No. 7 came some poetry but you neglected to give me the Author's name and I have supplied the offering with "Written by C.B.P." Am I not correct? I think I am. They are good and I prize them highly.

I read your letter to Nellie, it was an excellent letter—just such a one as she needs, and you did not offend her in the least. She admitted the truth of all you said, to me, but I hardly think she will to you. She will think it highly necessary to be on the contrary side; but I may be mistaken in this.

I have not seen Nettie yet. While I was in town, she and Roxy were away visiting. Roxy is paying the biggest kind of attention to her. All on Charlie's account, I wonder if she can see through a ladder. Roxy has been telling Nett that Nellie is not a friend to her, and she went right to Nellie with it, and learned the truth of the whole affair, for Nell did not hesitate to tell her many things Roxy had said about her, and then exacted a promise from Nett not to say anything to Roxy about it till she could be present. I imagine they will have a warm time when the three meet as Nellie declares she will not stand it, and Nett isn't over anxious to keep the peace. I would like be a witness of the scenes. Hope they won't come to blows.

I cannot sufficiently thank you for all the kind sympathy and counsel contained in No. 8. I wrote that I were a "child of God." I do beseech him earnestly to forget my transgressions and make me clear that the assurance was mine that I am owned and blessed by Him. I cannot see my way yet, I have so many doubts and fears. But I shall not give up and not be at rest till He claims me for his own. I do not read my Bible as I should. I will try to be more diligent in searching His Holy Word.

You will remember me in your prayers, my Brother, that I may be found among the "faithful few."

Well, I must close, as it is drawing near to noon. Mother seems a little better this morning.

Oh! Your proof! Don't you trouble over [it]? I was surprised to see so few black marks on my check. You may be right—in regard to spelling "Osier" but if so, No. 7 has it on the a.m. I cannot write "a very long letter time." There's an out for your sir. I find not exams typographical in no. 8. I ought to have left more margin around this letter but you take two "proofs" of it. My respects to Griff. I will write him soon.

I will write again as soon as possible—will try to write every week. But don't wait for me—What this letter lacks in quality is amply made up in quantity.

God bless and keep you, my Brother, Augusta.

From Belle Arnold Sleeper at Brooklyn to Charles Palmer at Fort Clay, Lexington, Kentucky, February 12, 1865, "No. 8 / Sabbath Morning 5:30"

My Dear Brother

I have got a few spare moments now, so I will commence this letter and finish it when I can. Now don't go to deceiving yourself, when you unfold this massive sheet thinking that this time you have got a long interesting letter.[32] Long it may be and interesting I would have it if I could. But as you don't anything know about the community which I am at present residing I shall be obliged to again make up in quantity what it lack in quality, though I believe this is contrary to the rules of letter writing headed to use by learned men. No, Sir, this is not apologizing, it is simply stating a fact. I have been up so much for nights for the last three weeks that its no wonder that there is a confusion of ideas running through my brain, or that I feel inadequate to render order out of the chaos. Mother Sleeper is getting some better, but she still needs constant care day and night; how long this will continue I can't tell; but the present prospect is not very favorable for a speedy lumination [?].

No letter from Charley this week, or from any one else. Out of my many correspondents I should think some one might have favored me with a letter, and there may be one at Berlin, but I don't feel as if there was. The fact is, brother mine, I haven't got feeling on any subject this morning, except it be a longing to rest from thought as well as care. I feel so utterly worn out—as if I could welcome relief I any way. I have hardly strength enough to hold myself erect. Yet I know I must, and I must smile and talk with a laughing air, for <u>his</u> Father and Mother's sake. O if I could go away all by myself for the next few weeks to come. But no, I must not shrink, I must go bravely forward. God give me strength.

Sunday night 11 o'clock Feb. 19, 1865

Dear Bub, little did I think one week ago that so long a time would elapse ere I should finish this letter. But when I tell you I have been ill you will overlook the delay. I am better now. I have tried to preserve my health for future need: but think the night watching together with the steep anxiety of mind was to much for my physical strength. Do not think me weak, Brother mine, as you read down the first page, remember I have many things to try my strength. I believe I am getting into the habit of showing you the weakest side of my nature. This will never do. For the future, no more if it.

Nellie called here for a few moments this morning; brought me my mail from Berlin. She and Wilson are on there way to Ripon. They returned toward night, bringing Maggie Cormic with them. They all called for a few moments. Nell seemed just as natural—oh so good—I just love that girl! You think I "have a misperception of her character" that I do not "quite understand her." Possible, but hardly probable. I have known her for a long time; and for the past year we have been almost inseparable friends. I have been with in her home circle and in society. I have seen her perplexed, annoyed, and provoked and in her gay moods, and I find her vastly superior to many of my lady friends. She is not perfect, and who among us is. She is true to her friends, and as you say, is blessed with a superior mind. I am glad that, contrary to my expectations, she answered that letter as she did. After she permitted me to read your letter, she inquired what I thought of it. I told her very plainly, and she agreed with me full; then she told me how she was going to answer it. And I assure you it was very different from the way she did answer it. I begged her not to do so, for I felt sure that you would judge her largely by the answer to that letter. She tried to look very sedate when she finally told me she "would be true to herself" when she answered it, but her eyes laughed so hard that I hardly expected it. I am really glad that you find her so interesting a Correspondent. When I tell you anything in regard to Nellie and Wilson, I can only tell you what <u>madam sermon</u>, or very little else. Though Nellie never says, when imparting anything to me, "don't tell," yet I know she trusts me, and I must not betray that "trust" even to my much loved Brother. "They say" she <u>will</u> marry him. Whether "they say" have it right or not, time will tell. They spend a great deal of time together. He is certainly very attentive. I have talked with her in regard to his mental caliber and so also has Lizzie and I can assure you that <u>if</u> Nellie marries him it with the knowledge that her intellect is far superior to his. Nor do I think that Nellie is at all frightened at the departure of her terms, or thinks it is necessary to dispose of herself at the first opportunity. Is she committing a wrong in accepting Wilson's attentions if he is willing to run all risks? I think I hear you say, you 'would not be a plaything to amuse any lady." I don't believe you would; but all are not alike. But here I am answering your No. 9 without telling you I have received it.

 I was not up when Nellie called this morning, so she came immediately to my room bringing me your letter, one from Lieut Wright, of the 38th Wisconsin, and one from A.D. Richardson, Correspondent of the N.Y. Tribune, all being thoughtfully received. Lieut Wright writes to one every now and then, just to let me know that he doesn't forget my husband. He gives it as his opinion that the War will not last over four months, and tries to encourage me to hope for the Best. A.D. Richardson can give me no particulars in regard to Hi—could not remember him, and it would be strange indeed if he could. He expressed deep sympathy and bids me hope for the best. Tells me if there is anything in his power that he can do for me that I have only to command him. He says, "If there is any <u>virtue</u> in <u>printer's ink,</u> we mean to keep the Authorities stimulate up to their duty in this most important matter." There I shall have to leave this now. Mother Colones [?] who has been spending the last week with us, has got up and says, "Bella must go to bed." I haven't got many objections to raise about the matter as it is nearly 3 o'clock and there is such a dizzy feeling in my head. Good night, my Brother. May the Goddess of slumber keep thee company tonight. And may good Angels guard well thy pillow from all harm, and into thy dreams my sweet visions of home be wafted, is the good night wish of Sister Gussie.

MARY

From Mary Burwell at Montello to Andrew Burwell, February 14, 1865

My Dear Husband,

Again I am seated to write a few lines to a loving husband that is far away. I am well and also little Lucy, but I can't say that I am in very good spirits just now. Went with Father and Till to Montello last Sunday to quarterly meeting, and while I was there, I heard that there had been a battle at Petersburg and that our loss was eight hundred killed and wounded, that they was fighting for a railroad, and I have not seen the paper yet, to know the particulars about it, but I am going to town tomorrow to find out. My dearest husband, you can just imagine my feelings now bout you. I know that you are down there where they say this battle was, and I don't know but you have been in the fight, and don't know whether you are alive or not. Oh my dear Andrew, how anxious I am to hear from you. If you are wounded and suffering, my dear one, do let me now the worst.

And if you are alright, do tell me that, and ease this aching heart of mine (no, it is yours.) O dear one, how earnestly do I ask God to keep you from ever having to go into battle. Wherever I am alone, I am whispering a prayer for you. You wished me to pay for your watch. Dear one, I will do so as soon as I get some money. I have not got much, but I have enough to last me, I guess, until I get some. Mrs. Hubble sent the order to me since I came home, but I did not have the money to spare. I was sorry, but I could not help it. I am glad you have got it. I hope you will live to bring it home. If anything should happen to you, dear one, will you have one of your friends send all that belongs to your home to me? But I hope and trust that you will live through the great trouble and bring your things yourself. It makes my heart ache to think of it. I can't bear to think that you won't come back to me again. This world will be a dark and lonely world to me, if you was gone. My dear little girl is a great comfort to me. She grows so much like yourself, in both looks and ways. She understands almost all I say to her, and begins to say a good many words. I imagine to myself sometimes how much comfort you will take with her, if you live and she lives, but I don't make up my mind to anything for certain, for I don't know how soon I may be deprived of either one of you. Our lives are uncertain here, as well as in the army, but it would seem better to us, to be together in our last moments, but dear husband, don't fret because I am fretful just now. I am in such suspense about you on account of what I have heard. I hope it ain't true, and if it is, I hope your Regiment was not there. Mr. Gage's folks are in great trouble about Leroy having to go to war. I guess they will stay there until he gets back, if he lives. They want to sell their property there if they could get a chance. I don't think he makes as much as he expected to on his apples. I am afraid he won't have your money ready for you by the time the year is up. He says if he knew Gaylord was going to move his store away, he would have bought dry goods instead of apples, but I hope he will get the money for you, for if you live to come home, we want a nice little farm somewhere. Oh dear one, how I hope it may be so that we shall live together again. Trust in the Lord, my dear one, that it may be so, and if we are not permitted to meet again in this world, I trust we shall meet in heaven, where we shall part no more.

Father and Mother send their love to you. He would write to you himself, but he is tired and wants to go to bed. Jane sends her love too. It is very late and all have gone to bed, so I must draw this to a close. I hope this will find you all right and safe. You can't think how bad I feel about you tonight, nor anyone else. My heart is heavy, but God is able to save you wherever you are. That comforts me a great deal. Accept this from your loving wife.

Mary to her darling Andrew

From Mary Burwell at Montello to Andrew Burwell, February 18, 1865

My Dearest Husband,

I am thankful that I have the privilege of writing to you once more. This week past has been a week of suspense to me, as I did not know nor could find out by the papers, or any other way, whether the 5th Regt., had been in the fight or not, until today. Father and I went to Montello and there found a letter from you written to father dated the 10th and while I was there in town, Reuben brought two for me that you had written the 3rd and 5th so I had relief about you. I expected you was in the battle, but did not expect you to come out all right. I think we have great reason to return thanks to God for keeping you safe through such a fight. Dear Andrew there is no one can tell how I have felt about you all the week, and how I still feel for you said it was not over with yet. I am afraid now they got you out they will keep you moving. Are they likely to have much fighting around there where the battle was? Oh dear Andrew, how I do hope and pray that the war will end this summer, but I don't know what to think of them. The Cabinets on both sides seems to be very dissatisfied, but I hope they will come to terms before long. I wish they would stop fighting while they make up their minds what they are going to do, and then if they make peace, there will be all these lives saved. How many women there is now waiting for the sad news of their husbands' deaths, and how many little children are calling their fathers' names in vain? It makes my heart ache. When I hear our dear little creature call her papa, and I didn't know whether she had one or not. The dear little creature knows nothing about the trouble her little parents is in, and I hope she never will see such a time as these. I hope you won't have to do any more fighting while you are there.

I read in the papers about the Vice-President, Stephens, that you spoke about in your letter, the other two men's names was Hunter & Campbell. They was trying to do something towards making peace, but the two Presidents don't seem to agree very well about it. But I hope they will come to the conclusion before many more lives is lost. I would hope they wouldn't keep you any longer than your time is out. I am afraid that the hardest part of it is to come. I dread the hot weather for you, and I am afraid that when there is any fighting going on, you will be called out now that you have commenced, but I hope not.[33]

The time does not look so long to me as it did awhile back, if you only keep well, and don't have to fight this summer would soon pass away. My dear husband I am glad you have got the watch, I want you to get whatever you want while you are away. You said you thought I would be satisfied if you come home in good health without being deprived of any of your limbs, whether you bring a watch or not. But if you bring it home you can sell it for something we need. I will pay for it, my dear one, as soon as I can get home.

I think of going back to Packwaukee next Wednesday and stay to Mr. Gages until Saturday and then take the Stage to Oxford. Mattilda is going with me to stay a week or two. You wanted to know what Regt. Leroy is in. I could not tell you, the last we heard he was on the march to someplace he did not know where himself, but I expect he would go where he was before if he could get there. Dr. Pratt enlisted and was thrown out twice and now he is at home.

Dear one, how I wish that it had been your lot to be thrown out, but it is no use to talk about that now. You have stayed almost half the time and I hope you will live to come back and cheer this lonely one that is waiting for you.

I miss you so in our cottage home
When the daylight cares are over
As I sit and watch the stars come out
Where we often sat before
And I listen in vain for thy welcome step
How I long to hear it once more.

Accept this from an ever loving Wife to her affectionate husband

From Mary Burwell at Montello to Andrew Burwell, February 23, 1865

Dear Husband,

It is now evening, and my little charge has gone to sleep, so I thought I would converse with a beloved husband that is far from me tonight, but I would give a good deal if we could be talking face to face, instead of writing. But it is a great satisfaction to hear from each other when we are far apart. Dear Andrew, tomorrow your time is half out. How thankful I am, dear one, that you have got along so well as you have so far. How earnestly do I ask God to keep you from all harm the next six months if you should have to stay, and I suppose you will. But if you live until your time is out without being hurt or get sick, I shall think the Lord has heard and answered my prayer. Dear one, he has kept you through one fight, and is able to keep you through many more, but still I hope you won't have to go into any more. You stayed almost six months without being in one, and you may stay the summer through without, but I suppose that is very unlikely. I am so much afraid there will be a very great battle when Grant gets ready to take Richmond, if that is what he intends to do, but I hope there won't be any more battles. Oh dearest one, how much I would give if this wicked war was over. Someone has got to lose a dear husband or father every battle or every week, whether battle or not. But I hope that it will not be my unhappy lot. Oh dearest one, my heart would be broke forever if you was taken away from me. This world would be empty to me without you, but I hope and trust for the best if you only keep well. I think the summer will pass away faster with me than the winter has. It seems a long time since you went away. How often do I think of the time we had last fall getting our things away from that place, and how bad I felt all the time. It did seem as if my heart would break in spite of me sometimes, and I could not help it either. I would cry myself to sleep every night and in the morning, my pillow would be wet with my tears for my dear absent one. I never shall forget this time as long as I live, and I hope and pray to the Lord that you can come home, so that I can tell you all my troubles. It seems that my trouble would be over if you was safe home with me again. We used to think we was having trouble enough before you went away, but I am willing to put up with almost anything, if you can only be with me once more, never to leave me again while we live. I am thankful, dearest Andrew, that you don't have to suffer as the southern men do that you write about.[34]

In your letter, you wanted to know if Cherry liked the heifer. I don't know, but I guess not very well. She acts just the same as she did last winter. She will hook her if she can, but the heifer seems to like her and stays by her when they are out together. I think they will come, the fore part of the summer anyway, and I hope you will be home to hunt cows for us in the fall. I will go with you. I won't let you go two rods without me when you do come. The pigs I told you we had done first rate for a while, and I thought they was such nice pigs, but they seemed to choke on everything they eat, until they died, but it was not for want of care, for I took as much care of them as I knew how to. But dearest, I know you won't think that I neglect anything. We have all the wood we want to burn. Mother agreed for twelve cord, and Bishop has agreed to cut it up for us this month, so I think we will have all we want until you come back. I hope we will have a nice little farm somewhere. Richard has bought Alvira Stimpson's place, and paid five hundred dollars for it. He paid a hundred and fifty down, and the rest in a year's time. Father is going to take me to Packwaukee tomorrow, and the next day I will go home with Reuben, if I don't get a chance without. I told you in my last letter that I was going in the middle of the week, but the weather is too bad. It rained, so I could not go. It is pleasant here now. I have had a good visit and enjoyed myself very good, with the exception of worrying so much about you being in a fight, but I felt better when I heard you was safe. Mattilda is going home with me for a week. Poor girl, she feels broken hearted enough. Dear little Lucy thinks so much of Father, she wants to go to him as soon as he comes in. She teases me all the time to carry her out to see the sheep. She thinks a good deal of Mother. She can keep her still when no one else can. Jane wishes me to write a few lines to you. She teases me for your picture. She says when you come home, she is going to have hers and yours taken together. Mother & Father send their love to you.

Accept this from your loving wife, Mary to her darling husband

From Mary Burwell at Oxford to Andrew Burwell, February 26, 1865

My Dear Husband

It is now Sunday and Lucy has gone to sleep, so I thought I would improve the time in answering your long letter of the 13th. How did you get the time to write so much at once! I tell you, my dear one, it done me good to come home and find such a long letter for me to read, and I am thankful that you are well and in such good spirits. We are all well and in good spirits here. I came home yesterday with Mr. Gaylord so I got down home and back without having it cost me a cent. Mattilda came back with me, we just got home in time to escape a snow storm. It commenced snowing right away when we got home and snowed all night and until almost noon today, but it won't last long.

I am glad that the two dollars arrived safe. I don't want you to think that you are calling too much on me for money for I don't think so at all. I am glad that I have it to send you when you are without. While I was gone I had five dollars of my State money sent me, so I am not without and I have a little besides. I hope they will pay you before long, for your own sake as well as many others.

Dear husband, my mind is a good deal easier about you now than it was at the time I heard of the battle. Oh darling one, I shall never forget how I felt when I found out you was there, but I cast all that on One that is able to save you. Let you be where you will and He has answered my prayers many times, and I dont forget to thank him for it. I guess you must have been scared, dear Andrew. How I do pity you. I think of you every hour in the day and wonder what you are doing, and hoping that you are all right. I think you was in a very dangerous position when you and the other corporal had to walk the line every half hour. I know there is nothing but dangers in the army but I hope and trust you will be spared through them all. You have been there half the time now. Oh how I do hope and pray that the next half will pass off as well with you as this has, for all I suppose this half has been hard enough, and much harder than I know anything about, but I am in hopes there won't be any more fighting if they are about making peace. Why can't they hold back a spell with their fighting?

I think that summer will pass away faster than the winter has for it will be pleasanter and we can get out more. But dear one, if you only keep well and don't have to go into battle, I can get along first rate. My health is very good and everyone tells me I am getting fat and I think likely I shall get rid of having the sick headache so much when I wean the baby. She seems too big to be called a baby now. I'll tell you, dear husband, we have got as nice a little girl as anyone has got. She grows so nice and fat. She knows most all we say, and talks a good deal about her papa. She will wake in the middle of the night sometimes and pat me on the face and say "Mamma, mamma, papa." Sometimes I think the dear little one knows what it means when we talk about papa, but I don't know. I hope you will live to come home and enjoy the dear little one's company.

I am so thankful that you are not a drafted man. I am glad now that you went when you did. There is a good many that wishes they went when you did. I hope that we shall never be sorry that you went. I am sure we will not be if you come out without being hurt, for I am in hopes we can get a small place of our own somewhere. I want to be as saving as [much as] possible of our money so as to have all we can when you come. I suppose Richard intends to make quite a farm of that place he bought, but I hope our turn will come next if our lives are spared for us.[35]

Mr. Marsden died today about noon. The men die here as well as in the army. I did not go to Mr. Rood's funeral, for Richard and mother were in a hurry to get home so I went right along with them. The sheep have grown since you seen them. Father manages them first rate. Fanny is about as big a baby as ever, her lamb is a ewe and a nice fat lamb it is too.

I must draw this to a close now for I want to write a little more on another sheet to you.

Accept this from your loving
Wife Mary to Andrew

P.S. I will go to the store tomorrow and get you some tobacco and send you if you don't get these letters let me know.

Belle

From Belle Arnold Sleeper at Brooklyn to Charles Palmer, Friday, February 26, 1865, "Afternoon"

Dear Charlie:

Two weeks ago this morning I seated myself to commence a letter to you, to be finished, I then thought in the course of a day or two. But the days have passed and this letter still lies unfinished. I am not well yet and when I have had anytime to devote to my Correspondents, I have been obliged to devote it to rest. I have spent a part of today on the bed, not sleeping, but thinking of my Soldier Husband, and my two brave Brothers—thinking until the thought becomes a burden that I could bear no longer, and now I have seated myself to the window to talk to you. The bright sunlight comes flooding in filling every crevice with a warm, joyous, dancing light. O that hearts might always live in the blessed sunshine. Though we may revel in the sunlight of today, some all <u>too</u> soon, may be plunged into clouds of deepest darkness. The bright thoughts of today will soon be obscured by the gathering of shadows. Sunlight and shadows—joy and sorrows—tears and smiles. Of such is life.

Since writing the above few lines, I have been thinking down deep, and now that I have come back to myself, I find that I cannot answer this letter of yours. I will write no more until, "Richard is himself again."[36]

Our people are going to Berlin tomorrow to carry my Mother home. I shall go with them, but not to stay, if am well enough when tomorrow comes. I have thought I would not send this letter to you, but I will. And when you have read it through, congratulate yourself, that is the last of the kind you receive, for sometime at least, from Augusta. I will not persecute my friends any longer with my thoughts and feelings, unless they are a different type than now, and then I trust it will not be a persecution.

Write to me, Brother mine, as often as your duties will permit. Your letters bring sunlight with them.

Hoping to hear from you soon and often. I remain

Your humble sister
Augusta

Mary

From Mary Burwell at Oxford to Andrew Burwell, March 1, 1865

My Dear Husband

Once more I am seated to write a few lines, to you to let you know that we are all about as well as usual, and I hope you are the same, for dear Andrew it is indeed a great blessing to enjoy good health, how uneasy I should be about you, if you were sickly and you would be the same about me, but you need not worry about me, my health is better this winter than it has been since the winter before we were married. And I hope it will continue to keep good. Mr. Hartson was in here last night and he said that his son that is in your company wrote home word, that he thought, the 5th

Regt was going to leave where you are and come further north to do garrison duty. I hope you will, it will seem better to have you come nearer home, then you won't be so apt to be called into battle as you are now, but after all it may not be true, when I hear a little good news, I hope.[37]

How I wish I could pop in to your camp someday and see what you are doing, wouldn't you jump? Father said he give a good deal to come and see you, but seeing he couldn't he prays earnestly every day for you to come home safe. How I wished I could come and meet you when you come home if I could know when you was coming. But it is a good way to look ahead but I can't help but think of the happy time if you live to see it. But dearest husband I must not think about coming to see you, it will cost so much. I will be thankful to have you come without meeting you. Oh how I wish I could look for you tomorrow, it seems a long time to look ahead to next fall, how many changes may take place before that time. Our dear little girl is so much company to me, she has got so she will climb up into a chair and she can climb upstairs herself. Father was telling me you wrote a letter to Columbus Cook [?], what did he want or don't he write to you? First I suppose you will wonder what I want to know for, but I thought that he wanted to sell his place to you, he wanted to graze. I have sent you a pound of tobacco this week.

I must draw this to a close now for it is bedtime again. Accept this from your loving wife,

Mary Burwell to her husband.

From Mary Burwell at Oxford to Andrew Burwell, March 5, 1865

My Dear Husband,

It is now Sunday, and I am seated to answer your letter of the 22nd. I did not write to you when I was home as often as I do here, on account of the mail not being so handy, but I will attend to it now, steady again. We are all well as usual here, and I am in hopes this will find you well, dear Andrew. What a great blessing it is that your health is so good. I hope you won't get sick when the warm weather comes. I want you to be very careful what you eat when the hot weather comes. I wished you could come home this spring to eat bread and milk with me. I tell you it seems good to have milk and good butter. How I would like to send you a nice roll of butter that mother has made. It tastes so much better than any one else makes.

Peggy has not come in yet, but I think she will before long. I hope her calf will be worth raising. I feel anxious to raise it, for if you live to come home, we want a little stock growing again. I will try and get it pastured somewhere near by, so that I can go and see to it.

You speak of so many Rebel deserters coming in. What do our men do with them? Do they put them in Reg't. with our men, or do they let them go? I wished they would all come into our lines and leave old Jeff alone. What would he do then? I guess they are all sick enough of this war but him. Some thinks that there won't be a battle when they take Richmond. I hope there won't be, for it makes me tremble when I think of it. You are so near by that you would be apt to be in, but still, dear Andrew, there is one thing that cheers me, God is able to provide a way for your escape, and if we put our whole trust in him and ask him to save you, I have faith enough to believe he will do it. Dear husband, I should like very much to have a picture of your camp, but I should like to have you out somewhere, so that I could tell you from the rest of the men. I expect there is an artist coming here in a short time. I should like to get Lucy's again, but I don't think I will have any more of mine taken, I had such a poor one the last time that I don't like to try it again. You said you did not know that I had any corn left. I have two boxes full, one is that long box that you used to keep iron in, and the other is a big square box. Father had to keep it in a box to keep it away from the rats. I believed I had 25 bushels for my share when it was husked. I had two hundred bushels ground into meal when I was home. I think I had better have father sell the oats when he thinks they will fetch the highest price, for the mice will eat a good many of them up, besides chawing the rest. They keep two cats in the barn most of the time. Your old cat looks so natural. She is just as kind as ever and just as pretty. I had a ride after Pete and Jim to quarterly meeting when I was home, and another to Packwaukee when I came back home. When I was on my way here, I saw Florentine Hotchkiss. He has got home safe and sound, and looks well.[38]

Oh dear husband, I wont' know how to be thankful enough if you get home. I will pay for your watch just as soon as I get some money, dear one. I did not like to borrow any of Mother, because I know she has not got much, and she would hate to send for more so quick after they sent her some, and I have only the five dollars of my state money. So you see, it won't do for us both to be out of money at the same time. But after I pay for the watch, I think I shall lay the rest away. My money will be enough with the money I get for the oats, to keep me and get what summer clothes

I want, and I am going to try and get some work to do, for I want a good many little things that I don't want to get if I have to pay the clear money for it. If cotton cloth comes down any, I would like to get some more sheets and pillow cases before we go to housekeeping again, if the Lord permits us to, and I think he will. At least I hope so.

I am glad Robert Camble wrote to you. Have you ever had a letter from Clarke? He said he would write to you, and Charley Osborne told Emma he would write, and got your directions. Most everyone enquires after you and all are glad you are so well. You have the best wishes of every one. Mrs. Hall's health is very poor, and has been all the winter. Well, dearest one, I must stop for it is bedtime. Excuse my poor writing, for my pen is bad, and the ink is miserable. Good night for this time. . . .

> In the deep midnight hush,
> When stars are brightly beaming.
> And whispering winds are still,
> I woke from pleasant dreaming.
> I looked into thy deep blue eyes,
> Like stars of midnight gleaming,
> And woke to find, alas, alas,
> That I was only dreaming.

From your loving wife, Mary, to her loving husband

Abraham Lincoln was inaugurated for his second term on March 4, 1865. In his stirring inaugural address he set the tone he desired for the reconciliation of North and South: "With malice toward none, with charity for all, with firmness in the right, as God gives us to see the right, let us strive to finish the work we are in, to bind up the nation's wounds, to care for him who shall have borne the battle, and for his widow and orphan—to do all which may achieve and cherish a just and lasting peace, among ourselves, and with all nations."[39]

BELLE

From Belle Arnold Sleeper at Brooklyn to Charles Palmer, March 7, 1865, "Tuesday morning"

Dear Brother

No. 10 is received. I see I am getting behind in numbers. But I will endeavor to catch up with you at no distant day. I went to Berlin, as I told you I thought of doing in my last, and it was then that I received No. 10, also a letter from Lieut O.N. Russell of the 36th Wis. Vol., which was quite a surprise. But what surprises me most is he wishes to Correspond with me. He was 2nd Reg't in Carleton's Co., when it left the State; but after a few months service, he obtained a "discharge," on account of physical disability. The Lieut writes a good letter and I do not think there is any wrong in our corresponding, though we are both married. I do not think his Wife will have the least objection to it, and I feel very certain that my Husband has confidence enough in me to allow me to correspond with whom I please. What does my Brother think about it?[40]

After I arrived in town I found that Nell and Wilson, Mr. & Mrs. Tripp, and Will Barnes, were all coming out that evening, partly for a sleigh ride, and the <u>rest</u> to see me. And as they all wished me to stay on in town the day and return with them, I finally concluded to do so. Nell went home with me to dinner. Very soon Mr. Terry made his appearance. He had met Father Sleeper in the street and from him learned that I was home, so came round for two or three hours. L.L. is not well. I fear he has taxed his energies too hard for the past year. He begins to look real old and care worn. He inquired after you with <u>real</u> interest. I believe he begins to know George as he is. Oh, George is talking real hard of enlisting. I suppose he had had a large bounty offered him.

Nell and I called on Mrs. Stansbury; her 'Pet" has gone and <u>no mistake</u>. Poor Mattie! Her dream of happiness has been short indeed. She has already learned that her husband is not true. What a horrible awakening for her trusting heart. But I suppose you have learned all the particulars, as Doner taking 'Through Base" of Mrs. Stansbury.

We enjoyed a pleasant half hour there, then went back to Tripps to tea, and to await the hour of starting there. Mr. Tripp could not come as his work detained him to a late hour; so the rest of us piled into a double sleigh and started. Arrived here about 8 o'clock, and at 10 o'clock they started on their homeward journey; and I seem to hear their merry laughter yet. I almost wished I was going back with them. Will Barnes was home from Winona where he is at work at the Photograph Art on a visit. He has now returned to Winona.

The next day (Tuesday) I received two letters from the Ripon P.O., that Mrs. Tripp had remailed there. One from Wiley and one from Dr. M. M. Marsh. Wiley's I have answered but Dr. Marsh can wait awhile. I have actually written two letters since I wrote you last. This is contrary to the usual order; your letters generally come every other one; but I shall try to write these before writing you again: to Lieut. Russell, to A.J. Richardson, & Dr. Marsh. The Dr. is unlike any other correspondent I have. Somehow I feel so strange like when I sit down to write him. I think he must be very dignified. He wishes me to keep him informed whether I do, or do not hear from my Husband, and of my own welfare. If he takes as much notice of me as every one who writes him a letter of inquiry to him, I should think his time must be nearly all taken with correspondents.

Wiley's letter was written last Dec. in front of Savannah. I could not remember his Brigade, so I addressed him 1st Division, 17th Army Corps, Beaufort, S.C.

MARY

From Mary Burwell at Oxford to Andrew Burwell, March 10, 1865

My Dearest Husband,

I received your letter of the 28th yesterday, and am now seated to answer it. On Tuesday, I received the letter with the receipt for the 90 dollars, and the next day I sent it to Portage by the stage driver, and on Thursday he brought the package with the money all safe. I had to pay two dollars for the express charges and 25 cents to the stage driver for his trouble. I have not sent any to Mrs. Hubble yet. You said in your letter that you expected more pay, so I thought I would wait, and if you was going to send any of that home, I would pay her all at once, and then I shouldn't that to trouble her for two receipts and it would be less trouble to me. But dear Andrew, don't think that it is trouble for me to do anything that you want me to do because I said it would be less trouble. No, dearest one, there is nothing in this world would be a trouble to me that I could do for you. I want you to be sure and keep enough money with you, for I don't suppose you will get paid again until your time is out. But I hope you will, so if you should get out, you won't have to wait, as you have the time. My dear husband, how I do hope and pray that you may be permitted to come home and enjoy that money yourself. If you was taken away from me, I never could take any comfort of that money. I should always be thinking of the dear life it had bought. I felt like sitting down and having a crying spell over it when I took it to put it away. You can rest easy, my dear one, about my spending it. I will pay for your watch with the tens, and the rest I will put away, and I will pay the odd four out of my money if you don't send any more home.

But don't you think it would come through safe in a letter? Two dollars seems to me to be a good deal to pay, but to be sure, it is better to pay that much than to lose the whole, and while I think of it, I want to ask you what you done with the receipts Wilkins gave you for the money you paid him for the wagon. I never heard a word about it, but I have wondered a good many times whether you took it with you, or give it to Gage's folks to give to me. I have asked them if you left any receipt there for me, and they could not remember anything about it. I heard when I was down home that Gage and Babcock was going to make a trade with their property. Jim Jones has been home on furlough, he don't want to take the farm of Mr. Babcock, and if he takes it back, he wants to trade the farm to Gage for his property there in town, and by what I heard Till say, I thought that Mr. Gage likes the plan very well. But I don't know how it will turn out. You need not say anything to any one there about, because it would go back to them and would tell me I had to write all I heard to you, and they would not be telling a lie there, for I do tell you all I hear that is fit to write. But no one down that way knows it, nor I don't want them to. If they make such a trade, what will be done with the mortgage you have on it. You would not take it up, would you? I should think that old Mr. Gage could make out to save enough to pay it at the end of the year. He has sold his place on the lake to Mr. Kingsley's brother that has just come up from Oshkosh.

I am glad, my dear husband, that you are blessed with the privilege of having such meetings. How I would like to see you all, but I don't suppose I would like to stay there a great while, but it seems to I would be contented most anywhere so long as I could be with you, if it was but a bush shanty, as we used to talk about. My dearest husband, don't let it worry you about swearing at me. I don't know that you ever did swear at me in your life, but my darling one, if you did, it never was laid up in my mind at all. I think I have more occasions to ask you to forgive for being cross and petty to you then you have to ask me to forgive. But darling, with all my heart I forgive all your swearing, and I feel as if God had forgiven you too. How happy it makes me feel to think you have made that resolve not to swear any more. May God help you to guard against all evils, so that you may live in this world as you would wish you had when he calls you to die. But dearest one, it is my prayer that your life may be spared to come home and live a long happy life with me and your dear sweet girl that is waiting for you.

Goodbye for tonight, from your loving wife, Mary.

From Mary Burwell at Oxford to Andrew Burwell, March 12, 1865

Dearest Husband,

Sunday evening has come again and I have felt very lonesome all day so I thought I would expend an hour or two in writing to a loved one far away. How much I would give, dear Andrew, if I could see you come in on the Stage tomorrow. I do get so impatient sometimes, that is seems as if time stopped moving and yet I know that the time is flying away fast. It don't seem possible to me when I think of it, that you have been gone six months, and have commenced on the seventh, but it is so. We have lived through the winter apart and I am very thankful that we have gotten along so well. I don't mind the work nor any chores, or anything of that kind, but if I knew you was safe from battles I would not feel so bad. It is the worry and suspense that I have to be in, that is the worst, but darling, I am in hope they will end the trouble this spring. It seems to be the idea of most everyone but I do hope it will be done without any more lives being lost. How do they seem to feel about the war down there? Do they talk about doing any more fighting? I hope not, I did hear a while ago that your Regt was coming farther north. Have you heard any thing about it? I wished you might come.

I have been reading over the letters today that you wrote to me before we were married. Oh, dear Andrew, it brought back to mind the many happy hours we used to spend together talking about how happy we should be when we could be together all the while, but we did not say, we was going to be separated so long as this.

My thoughts has been away ahead to next August, and back again to day, I guess you will think my mind has been wandering today when you read this but I can't help but think of these things. Sometimes I think it is an awful long time to next fall and when I think of it again and think how fast the summer months pass away, it don't look long, but my dear husband, if you only can keep well and not have to got into battle, I can get along with anything else. Oh, dear one, it will seem so good to see your dear face once more, and more than all for our dear little girl to know her papa and love you as she does me, and the rest of us. How I would like to know when you are coming, so that I could meet you at the stage. That would be nice, but I don't suppose I could know, the day to be there, but this is looking a good ways ahead, the Lord only knows who will be alive to see that time come, but we can ask him to spare our lives, and believe in him faithfully and he will answer our prayers. How does your meetings prosper now? I should think that Stephen Chapel would be quite a help to talk if nothing more. Our preacher has been quite sick with inflammation on the lungs, so we have been without preaching for several weeks. It makes it seems so dull Sundays, without any meeting to go to.[41]

There is a man here in town that many people use, so he came to see us yesterday but he did not want to insure Mother or Emma but mine he could and he left me a book to read, and left me to make up my mind about it, but I had already made up at the time. It would be a good thing if I had the money to spare but I have not and then is no telling whether my child would be any the better for it after I am dead or not. I don't believe in paying out so much money on such uncertainty, these hard times, do you?

Mrs. Hall is very miserable. I doubt that she will live a great while. I don't know what will become of him or the children. Eliza Reynolds and her man is going to Minnesota in a few weeks. I hope you won't want to go to a new country when you come back. I don't worry any at all about it.

I haven't seen Aunt Eliza since she was up here in the winter. I suppose she does not like it because we don't go down there, but I don't go anywhere out of town, only down home. I have not been across the creek but once since I came here and that was on business. I tell you, dear one, it is about all we want to tend to is our own business and our cows.

But I must give up for my paper is giving out. I am ashamed of such writing as I send you lately but my pen is about wore out. I must get me a new one and the ink, I think, has been fine. It is some I got a little while ago, but excuse it all.

I hope to get a letter from you tomorrow.

Good night, dear Andrew, from your loving Wife Mary Burwell

BELLE

From Belle Arnold Sleeper at Berlin to Charles Palmer, March 12, 1865, "Sunday Eve"

Home once more! I am glad to be here I assure you. Came yesterday, and I am going to stay for some while too. Don't think, Brother mine, that because I am so glad to be home, I was wearied of taking care of my Husband's Mother. Far from that. But she does not need my undivided care now. I owe my duty to my own Mother. I have with been with Father and Mother Sleeper since the first of Sept. last; and I have been happier ministering to their wants than I otherwise have been. Though I could not be what their son was to them yet I have tried hard to be in all respects a daughter to them, and I believe I have not failed. I would not be quite contented so far from town. It is here my Husband will come first, and I must be among the first to greet him.

Nellie took tea with me last evening. Dick came around and spent the evening with us and attended Miss Nellie home. He talked of leaving town this week I believe he will go, as he has stopped work. Rumor says they will be married soon; and encourages the same with regard to Oren and Dora.

This is not a letter, Ben, I hardly know what you will call it, but I shall send it to you, and write to you in a day or two when I shall endeavor to answer No. 10. Nell says three weeks passed without you receiving a line from me and I can't allow that to happen again.

I think of you very often and pray that God will keep you from all harm. Write to me soon and write often.

Yours with much love,
Augusta

From Belle Arnold Sleeper at Berlin to Charles Palmer at Fort Clay, Lexington, Kentucky, March 16, 1865, "No. 10"

My Brother

I have just finished a letter to Dr. Marsh and I'll tell you what a feeling came over me as I took up my pen to commence this to you. I thought first of the two or three last letters I had written you, then I wondered if I could make this any more interesting then the others were, I felt that I could not and I would not write at all to you. Then straight I go ashamed of myself, and now that I have confessed to you my weakness, I believe that I can go on and finish this letter with a better grace.

I have read and reread No. 10, a great many times and tears of joy and thankfulness fell from my eyes, and I have fervently thanked God, the giver of all good, that my brother is thus pure and noble. You have great reason to be thankful that you have escaped from the many sins and temptations, into the arms of which so many fallen. How few, how very few live to half your age and remain free from the sin of intoxication. O Charlie, great indeed has been the work wrought in you. How proud I feel of my Brother, and how very glad that you have given me a Sister's place in your heart.

I must close now, and go down to the Post Office. The mail has not come in now until 8 o'clock, and this makes it very late for me to go to the P.O.

but I can't stay till morning. To think of letting a letter remain there all night, drives me out much darker nights than this. I am looking for a letter from Hi; this week, certain. What shall I do if no tidings come! O Charlie, it is so hard to wait patiently.

MARY

From Mary Burwell at Oxford to Andrew Burwell, March 16, 1865

My Dear Husband,

I received your letter written the 7th today. It found us all well as usual, and I hope this will find you well and enjoying yourself as well as your circumstances will admit you to. I am very thankful that we all enjoy such good health as we do, while we are apart. I hope we shall continue so, especially you. It would be so much harder for you to be sick away off there, without any friends near you to take care of the other. But I hope we shan't any of us be out of health this summer. Dear Andrew, I want you to be as careful as can of your self, now it is coming spring. And when the very hot weather comes, be careful what you eat and drink. I tell you, we have had a hard storm here for the past three days. It has snowed 6 inches on the level and it rained with all the rest and then froze on to the snow, making a crust about an inch thick, and today the wind has blown a perfect gale. But today, I made out to go to the Post Office. It took two days for the Kilbourn Stage to go and come in, the roads was so bad, and it got in after I had gone to bed (Lucy was so cross, I had to go before the rest did), but when I found out the stage had come, I hopped out of bed and Em and I went to the Office, and I did not get a letter. Wasn't that too bad? I do hope that this is the last of our winter. I am most tired of winter weather, but we have got along bravely, a great deal better than I expected to. Our cows are going to turn out good this spring. We have had to buy some hay of Wm. Knox, and we had to pay a dollar a hundred for it, and another dollar for getting it hauled. I am in hopes we shall have enough now, but I don't know. It will be owing to thaw soon the ground will be bare, so that the grass will begin to grow, but it don't look like much like it here now. The ground is all covered with snow, and it makes it look quite wintry here now. Jaeger is having his store all torn down and hauled to Portage. I tell you it will leave a bad looking spot there when it is all gone. I am in hope there will somebody come in here and build up new buildings in place of these that is torn down, but I am afraid Oxford has seen its best days. My dear husband, I am so glad you are having such good meetings down there. I would like to be there with you and help you to enjoy them. Dearest one, how much better it is to live that way, then it would be to give way to gambling and drinking as a great many do when they get into the army. Oh dear one, you can't think how happy it makes my heart feel to think that you have taken this course while you was away. I hope and pray, dear Andrew, you never will turn back any more. If we never see each other in this world, let us try and live so as to meet in heaven, but I can't bear that thought that we shan't see each other here again. But it would be more satisfaction if you should be taken away down there, to think that you was prepared to go, than it would be if you died as some that I heard of. I hope, my dearest one, that you will be spared to come home, so that I can enjoy a happy life with you and have you to help me to bring up this dear little girl. I have quite a time making her mind once in a while, but I don't think she is going to be very hard to conquer. She is getting to be such a big girl, and she acts so old. She will take up a slate and pencil and sit down and mark away, just as handy as I will, and she plays with her dolls. Jane gave hers to her when I was down home, and she has a nice time playing with them. And she thinks so much of pictures, she was bound to have the letter that I got today with the picture on it. She thought that was very nice. Dear one, how I wished you could write and tell me you was coming home. That would cheer me more than anything else, but I hope before many months shall pass away, you can be free. Oh how I do look ahead some days and think how long it is going to be before your time will be out and how much longer you will have to stay, I can't tell, but hope not any, if you can't come before. But my darling one, take good care of yourself and strive to serve God now every day, and pray for me, and I will and do pray for you every day. My darling one, I shall have to stop, for baby is waking up and I must go to bed. Good night, dearest, for this time.

From Your Mary

BELLE

From Belle Arnold Sleeper at Brooklyn to Charles Palmer at Fort Clay, Lexington, Kentucky, March 19, 1865, "Sabbath morning, Father Sleeper's"

My Brother:

Many things have transpired since writing the above to render it impossible to finish this letter. My Mother has sold her house and lot and we have been moving for the last two or three days. Mother is going to leave town in a week or two, to spend the Summer visiting among her friends. She will stay with me until she leaves. Father and Mother [Sleeper] have not come home, thought I am looking with all my eyes for them today.

Nellie came home with me last night; spent the night, and now sits at the opposite side of the table writing to a lady friend of hers. She just enquired who I was writing to; when I told her Charlie she said, "Why I must write to Charlie today, so its no use for me to tell you that Dick 'has left' town as Nell will probably give you the particulars."

Nell and I went to the P.O. last night. She got nothing and I got a letter from "Brother Charlie," and one from a friend in Fond du Lac: a lady who was an intimate friend of mine in years gone by. She is now married, and knows not what it is to be separated from her husband, but a few hours at a time. She tells me that she is "so happy." Of course, she is, I would like to know who couldn't be happy with one's husband near them all the time.

Such a good letter from my Soldier Brother. I did miss your letter last week sadly. But I kept thinking "Charlie must be very busy or else he would certainly write me," and I see I was right. So you learned Theater Action for a short space of time, did you? Of course, you succeeded with the "Zouave Drill?" I don't believe you know what the word "fail" means. If you do, I am certain you haven't learned from experience. How well I would have liked to witness the closing scene; and I would not have objected to being witness to the whole performance.[42]

Now that your duties are multiplying I shall not object to your dealing out "Homeopathic doses," providing you deal them out very close together. I shall try to be more punctual in the future in writing to you. I have had many duties to occupy my time but through all I have tried hard to take care of my health, for I felt that I should need all my strength to care for my Husband when he returned. But now, I sometimes feel that he will never need my care. The week has passed and no word from him. Can it, oh can it be, that he slowly starved to death in that loathsome prison den! I <u>will not</u> believe it! He will come back to me! And yet, as the days pass by, and no tidings come, there seems settling around me a cloud so thick in its awful blackness that I shudder to think that soon, very soon, it may shut out every ray of light. God help me to bear this heavy burden. I gave him to his Country ere I scarcely learned to call him mine, and if he must be sacrificed, I must bear it, though I can not but feel that it is a needless sacrifice.

No, no, Charlie, you must not put on a "stern exterior" with me. You will drive me from you entirely if you do. I like to come to you in all my moods, but times I fear that I shall weary you with my murmurings and you will think me weak and selfish. The "peep behind the scenes" that you have allowed me to take, has made me feel free to write to you, just my thoughts and feelings. No, No! Do not draw the curtains so closely now that I cannot get a glimpse of your life. Be "stern" as you like to others, but not to me, I would feel that I had lost my brother entirely.

I see we slightly differ in regards to Nellie. I drew my inferences from the conversations we had held together—from many remarks she has made to me at different times. And, Charlie, though I will not discuss the subject longer with my pen, sometimes we shall meet face to face, we will just take a hasty review of it, for I still think that I have had good reason to believe that at one time, she prized wealth and position more than a living heart. If her opinions and feelings have undergone a change no one will rejoice more than I shall.

Perhaps, Dick would not be a "plaything" without an end in view. And I cannot say he has not accomplished that end. Your know our best Generals sometimes deem it best to take a City by regular siege, and often win in this way, when if they attacked by storm they would have failed entirely.

I was around to Col. Carelton's [sic: Carlton] a few mornings ago, and while there was informed that "Charlie was soon to be married." Now, Sir, what have you to say about this <u>serious charge</u>? Roxy did not hardly believe it, but Emma though it quite likely. I neither contradicted nor affirmed the statement for I felt they wished to "draw-me-out" and I hardly thought they would do it. I did not see Wright at all. The Carletons told me how highly he spoke of you, and how much you had done for him. I have heard many speak of his improved appearance. I would liked to have seen him right well.

Now I have got a secret to tell you. Don't tell anyone, if you do, tell them not to tell. Mrs. Stansbury is going to have a "married sociable" or perhaps it should be termed a "concert," made up of her music class. But it isn't to be known till just before it comes off. I wouldn't want to wager a large amount that half of the town don't know it already. I do not belong to the "class," but I did once, as I was honored with an invitation. I am to sing in a "quartette" with Dora. Now don't go to pitying her, for if I find I can't do my part well, I shall sort-a-slide out. Nell and Nettie are going to sing a piece of Opera I believe. Oh, I expect it will be a grand affair. Nell just sits here making all sorts of suggestions in regard to my style of writing and the blunders on this page you may just credit to her. I want her to stay tonight with me; and if she does, she says she can't write to you. But I am so selfish that I shall keep her if I can. I don't want to stay alone.

Be careful of your health, Brother mine, and not tax your energies too hard. Your "time" is half expired. It cannot be that it will be necessary for you to remain a year and a half longer.

I do not hear from Wiley. His Wife has come back into town to live. I discover but one error in your "proof"—an out of one word only. This has been a beautiful Sabbath day. Beautiful overhead, but rather wet under foot. Quite an amount of snow fell last week and the warm sun yesterday and today has had a very softening influence on it. Summer will soon be here and I care not how soon.

Write soon and often, but do not let me intrude on your duties.

God bless and keep thee, my Brother, is the prayer of Augusta.

P.S. Excuse the variety of the writing fluid. I got Mother's bottle when I commenced, but soon had to deliver it up to her.

From Belle Arnold at Berlin to Charles Palmer, March 21, 1865, "No. 2 [?], Evening, 10 O'clock"

My Dear Brother:

I am almost ashamed to write to you with a pencil and so hurriedly as I must after waiting so long and having received such a good letter from you. But Charlie, my dear brother, I remember that you once wrote me that a few lines written crosswise and a sheet of paper would be acceptable from me. So I shall not apologize in the least. I have just come in from evening meeting and I feel that I must write you a few lines before retiring and the ink is so thick it is almost impossible to use it. Am going to serve on a committee, tomorrow, that is laboring here for the American Bible Society. The labor consists of canvassing the City to ascertain who has a Bible and who has not; those that have not and cannot buy, we shall furnish gratis, and those who wish to buy we will sell to. Sister Goodwin and myself were appointed from the M.E. Church, and I believe there are two from each of the other churches. Our district is the South Side of the Main St. on the west side of the river, and extends to the limits of Berlin.

What shall I say in answer to your letter: It is so good all the way through, and I want to say as much. I did commence writing as the spirit moved but it is so old now that it would not be interesting. I shall try to do more in the writing line. I am actually ashamed to tell you when I wrote to Nellie. But I have a letter almost finished now. That exhibition took four weeks then I went north the next morning and stayed a week, and then since I came home so much to attend to! Charlie, don't you scold me now, I will try to do better! Don't forget that "good long letter" in vacation. I will see about that 'card' right off-will speak to T.L. about it. The latest is that Roxy is married to Farmer—married last night. Wiley was invited but Bell was left out. Wiley did not attend. Write soon to Belle.

From Belle Arnold Sleeper at Berlin to Charles Palmer at Fort Clay, Lexington, Kentucky, March 24, 1865, "No. 11 / Saturday night, 10 o'clock"

My Brother,

I cannot "lay one down to rest" tonight without telling you how sad and disappointed I am feeling, Charlie it is so dark tonight. Not a single ray of sunshine. I am almost ready to sink down in despair. O my Brother, I pray God that you may never know what it is to feel that the one who is all in all to you, for whose life you would willingly yield up your own, has died, or is dying by degrees, that most horrible of all horrible deaths, slow starvation. O must—I give up! Shall I never know how or when he died! Will no one ever bring me tidings of him! O must, must I drink of this bitter, bitter cup! I encouraged him to go. I told him it was right—that he was dearer, aye, a thousand times dearer to me because of his determination to go. And felt proud of him when I saw that he never flinched, but went bravely forward in the path of duty and right; allowing not even the one tie, to bind him to his home. Where now is my pride? I fear it has nearly fled from me. Charlie, had he died in the battlefield, I could bear it. And I must bear it as it is, but oh, 'tis very hard. I felt so sure of a letter this week. It did not seem possible that another Sabbath would roll around and yet no tidings from him. I felt so sure! But now I must give up. The week has passed, and tonight, all hope seems fled. Half of my existence is crushed out. For the past year, every hope and every thought of the future has been linked with him. O I would tried so hard to have made his life bright and happy; but now, now all is past. My short dream of the future has faded, and in its place is naught but darkness, so steep and awful that I can feel it in my inmost soul. O for one ray of light!

You will wonder why I have given up my husband's return. It is because all the Prisoners are now exchanged who were at Salisbury, and he has not come, and I have reason to believe that none were taken from the Salisbury clink to any other place. Today I saw a list of 1300 prisoners who died in the Hospitals at S. Hi's name was not there, but the writer states that many died in the clink and many were shot by the guards whose names would never be known. If I would only know, but I cannot. I can only wait and suffer on. Almost 12 o'clock. For nearly two hours, I have sat here. And I have told you some of the sadness in my heart. I don't why of late, I think of you when I am sad, and wish so much to see you. I cannot go to my Mother, I prefer the quiet of my own room. Mother tries to talk me out of my sadness to make me forget. My sisters each have their own families to think of and care for. I must either lock up this great sorrow in my heart or my brother Charles must help me to bear it.

The clock strikes 12. Good night, my Brother, may good Angels guard thee, is the prayer of your sister.

Sabbath morning, 11 o'clock

I have not been to Church this morning for several reasons. One is my Mother being quite ill last night I did not get any sleep till nearly morning, consequently I slept quite late. After I finished writing you last night, I sat here till I dare not stay in this little room any longer. It is Hiram's room, and one we have occupied together. I am getting cowardly. I am almost afraid of my own shadow; and the rustling of trees against the low roof sends a cold chill to my heart. You will wonder at this and I will tell you. A short time before Hi went away, we were speaking of the possibility of our never meeting again. And after conversing for some time, he turned and so seriously that his words made a deep impression on my mind, "Belle, my wife, if I die, you shall know it, for I, myself will tell it to you." And now I hardly dare to be alone. Not because I fear to see him, or fear to feel his presence, but because my cowardly heart shrinks from the confirmation of its worst fears. And this is why I crept softly downstairs and to my Mother's bed. I found her suffering from pain, which soon grew worse, but toward morning the distress left her and she slept. Another reason Why I did not care to go to Church, is that not half the people who gather in the House of prayers, gather there to worship God. I do not care for the pity of the idle crowd, and their charitable remarks, and glances do not add god to my devotions. I thought a week ago last Sabbath that I would not go again. It was wrong I know; but the discourse afflicted me deeply, and the multitude or questions, asked out of idle curiosity, which I was compelled to answer before I would get egress from the Church, jarred terribly on the cords of my heart. It is so hard for me to keep up a stern exterior. Then there are those who think, "Mrs. Sleeper does not care for her husband." Pray one and I shall have help to bear my burden—Nellie has come and thinks it about time to retire. So my brother I must leave you.[43]

Write as often as possible to me. But do not let my sad thoughts and feeling affect you or I shall feel that I should not come to you in my sorrow.

Good night.
Augusta

Monday

You will think this letter long I fear but I fear after reading it over that I have omitted to mention anything that I intended to speak of. I add this P.S. just to let you know though this letter is long, I could have made it much longer.

Andrew Burwell's 5th Infantry led the charge in the final battle of the Petersburg siege and was the first unit to plant its battle flag on the Confederate defenses. Andrew Burwell was wounded on April 2, 1865, during this battle; he was first taken to City Point Hospital, Virginia, and later transferred to a hospital in Washington, DC, where he recovered from his wounds and was mustered out of service on July 12, 1865.[44]

Belle Arnold at Berlin to Charles Palmer at Fort Clay, Lexington, Kentucky, April 2, 1865, "No. 13 / Sunday night, 9 o'clock"

My Brother:

Your No. 18 came to hand last night. I was obliged to turn it over a number of times, in order to be sure it came from you, but when I commenced reading it I doubted no longer. It was Brother Charlie all the way through, but so short. Please don't get into a hurry often when you write. But, I would rather you would write in a hurry that not write at all. Much rather, I assure you.

Father and Mother Sleeper came home today, and I have been so busy that I could not get around to write till I came to my room for the night. I did not want to miss writing this week so I have taken a small sheet, not because, I haven't much to say to you, but because I haven't much time to say it in.

I do not mean to "keep making excuses"; I think it is from force of habit. I'll try to "stop."

No, I did not mean to withdraw my confidence from you. But when I stopped to realize how full of murmurs and darkness so many of my letters had been I was fearful you would weary of them. But I cannot <u>keep up appearances</u> with those who are dear to me. Your "retaliation" quite brought me to my senses again. No, sir, I didn't like it one bit. I should feel that I had lost you, and beneath a "stern exterior" I could never find my Brother again. I shall not tell you how glad I am that you do not tire of my letters though they are fill entirely of my own heartaches, for you would say "making excuses" again. And I want it <u>distinctly</u> understood, that I make no more <u>excuses</u>.

The "Concert" does not come off till the 13th this month—I have concluded to play an intermediate piece—a waltz and let it go at that. I have not made an effort to sing. Dora is very busy indeed. The "Concert" of the flowers came off last Friday night and was a decided success. Great praise was given Dora for her able management. The Hall was crowded.

I often meet Oren and Dora together as of late. He pays her very decided attention. I hear many speak of his entire devotion to her. Will it always last. I hope so. Oren and I are friends again. The key to it is I have paid him the $15 I borrowed of him. Perhaps I judge him harshly. But it was very hard for me to ask him for the money and his strange manner stung me sharply. It may be because I am not used to dealing with businessmen.

I am very glad that you intend on coming home next Fall, on a visit. And I seriously hope there will be no need of you returning to "service" again.

My Mother has sold her little home. Wiley thought it best. And under the circumstances I am glad of it. She will visit among our relatives this Summer, and then I hope to be able to take her to a home of my own which would never be complete without her presence there. She is still with me. I hardly know what to do with myself this Summer. But if I do not hear from my Husband soon, I think I will go into some kind of employment. Nell and I have been talking about leaving this little city and trying our fortune elsewhere at typesetting. Wilson came up from Oshkosh last night. Nell and him gave me a short call today. He returns in the morning.

Charlie, please don't criticize this letter. If you knew how tired I am, I am sure you would not.

Write soon, to your lonely sister.
Augusta

MARY

From Mary Burwell at Oxford to Andrew W. Burwell, April 2, 1865

My Dearest Andrew,

Sunday evening has again come and finds me as usual writing to a beloved husband that is far away. We are all well at present, and I hope this will find you well and safe, we have just heard of a battle between Grant and Lee, but have not heard any particulars yet. Oh my dearest one, my heart thumps so that it jars my hand as I write, for fear you was there, but still I have a little hope that you was not for I have just been to George Bell's to see what they knew about it and he said the 2nd and 9th Corps was all that was spoke of being in, so that is better than not hearing anything. I don't know whether it is true or not, but I hope to get a letter from you tomorrow that will be later date than the battle. The last letter I got from you was written on the 22nd of March, I got it last Friday night, and with it your Company Register.

But my dearest Andrew, I am sorry to tell you that the stock was broken into and consequently the register is torn apart right through the middle. It was too bad, I feel so bad about it I could have cried, if it would do any good, how pretty it is. I will get some gum [illegible] and mend it again and if I have money enough when I go to Portage, I will get it framed and glass over it, or else I will keep it covered until you come home, if God is willing you should. Did you buy that or was it gave to you?

Dear husband, you spoke in your letter of having lonesome spells, I know all about such feeling. I get lonesome for you very often, it is as you say I can't hardly believe sometime that we are so far apart, when I get to thinking about it, it seems as if I could not stay here any longer, I must fly to you, but I know that is impossible. So I will think, all things over and think may be there will something turn up, and they will make peace before long, and my dear one can be home by the time his year is up, But you see this is only my thoughts. I try to flatter myself for the best, and then I think why do I doubt, when I feel so satisfied that the Lord does hear my prayers and will answer them. It is as you said in your letter, he has spared many others and I know he will spare you if we both ask him faithfully and trust it all to Him. I am so thankful my own dear one, that you do put your trust in Him.

It was so good to read your letters, they are such good ones. How I do find hope you will live to come home, what comfort we will take reading them. I tell you that I take some comfort reading your old letters that you wrote me before we was married. It makes me think of the good old times we used to have. Oh, dear one, how I long for the time to come when I can watch for you to come home. I see a soldier come in from Portage tonight. He stopped at the tavern, and he had a big bundle of clothes tied up in his oilcloth blankets. Oh darling, how I did wish that was you. I just imagined you coming to the house, and me running out to meet you. Well, dear Andrew, let us try and wait with all the patience we can putting our trust in God for we know that He is able and willing to hear and answer of those that put their trust in Him. You have commenced on your eighth month after the 24th of this month there will be only four more until the year from your enlistment date will be up. How much longer you will have to stay, I can't say but I only hope you can come next quarter, and so much sooner as they have a mind to let you. I would be glad if it was this week.

Our dear little girl is growing so nicely. She runs out in the dooryard and chases the cat around. She loves to have little girls come to play with her. She will cry after them if she sees them in the street. I am going to wean her daytime this week, and next week I will take her off nights. Mother is going to take her and have her sleep with her. She can reach the door latch and shut herself out and she will say bye-bye. She is a timid little thing, she is afraid of the chickens when they make a very loud noise, and she is afraid to look out of the window when it is dark, or go into a cloak room, but I am very careful about scaring her. I think she will outgrow that after awhile.

I have not heard of that box of clothes you spoke of but I have written to Mr. Gage to have him send your bundle along to me when it does come. I hope it will get through safe.

Peggy has not come in yet, but I am waiting supportively for her. We have a heifer calf that Ed Hall gave Emma, so we have one to feed and I hope we shall have another in a day or two. I do not think of any more for now so I will have to stop for this time accept this from your

Loving Wife Mary E. Burwell

Give my respects to Mr. Thompson and tell him to keep up good courage. His time is passing away as well as your when he can go home too.

From Mary Burwell at Oxford to Andrew W. Burwell, Tuesday, April 4, 1865

My Dearest Husband,

I feel very much unnerved tonight for we have just heard today of the great battle at Richmond. The men and boys have been firing off the anvil all afternoon, but oh, my darling husband, what thoughts passed through my mind tonight. I feel as if I could fly to you, and see if you are safe. You must have seen some hard fighting, but I am so very much afraid that you are hurt, that it does seem almost impossible to wait for a paper or letter. But if you are not hurt or alive, I shall have news from you before you get this. I just received a letter from you written the 28th but, dearest one, you have seen some hard times since then, I know and I shall have to wait until Thursday before I can know any more about it. Oh dear one, how I do hope this is the last of this war, but I am afraid all ain't true that is told. Oh how I do hope and pray, that God has spared you for I know that what He wills is best, but it would seem hard to think that what is best for you to be taken away. But dear one, I can't think that you are hurt or that you won't come back to me again. Oh my dear one, how much I would give to know how you are tonight but I can't know. I know there is a great many that is deprived of loved ones this last week, but oh, I hope and pray that my dear husband is alive and well. I shan't know how to be thankful enough if you have gone through safe. Adelbert Eastman and David Bishop has got home. How I wish you was home tonight but I will have to close this for it is getting late. I must go to my bed and lay and wonder if my dear one is alive or not or is he suffering from his wounds.[45]

Oh darling, what a time this is. I hope this is the last of the trouble, well dear one, good by for the present from you most true and loving wife

Mary E. Burwell

From Mary Burwell at Oxford to Andrew W. Burwell, April 7, 1865

My Dear Husband,

Once more I take my pen in hand to write to you. We are all well, and I hope and trust that this will find you well and safe. My dear Andrew, we are in great fear about you just now. I know you have been in that great battle, and that is all we know about you. Oh my dear one, you can't tell how I feel. When I first heard that Richmond was taken, it seemed to me as if I must sink through the floor. I trembled so, that I could not keep a limb still. We heard of the battle on Tuesday, and now it is Friday night, and I don't know yet whether you are dead or alive.[46] I expect to get a letter tonight. Oh my dearest one, I try to think or imagine what awful scenes you have had to pass through within the last week, and while I think, it seems as if I could not endure the thoughts of you being in such a place, let alone getting wounded or being killed. It seems to take my strength all away for me to think of it. Well, dear husband, I have been to the Post Office, and did not get any letter. Now I shall have to wait until Monday before another mail will come in, but I suppose I had not ought to expect a letter right away now, for I guess may be you ain't where you can write, if you are able, but still it seems almost impossible for me to wait, but I shall have to. There is no other way for me to do, only to pray to God to be with you wherever you are, and I do ask Him every day and every night to keep you and shield you in the hour of danger. And oh my dearest Andrew, how earnestly I have asked him to spare your dear life through these past battles, and dear one, I do hope and trust that God has answered my prayer. Oh how anxiously I am waiting for a letter from you. I can't bear to think that I ain't going to get any more letters from you. Oh no, it can't be that my darling husband is taken away from me, never to come back in this world. I hope not, dearest.

I do hope now that the war will be ended. I should think the fighting was about done now. I hope so anyway. We have heard today that Grant was chasing Lee, and I am wondering if you are with him, or whether you are left to guard Richmond, for I suppose it will have to be guarded. Of course, if you are with Grant, it is not to be wondered at about me not getting a letter from you since the battle. The last I got was written the 28th of March.

I went and told Jane Fish about Arte Foote, and speaking of him makes me think of telling you that Ovando English is wounded in his shoulder, and Del Eastman and David Bishop has got home.[47]

There is several other soldiers that is home that I don't know. They are going to have a dance here next Friday for these returned soldiers. My dear husband, I think if you live to get home, we will rejoice in your return in a better way than that. I know, dear Andrew, that is too bad that I sold that hay. I am sorry now, but hay seemed to be plentiful enough the fore part of the winter, and every body that we asked told us that what we had here would winter the two cows, and it cost so much to get a team here, that I thought I had better sell that down there, and that would save hunting up a team to haul it, and save the expense. But it did not turn out as I expected, but I can't help it now. I will try to be more thoughtful another time, and about me breaking into that 50 dollars, I would not do it for anything. I don't think of using it no more than if I had not got it. I think it is money that is hard earned, and I will save all I can of your money that you sent home, for you to use your own self, if you live to come home. You wanted to know if I had heard any more about that trade of Mr. Gage and Babcock. No, I have not. May be they won't do anything about it until Leroy gets back, but I don't know, and as you say, all I want is our money and the interest all right, for indeed my darling one, you have suffered enough to have something to show for it, and it is my daily prayer to God that you may live to come home to enjoy it. I have got a very bad headache tonight, so I think you will excuse me if I don't write another sheet. Dear husband, I thought I would write a private letter this time. May you be more settled by and by, and then I will write you one. I hope you will be alive and well, so as to read a good many letters yet, but I would rather have you come home where you would be safe from the horrible battlefield, but I hope the time is not far off. Well, dearest one, I must say good night for this time, from your ever true and loving wife,

Mary Burwell to her darling Andrew

Aware that the Army of Northern Virginia would soon be defeated, on April 7 Grant sent a message to Lee: "The result of the last week must convince you of the hopelessness of further resistance on the part of the Army of Northern Virginia in this struggle. I feel that it is so, and regard it as my duty to shift from myself the responsibility of any further effusion of blood, by asking of you the surrender of that portion of the C.S. Army known as the Army of Northern Virginia." Lee declined to surrender but inquired about the terms of surrender.[48] Undeterred by the sight of eighty thousand Union campfires in the distance, Lee and his generals determined to attack cavalry commanded by Philip H. Sheridan. On April 9, the Confederates moved the cavalry from their position near Appomattox Courthouse, only to realize that a massive number of federal troops were directly behind Sheridan's cavalry. Lee conceded to his staff, "There is nothing left for me to do but to go and see General Grant and I would rather die a thousand deaths."[49]

ANNIE

From Annie Cox at Madison to Gideon Winans Allen at Sturgeon Bay, Wisconsin, April 9, 1865

... Jeff Davis has gone to Augusta and would attempt to carry on the government there but the latest news is that he had been captured with his army.... The hills sang out merrily and the cannons boomed.

Annie's joy at the surrender of Lee, and the joy of much of the nation, turned to sorrow on April 14, when Abraham Lincoln was shot by John Wilkes Booth at 10:00 p.m. Lincoln succumbed to his wounds at 7:22 the next morning.[50]

Belle Arnold Sleeper did not share the joy that others felt at the news of Lee's surrender to Grant on April 9. The day before the surrender at Appomattox, Belle had learned that Hiram Sleeper had perished at Salisbury Prison on December 28, 1864, and that her months of hoping for his safe return had been for naught.[51] Hiram Sleeper was but one of the nineteen thousand Confederates and twenty-six thousand federal prisoners who perished in the squalid conditions of wartime prisons.[52]

BELLE

From Belle Arnold Sleeper at Berlin to Charles Palmer at Fort Clay, Lexington, Kentucky, April 16, 1865, "No. 18 I don't know whether I have numbered this right or not / Sunday Evening"

My Brother,

Both No. 14 and 15 have been received. No. 14 last Monday night or either Tuesday morning and No. 15 came to the house this morning. I did not write to you a week ago today. I could not and there has been no time through the week that I could have written to you though I have longed for your presence many times.

Charlie, my Brother, I have no husband now. A week yesterday, since the terrible news reached me. I thought I was prepared for this news but the blow has nearly crushed me. For seven long scary months, I have watched and waited, and this, this is my reward! I have tried many times to feel that all hope was useless, and that I must give up. But oh, I did not know how large my hope was 'til now. I have no longer room for hope.

My informant was a Mr. Mullin, a comrade of Hiram's. He wrote me but a few lines, telling me that my husband died at Florence, S.C., the 28th of last Dec. Disease, Chronic Diarrhea. That his last words were, "tell my wife to meet me in heaven." He gave him my likeness with the request to send it to me when he was no more. He has sent it to me, with his Srg't certificate and two letters received from me, one of which I wrote him after he was captured directing to Libby Prison. Mr. Mullin bade me write him for any particulars I wished, and he would send me all of the information in his power. I have written him and hope tomorrow's mail will bring me the wished for information. He is in Illinois at present.

If my Husband must go, I am glad he went so soon, for his sufferings must have been extreme. But 'tis hard, very hard to know he died for want of the care I would have been so glad to have bestowed upon him for the want of the necessaries of life of which I had an abundance! While I was surrounded by all the comforts and many of the luxuries of life, he, my husband, was slowly dying for the want of a bare necessity. O, my Brother, as these thoughts come rushing through my head, my brain reels, and my heart seems bursting! O was it right to take my husband from me, and leave me in this cold world, alone! God alone knows how dark my life was, how selfish and exacting I was fast becoming, when my husband took me to his heart and generously forgave my every wrong thought. For nearly one whole year he bore with my capriciousness well, and when at last I promised to be his, he took me to his heart never chiding me for the past, though many times I must have pained him deeply. I had thought to make reparation for all the past—to render all his future bright and happy. But God has taken him from me. It may be I could not be entrusted with his happiness, that I could not render his future bright. But O, I would have devoted my life to him next to my God! With him has every thought of the future has been entwined! Now I am alone! No not alone, for I believe his spirit hovers near me, and I will meet him in heaven. At first, I could not have it so. It seemed that I must have my husband—that I could not give him up. Now I must give him up, and so I have waited patiently for him to come to me, as I must wait for the time when I can go to him.

You need not fear to tell me that wish now, though wait till we meet if you choose. When I first found the ring was broken, a cold chill crept over me, but I succeeded in shaking off the impression it first made upon me. I use to feel, at times, so sure that Hiram would come back to me, that I would not often allow myself to look on the dark side. He was so hopeful of the future that it wrong of me to disband. But the dark side is now turned to me, and oh so dark. My hopes of the happy future are crushed and joy seems forever fleet. I have cared for myself, because he wished it. Now what is life to one with its one object gone! O, this is so hard to bear, but God helping me, I will be patient.

Col. Castleton has been home on "furlough." He leaves tomorrow morning for the "front" I was over there toward night to carry a pack for Wiley.

The Col. thinks and says that Wiley will soon come home. I hope both my brothers will come back home and remain with us.

The whole city is in mourning for our President. What may we expect now.

I must bid you good night. I am not "feeling well" tonight, and will not attempt to answer your letters, for I could not do them justice.

God protect and keep thee is the prayer of

Your sister,
Belle.

Aftermath of War

April 16, 1865

The sun's rays spread softly across cities, towns, and farms of Wisconsin as the women of Wisconsin awoke to futures changed both by national events and by their wartime experiences. The women whose voices have been revealed in this book ventured forth into lives diminished by loss and bereavement but also into a world that had been enriched by the contributions they, and countless other women, had made during the war.

The Civil War was a transformative event for Wisconsin women as legislation expanded opportunities for girls and women in education, changed transportation, and accelerated the westward movement. Women's leadership in civic organizations altered their role from serving as volunteers at the local level to being part of a coordinated national movement. The absence of men during the war and the deaths of so many men impacted family life and marriage. The deaths of 600,000 soldiers altered funeral and burial practices.

EXPANSION OF EDUCATION:
EMILY QUINER AND ANNIE COX

The growth in educational opportunities for women enabled Emily to make contributions in education that may have helped to fill her heart and head after she was unable to return to nursing her wounded and ill soldiers in Memphis. Emily completed her degree at the University of Wisconsin in 1869, a result of the decision of the university to admit women as a means of sustaining the university's existence during the war. This wartime decision was extended by a Wisconsin legislative act of 1866 that stipulated that "the university in all of its departments and colleges" be "open alike to male and female students." Despite this legislative mandate, the new UW president, Paul Chadbourne, did not favor coeducation, and the legislature amended the law to set up a "Female Department." Chadbourne convinced the legislature to allocate $50,000 to construct a building for women students, the first funding the state of Wisconsin had ever provided for a university building. This gender-based segregation of students would last until Chadbourne left, in 1870.[1]

Emily continued to contribute to society as a teacher in the Chicago schools from 1869 through 1879 and in the Denver public schools from 1879 through 1904. In her last years, Emily returned to Chicago to live with her sister Maria. Emily died at the age of seventy, a year after the conclusion of America's next great war, on October 22, 1919. She is buried at Forest Hill Cemetery in Madison.[2]

Annie Cox married her "Winans" on May 16, 1865, and moved to Sturgeon Bay, where the couple had five children, three of whom grew to adulthood. In 1909, at the age of thirty, their daughter Ruth Florence Allen became the first woman to complete a doctorate in botany at the University of Wisconsin. Ruth's accomplishment was a direct result of the Morrill Act, passed by the United States Congress in 1862, which greatly expanded higher education and further opened higher education to women. Before the war the study of topics related to Wisconsin's major economic base was very limited, for in 1860 only 3 percent of the 397 colleges in the United States had a department of agriculture.[3] Under the Morrill Act, colleges of agriculture, home economics, and mechanics were opened, and by 1890 the total number of colleges and universities grew to 998. In the years between 1869–70 and 1909–10, the proportion of bachelor's degrees earned by women rose from 15 percent to 23 percent.[4] In the United States in 1880 the first 11 women earned their master's degrees while 868 males met the same goal. That same year 3 women and 51 men earned doctoral degrees. In 1909, the year in which Annie's daughter Ruth earned her doctorate, 44 women and 399 men nationwide were awarded doctoral degrees.[5]

Annie was not granted "the sunny side of life" that she had wished for in her January 25, 1863, letter; the home she and Winans shared in Sturgeon Bay was built among "tall white pines [that rested] their shade over [their] house, the shades were drawn, the rooms were dark." Annie and Winans continued to disagree on many issues as Annie retained her faith and Winans declared himself an atheist late in his life. Annie did not live to see her daughter Ruth earn her doctorate; she died of tuberculosis in 1895. Gideon Winans Allen was district attorney in Sturgeon Bay and also served in the State Assembly. He died in Sturgeon Bay in 1912.[6]

The Transcontinental Railroad: Susan Brown

The passage of the Pacific Railroad Act on July 1, 1862, allowed Susan Brown to escape from the responsibilities she had borne since her childhood years. From 1888 to 1895 Susan lived a life of adventure and travel and took great pride in making trips on all four transcontinental railroads. Her journeys not only reflected the spirit of this independent and intrepid woman but also are testimony to the impact the coast-to-coast extension of the railroads had on the American people and nation.

In November 1888, Susan traveled by the Northern Pacific Railroad to visit her son Will in Washington State, where she stayed for a year and was a witness to the Great Seattle Fire. She returned to Minnesota (where the Waldo Brown family had moved in 1869) to attend her daughter Emily's high school graduation. Emily and Susan were "determined to see California" and traveled there on the Union Pacific Railroad (with a stop to see the Corn Palace in Sioux City, Iowa). Susan stayed on the West Coast visiting her brother George and again traveled to Washington State to visit Will. Susan traveled on her third transcontinental railroad when she took the Canadian Pacific back to Minnesota in 1892 for Emily's wedding. Susan then returned to the Pacific coast to celebrate Christmas with her son. Even after she broke her hip in a fall, the sixty-five-year-old Susan's passion for travel was not quelled, and she returned to the East in 1895 by the fourth of the transcontinental railroads, the Great Northern Railroad. Susan's last recorded travel was to New York State in 1896, where she wrote her life story as a gift to her children and grandchildren. The autobiography of this amazing woman ends with the statement "If I live to make more history, I may record it."[7]

The transcontinental railroads that were such a vital part of Susan Brown's post–Civil War life were first proposed in 1845, but Congress, divided by sectional differences, did not approve this idea. By 1860 the United States had 30,600 miles of railroad, with the vast majority in the north, where rail was used to transport farm products and manufactured goods, as well as passengers. The South relied on its rivers for transport and had only 8,500 miles of railroad. Only one railway ran south from Richmond to Mississippi, and it was routed through Memphis and Chattanooga, adding 600 miles and ten hours of travel to the route.[8]

In 1862, with the Southern states no longer in Congress to block legislation, the Pacific Railroad Act was approved on July 1.[9] The Union Pacific began building from Sacramento east, and the Central Pacific began building west from near the Iowa–Nebraska border. The two railroads met in Promontory Point, Utah, on May 10, 1869, with a total of 1,776 miles of track having been laid in the seven years of construction. The completion of the railroad made travel from the Atlantic to the Pacific much more affordable, with the cost dropping from $1,000 to $150. The Union Pacific was just a small portion of the postwar growth of railroads. From 1865 to 1873, thirty-five thousand miles of railroad track were constructed.[10]

Civic Engagement: Emily Quiner

Many of the early pages in Emily's diary recount her contributions to the war effort—making flags, sewing shirts for the soldiers, knitting soldier's mittens, and preparing packages to send to the warfront. She also recounts her role as a leader for the local temperance lodge and soldier's aid society. Emily's contributions were just part of the larger story of the increased civic engagement among women throughout the North, which did not cease with the end of the Civil War. During the course of the war, Wisconsin Soldiers' Aid Societies contributed six thousand boxes of supplies worth more than $200,000 ($5.7 million in 2017 dollars).[11]

The work of Northern women in sewing flags and through Ladies Aid Societies allowed them to contribute to the war effort while staying within the domestic sphere. Moreover, the very public work of the Sanitary Fairs, while conducted under the legal auspices of their husbands or male family members, demonstrated the ability of women to plan and implement large-scale public projects and gave a new voice and prominence to women. The work of the United States Sanitary Commission, although led by men, moved women's role as volunteers from the local to the national level.[12]

Volunteer activities during the war also moved the role of women from a focus on the individual to a wider focus on society. The postwar Temperance Movement continued the commitment to abstinence from alcohol that was so much a part of Emily Quiner's life. However, postwar temperance activities moved from "the lodge," with an emphasis on individual pledges, to public activities that had as their goal to rid communities of establishments that sold alcohol. In February 1874, the Ladies Temperance Alliance made plans to invade all seventy-four of Madison's saloons with female praying bands. This tactic was abandoned after the bands visited four or five saloons.[13]

The contributions of women during the war led to a new understanding of their ability to contribute to society as a whole, a sentiment expressed by Henrietta Colt of the Milwaukee Soldier's Aid Society when she stated, "I know now that love of country is the strongest love, next to the love of God, given to man."[14]

Henrietta Colt's statement is echoed by modern scholars who see the Civil War as positioning women for an expanded civic role: "The war situated Northern women in a new civic setting and placed a higher value on their ideological commitment to the nation-state, their economic contributions to home and family, and even their partisan affiliations."[15]

The changing expectations related to the civic role for women was recognized by Elizabeth Cady Stanton, who said, in 1884, that the Civil War "had created a revolution in woman herself, as important in its results as the changed condition of former slaves."[16] Cady Stanton wished to tie women's suffrage to black suffrage because women's former allies in the abolitionist movement were congressional leaders for black suffrage.[17] The Wisconsin Women's Suffrage Association was established in 1869, but Wisconsin women did not win the right to vote until the passage of the Nineteenth Amendment to the US Constitution, in 1919.[18]

Westward Expansion and Agricultural Changes: Margaret Patchin

Margaret and Augustus Patchin remained on their farm near Wyocena, where their sons Herbert and Orlo worked with them. The impact of the Patchin family on the Wyocena area is reflected by the existence of Patchin Road, outside Wyocena, where small farms are still located. Margaret died on February 14, 1893, and Augustus died on February 14, 1902. Herbert and Orlo lived in Wyocena until their deaths; Orlo died in 1929 and Herbert in 1948.[19]

Margaret's venture into beekeeping may not have been the only change in farming for the Patchin family. The Homestead Act, another legislative proposal that had been blocked by senators and representatives from the Southern states, encouraged the growth of small farms in the western states. After the Homestead Act was finally approved, in 1862, more than 1.261 million acres were allocated in 160-unit parcels to farmers who had lived on the land for five years. The growth of the railroads and the settling of the West facilitated by the Homestead Act changed the face of agriculture in Wisconsin. Wheat production shifted west to Minnesota and the

The site of the Patchin family farm on Patchin Road, 2017. (Photo courtesy Terrie Pease, Wyocena and Pardeeville historian)

Dakotas, while Wisconsin transitioned to dairy farming.[20] By 1870 Wisconsin was home to fifty-four cheese factories, the sixth highest number among the states. In 1875, Wyocena's cheese factory produced forty-six thousand pounds of cheese.[21]

Marriage, Divorce, and Widowhood: Sarah Powers, Mary Burwell, and Rosabella Arnold Sleeper

Sarah Powers, Mary Burwell, and Rosabella Arnold Sleeper's post–Civil War lives demonstrate different facets of marriage and family life after the war ended. Sarah Powers, widowed by the war, faced an uncertain future in a world in which the limited employment opportunities for women were further constrained by the return of soldiers to civilian roles. As a young widow with three children, Susan faced a life of poverty despite the pensions granted by the US government to Civil War widows. The 200,000 Union women who were widowed were granted pensions of $8.00 per month, the equivalent of $121 in 2017 dollars. Even when this sum was increased by $2.00 a month for each child under the age of sixteen, war widows had to rely on the kindness of others, employment outside the home, or remarriage for survival.²²

Sarah married again on Christmas Day 1867 and gave birth to another child from this marriage.²³ This marriage was far from happy; Sarah was subjected to "brutal treatment by her second husband and applied for and granted a divorce." The people of Fox Lake were so aware of the horrors of her marriage that sixty-five citizens signed a petition asking that she be granted custody of the children she had borne with Norman as well as the child of her second husband. In an unusual move, the Wisconsin legislature approved the restoration of her widow's pension, a sum she had forfeited when she married.²⁴ Following her divorce, Sarah reverted to the name Powers and changed the surname of the child fathered by her abuser to Powers. Sarah died on September 10, 1907, and is buried at Riverside Memorial Park in Fox Lake, where a memorial stone to her beloved Norman lies beside her grave.²⁵

Sarah was among many women who turned to divorce in the period between 1867 and 1888, when the rate of divorce increased by 150 percent. This increase may have been the result in part of husbands' and wives' difficulties adjusting to their changed roles as well as to a limited understanding of the psychological effects of war. Out of more than 2 million Union soldiers, only 819 were declared insane.²⁶

Andrew Burwell lived to come home and "enjoy his dear little one's company" on their farm in Endeavor, Wisconsin. Five children were born to this marriage. Lucy Mathilda Burwell (1863–1901) is the "little one" who so looked forward to the arrival of "papa's" letters in the heartfelt, poetic epistles authored by Mary Burwell. After Andrew's return, four more children joined this family: William Henry (1867–1948), Carrie E. (Hume) (1868–1950), Robert Andrew (1872–1952), and Nellie Winifred (Bartels) (1883–1974). Mary Burwell died on April 8, 1899, after thirty-four years of marriage with her dearest husband, Andrew. Andrew then married her sister Ellen, who died in 1925. Andrew, born in 1841, lived until 1926. Emma, mentioned in the letters, was Andrew's sister; she married Mary and Ellen's brother, Richard. Till and Leroy were Mary's sister and brother-in-law. This close-knit family continues to be united in death as they were in life, as all except Carrie are buried in the Hill Crest Cemetery in Endeavor, Wisconsin.

Rosabella A. (Belle) Arnold Sleeper, who was widowed by the war, initially made postwar plans to live with her brother, Wiley Arnold, whose wife had left him, and to help care for his daughter, Clara. When Wiley remarried, Belle once again felt at loose ends and vacillated between returning to school and buying a home with her mother but then married Oscar Benedict when he asked her "to come into his heart and home and abide forever."[27] Oscar Benedict of Farmington had been a member of the 38th Infantry and had served from March 1864 to June 1865. Belle and Oscar had three children: Mary (1867), Julia (1872), and Paul in 1876. After Oscar died, in 1881, Belle married George Lovejoy Richardson, who had served in the 7th Minnesota, and resided with him in Waupaca, Wisconsin, until their deaths in 1920. Belle died on February 21, and George died on November 30.[28]

Funeral and Burial Practices: Mary Burwell and Belle Arnold Sleeper

Mary and Andrew Burwell and their children are buried in the family plot in Endeavor, Wisconsin. Family plots, often enclosed with a small wall that resembled the foundation of a home, were an important part of the rural or garden cemetery movement, which allowed a family to lie together in death as they had in life.[29] These garden cemeteries, exemplified by Elmwood Cemetery, which was visited by Emily Quiner, were designed with curving driveways to provide access to family plots.

Belle Arnold Sleeper did not have the comfort of visiting Hiram's gravesite or of being with him when he died. Before the Civil War, death was part of family life and was regarded as "the final scene of life's drama as written by God."[30] The occurrence of so many deaths far from home and the lack of burial rites for twelve thousand unknown soldiers and twenty-five thousand unburied soldiers led to uncertainty about the spiritual state in which the deceased had met their deaths. One important aspect of having the family present at the time of death was the assurance that the deceased had been saved and was thus assured of immortality at the time of death.[31] Accounts of the dying seeing visions of angels or the heavenly portal brought great comfort to the surviving family. When soldiers died far from home, deathbed letters written by nurses or fellow soldiers could provide comfort. Belle Arnold Sleeper's need for assurance that Hiram was in a state that granted him immortality was met when she learned that Hiram's last words were that he would meet her in heaven. The large number of dead and uncertainty about their spiritual state resulted in a greater exploration of the afterlife. Between 1832 and 1866 only nine books were published on the afterlife; between 1871 and 1876 the afterlife was the topic of more than eighty books.[32]

When soldiers died far from home, the family could not prepare the body for burial as had been done in the past. A family whose loved one could be identified and that had the money to pay the cost of transporting the body would hire an embalmer, often a doctor, to inject the body with arterial embalming fluid and ship the body home for burial. This new practice gave rise to the profession of undertakers, as the carpenters and cabinetmakers who had previously assisted families by making caskets did not have the skills necessary to prepare bodies for burial.[33]

The importance of the gravesite to family members was described by Nellie in a letter to Charles Palmer: "How sad for Belle and his parents. Today they have done the last and all they can do. No grave by which to shed tears, to stand by and feel that he is nearer, or to plant flowers and mosses. Beautiful emblems we so love to decorate the graves of those near and dear to us. All these are deprived them."[34]

Adding to the pain caused by the lack of a gravesite at which the family could mourn was the callous manner in which many Civil War soldiers were buried. Colonel Oscar A. Mack, the Confederate inspector of cemeteries, reported in 1870–71 that "The bodies [of prisoners] were placed one above the other, and mostly without coffins." The lack of certainty about the names of the deceased was also a source of pain: "Even in the years immediately after the Civil War, the federal government was unable to verify the number of dead or compile a credible list of interments to a degree that would have allowed them to inscribe names on a single memorial or on individual headstones." Adding to Belle's pain was the absence of Hiram Sleeper's name on the Roll of Honor for Salisbury Prison, which had the largest number of unidentified dead of any Confederate prison.[35] Sarah Powers, whose husband Norman had died in July 1863, could at least take comfort in the knowledge that Norman "had been put in a coffin and decently buried."[36]

Belle may have also suffered because the circumstances of Hiram's death were so uncertain. Following the war, Hiram was identified as defecting while a prisoner at Salisbury Prison.[37] He was among the more than 2,500 prisoners from Salisbury Prison who joined the Confederacy. Following a failed escape attempt on November 25, 1864, 350 Union prisoners pledged allegiance to the South in a last, desperate measure to escape starvation and death. Hiram may have been among these defectors, adding the shame of marrying a traitor to Belle's loss.[38]

Voices of Wisconsin Women

Although Emily stopped writing in her diary when she acceded to her father's wishes to remain in Madison, her writing "on his history" is critical to scholars of the role of Wisconsin men in the Civil War. Edwin Quiner's *Military History of Wisconsin: A Record of the Civil and Military Patriotism of the State* is still the most frequently cited book about Wisconsin's role in the Civil War.[39] The work of Emily and her sisters on this history was neither acknowledged nor cited by their father; although the Quiner history did acknowledge the contributions of the "Soldiers Aid Societies," it lamented the lack of opportunity in the book to relate "what the women of Wisconsin have done to sustain the government in the recent war."[40]

As part of the collective contribution of Wisconsin women during the Civil War, the women whose words are reflected in this book made vital individual contributions. Emily Quiner used her domestic skills to clothe soldiers, offered care and compassion as a nurse on the warfront, and made an uncredited contribution to the recorded history of the Civil War. Annie Cox argued vehemently and effectively for freedom for enslaved Americans. Mary Burwell and Margaret Patchin assumed new responsibilities in farm management for the benefit of their families, their communities, and Union soldiers. Sarah Powers was robbed of a happy marriage and suffered cruel torment as she attempted to provide a home for her children. Belle Arnold Sleeper sacrificed her carefree girlhood, her health, and her husband. Susan Brown sacrificed family and comfort. Ann Waldo, like so many who were called to the battlefront in the years from 1861 to 1865, gave her very life in service to her country.

Emily and Annie; Susan and Ann; Margaret, Sarah, Mary, and Belle each made one other noteworthy contribution. Through their diaries and letters, they have deepened our understanding of the Civil War and extended our knowledge of this critical period in the history of our nation and of its citizens.

Notes

PREFACE

1. "Population of the United States in 1860: Wisconsin."
2. Thomas R. Flagel, *The History Buff's Guide to the Civil War*, 139.
3. John Zimm, *This Wicked Rebellion: Wisconsin Civil War Soldiers Write Home*, vii.

INTRODUCTION

1. Richard N. Current, *The Civil War Era, 1848–1973*, 355.
2. Frank L. Klement, *Wisconsin in the Civil War: The Home Front and the Battle Front, 1861–1865*, 11.
3. Current, *Civil War Era*, 355.
4. Current, *Civil War Era*, 343; Wisconsin Historical Society, "Wisconsin Troops Help Capture Jefferson Davis."
5. Wisconsin Historical Society, "Iron Brigade."
6. Current, *Civil War Era*, 355.
7. Mary Pipher, *Reviving Ophelia: Saving the Selves of Adolescent Girls*, 225.
8. David Kaser, *Books and Libraries in Camp and Battle: The Civil War Experience*, 27.
9. Nancy Mulhern, comp., *Population of Wisconsin, 1850–2000: Population Statistics Were Taken from the United States Federal Census*, 29.
10. "United States Census, 1860," *FamilySearch*, https://familysearch.org/ark:/61903/1:1:MWMY-QMM, October 2, 2017, Jane E Quiner in entry for CC Hayes, 1860.
11. Bertel Wernick Suckow, *Madison City Directory: A City and Business Directory for 1866*, 127.
12. "Inventory of the Allen Family Papers."
13. Suckow, *Madison City Directory*, 90; Historic Madison Inc., "Canal across the Isthmus."
14. "United States Census, 1860," *FamilySearch*, https://familysearch.org/ark:/61903/1:1:MWMT-G9H, December 13, 2017, Charles J Cox, 1860.

15. Susan Appleton Brown, *Autobiography*.

16. "Summary," Waldo-Henderson Family Papers.

17. "United States Census, 1860," *FamilySearch*, https:familysearch.org/ark:/61903/1:1:MW9V-2X2, December 12, 2016, Susan Brown in entry for William Brown, 1860.

18. Mulhern, *Population of Wisconsin, 1850–2000*, 55; Michael J. Goc and Geraldine N. Dricoll, *Winneconne: History's Crossing Place*, 8.

19. Mulhern, *Population of Wisconsin, 1850–2000*, 150.

20. Patchin Family Papers.

21. Mulhern, *Population of Wisconsin, 1850–2000*, 25.

22. Mulhern, *Population of Wisconsin, 1850–2000*, 33.

23. Elaine Reetz, *Come Back in Time*, 87–89.

24. Charles Bennett Palmer Papers, 1862–1900.

25. Mulhern, *Population of Wisconsin, 1850–2000*, 55.

26. "Demographics," in *The Wisconsin Mosaic: A Brief History of Wisconsin*.

27. Robert C. Bieder, *Native American Communities in Wisconsin, 1600–1960*, 158.

28. "Demographics."

29. Pipher, *Reviving Ophelia*, 225.

Chapter 1. April 1861 to April 1862

1. David V. Mollenhoff, *Madison: A History of the Formative Years*, 85.

2. Emily's dates in her original diary do not match the correct days of the week for April 14–28. They have been corrected in the text.

3. Jeanie Attie, *Patriotic Toil: Northern Women and the American Civil War*, 26.

4. Steve Drake, e-mail messages to the author, September 22–24, 2017.

5. Robert E. Sterling, "Civil War Draft Resistance in the Middle West," 15. Lincoln based his call for troops on a 1792 statute that authorized the president to activate militias in the event of insurrection or invasion. Phillip Shaw Paludan, *A People's Contest: The Union and the Civil War, 1861–1865*, 15.

6. Reuben Gold Thwaites, *Civil War Messages and Proclamations of Wisconsin War Governors*, 51.

7. John C. Fredriksen, *Civil War Almanac*, 23; J. Matthew Gallman, *The Civil War Chronicle*, 52; James D. McCabe, *Life and Campaigns of Robert E. Lee*, 32.

8. John S. Bowman, *The Civil War Almanac*, 52.

9. Judge Spooner was the 90th District representative from Elkhorn. Louis H. D. Crane, ed., *A Manual of Customs, Precedents, and Forms in Use in the Assembly of Wisconsin*, 10.

10. Wisconsin's expenditures during the war would far exceed this initial allocation. From 1861 to 1867 the state of Wisconsin expended $2,698,999 on the war, and local governments spent $7,752,506. Individual soldiers made additional expenditures of $1,051,520 to the war. Current, *The Civil War Era*, 395.

11. Holly Berkley Fletcher, *Gender and the American Temperance Movement of the Nineteenth Century*, 74.

12. A. J. Craig was assistant superintendent of public instruction for the State of Wisconsin. John S. Dean and Frank M. Stewart, eds., *The Legislative Manual of the State of Wisconsin*, 138.

13. The Governor's Guard was a company of local militiamen that had formed early in 1861. Walter Glazer, "Wisconsin Goes to War," 83–84.

14. Emily's diary contains the full text of the "Star Spangled Banner" as well as the poem recounting the thoughts of Ralph Farnham, the last surviving Revolutionary War soldier as he contemplated the Civil War. Perhaps tiring of writing, Emily did not include the texts of other readings and songs.

15. The report of a ship being seized appears to be one of many false rumors that spread in the early days of the war.

16. As the 6th Massachusetts Infantry marched through Baltimore, citizens loyal to the Confederacy attacked the regiment, killing seven soldiers as well as nine civilians. Bud Hannings, *Every Day of the Civil War: A Chronological Encyclopedia*, 36.

17. Fort Pickens in Pensacola, Florida, was not attacked on this day. It was one of the few forts in the South to remain in Union control throughout the war. Edwin S. Bearss, "Civil War Operations in and around Pensacola," 165.

18. Both Drs. Brisbane served in the 1st Wisconsin Infantry from April 17 to August 21, 1861, and returned safely home. Wisconsin Veterans Museum, Civil War Roster Database.

19. The Randall Guards were members of the 2nd Infantry who came from Madison and other areas of Dane County. Jeffrey D. Wert, *A Brotherhood of Valor: The Common Soldiers of the Stonewall Brigade, C.S.A, and the Iron Brigade, U.S.A.*, 22.

20. Current, *The Civil War Era*, 337–38.

21. H. A. Tenney was a publisher, legislator, and comptroller for the state treasury. Mollenhoff, *Madison*, 94, 422n110.

22. Catherine Clinton, *The Other Civil War: American Women in the Nineteenth Century*, 114.

23. Thwaites, *Civil War Messages and Proclamations*, 69–70.

24. The Beloit Rifles were also part of the 2nd Infantry and included graduates and students of Beloit College. Wert, *A Brotherhood of Valor*, 22.

25. Colonel Elmer Ellsworth had gone to high school in Kenosha, Wisconsin, had been employed in Abraham Lincoln's law office in Springfield, Illinois, and accompanied the Lincolns to the White House. He was part of the force sent to secure Alexandria, Virginia, across the Potomac from Washington, DC. On May 24, James Jackson, the proprietor of the Marshall House Inn, shot Colonel Ellsworth at point-blank range while Ellsworth was removing a large Confederate flag from the hotel's roof. Upon hearing of his death, President Lincoln cried, "My boy, my boy! Was it necessary that his sacrifice be made?" The South also gained its first hero of the war through this event when Confederate accounts of the incident claimed that Jackson had perished "among a pack of wolves." Owen Edwards, "The Death of Colonel Ellsworth."

26. Emily had passed an examination to qualify as a teacher in the town of Madison schools. See Susan Brown entry for April 20, 1862, for a description of the content of this examination. Dorothy Dennison Volo and James M. Volo, *Daily Life in Civil War America*, 320.

27. Fannie, Emily's sister, was an assistant teacher in the City of Madison's first ward school during the summer and winter terms in 1861–62. *Annual Report of the Board of Education of the City of Madison, for the Years 1861 and 1862, adopted Dec. 16. 1862*, 15.

28. Stephen A. Douglas, US senator from Illinois and the Democratic candidate in the 1860 presidential election, had died of typhoid fever on June 3.

29. Enrollment at the university declined from three hundred in 1861 to sixty-three by 1863. Fearing that the university would be forced to close, officials allowed women to enroll in normal school programs there. This was the second time women had been admitted to the university. In April 1860 the university had admitted thirty women and twenty-nine men to a ten-week "normal school" program that was suspended by the end of 1860. Current, *The Civil War Era*, 400; Marian J. Swoboda and Audrey J. Roberts, *They Came to Learn, They Came to Teach, They Came to Stay*, 2.

30. The representation of all thirty-four states demonstrated the view of the Union that the secession of the Southern states was not legal and therefore did not diminish the integrity of the Union. The soldiers marching in the procession were not as enthused as Emily was about their participation in the parade. July 4, 1861, was an extremely hot day, and they were required to march from 9:00 a.m. until 2:00 p.m. When they returned to Camp Randall, the soldiers were incensed to learn that their Independence Day meal was cold beef and hard bread. They rose in protest, throwing food and plates about until they were promised that the food would be improved. Kerry A. Trask, *The Fire Within: A Civil War Narrative from Wisconsin*, 58–59.

31. Madison residents provided the soldiers' picnic as a way to atone for the fiasco of the July 4th celebration. More than six thousand residents marched to Camp Randall bearing great quantities of food and, with bands playing, hosted a grand dinner for those stationed at Camp Randall. Trask, *The Fire Within*, 60.

32. Hannings, *Every Day of the Civil War*, 63.

33. Mollenhoff, *Madison*, 87.

34. The 2nd Infantry was the only Wisconsin regiment to fight at Bull Run. This regiment suffered 19 men killed and 114 wounded; 38 were held as Confederate prisoners until early in 1862. Wisconsin Historical Society, "This Day in Wisconsin History."

35. On Saturday, August 10, General Lyon led 5,400 Union troops into the Battle of Wilson's Creek and Oak Hill, near Springfield, Missouri, facing 11,000 Confederate soldiers. The gallant General Lyon was wounded in the leg and in the head but continued to lead his troops into battle. A third wound proved fatal, and the command passed to Major Samuel Davis Sturgis. After six hours of battle the Union troops were repelled and forced to retreat to Springfield. Confederate general Sterling Price survived the battle and arranged for General Lyon's body to be returned to Springfield for temporary interment. Union troops suffered 223 killed, 721 wounded, and 291 missing. Confederate troops suffered 265 killed, 800 wounded, and 30 missing. Hannings, *Every Day of the Civil War*, 69–70; Robert E. Denney, *The Civil War Years: A Day-by-Day Chronicle of the Life of a Nation*, 66; E. B. Long and Barbara Long, *The Civil War Day by Day: An Almanac 1861–1865*, 107.

36. A week after the soldiers of the 1st Infantry were mustered out, they were ordered to reorganize for a three-year term, and they departed for the battlefront in October 1861. Both Benjamin L. Brisbane and William H. Brisbane were members of the 1st Infantry. Neither returned to service when the 1st Infantry reorganized. Wisconsin Veterans Museum, Civil War Roster Database.

37. The US Sanitary Commission provided instructions for "short shirts made like long, only 1 yard long, and open in front." As the war progressed and uniforms were centrally provided, the work of making shirts became a source of income for seamstresses, who received a dollar for a dozen shirts. Attie, *Patriotic Toil*, 116; Susan Estabrook Kennedy, *If All We Did Was to Weep at Home: A History of White Working-Class Women in America*, 70.

38. Six weeks earlier, President Lincoln had appointed the "last Thursday in September next as a day of humiliation, prayer, and fasting for all the people of the nation." In a spirit of ecumenicity, the president further declared, "And I do earnestly recommend to all the people, and especially to all ministers and teachers of religion, of all denominations, and to all heads of families to observe and keep that day, according to their several creeds and modes of worship, in all humility and with all religious solemnity, to the end that the united prayer of the nation may ascend to the throne of Grace, and bring down plentiful blessings upon our country." Abraham Lincoln, "Proclamations of Days of Thanksgiving, Fasting, and Prayer."

39. Mrs. Fairchild was probably Mrs. Sally Blair Fairchild, mother of Lucius Fairchild, who was wounded at Gettysburg and later in life became governor of Wisconsin.

40. The number of officers for Emily's Aid Society was substantially smaller than that for larger organizations, which sometimes had up to five vice presidents as well as a committee on cutting and a committee on packing. More than twenty thousand Ladies Aid Societies had been formed in the North during the first two weeks of the war. Ethel Alice Hurn, *Wisconsin Women in the War between the States*, 23; Mary Elizabeth Massey, *Bonnet Brigades*, 32.

41. A seton was a long strip of linen or cotton thread passed through the skin by a needle to apply medications or to provide a drain after surgery.

42. Soldiers' mittens were knit with two spaces for the index finger and thumb in addition to a space for the three remaining fingers so the wearer could still shoot a gun while wearing them. The Milwaukee Mitten Society popularized the knitting of these mittens and knitted thousands of mittens with this specialized pattern. "Soldier's Mittens"; Karen A. Kehoe, "'Not a Moment for Delay': Benevolence in Wisconsin during the Civil War Era," 148.

43. The Myrmidons Society was a dining club at the university named after the Myrmidons described in the *Iliad*. These legendary people were brave warriors created from ants by Zeus.

44. Prior to 1861, each state set its own Thanksgiving Day. In 1861 President Lincoln established Thursday, November 28, as a National Day of Thanksgiving. In his proclamation, Lincoln addressed his proclamation to his "fellow citizens in every part of the United States." Governor Randall's proclamation was less magnanimous as he invoked Jeremiah 6:21: "Behold, I will lay stumbling blocks before

this people [e.g., the citizens of the Southern states], and the fathers and sons together shall fall upon them; the neighbor and his friend shall perish." Abraham Lincoln, "Proclamation of Thanksgiving"; Thwaites, *Civil War Messages and Proclamations*, 76.

45. President Lincoln delivered his first State of the Union to Congress on this date. In his message he stated, "The Union must be preserved, and hence, all indispensable means must be employed," noting the struggle "was not only for today but for the future as well." Long and Long, *The Civil War Day by Day*, 146.

46. Wallace W. LaGrange of Ripon was captain of the 1st Cavalry. On October 2, 1862, Captain LaGrange died of wounds sustained in battle at Dandridge, Tennessee, after singlehandedly capturing four rebels. Wisconsin Veterans Museum, Civil War Roster Database.

47. The "machine" in question was probably a reaper, as mechanical equipment was being incorporated into farming in the early 1860s because of the lack of farmhands. Much machinery was manufactured by Wisconsin firms including Fish Brothers and J. I. Case in Racine. The efficiency of this equipment changed farming forever. The September 1863 *Merchant's Magazine and Commercial Review* rhapsodized about the wonders of farm machinery: "We have seen in the past few weeks, a stout matron whose sons are in the army, with her team cutting hay at seventy-five cents per acre, and she cut seven acres a day with ease, riding leisurely upon her cutter." See Sarah Powers letter of July 12, 1863, for discussion of the use of machinery in farming. R. Douglas Hurt, "The Agricultural Power of the Midwest in the Civil War," 71; Gallman, *The Civil War Chronicle*, 354.

48. Emily, with her commitment to temperance, would have been appalled to learn that on this sacred day Union troops were given unsolicited gifts of liquor. Karen Abbott, *Liar, Temptress, Soldier, Spy: Four Women Undercover in the Civil War*, 122–23.

49. "James Henry Lane."

50. The regimental surgeon for the 1st Cavalry, Thomas W. Johnson, was captured at Bloomfield, Missouri. After his release he was transferred to the 1st Missouri Cavalry, where he served until January 1, 1863. Wisconsin Veterans Museum, Civil War Roster Database.

51. The state officers were Governor Louis P. Harvey, Lieutenant Governor Edward Salomon, Secretary of State James T. Lewis, Secretary of the Treasury Samuel D. Hastings, Attorney General Winfield Smith, and Superintendent of Public Instruction Josiah L. Pickard. Dean and Stewart, *The Legislative Manual of the State of Wisconsin*, 138.

52. William Barstow, Wisconsin's third governor, who had been forced to resign because of a fraudulent election, organized Company S of the 3rd Cavalry and served as its leader until he was mustered out of service on March 4, 1865. See Annie Cox's September 15–16, 1863, letter for additional information on William Barstow. Wisconsin Historical Society, "Barstow, William Augustus (1813–1865)."

53. Tom Thumb, also known as the Little General, was only two feet eleven inches tall and was one of the most famous touring acts of the mid-nineteenth century. His distant relative, Phineas T. Barnum, had adopted Tom Thumb as a child

and became the manager of his career. Barnum was directly impacted by the war in November 1864.

54. Bayard Taylor was an American travel writer born in Pennsylvania who wrote five books between 1846 and 1857. During the Civil War he was a correspondent for the *New York Tribune*. Late in the war he was named as a member of the diplomatic staff of the American minister to St. Petersburg. Taylor died in Germany on December 19, 1878.

55. Richard H. Chittenden of Ripon, the captain of the 4th Cavalry, enlisted on October 2, 1861, and resigned on July 14, 1862. Wisconsin Veterans Museum, Civil War Roster Database.

56. John Stacy enlisted in the 1st Cavalry on November 8, 1861, and died a year later, on November 16, 1862, at Cape Girardeau, Missouri. Wisconsin Veterans Museum, Civil War Roster Database.

57. Some letters between spouses contained separate papers with their private thoughts. These "privates" were not preserved in their archive of letters from the war.

58. On February 12, Fort Donelson fell to U. S. Grant, who when asked the terms of surrender answered, "No terms except unconditional and immediate surrender can be accepted." This phrase gave a new meaning to the initials of Ulysses Simpson Grant. The Battle of Fort Donelson was a decisive Union victory, in part because of the efforts of the Third Infantry. This victory led to Grant's promotion to major general. The estimates of the number of Confederate troops that surrendered with General Buckner at Fort Donelson range from 5,000 to 15,000. Confederate casualties were around 1,200. The Union had 27,000 troops engaged; 500 were killed, 2,108 were wounded, and 224 were captured. General Gideon Johnson Pillow fled Fort Donelson prior to the surrender and was relieved of his command on March 11 as a result of his actions. General Albert Sidney Johnston was safely ensconced in Nashville during this battle but died at the Battle of Pittsburg Landing on April 6, 1862. Denney, *The Civil War Years*, 134; Long and Long, *The Civil War Day by Day*, 170–72, 194.

59. Jane Swisshelm, a journalist from St. Cloud, Minnesota, spoke on abolition and women's rights.

60. David G. Purman was a 1st lieutenant in the 1st Infantry. He enlisted October 2, 1861, was promoted to 2nd lieutenant on December 10, 1861, was wounded at Shiloh, and resigned on November 6, 1862. He reenlisted as a lieutenant colonel on May 20, 1864, in the 41st Infantry; that regiment was not filled, and he was mustered out of service on September 24, 1864. Wisconsin Veterans Museum, Civil War Roster Database.

61. Gerry W. Hazelton was a state senator representing Columbus, Wisconsin; E. L. Brown represented Waupaca, Wisconsin. Dean and Stewart, *The Legislative Manual of the State of Wisconsin*, 72.

62. Wendell Phillips, a highly regarded but controversial abolitionist from Boston, had been pelted with rocks and eggs when he spoke in Cincinnati in March. Senator Joseph A. Wright of Indiana espoused the view that the 1862 Union ticket would gain twenty thousand votes if Lincoln would jail Phillips for his "traitorous

speeches." Abolition was not Phillips's only cause—he also championed women's rights, Native American rights, labor reform, and prohibition. Bowman, *The Civil War Almanac*, 92; V. Jacque Voegli, *Free but Not Equal: The Midwest and the Negro during the Civil War*, 37; Flagel, *History Buff's Guide to the Civil War*, 43.

63. Historic Madison, Inc., "Camp Randall Prison Camp." Over the course of the war, 211,411 Union soldiers were taken prisoner, with 16,668 paroled without going to a prison camp and another 30,218 dying in prison. A much larger number of Confederate soldiers were captured and paroled (462,634 captured, 247,769 paroled), with a slightly smaller number dying in prison camps (25,976). Margaret Wagner, Gary W. Gallagher, and Paul Finkelman, eds., *The Library of Congress Civil War Desk Reference*, 583.

64. Thwaites, *Civil War Messages and Proclamations*, 89–91.

65. Thwaites, *Civil War Messages and Proclamations*, 116–17.

66. Wisconsin Historical Society, "This Day in Wisconsin History."

67. Wisconsin Historical Society, "This Day in Wisconsin History."

68. Stewart M. Brooks, *Civil War Medicine*, 43–44.

69. The Battle of Pittsburg Landing (Shiloh) was the bloodiest battle fought to date, with 24,000 casualties. The Union Army suffered 1,754 fatalities, and the Confederate Army suffered 1,723 fatalities, including the Confederate general Albert S. Johnston. The 14th and 16th Wisconsin Infantries were involved in this battle. The 18th Wisconsin, one week out of training in Madison, battled the enemy in a peach orchard at the left of the Union line. As the soldiers fell, peach blossoms drifted down to cover their bodies. A total of 174 members of the 18th were captured. The 17th Infantry, also known as the Irish Regiment, had refused to leave Madison until its soldiers were paid. Their recalcitrance may have saved them from carnage. The United States Sanitary Commission demonstrated its power when the battle was over by bringing in more than 11,000 shirts, 3,700 pairs of drawers, 3,500 pairs of socks, 2,800 bedding kits, 1,100 bottles of "medicinal spirits," and more than seventeen tons of food. Robert W. Wells, *Wisconsin in the Civil War*, 20; Denney, *The Civil War Years*, 153, 155.

70. Elias Hill of Menasha enlisted on September 18, 1861, in the 10th Infantry and died on February 28, 1862, in Bowling Green, Kentucky. Gilbert Fish of Winneconne was captured at the Battle of Pittsburg Landing; he was released and mustered out of service on July 18, 1865. John Conderman of Winneconne was also a member of the 18th Infantry. A musician, Conderman was discharged on July 14, 1862. The 14th Infantry had indeed fought at Pittsburg Landing (see Emily Quiner's April 9, 1862, diary entry). Wisconsin Veterans Museum, Civil War Roster Database.

71. Captain Oliver D. Pease of Watertown died of the wounds sustained at Pittsburg Landing on April 11, 1862; Lieutenant David G. Purman's wounds led to his resignation from the army on November 6, 1862. Wisconsin Veterans Museum, Civil War Roster Database.

72. Cousin Joseph's wounds proved fatal; he succumbed to his injury on April 28, 1862, in Savannah, Georgia. Seventy percent of Civil War wounds were to the extremities as soldiers on both sides were trained to aim for arms and legs to

impede the advance or retreat of the army transporting wounded soldiers with a chance of survival. Amputation was usually the only "cure" provided for those who were shot in an extremity. The transfer of pus, which was thought to have lifesaving benefits, often transferred infection from one injured soldier to the next, increasing the rate of death from amputations. Wisconsin Veterans Museum, Civil War Roster Database; Brooks, *Civil War Medicine,* 97; "Why Did Civil War Officers Tell Their Men to 'Aim Low'?"; "Talking Spirits Tour Performance."

73. Fredriksen, *Civil War Almanac,* 145.
74. Long and Long, *The Civil War Day by Day,* 205.
75. Mollenhoff, *Madison,* 87.

Chapter 2. May 1862 to April 1863

1. Harvey's successor, Governor Salomon, declared May 1 a "day of public rest and cessation of business, and recommended to the people of this State, that, on that day, between the hours of 10 and 12 o'clock in the morning, they assemble in their respective towns, cities, and villages, then and there to commemorate the death of the late Governor, the Hon. Louis P. Harvey." Thwaites, *Civil War Messages and Proclamations,* 116.
2. Wisconsin Historical Society, "This Day in Wisconsin History."
3. Thwaites, *Civil War Messages and Proclamations,* 124.
4. Sterling, "Civil War Draft Resistance in the Middle West," 54–57.
5. Sterling, "Civil War Draft Resistance in the Middle West," 54–57.
6. Wagner, Gallagher, and Finkelman, *The Library of Congress Civil War Desk Reference,* 150.
7. Bowman, *The Civil War Almanac,* 107.
8. "Kingdom Coming" was a Civil War song with minstrel show influences that had been composed by Henry Clay Work. "Old Southern Gentleman" originated in 1668 as a tribute song to a courtier to Queen Elizabeth I. By the Civil War the lyrics had been adapted to honor General Zachary Taylor. The Confederates developed a parody of the song called "The Yankee President." "Kingdom Coming (Work, 1862)."
9. The new building, Main (now Bascom) Hall, was built in 1859 and topped with a dome that mirrored that of the Wisconsin Capitol, which is 1.5 miles down State Street. Stuart D. Levitan, *Madison: The Illustrated Sesquicentennial History,* 35.
10. Edward Everett was one of the most noted speakers of the Civil War era. He was selected to be the keynote speaker at the dedication of the cemetery at Gettysburg, in November 1863. After Everett's two-hour oration, President Lincoln delivered his eloquent, two-minute-long Gettysburg Address.
11. "Bullet-proof" vests with a thin sheet of metal sewn between two layers of fabric were advertised to soldiers during the Civil War at a cost of between five and eight dollars. The efficacy of these vests was suspect as some vests were found postbattle with an indentation where a bullet had hit the vest and others were found on the bodies of mortally wounded soldiers. "Failed Objects: Bullet Proof Vests and Design in the American Civil War."
12. Julius Stevens was a member of the 14th Infantry who enlisted on September 8, 1861, and was discharged from service on August 31, 1862. He enlisted again on

September 13, 1864, in the 1st Cavalry (Morris Waldo's regiment) and was mustered out on April 19, 1865, when he was reported absent because of sickness. Joseph Post was a member of the 14th Infantry, enlisting on September 21, 1861; as Ann recounted, he died of his wounds on May 27, 1862. Wisconsin Veterans Museum, Civil War Roster Database.

13. John G. Hutchinson led a family of singers who had received permission to sing to soldiers along the Potomac following the first battle of Bull Run. Hutchinson chose to sing John Greenleaf Whittier's "Ein Feste Burg ist Enser Gout." The assembled soldiers became agitated when he sang the lines "What whets the knife for the Union's life? Hark to the answer, Slavery!" When the Hutchinson family was forbidden by Generals Philip Kearny, William B. Franklin, and George B. McClellan to sing to the soldiers again, John Hutchinson appealed directly to Secretary of the Treasury Salmon P. Chase, who then shared the lyrics with President Lincoln. Lincoln remarked that these "were just the sort of songs he wanted soldiers to hear," and the Hutchinson family was again allowed to sing to Union soldiers. Samuel Pickard, *Life and Letters of John Greenleaf Whittier*, 467–68.

14. Mollenhoff, *Madison*, 87.

15. Sterling, "Civil War Draft Resistance in the Middle West," 70–72.

16. Sterling, "Civil War Draft Resistance in the Middle West," 139.

17. Mollenhoff, *Madison*, 89.

18. Leonard Bradley enlisted in the 23rd Infantry and was mustered out on October 11, 1863. McHenry is not listed in Wisconsin's Civil War Roster. Wisconsin Veterans Museum, Civil War Roster Database.

19. Chris Bishop and Ian Drury, *1400 Days: The US Civil War Day by Day*, 93.

20. Colonel Edward Daniels from Ripon was not killed and served until his resignation on February 3, 1863. Matthias J. Bushnell of Omro and Chaplain George W. Dunmore were both killed at Languelle Ferry, Arkansas. Thomas F. Allen of Waupun was taken prisoner during this same battle and was discharged from service on November 17, 1862. Wisconsin Veterans Museum, Civil War Roster Database.

21. Hiram Baker, a member of the 1st Cavalry, died at Bloomfield, Missouri, on August 5, 1862. Wisconsin Veterans Museum, Civil War Roster Database.

22. Emily's September 1862 visit to the camp was unusual, for "by this time Camp Randall had become passé and the Ladies Aid no longer hosted dinners and delicacies." Mollenhoff, *Madison*, 98.

23. This special session was called to address legislation on military organization, rights of soldiers to vote, and the "Indian uprising." The "Indian uprising" had begun when, following the government's unsuccessful attempt to remove long-time Winnebago (Hoocąągra) residents from the state, the Winnebago murdered white settlers in the New Lisbon area. Legislative Reference Bureau, "Special and Extraordinary Sessions of the Wisconsin Legislature," 7; Current, *The Civil War Era*, 322.

24. Emily's quiet day is in contrast to the deadly battle that occurred on this date. Union and Confederate troops met at Antietam on the "bloodiest day in U.S. military history." The Iron Brigade was critical to the success of the Union Army, which stopped the first attempted Confederate invasion of the North, but the Brigade lost almost half of its eight hundred members to death or injury. This bloody conflict

was the first real test of the Union's newly established ambulance corps and field hospitals. Wisconsin Historical Society, "This Day in Wisconsin History"; Agnes Brooks Young, *Women and the Crisis: Women of the North during the Civil War*, 214–15.

25. Wagner, Gallagher, and Finkelman, *The Library of Congress Civil War Desk Reference*, 23.

26. Letter from Maggie Swem to Susan Brown, September 27, 1862. Waldo-Henderson Family Papers, Wisconsin Historical Society Archives.

27. Susan was referring to the Battle of Perryville, in which the 21st Infantry had fought on October 8. Wisconsin Historical Society, "This Day in Wisconsin History."

28. Macaulay's *History of England* was published in five volumes beginning in 1848. The last volume was published posthumously in 1861. This history was noteworthy for incorporating social history with political and military history. "Thomas Babington Macaulay."

29. The Quiner family compiled ten volumes of scrapbooks containing letters written by Wisconsin soldiers and published in Wisconsin newspapers. This collection is available online from the Wisconsin Historical Society, http://content.wisconsinhistory.org/cdm/ref/collection/quiner/id/19537.

30. The fourth Thursday in November was not set as the permanent date for Thanksgiving until 1863. President Lincoln had issued a proclamation declaring November 27, 1862, a day of Thanksgiving for victory in battle and encouraged the people of the United States to "reverently invoke the divine guidance for our national counsels, to the end that they may speedily result in the restoration of peace, harmony, and unity throughout our borders and hasten the establishment of fraternal relations among all the countries of the earth." Governor Salomon's Thanksgiving proclamation reflected the abatement of war fever since the previous year, recommending to the people of the state that they "pray for a speedy suppression of the rebellion, and for peace to our distracted country." Pilgrim Hall Museum, "Presidential Thanksgiving Proclamations"; Thwaites, *Civil War Messages and Proclamations*, 147.

31. Bowman, *The Civil War Almanac*, 121.

32. Wisconsin Historical Society, "This Day in Wisconsin History."

33. Wisconsin Historical Society, "This Day in Wisconsin History."

34. Thwaites, *Civil War Messages and Proclamations*, 180–81.

35. Klement, *Copperheads in the Middle West*, 45.

36. Wagner, Gallagher, and Finkelman, *The Library of Congress Civil War Desk Reference*, 152.

37. Wagner, Gallagher, and Finkelman, *The Library of Congress Civil War Desk Reference*, 26.

38. Annie Cox, "February 1, 1863 letter to Gideon Allen," Allen Family Papers, 1862–1964.

39. Phineas J. Clawson of Madison of the 20th Infantry was wounded on December 7, 1862, at the Battle of Prairie Grove, which secured Arkansas for the Union. He was promoted to 2nd lieutenant before being discharged on December 31, 1862. Wisconsin Veterans Museum, Civil War Roster Database.

40. The Democrats were not seen as cursing land, homes, and nation in six Wisconsin counties whose foreign-born populations were largely opposed to the draft. Their sentiment was echoed by the editor of the *Sheboygan Diary*, who wrote, "In Heaven's name, let us have no more of this conscription—a system which the most proscriptive monarchial government would scarce resort to." On November 10, 1863, citizens of Ozaukee County, Wisconsin, attacked William Pors, the Ozaukee County draft official, at the courthouse, threw him down the stairs, and chased him to the post office. He was spirited out of town and taken to Milwaukee. His home was attacked and destroyed, his wife and three-year-old child barely escaping. Attacks continued on the homes of other leading citizens through the next day. At least one rape was reported. On November 11, forty men from Saukville organized a peaceful, nonviolent antidraft demonstration and quelled the violence. By Wednesday six hundred soldiers from the 28th Infantry were sent to Port Washington, where they arrested two hundred persons. One hundred thirty were convicted and transported to Camp Washburn in Milwaukee, and forty were transported to Camp Randall in Madison. One hundred were paroled by December 12, and the ringleaders were released early in March 1863, following a successful lawsuit in which the Wisconsin Supreme Court ruled that suspension of habeas corpus for these men was unconstitutional. The draft in Port Washington continued peacefully under the watch of the 28th Infantry, and the city established the Ozaukee Guards to protect against future draft riots. The Ozaukee Guards were reluctant to arrest friends and neighbors and soon disbanded. Klement, *The Copperheads in the Middle West*, 26–27, 67–68; Sterling, "Civil War Draft Resistance in the Middle West," 99–120.

41. Wells, *Wisconsin in the Civil War*, 32.

42. Thwaites, *Civil War Messages and Proclamations*, 157.

43. Helen R. Olin, *The Women of a State University: An Illustration of the Working of Coeducation in the Middle West*, 169.

44. Madison may have been the home of the first national Ladies Union League, which looked after soldiers' families and wrote letters to soldiers to boost their morale. Genevieve McBride, *On Wisconsin Women: Working for Their Rights from Settlement to Suffrage*, 30.

45. Annie's "Pa" was her stepfather; she used "father" to refer to her biological father, Michael Poad.

46. Nancy and Amelia, the two eldest Patchin children, had died within a month of one another when Nancy was six and Amelia was not yet five. Horatio was their eldest son; he died at age eight. https://www.findagrave.com/memorial/71908353/margaret-a-patchin#.

47. Wagner, Gallagher, and Finkelman, *The Library of Congress Civil War Desk Reference*, 29.

48. Bishop and Drury, *1400 Days*, 127; Hannings, *Every Day of the Civil War*, 301; Long and Long, *The Civil War Day by Day*, 343.

CHAPTER 3. MAY 1863 TO APRIL 1864

1. Denney, *The Civil War Years*, 279.

2. Fredriksen, *Civil War Almanac*, 294.

3. Wisconsin Veterans Museum, Civil War Roster Database.

4. Wisconsin was a major grower of wheat during the Civil War, and good weather led to record midwestern harvests with yields of 33 percent more wheat, 25 percent more corn, and 15 percent more oats than in the previous year. As a result, Milwaukee surpassed Chicago as a shipper of grains, with ships using Canadian waterways to move products to the East and to Europe. Hurt, "The Agricultural Power of the Midwest in the Civil War," 72; D. Balasubramanian, "Wisconsin's Foreign Trade in the Civil War," 259–62.

5. Margaret was forty-five years old when she wrote this letter and had given birth to eight children. She would live for another thirty years. https://www.findagrave.com, accessed April 27, 2019, memorial page for Margaret Patchin (18 Mar 1834–17 Aug 1912), Find a Grave Memorial no. 75408673, citing Story Cemetery, Oregon, Dane County, Wisconsin, USA; Maintained by McFarland (contributor 47349869).

6. The June 1864 University of Wisconsin commencement was canceled as all but one member of the graduating class had enlisted in the army when Lincoln issued a call for one-hundred-day volunteers. One hundred fifty students formed the University Guards under the leadership of a faculty member, leading one student to comment, "Only cripples and copperheads were left." Mollenhoff, *Madison*, 91.

7. In his June 9 letter, Winans wrote, "I have just been enrolled as one of the militia of this district. If I am drafted you can be sure of one thing—there will be a battle soon after. Perhaps, though, I'll just make a speech denouncing the administration and the war when the spies of the Star Chamber will be set upon my track, I'll be arrested, have a mock trial, make myself notorious, be sent South, refuse to take the Oath of Allegiance to the Confederacy, and be sent back ala Vallandigham. . . . Our government is in the hands of either fools or traitors." The Star Chamber was a court established in British law that became known in the reign of Charles I as a symbol of oppression. Winans saw the courts that enforced conscription law as being as oppressive as the court of Charles I. Clement Vallandigham was an Ohio Democrat who was charged with treason on May 5, 1863, and sentenced to "close confinement for the duration of the war" for his antiwar views and statements. His appeal to the Supreme Court for a writ of habeas corpus was denied on May 11. Later in the month, the Secretary of War ordered that Vallandigham be expelled from Union territory until the war ended. In an act of defiance, Ohio Democrats nominated Vallandigham for governor on June 11. When Vallandigham reached the South he was detained in Wilmington, North Carolina, as an enemy alien and later shipped to Canada. Gideon Allen, "June 9, 1863 letter to Annie," Allen Family Papers, 1862–1964; "Court of Star Chamber"; Bowman, *The Civil War Almanac*, 145–46, 148, 152; Fredriksen, *Civil War Almanac*, 304, 308; Bishop and Drury, *1400 Days*, 364.

8. Wells, *Wisconsin in the Civil War*, 53.

9. Norman Powers, *The Civil War Letters of Norman Powers of Fox Lake, Dodge Co. Wisconsin and Other Related Family Letters*, 29.

10. Powers, *The Civil War Letters of Norman Powers*, 34. Charles Kendall from Burnett had enlisted August 21, 1862; he was wounded at the Battle of Champion

Hill on May 16, 1863, and was discharged on May 19, 1865. Oscar Lawrence enlisted on August 13, 1862, was promoted to 1st lieutenant on July 20, 1864, and was discharged on June 22, 1865. Wisconsin Veterans Museum, Civil War Roster Database.

11. Powers, *The Civil War Letters of Norman Powers*, 35–36. The 29th Infantry fought "three heavy battles" on May 14, 16, and 17 at Jackson, Champion Hill, and Big Black River, Mississippi. Bowman, *The Civil War Almanac*, 147; Wisconsin Historical Society, "This Day in Wisconsin History."

12. As Emily began her trip south, the 2nd Wisconsin Infantry was the first to engage Confederate troops at Gettysburg in a fierce engagement that presaged the next three days of battle. The 2nd lost almost one-third of its troops to death or injury in this initial engagement. Other Wisconsin troops that fought at Gettysburg included the Iron Brigade, the 3rd, 5th, and 26th Infantry, and the 1st US Sharpshooters, Company G. Despite orders from General Lee, General Ewell rested his troops after this initial engagement, allowing the Union forces to gain a strategic advantage on Cemetery Hill. On the first day of battle 9,000 Union soldiers and 6,800 Confederate soldiers were lost. Of the remaining 302 members of the 2nd Infantry, 116 were among those lost. Wisconsin Historical Society, "This Day in Wisconsin History."

13. The November 7, 1861, battle at Belmont was one of the first under the command of Grant. The Union forces lost 120 killed and 383 wounded. Bowman, *The Civil War Almanac*, 71.

14. A statue of President Andrew Jackson erected in Memphis was similar to the statue of him in New Orleans, which had been inscribed by orders of General Butler in 1862 with the statement Emily quotes. Mary Ann Wegman, "Battle of New Orleans: Jackson Square."

15. Powers, *The Civil War Letters of Norman Powers*, 43–44. The Confederate Army reported 3,903 killed, 18,735 injured, and 5,425 missing. Union losses totaled 3,155 killed, 14,529 injured, and 5,365 missing. Lee's army retreated to Virginia over the next ten days with Meade's army in desultory pursuit. Bowman, *The Civil War Almanac*, 160–62.

16. The Gayoso was a Memphis hotel that had been turned into a Union hospital. "Memphis and the Civil War in Vintage Drawings and Photos."

17. Emily's reference to four nurses and one female nurse reflected the differing views of men and women with the same title. Men were key members of the medical team, whereas "the industrious nurse/secretary functions more as a symbol of home than as a skilled medical worker." Christine Ann Bell, "A Family Conflict: Visual Imagery of the 'Homefront' and the War between the States, 1860–1866."

18. Over the course of the war, 44,558 Union soldiers died from diarrhea. Wagner, Gallagher, and Finkelman, *The Library of Congress Civil War Desk Reference*, 644.

19. Phineas B. Gates was Sarah's brother and a member of the 19th Illinois Infantry. National Park Service, "The Civil War: Search for Soldiers"; Powers, *The Civil War Letters of Norman Powers*, 47–48.

20. The siege of Charleston began on July 10 as 3,700 federal troops landed on Morris Island and constructed fortifications of sand and palmetto leaves. Fredriksen, *Civil War Almanac*, 327.

21. A New York City mob of fifty thousand rioted in protest after predominantly Irish names were drawn in response to the March 3 Conscription Act. They overwhelmed the draft office, from which the superintendent barely escaped with his life, and burned an orphanage for black children and the offices of Horace Greeley's *Tribune*. As the riot continued, the fury of the mob turned on the African American population. Union soldiers, including the 3rd Wisconsin Infantry, were brought from Gettysburg to quell the rioters but not before more than one thousand citizens, including rioters and black citizens, were killed and injured. Smaller riots also broke out in Boston as well as in other eastern cities. Bowman, *The Civil War Almanac*, 162; Wells, *Wisconsin in the Civil War*, 64; Powers, *The Civil War Letters of Norman Powers*, 49.

22. The Winnebago, now known as the Hoocąągra, members of the Ho-Chunk Nation, are Wisconsin Native Americans.

23. Michael J. Cantwell of Madison served in the 12th Infantry from November 1, 1861, to January 16, 1865. He was promoted to 1st lieutenant on April 29, 1862. James H. Howe from Green Bay served in the 32nd Infantry from August 30, 1862, to July 6, 1864. Wisconsin Veterans Museum, Civil War Roster Database.

24. John Barnard of the 14th Infantry enlisted on October 7, 1861, was wounded at Vicksburg, recovered, and was mustered out of service on October 9, 1865. James Farrell may have been a member of the 27th Infantry from Franklin who had enlisted on December 2, 1862, and drowned in the Arkansas River on March 12, 1864. Another James Farrell of the 2nd Cavalry could also have been Emily's patient. He enlisted on November 1, 1861, and deserted on July 1, 1864. Wisconsin Veterans Museum, Civil War Roster Database.

25. Truman Tyrell was a member of the 29th Infantry who was taken prisoner at the Battle of Sabine Cross Roads. He survived and was mustered out of service on May 22, 1865. George W. Burchard from Fox Lake, a member of the 29th Infantry, was promoted to Major of the Second United States Colored Troops on June 22, 1863. He served in this capacity until 1866. From 1878 to 1882 he was the private secretary to Governor William E. Smith and was State Adjutant General from 1889 to 1891. Burchard died in 1921. Wisconsin Veterans Museum, Civil War Roster Database; Wisconsin Historical Society, "Burchard, George Washington, 1835–1921"; Powers, *The Civil War Letters of Norman Powers*, 54–55.

26. William Richardson of the 11th Infantry was killed in Jackson, Mississippi, on July 11, 1863. Wisconsin Veterans Museum, Civil War Roster Database.

27. William G. Pitman served from August 21, 1862, until December 16, 1863, in the 23rd Infantry. Wisconsin Veterans Museum, Civil War Roster Database.

28. Lieutenant Colonel Jeremiah M. Rusk served in the 26th Infantry from July 22, 1862, to June 7, 1865. William I. Henry of Ahnapee served in the 14th Infantry from October 14, 1861, to May 31, 1866. Wisconsin Veterans Museum, Civil War Roster Database.

29. Lieutenant Levi J. Billings of the 8th Infantry served from December 24, 1861, to December 30, 1864. William H. H. Townsend of Hazel Green served in the 16th Infantry from October 2, 1861, to December 20, 1864, and was wounded at the

Battle of Pittsburg Landing in 1862. Wisconsin Veterans Museum, Civil War Roster Database.

30. Elmwood Cemetery in Memphis was established as one of the first garden-style cemeteries in America in 1852. Today it is on the National Register of Historic Places. "Elmwood Cemetery."

31. Powers, *The Civil War Letters of Norman Powers*, 57–58.

32. Powers, *The Civil War Letters of Norman Powers*, 1; Brooks, *Civil War Medicine*, 119.

33. Powers, *The Civil War Letters of Norman Powers*, 50.

34. Powers, *The Civil War Letters of Norman Powers*, 119, 50, 56.

35. Wisconsin Veterans Museum, Civil War Roster Database.

36. Powers, *The Civil War Letters of Norman Powers*, 59–60.

37. There were nine John Reeds who served in Wisconsin Infantry during the war. Homer S. Jones of the 29th Infantry was wounded May 16, 1863, at the battle of Champion Hill and mustered out on June 22, 1865. William Welch of Brothertown served from August 14, 1862, to June 8, 1865, as a member of the 21st Infantry and was wounded at both Chickamauga and Dallas. James Hodges of Muscoda, who was wounded at Petersburg, served in the 11th Infantry from August 5, 1861, to September 1, 1864. Wisconsin Veterans Museum, Civil War Roster Database.

38. Frederick Wardrobe from Waukesha enlisted in the 28th Infantry on August 7, 1862, and resigned to become a hospital steward on May 24, 1864. Wisconsin Veterans Museum, Civil War Roster Database.

39. Mortimer B. Pierce, captain of Company A in the 32nd Infantry, served from September 26, 1862, to June 12, 1865. Wisconsin Veterans Museum, Civil War Roster Database.

40. George Wick was a soldier from Madison who served in the 2nd Infantry from January 29, 1862, until January 29, 1865. Wisconsin Veterans Museum, Civil War Roster Database.

41. Fort Pillow later became the site of the April 12, 1864, massacre of African American troops by Confederate forces. Captain James Berry of Springville served in the 25th Infantry from August 16, 1862, until November 28, 1863. Wisconsin Veterans Museum, Civil War Roster Database.

42. Joseph Curtis was a hospital steward in the 12th Infantry and served from September 27, 1861, until November 23, 1864. Wisconsin Veterans Museum, Civil War Roster Database.

43. Mr. Bond may have been Richard H. Bond, who served in the 41st Infantry from May 17 to September 23, 1864. Wisconsin Veterans Museum, Civil War Roster Database.

44. On June 1, 1863, General Burnside of the Department of the Ohio ordered the suppression of the *Chicago Times* due to "repeated expressions of incendiary and disloyal statements." Bowman, *The Civil War Almanac*, 150.

45. Benjamin A. Taft of Madison served from August 12, 1862, to September 2, 1863, and was wounded at Arkansas Post, Arkansas. Wisconsin Veterans Museum, Civil War Roster Database.

46. William Vilas from Madison served as captain and then lieutenant colonel in the 23rd Infantry from August 14, 1862, to August 29, 1863. After the war, Vilas

served as professor of law at the University of Wisconsin and as a cabinet member in the administrations of Grover Cleveland. Later in life he served one term as a US senator from Wisconsin. Wisconsin Historical Society, "Vilas, William Freeman, 1840–1908: Lawyer, Politician, Senator, Cabinet Officer, and Philanthropist."

47. Annie Cox, "September 23, 1863 letter to Gideon Allen," Allen Family Papers, 1862–1964.

48. David Libscomb was a writer who also wrote on Christian pacifism.

49. Victoria Brown, *Uncommon Lives of Common Women: The Missing Half of Wisconsin History*, 3.

50. Wiley Arnold, a captain in the 32nd Infantry, served from August 2, 1862, until June 12, 1865. Wisconsin Veterans Museum, Civil War Roster Database.

51. George Clayton had assumed responsibility for the *Courant* in Charley's absence and was the source of much conflict for Belle and the other typesetters.

52. An em is a unit in typography based on the specified point size.

53. Hi is Hiram Sleeper, whom Belle married in 1864. Hiram enlisted as a sergeant in the 38th Infantry on March 25, 1864. Wisconsin Veterans Museum, Civil War Roster Database.

54. Annie Cox replied to letters from Winans in which he complained that his sister had called him a traitor, asserting, "Democrats are not traitors, that is a miserable partisan slander." Winans's sister, Martha, and her husband had been forced out of their Kansas home and had moved to Fort Scott, Missouri, as they were among the few non-Copperheads in Kansas. They were then forced to flee again when Confederates threatened to capture the fort. Bitter about Winans's political views, Martha had sent him a letter calling him a villain and a traitor. Klement, *Copperheads in the Middle West*, 39; Gideon Allen, "November? 1863 letter to Annie Cox," Allen Family Papers, 1862–1964.

55. George B. Smith was a Wisconsin politician who was critical of Lincoln. Klement, *Copperheads in the Middle West*, 39.

56. Bowman, *The Civil War Almanac*, 175; Bishop and Drury, *1400 Days*, 145.

57. Thwaites, *Civil War Messages and Proclamations*, 198.

58. The first sanitary fair was held in Chicago, drawing five thousand visitors over two weeks and raising a total of $100,000 (the equivalent of $2 million in 2018). Wisconsin members of the executive committee were Mrs. Governor Harvey, Mrs. Governor Salomon, Mrs. Dr. Carr, and Miss Lottie Ilsey of Madison, Mrs. L. Fisher of Beloit, Mrs. J. H. Turner of Berlin, Mrs. J. S. Colt and Mrs. Judge Hubbell of Milwaukee, and Miss Emma Brown of Fort Atkinson. Mrs. Salomon solicited items from the Germans, and Mrs. Colt visited "towns by the score." The German department included much fine needlework and generated $4,000 in sales. Mrs. B. F. Hopkins, secretary of the Madison Soldiers Aid Society, provided donations, as did Mrs. Dr. Carr and Mrs. Dr. Hoyt. Ladies of Janesville, Beloit, Racine, Green Bay, Berlin, and Keshena made donations of needlework and Indian curiosities. Shullsburg sent collections of minerals. Phillip Katcher, *The Civil War Day by Day*, 117; *History of the North-western Soldiers' Fair, Held in Chicago the Last Week of October and the First Week of November, 1863*, 8–9, 12, 14, 24, 57, 58.

59. "The President's Hymn," composed by William Augustus Muhlenberg in honor of Lincoln's 1863 Thanksgiving Proclamation, exhorted all people of "east and west, north and south" to sing one Thanksgiving song. Neil A. Cook, "'The President's Hymn': A Thanksgiving Song."

60. Annie was responding to Winans's sharing of his notes on the law regarding the status of a husband and wife: "The husband has control over his wife. He may supervise and enforce her labour. He may restrain her extravagance, her inordinate propensities to travel, and her keeping bad company. He may use moderate correction, and, as the courts say, with a rod as big as his thumb." Gideon Allen, December 7, 1863, Letter to Annie Cox, Allen Family Papers, 1862–1964.

61. Emerson David Fite, *Social and Industrial Conditions in the North during the Civil War*, 238.

62. Gallman, *The Civil War Chronicle*, 71.

63. Denney, *The Civil War Years*, 355.

64. Annie and her family were living in Dr. Morse's home in exchange for working as household servants. Ruth Allen, "Biography Manuscript by Mabel Nebel. Part 1 [Unpublished, 1960s]," Allen Family Papers, 1862–1964.

65. Nelson F. Beckwith was one of Berlin's wealthiest and most prominent citizens. He made his fortune in lumbering, and his fine home and hotel figured in his $9,000 estate. *Home Town Ties: Berlin, Wisconsin, 1848–1998*, 50.

66. Ransom VanNorman of the 5th Infantry enlisted on April 25, 1861, was wounded on June 27, 1862, and was killed in action at Spotsylvania on May 10, 1864. Wisconsin Veterans Museum, Civil War Roster Database.

67. Thomas J. Griffith of Berlin was a member of the 1st Heavy Artillery who served from July 27, 1863, until August 30, 1865. Wisconsin Veterans Museum, Civil War Roster Database.

68. Annie and Winans's correspondence continued until they were married, on May 5, 1865. Except for one letter late in the war, their subsequent correspondence avoided discussion of the war, soldiers, politics, or local activities and instead recounted Annie's desire for a home of their own and Winans's search for employment.

69. In the greeting of this letter Belle addressed Charles Palmer by a diminutive of his middle name, Bennett.

70. Fredriksen, *Civil War Almanac*, 583.

Chapter 4. May 1864 to April 1865

1. Bishop and Drury, *1400 Days*, 195. Wisconsin Historical Society, "This Day in Wisconsin History."

2. Lysander Cutler was commissioned colonel on July 16, 1861, and rose to the rank of brevet general before resigning on June 30, 1865. "Total Civil War Casualties in Killed and Mortally Wounded."

3. Wisconsin Veterans Museum, Civil War Roster Database.

4. In the greeting of this letter Belle addressed Charles Palmer by a diminutive of his middle name, Bennett.

5. Sidney D. Woodworth first enlisted in the 18th Infantry on January 4, 1862, was taken prisoner at Shiloh, and was mustered out on March 30, 1863. He

reenlisted in the 38th Infantry on April 14, 1864, transferred to the Veterans Reserve Corps on October 13, 1864, and was mustered out of service on November 9, 1865. The Veterans Reserve Corps began in 1863 as an organization in which wounded soldiers unable to return to the front after recovering from their injuries could serve in military hospitals. Wisconsin Veterans Museum, Civil War Roster Database. Paul A. Cimbala and Randal M. Miller, *An Uncommon Time: The Civil War and the Northern Homefront*, 202.

    6. Eugene Wheelock of Marquette was a member of the 37th Infantry. He was killed on July 30, 1864, at Petersburg, Virginia. Wisconsin Veterans Museum, Civil War Roster Database.

    7. The 42nd Infantry was mustered in on September 7, 1864, and left Camp Randall for guard duty in Cairo, Illinois, on September 22–24, 1864. During the next nine months the 42nd served on guard duty and provost (military police) duty in Illinois, losing fifty-eight members to disease before being mustered out on June 20, 1865. Wisconsin Historical Society, "42nd Wisconsin Infantry History."

    8. The remainder of this letter is missing.

    9. Fredriksen, *Civil War Almanac*, 518.

    10. Thwaites, *Civil War Messages and Proclamations*, 239.

    11. Bishop and Drury, *1400 Days*, 594.

    12. Because they lacked standard identification, only 58 percent of Civil War bodies could be identified. To spare their families the fate of not knowing whether they were dead or alive, many soldiers would carry a slip of paper on their person to assist in identification. To meet this need, merchants and sutlers began selling "identification discs." The exact date they were made available cannot be determined, although they were probably available during the winter encampments of 1861–62. In February 1862, Henry L. Franklin wrote home about purchasing his "medal for soldiers to wear around their necks." Larry B. Maier, *Identification Discs of Union Soldiers in the Civil War: A Complete Classification Guide and Illustrated History*, 9.

    13. Rumors that guerrillas would attack Milwaukee and Chicago had raised alarm in central Wisconsin when federal agents arrested one hundred men in Chicago for plotting against the US government. Confederate sympathizers from Canada did succeed in setting fire to ten hotels and P. T. Barnum's museum in New York City on November 25, and Confederates raided St. Albans, Vermont, on October 19. Fredriksen, *Civil War Almanac*, 523; Denney, *The Civil War Years*, 492; Bowman, *The Civil War Almanac*, 229, 232.

    14. Sidney Gifford, who enlisted in the 1st Heavy Artillery on September 5, 1864, is the only one of the "draftees" listed here who is identified in the Wisconsin Veterans Museum's Civil War Roster Database. Henry A. Conger of Oxford served in the 19th Infantry from February 27, 1862, until May 11, 1865, and was captured at Fair Oaks on October 27, 1864. Charles Allen was a member of the 22nd Infantry and was killed at Fair Oaks on October 27, 1864. Wisconsin Veterans Museum, Civil War Roster Database.

    15. Mary's fears regarding election day violence were shared by Abraham Lincoln, who was concerned about violent elections in Maryland and other states because of the ridicule he had experienced during the campaign. Bishop and Drury, *1400 Days*, 429.

16. Harmon S. Kribbs was a 1st lieutenant in the 5th Infantry, Company H. He served from September 1864 to June 20, 1865. Wisconsin Veterans Museum, Civil War Roster Database.

17. Ebenezer Wright was a member of the 16th Infantry from Janesville. He died of wounds sustained at the Battle of Atlanta on August 2, 1864. Wisconsin Veterans Museum, Civil War Roster Database.

18. H. Levander Farr from Cottage Grove served in the 5th Infantry from August 20, 1862, until June 20, 1865, and was promoted to 2nd lieutenant on August 22, 1864. Wisconsin Veterans Museum, Civil War Roster Database.

19. Mark Mielz of Fox Lake, Wisconsin, and the 29th Infantry also survived the war. Wisconsin Veterans Museum, Civil War Roster Database.

20. Andrew Fish was a member of the 38th Infantry. He served from August 27, 1864, until June 17, 1865, and was wounded at Petersburg, Virginia, on April 2, 1865. Wisconsin Veterans Museum, Civil War Roster Database.

21. Fredriksen, *Civil War Almanac*, 537.

22. William Pierson was a member of the 36th Infantry. He enlisted on February 29, 1864, and was discharged due to disability on June 2, 1865. Wisconsin Veterans Museum, Civil War Roster Database.

23. General Benjamin F. Butler attempted to construct a canal to permit Union vessels to make a detour around Richmond on the James River in Virginia. After twelve thousand pounds of dynamite merely threw the excavated dirt back into the canal, Butler abandoned this effort. Fredriksen, *Civil War Almanac*, 538.

24. Thwaites, *Civil War Messages and Proclamations*, 223–27.

25. George Leroy Gage enlisted November 18, 1861, in the 3rd Infantry and was discharged April 16, 1863, due to a disability. Mary's brother, Richard Swannell, if drafted, did not serve in the army. Wisconsin Veterans Museum, Civil War Roster Database.

26. Wisconsin Veterans Museum, Civil War Roster Database.

27. Louis A. Brown, *The Salisbury Prison: A Case Study of Confederate Military Prisons, 1861–1865*, 13, 28, 61.

28. Hiram's mother, Nancy Sleeper, recovered from her wartime illness and died on March 23, 1879, at the age of seventy-four. "Wisconsin Death Index, 1820–1907," *FamilySearch*.

29. Charles A. Sleeper served in the 4th Cavalry from May 20, 1864, until April 10, 1862, when he was discharged. He enlisted in the 41st Infantry on April 20, 1864, and served until September 23, 1864. As Belle reported, he enlisted for a third time on February 4, 1865. After providing garrison and guard duty in St. Louis, the 49th Infantry was mustered out of service on November 8, 1865. Wisconsin Veterans Museum, Civil War Roster Database.

30. A. D. Richardson, who was held at Salisbury from February 3, 1864, until he and others escaped on December 18 of that year, described the prisoner rations of corn bread and beef and also reported that food could be purchased outside the prison. A Union sympathizer, Luke Blackmer, spent $8,000 to $10,000 for supplemental food for the prisoners. Conditions and rations for citizen prisoners such as

Richardson were better than those for soldiers held prisoner; they were housed in interior spaces and, if they died, were buried in coffins and not dumped by the wagon load into trenches, as was the fate of soldiers. The beef provided to soldiers was usually offal, part of a daily ration of five hundred calories per day. Some prisoners supplemented their rations by taking rations from deceased comrades whose deaths had not yet been discovered by their guards. Brown, *The Salisbury Prison*, 51–52, 100–104.

31. Belle's fears about conditions at Salisbury Prison were confirmed in letters written by one of the Confederate guards, David McRaven, to his wife, Amanda. Many of McRaven's letters refer to the cold experienced by the guards in their quarters, the dozens of lice he killed when he changed his clothes, and how he tramped miles every day in an effort to keep warm. In October 1864, he wrote, "Sometime I feel a touch of sorrow when I look off my stand of the garrison and see the amount of suffering and wretchedness in the space allotted to the Yankee prisoners. There are 10–25 buried here every day." In late November McRaven reported on an attempted escape by the Yankees: "our men . . . killed 18 to 20 and wounded a good many more, the yankies . . . fell down on their bellies and begged like dogs." And later, "I saw one shot down like beef" and "They fight each other like dogs." After the prisoners were released, in February 1865, McRaven visited the Yankee tents and reported he had "found it a stinking place and old shoes and rags enough to breed a pestilence." Louis A. Brown, "The Correspondence of David Olando and Amanda Nantz McRaven, 1864–1865," 57.

32. This letter was written on a larger folio than those used for all other letters.

33. Vice President Alexander H. Stephens, Senate President Pro-Tempore Robert M. T. Hunter, and Assistant Secretary of War John A. Campbell represented the Confederacy in peace talks with President Lincoln and Secretary of State William H. Seward on February 3. These talks did not bring peace, because the South demanded an armistice and Lincoln would not yield on Southern recognition of federal authority. Long and Long, *The Civil War Day by Day*, 633.

34. Food had become increasingly scarce for the Confederate army. As early as January 1864, Davis had authorized the army to requisition food from civilians. This supply problem was exacerbated when Sherman, from February 1864 on, continued to destroy railroad lines needed to get supplies to Confederate troops. Sherman's march throughout Georgia and the Carolinas further depleted the food available to Confederate soldiers and civilians. Eliza Andrews, a young woman who was traveling in Georgia following Sherman's march, described the destitution of the Confederate troops: "I saw numbers of them seated on the roadside greedily eating raw turnips, meat skins, parched corn—anything they could find, even picking up the loose grain that Sherman's horses had left." Gallman, *The Civil War Chronicle*, 483.

35. Draftees were viewed by some as "cowards, who set at home [and] ridicule everybody and too cowardly to go themselves." Quoted in Melissa Traub, "'$300 or Your Life': Recruitment and the Draft in the Civil War."

36. Although not a Shakespearean quote, this phrase was used to refer to Richard the Lionheart.

37. Frederick Hartson of Fox Lake served in the 5th Infantry from August 30, 1864, until June 7, 1865. Wisconsin Veterans Museum, Civil War Roster Database.

38. Sergeant Florentine A. Hotchkiss, a member of the 3rd Cavalry from Montello, enlisted on November 1, 1861, and was discharged on February 17, 1865. Wisconsin Veterans Museum, Civil War Roster Database.

39. Fredriksen, *Civil War Almanac*, 561.

40. Oliver N. Russell was wounded at Reams Station on August 25, 1864, was promoted to captain on October 18, 1864, but was not discharged from the 36th Infantry until July 12, 1865. Wisconsin Veterans Museum, Civil War Roster Database.

41. Stephen Chapel of Blooming Grove served in the 5th Infantry from September 8, 1864, to June 30, 1865. Wisconsin Veterans Museum, Civil War Roster Database.

42. The Zouave Drill was a very detailed manual of arms developed by Colonel Elmer Ellsworth for the musket, percussion cap, sword, and saber. Elmer E. Ellsworth, *The Zouave Drill: Being a Complete Manual of Arms for the Use of the Rifled Musket, with Either the Percussion Cap, or Maynard Primer*.

43. Churchgoers who did not share Belle's belief that Hiram was still alive may have seen her lack of mourning dress as evidence that she "did not care for her husband." Social mores dictated that a widow wear mourning dress for two and half years, beginning with a six-month period of heavy mourning, during which the widow would wear only black, followed by full mourning, in which the black clothes could be adorned with black lace and the face no longer had to covered by a veil, and the final stage, half-mourning, when gray or lavender could also be worn. Volo and Volo, *Daily Life in Civil War America*, 334.

44. Andrew Burwell and Mary E. Burwell, "Overview of the Collection," McCain Library and Archives.

45. Adelbert Eastman of the 37th Infantry was discharged on March 25, 1865, due to disability. David B. Bishop was mustered out of the 19th Infantry when his term expired, on April 29, 1865. Wisconsin Veterans Museum, Civil War Roster Database.

46. Unaware that Andrew had been injured, Mary wrote to him once again as she had heard the news of the great battle at Richmond. The Confederate capital had fallen to Union troops, including the 5th Infantry, on April 3. Many Wisconsin regiments, including the 5th, 6th, 7th, 19th, 36th, 37th, and 38th Infantries, occupied the cities of Petersburg and Richmond. Wisconsin Historical Society, "This Day in Wisconsin History."

47. Ovando English of the 32nd Infantry was wounded on March 21, 1865, at Bentonville, North Carolina. Wisconsin Veterans Museum, Civil War Roster Database.

48. Denney, *The Civil War Years*, 555–56.
49. Fredriksen, *Civil War Almanac*, 581.
50. Denney, *The Civil War Years*, 559.
51. Wisconsin Veterans Museum, Civil War Roster Database.
52. Brooks, *Civil War Medicine*, 6.

AFTERMATH OF WAR

1. Levitan, *Madison*, 61.
2. Wisconsin Historical Society, "Quiner, Emily (or Emilie) 1839–1919."
3. Wagner, Gallagher, and Finkelman, *The Library of Congress Civil War Desk Reference*, 683.
4. Thomas D. Snyder, ed., *120 Years of American Education: A Statistical Portrait*, 75.
5. National Center for Education Statistics, "Table 301.20: Historical Summary of Faculty, Enrollment, Degrees, and Finances in Degree-Granting Postsecondary Institutions."
6. "Inventory of the Allen Family papers, 1862–1964"; Ruth Allen, "Biography Manuscript by Mabel Nebel," 1, 104.
7. Susan Appleton Brown, *Autobiography*.
8. Katcher, *The Civil War Day by Day*, 13.
9. Long and Long, *The Civil War Day by Day*, 236.
10. Wagner, Gallagher, and Finkelman, *The Library of Congress Civil War Desk Reference*, 788.
11. Hurn, *Wisconsin Women in the War between the States*, 57.
12. Rajean Attie, "'A Swindling Concern': The United States Sanitary Commission and the Northern Female Public, 1861–1865," 1.
13. Mollenhoff, *Madison*, 151.
14. Kehoe, "'Not a Moment for Delay,'" 138.
15. Nina Silber, *Daughters of the Union Fight the Civil War*, 10–12.
16. Judith Giesberg, *Army at Home: Women and the Civil War on the Northern Homefront*, 10.
17. Bell, "A Family Conflict," 75.
18. Current, *The Civil War Era*, 531–33; Wisconsin Historical Society, "The Women's Suffrage Movement."
19. https://www.findagrave.com, accessed December 7, 2018, memorial page for Herbert E. Patchin (1862–1948), Find a Grave Memorial no. 71908345, citing Wyocena Cemetery, Wyocena, Columbia County, Wisconsin, USA; https://www.findagrave.com, accessed December 7, 2018, memorial page for Orlo C. Patchin (1851–1929), Find a Grave Memorial no. 71908357, citing Wyocena Cemetery, Wyocena, Columbia County, Wisconsin, USA.
20. Bishop and Drury, *1400 Days*, 247.
21. Terry D. Pease, *A History of the Pardeeville-Wyocena Area*, 16.
22. Volo and Volo, *Daily Life in Civil War America*, 355; Gallman, *The Civil War Chronicle*, 183.
23. Wisconsin Historical Society, "Wisconsin Genealogy Index: Marriage Record Entry for Dane County."
24. "Civil War Records of Norman Powers," 61.
25. https://www.findagrave.com/memorial/61776203/sarah-jane-powers.
26. Massey, *Bonnet Brigades*, 328–39; Flagel, *History Buff's Guide to the Civil War*, 156.

27. Letter from Bella, September 30, 1866, Charles Bennett Palmer Papers, 1862–1900.

28. Ancestry.com, "U.S. Find a Grave Index, 1600s–Current."

29. Volo and Volo, *Daily Life in Civil War America*, 330–33.

30. Volo and Volo, *Daily Life in Civil War America*, 330.

31. Maggi M. Morehouse and Zoe Trodd, *Civil War America: A Social and Cultural History*, 279.

32. Paludan, *A People's Contest*, 366–67.

33. Volo and Volo, *Daily Life in Civil War America*, 341.

34. Letter from Nellie, May 7, 1865, Charles Bennett Palmer Papers, 1862–1900.

35. U.S. Department of Veterans Affairs, "Salisbury National Cemetery"; Louis A. Brown, *The Salisbury Prison*, xvi.

36. Powers, *The Civil War Letters of Norman Powers*, 56.

37. Joyce Bennet Stemler, *They Went South: Biographical Sketches of the Civil War Veterans from Berlin, Wisconsin*, 103; National Archives, Pvt-Sgt Hiram H. Sleeper, Military Service Record.

38. Brown, *The Salisbury Prison*, 89.

39. Wisconsin Historical Society, "Quiner, Edwin Bryant (1816–1868): Wisconsin Civil War Historian and Author."

40. Edwin Quiner, *Military History of Wisconsin: A Record of the Civil and Military Patriotism of the State*, 239.

Bibliography

Writings of Wisconsin Women

Allen, Gideon W. Allen Family Papers, 1862–1964. Box 1, folders 2–8. Newberry Library, Chicago.
Burwell, Andrew, and Mary E. Letters. Box 1, folders 1–8. McCain Library and Archives, University of Southern Mississippi.
Charles Bennett Palmer Papers, 1862–1900. Box 1, folders 7–8. Wisconsin Historical Society, Division of Library, Archives, and Museum Collections.
Patchin Family Papers and Photographs. WVM Mss 1386. Wisconsin Veterans Museum.
Powers, Norman. *The Civil War Letters of Norman Powers of Fox Lake, Dodge Co. Wisconsin and Other Related Family Letters*. Letters owned by Jean Selden Bastian of Chippewa Falls, Wisconsin, transcribed by Jackie Selden Riley, December 1982.
Quiner, Emily. *Emily Quiner's Diary, 1861–1863*. http://content.wisconsinhistory.org/cdm/ref/collection/quiner/id/32026.
Waldo-Henderson Family Papers, 1829–1979. Box 2, folder 6. Wisconsin Historical Society, Division of Library, Archives, and Museum Collections.

Background Material

Abbott, Karen. *Liar, Temptress, Soldier, Spy: Four Women Undercover in the Civil War*. New York: Harper, 2014.
Andrews, Sarah E. *Postmarked Hudson: The Letters of Sarah A. [sic: E.] Andrews to Her Brother, James A. Andrews, 1864–1865. With a Genealogy of the Andrews Family*. Hudson, WI: Star-Observer Publishing Company, 1955.
Annual Report of the Board of Education of the City of Madison, for the Years 1861 and 1862, Adopted Dec. 16, 1862. Madison: Atwood and Rublee, Book and Job Printers, 1861–62.
Attie, Jeannie. *Patriotic Toil: Northern Women and the American Civil War*. Ithaca: Cornell University Press, 1998.

Attie, Rejean. "'A Swindling Concern': The United States Sanitary Commission and the Northern Female Public, 1861–1865." PhD dissertation, Columbia University, 1987.

Balasubramanian, D. "Wisconsin's Foreign Trade in the Civil War." *Wisconsin Magazine of History* 46, no. 4 (Summer 1963): 257–62.

Bearss, Edwin C. "Civil War Operations in and around Pensacola." *Florida Historical Quarterly* 36, no. 2 (1957): 125–65.

Bell, Christine Anne. "A Family Conflict: Visual Imagery of the 'Homefront' and the War between the States, 1860–1866." PhD dissertation, Northwestern University, 1996.

Bieder, Robert C. *Native American Communities in Wisconsin, 1600–1960.* Madison: University of Wisconsin Press, 1995.

Bishop, Chris, and Ian Drury. *1400 Days: The US Civil War Day by Day.* North Dighton, MA: JG Press, 1998.

Bowman, John S. *The Civil War Almanac.* New York: Facts on File, 1982.

Brooks, Stewart M. *Civil War Medicine.* Springfield, IL: C. C. Thomas, 1966.

Brown, Louis A. "The Correspondence of David Olando and Amanda Nantz McRaven, 1864–1865." *North Carolina Historical Review* 26, no. 1 (January 1949): 41–98.

Brown, Louis A. *The Salisbury Prison: A Case Study of Confederate Military Prisons, 1861–1865.* Wendell, NC: Avera Press, 1980.

Brown, Susan Appleton. *Autobiography.* Unpublished, 1898. Waldo-Henderson Family Papers, 1829–1979, box 1, folder 1. Wisconsin Historical Society, Division of Library, Archives, and Museum Collections.

Brown, Victoria. *Uncommon Lives of Common Women: The Missing Half of Wisconsin History.* Madison: Wisconsin Feminists Project Fund, 1975.

Burwell, Andrew, and Mary Burwell. "Letters. Overview of the Collection." Southern Mississippi Library. http://lib.usm.edu/spcol/collections/manuscripts/finding_aids/m100.

Cimbala, Paul A., and Randal M. Miller. *An Uncommon Time: The Civil War and the Northern Home Front.* New York: Fordham University Press, 2002

Claflin, Gilbert, and Esther Claflin. *A Quiet Corner of the War: The Civil War Letters of Gilbert and Esther Claflin, Oconomowoc, Wisconsin, 1862–1863.* Edited by Judy Cook. Madison: University of Wisconsin Press, 2013.

Clinton, Catherine. *The Other Civil War: American Women in the Nineteenth Century.* Rev. ed. New York: Hill and Wang, 1999.

Clinton, Catherine, and Nina Silber. *Divided Houses: Gender and the Civil War.* New York: Oxford University Press, 1992.

Cook, Neil A. "'The President's Hymn': A Thanksgiving Song." *American Civil War Forum.* https://www.americancivilwarforum.com/the-presidents-hymn-a-thanksgiving-song-225184.html.

"Court of Star Chamber." *Encyclopedia Britannica.* https://www.britannica.com/topic/Court-of-Star-Chamber.

Crane, Louis H. D., ed. *A Manual of Customs, Precedents and Forms, in Use in the Assembly of Wisconsin; Together with the Rules, the Apportionments, and Other Lists and Tables for Reference, with Indices*. 3rd annual ed. Madison: James Ross, State Printer, 1861.

Current, Richard N. *The Civil War Era, 1848–1973*. Volume 2 of *The History of Wisconsin*, edited by William Fletcher Thompson. Madison: State Historical Society of Wisconsin, 1976.

Dean, John S., and Frank M. Stewart, eds. *The Legislative Manual of the State of Wisconsin; Comprising Jefferson's Manual, the Rules, Forms and Laws for the Regulation of Business; also, Lists and Tables for Reference*. 2nd annual ed. Madison: Atwood and Rublee, State Printers, 1863.

"Demographics." *The Wisconsin Mosaic: A Brief History of Wisconsin*. http://dalbello.comminfo.rutgers.edu/FLVA/background/demographics.html.

Denney, Robert E. *The Civil War Years: A Day-by-Day Chronicle of the Life of a Nation*. New York: Sterling Publishing Company, 1992.

Edwards, Owen. "The Death of Colonel Ellsworth." *Smithsonian Magazine*. April 2011. http://www.smithsonianmag.com/history/the-death-of-colonel-ellsworth-878695/.

Ellsworth, Elmer E. *The Zouave Drill: Being a Complete Manual of Arms for the Use of the Rifled Musket, with Either the Percussion Cap, or Maynard Primer; Containing also the Complete Manual of the Sword and Sabre*. Philadelphia: T. B. Peterson and Brothers, 1861.

"Elmwood Cemetery." http://www.elmwoodcemetery.org.

"Failed Objects: Bullet Proof Vests and Design in the American Civil War." *O Say Can You See: Stories from the National Museum of American History*. http://americanhistory.si.edu/blog/2013/04/failed-objects-bullet-proof-vests-and-design-in-the-american-civil-war.html.

Fite, Emerson David. *Social and Industrial Conditions in the North during the Civil War*. New York: Macmillan, 1910.

Flagel, Thomas R. *The History Buff's Guide to the Civil War*. Nashville, TN: Cumberland House, 2003.

Fletcher, Holly Berkley. *Gender and the American Temperance Movement of the Nineteenth Century*. New York: Routledge, 2008.

Fredriksen, John. *Civil War Almanac*. New York: Facts on File, 2010.

Gallman, J. Matthew. *The Civil War Chronicle: The Only Day-by-Day Portrait of America's Tragic Conflict as Told by Soldiers, Journalists, Politicians, Farmers, Nurses, Slaves, and Other Eyewitnesses*. New York: Crown Publishers, 2000.

Giesberg, Judith Ann. *Army at Home: Women and the Civil War on the Northern Homefront*. Chapel Hill: University of North Carolina Press, 2009.

Glazer, Walter. "Wisconsin Goes to War." MS thesis, University of Wisconsin, 1963.

Goc, Michael A., and Geraldine N. Dricoll. *Winneconne: History's Crossing Place*. Winneconne, WI: Winneconne Historical Society and New Past Press, 1987.

Hannings, Bud. *Every Day of the Civil War: A Chronological Encyclopedia*. Jefferson, NC: McFarland Publishing, 2010

Historic Madison Inc. "Camp Randall Prison Camp." http://www.historicmadison.org/madison%27s%20past/connectingwithourpast/camprandallprisoncamp.html.

Historic Madison Inc. "Canal across the Isthmus." http://www.historicmadison.org/Madison%27s%20Past/connectingwithourpast/downtownmadisonscanal.html.

History of the North-western Soldiers' Fair, Held in Chicago the Last Week of October and the First Week of November, 1863: Including a List of Donations and Names of Donors, Treasurer's Report, &c &c. Chicago: Dunlop, Sewell & Spalding, 1864.

Home Town Ties: Berlin, Wisconsin, 1848–1998. Berlin, WI: Berlin Diary Newspapers, 1998.

Hurn, Ethel Alice. *Wisconsin Women in the War between the States.* Madison: Wisconsin History Commission, 1911. http://www.wisconsinhistory.org/turningpoints/search.asp?id=94.

Hurt, R. Douglas. "The Agricultural Power of the Midwest in the Civil War." In *Union Heartland: The Midwestern Homefront during the Civil War,* edited by Gillette Aley and J. L. Anderson, 68–96. Carbondale: Southern Illinois University Press, 2013.

"Inventory of the Allen Family Papers." Newberry Library, Chicago. https://mms.newberry.org/xml/xml_files/Allen.xml#bio1.

"James Henry Lane." *The Civil War Muse.* http://www.thecivilwarmuse.com/index.php?page=james-h-lane.

Kaser, David. *Books and Libraries in Camp and Battle: The Civil War Experience.* Westport, CT: Greenwood Press, 1984.

Katcher, Phillip. *The Civil War Day by Day.* St. Paul, MN: Zenith Press, 2007.

Kehoe, Karen A. "'Not a Moment for Delay': Benevolence in Wisconsin during the Civil War Era." PhD dissertation, Marquette University, 2003.

Kennedy, Susan Estabrook. *If All We Did Was to Weep at Home: A History of White Working-Class Women in America.* Bloomington: Indiana University Press, 1969.

"Kingdom Coming (Work, 1862)." *The Hardtacks: Folk Music of the Antebellum and Civil War Eras.* https://civilwarfolkmusic.com/2013/02/23/1862-kingdom-coming-work/.

Klement, Frank L. *The Copperheads in the Middle West.* Chicago: University of Chicago Press, 1960.

Klement, Frank. L. *Wisconsin in the Civil War: The Home Front and the Battle Front, 1861–1865.* Madison: State Historical Society of Wisconsin, 1997.

Legislative Reference Bureau. "Special and Extraordinary Sessions of the Wisconsin Legislature." *Informational Bulletin* 14, no. 2 (2014): 7. http://legis.wisconsin.gov/eupdates/sen07/special_and_extraordinary_sessions_of_the_wisconsin_legislature_aug_2014.pdf.

Levitan, Stuart D. *Madison: The Illustrated Sesquicentennial History, Volume 1, 1856–1931.* Madison: University of Wisconsin Press, 2006.

Lincoln, Abraham. "Proclamation of Thanksgiving." *Abraham Lincoln Online.* http://www.abrahamlincolnonline.org/lincoln/speeches/thanks.htm.

Lincoln, Abraham. "Proclamations of Days of Thanksgiving, Fasting, and Prayer." *World Challenge Pulpit Series.* http://www.tscpulpitseries.org/english/1990s/ts910201.html.

Long, E. B., and Barbara Long. *The Civil War Day by Day: An Almanac 1861–1865.* Garden City, NY: Doubleday, 1971.

Maier, Larry B. *Identification Discs of Union Soldiers in the Civil War: A Complete Classification Guide and Illustrated History*. Jefferson, NC: McFarland, 2008.

Massey, Mary Elizabeth. *Bonnet Brigades*. New York: Knopf, 1966.

McBride, Genevieve. *On Wisconsin Women: Working for Their Rights from Settlement to Suffrage*. Madison: University of Wisconsin Press, 1993.

McCabe, James D. *Life and Campaigns of General Robert E. Lee*. Atlanta: National Printing Co., 1870.

"Memphis and the Civil War in Vintage Drawings and Photos." *Historic Memphis*. http://historic-memphis.com/memphis-historic/civil-war-memphis/civil-war-memphis.html.

Mollenhoff, David. *Madison: A History of the Formative Years*. 2nd ed. Madison: University of Wisconsin Press, 2003.

Moore, Frank. *Women of the War: Their Heroism and Self-Sacrifice*. Hartford: S. S. Scranton, 1866.

Morehouse, Maggi M., and Zoe Trodd. *Civil War America: A Social and Cultural History*. New York: Routledge, 2013.

Mulhern, Nancy, comp. *Population of Wisconsin, 1850–2000: Population Statistics Were Taken from the United States Federal Census*. Madison: Wisconsin Historical Society Library, 2009.

National Archives and Records Administration. Pvt-Sgt Hiram H. Sleeper, Military Service Record. Document ordered from https://www.archives.gov/research/military.

National Center for Education Statistics. "Table 301.20: Historical Summary of Faculty, Enrollment, Degrees, and Finances in Degree-Granting Postsecondary Institutions: Selected Years, 1869–70 through 2011–12." *Digest of Education Statistics*. https://nces.ed.gov/programs/digest/d13/tables/dt13_301.20.asp.

National Park Service. "The Civil War: Search for Soldiers." https://www.nps.gov/civilwar/search-soldiers.htm.

Olin, Helen R. *The Women of a State University: An Illustration of the Working of Coeducation in the Middle West*. New York and London: G. P. Putnam's Sons, 1909.

Paludan, Phillip Shaw. *A People's Contest: The Union and the Civil War, 1861–1865*. New York: Harper & Row, 1988.

Pease, Terry D. *A History of the Pardeeville-Wyocena Area*. [Wisconsin]: T. D. Pease, 1997.

Pickard, Samuel Thomas. *Life and Letters of John Greenleaf Whittier*. Vol. 1. Boston: Houghton Mifflin, 1895.

Pilgrim Hall Museum. "Presidential Thanksgiving Proclamations." http://www.pilgrimhallmuseum.org/pdf/TG_Presidential_Thanksgiving_Proclamations_1862_1869.pdf.

Pipher, Mary Bray. *Reviving Ophelia: Saving the Selves of Adolescent Girls*. New York: Ballantine Books, 2001.

"Population of the United States in 1860: Wisconsin." https://www2.census.gov/library/publications/decennial/1860/population/1860a-37.pdf?#.

Quiner, Edwin. *Military History of Wisconsin: A Record of the Civil and Military Patriotism of the State*. Chicago: Clarke & Co., 1866.

Reetz, Elaine. *Come Back in Time*. Vol. 1, *Communities*. Princeton, WI: Fox River Publishing, 1981.
Silber, Nina. *Daughters of the Union: Northern Women Fight the Civil War*. Cambridge, MA: Harvard University Press, 2005.
Snyder, Thomas D., ed. *120 Years of American Education: A Statistical Portrait*. Washington, DC: Office of Educational Research and Improvement, National Center for Education Statistics, [1993].
"Soldier's Mittens." *Ravelry*. https://www.ravelry.com/patterns/library/soldiers-mittens.
Stemler, Joyce Bennet. *They Went South: Biographical Sketches of the Civil War Veterans from Berlin, Wisconsin*. Berlin, WI: Berlin Historical Society, 1966.
Sterling, Robert E. "Civil War Draft Resistance in the Middle West." PhD dissertation, Northern Illinois University, 1974.
Suckow, Bertel Wernick. *Madison City Directory: A City and Business Directory for 1866*. Madison, WI: B. W. Suckow, 1866.
Swoboda, Marian J., and Audrey J. Roberts. *They Came to Learn, They Came to Teach, They Came to Stay*. Madison: Office of Women, 1980.
"Talking Spirits Tour Performance." Presented by the Wisconsin Veterans Museum, Forest Hill Cemetery, Madison, October 4, 2015.
"Thomas Babington Macaulay." *Age-of-the-Sage: Transmitting the Wisdom of the Ages*. http://www.age-of-the-sage.org/history/historian/thomas_macaulay.html.
Thwaites, Reuben Gold. *Civil War Messages and Proclamations of Wisconsin War Governors*. Madison: Wisconsin History Commission, 1912.
"Total Civil War Casualties in Killed and Mortally Wounded." http://thomaslegion.net/battles.html.
Trask, Kerry. *The Fire Within: A Civil War Narrative from Wisconsin*. Kent, OH: Kent State University Press, 1995.
Traub, Melissa, "'$300 or Your Life': Recruitment and the Draft in the Civil War." Thesis, University of Connecticut–Storrs, 2015.
US Department of Veterans Affairs. "Salisbury National Cemetery." *National Cemetery Administration*. https://www.cem.va.gov/cems/nchp/salisbury.asp.
Voegli, V. Jacque. *Free but Not Equal: The Midwest and the Negro during the Civil War*. Chicago: University of Chicago Press, 1967.
Volo, Dorothy Denneen, and James M. Volo. *Daily Life in Civil War America*. Santa Barbara, CA: Greenwood Press, 2009.
Wagner, Margaret, Gary W. Gallagher, and Paul Finkelman, eds. *The Library of Congress Civil War Desk Reference*. New York: Simon and Schuster, 2002.
Wegman, Mary Ann. "Battle of New Orleans: Jackson Square." http://neworleanshistorical.org/items/show/623?tour=56&index=1.
Wells, Robert W. *Wisconsin in the Civil War*. Milwaukee: Milwaukee Journal, 1962.
Wert, Jeffrey D. *A Brotherhood of Valor: The Common Soldiers of the Stonewall Brigade, C.S.A, and the Iron Brigade, U.S.A*. New York: Touchstone, 2000.
"Why Did Civil War Officers Tell Their Men to 'Aim Low'?" *History Beta*. https://history.stackexchange.com/questions/2014/why-did-civil-war-officers-tell-their-men-to-aim-low.

Wisconsin Historical Society. "42nd Wisconsin Infantry History." https://www.wisconsinhistory.org/Records/Article/CS2484.

Wisconsin Historical Society. "Barstow, William Augustus (1813–1865)." https://www.wisconsinhistory.org/Records/Article/CS2079.

Wisconsin Historical Society. "Burchard, George Washington, 1835–1921." https://www.wisconsinhistory.org/Records/Article/CS5920.

Wisconsin Historical Society. "Iron Brigade." https://www.wisconsinhistory.org/Records/Article/CS1606.

Wisconsin Historical Society. "Quiner, Edwin Bryant (1816–1868): Wisconsin Civil War Historian and Author." https://www.wisconsinhistory.org/Records/Article/CS2580.

Wisconsin Historical Society. "Quiner, Emily (or Emilie) 1839–1919." https://www.wisconsinhistory.org/Records/Article/CS12133.

Wisconsin Historical Society. "Vilas, William Freeman, 1840–1908: Lawyer, Politician, Senator, Cabinet Officer, and Philanthropist." https://www.wisconsinhistory.org/Records/Article/CS2032.

Wisconsin Historical Society. "Wisconsin Genealogy Index: Marriage Record Entry for Dane County." Vol. 1, p. 573; viewed online at https://www.wisconsinhistory.org.

Wisconsin Historical Society. "Wisconsin Troops Help Capture Jefferson Davis." https://www.wisconsinhistory.org/Records/Article/CS3521.

Wisconsin Historical Society. "The Women's Suffrage Movement." *Turning Points in Wisconsin History.* https://www.wisconsinhistory.org/turningpoints/tp-032/?action=more_essay.

Wisconsin Veterans Museum. Civil War Roster Database, https://www.wisvetsmuseum.com/research/civil-war-database/.

Young, Agnes Brooks. *Women and the Crisis: Women of the North during the Civil War.* New York: McDowell, Obolensky, 1959.

Zimm, John. *This Wicked Rebellion: Wisconsin Civil War Soldiers Write Home.* Madison: Wisconsin Historical Society Press, 2012.

Index

1st US Sharpshooters, 314n12

abolition, 105, 190, 295, 307n59, 307–8n62
African Americans, xii, 7, 49, 105, 175, 182; Fort Pillow Massacre, 316n41; United States Colored Troops, 315n25; victims of riots, 315n21
Allen, Annie Cox. See Cox, Annie
Allen, Charles, 319n14
Allen, Gideon Winans (Annie's fiancé): Copperhead activity, 106, 120–21, 188–89; draft resistance, 313n7; engagement, 120; letters to Annie Cox, 106, 170, 318n68; political beliefs, 175, 186, 187, 188–89, 190–91, 193, 317n54; postwar life, 292–93; wife's role, 318n60. See also Cox, Annie: letters to Gideon Allen
Allen, Martha (Gideon's sister), 186, 317n54
Allen, Mr. (instructor at University of Wisconsin), 43, 88, 90, 109, 114
Allen, Ruth Florence (Annie's daughter), 292–93
Allen, Thomas F., 310n20
ambulance corps, 203, 310–11n24
Appomattox Courthouse, 287, 288

Appleton, Orange (Ann and Susan's brother), 47, 100
Arnold, Clara (Belle's niece), 298
Arnold, Clarence (Belle's brother), 6, 183, 184
Arnold, Georgie (Belle's nephew), 192
Arnold, Mother (Belle's mother), 6, 183, 192, 202, 275–76, 280, 282, 298. See also Sleeper, Belle: letters to Charles Bennett Palmer
Arnold, Rosabella August. See Sleeper, Belle
Arnold, Wiley (Belle's brother), 6, 183, 203, 252, 268, 278, 297–98, 317n50; son's death, 192. See also Sleeper, Belle: letters to Charles Bennett Palmer; Wisconsin Regiments: 32nd Infantry
Augustus (Gus; Emily's cousin), 31, 36, 97, 102; as dentist, 98, 104, 167, 169; temperance activities, 169, 170, 173. See also Quiner, Emily: diary entries

Baker, Elizabeth. See Cox, Elizabeth Baker Poad
Baker, Hiram, 96, 310n21
Baltimore, Union attack on, 13, 303n16
Barnard, John, 147, 315n24

Index

Barnum, Phineas T., 306–7n53, 319n13
Barstow, William, 306n52
Barstow Cavalry, 53, 306n52
battles: Antietam, 3, 310–11n24; Arkansas Post, 316n45; Atlanta, 196, 320n17; Belmont, 136, 314n13; Big Black River, 130, 314n11; Bloomfield, Missouri, 100, 306n50, 310n21; Bowling Green, Kentucky, 308n70; Bull Run, 26, 27, 304n34, 310n13; Champion Hill, 130–31, 313–14n10, 314n11, 316n37; Chancellorsville, 119, 120; Charleston, 314n20; Chickamauga, 120, 316n37; Dallas, 316n37; Dandridge, Tennessee, 306n46; Fair Oaks, 319n14; Fort Donelson, 67, 307n58; Fort Pillow, 316n41; Fort Sumter, 3, 7, 9, 10; Island No. 10, 73, 81, 137; Jackson, 130, 314n11, 315n26; Langueille Ferry, Arkansas, 94, 310n20; New Madrid, 137; North Anna River, 196; Perryville, 101, 311n27; Port Gibson, 129, 130, 157; Prairie Grove, 311n39; Reams Station, 322n50; Richmond, 260, 283, 286; Sabine Cross Roads, 315n25; Seven Pines, 82; Spotsylvania Campaign, 196, 318n66; Stones River, 105; Wilderness Campaign, 196; Wilson's Creek and Oak Hill, 304n35. *See also* Gettysburg, Battle of; Petersburg, Battle of; Pittsburg Landing, Battle of; Vicksburg Campaign
Beckwith, Norman F., 192, 252, 318n65
Beckwith Hall/Hotel (Berlin, Wisconsin), 184, 318n65
Beloit Rifles, 18, 303n24. *See also* Wisconsin Regiments: 2nd Infantry
Benedict, Julia (Belle's daughter), 298
Benedict, Mary (Belle's daughter), 298
Benedict, Oscar (Belle's second husband), 298
Benedict, Paul (Belle's son), 298

Berlin, Wisconsin, 6, 41, 317n58, 318n65. *See also* Arnold, Wiley; Palmer, Charles Bennett; Sleeper, Belle; Sleeper, Hiram
Berlin Courant, 6, 64, 182, 317n51
Berry, James, 165, 316n41
Billings, Levi J., 153, 315–16n29
Bishop, David B., 285, 322n45
Blackmer, Luke, 320–21n30
Bloody Angle. *See* battles: Spotsylvania Campaign
Bond, Richard, 169, 316n43
Booth, John Wilkes, 288
Boston, Massachusetts, 315n21
Bradley, Leonard, 92, 310n18
Brisbane, Benjamin L., 13, 14, 30, 303n18, 305n36
Brisbane, William H., 12, 13, 15, 17, 19, 23, 32, 35, 303n18, 305n36
Brown, Edward (Susan's son), 6, 60, 69, 71, 78, 94, 95, 101. *See also* Brown, Susan: letters to Ann Waldo; Waldo, Ann: letters to Morris
Brown, E. L., 54, 307n61
Brown, Emily (Susan's daughter), 293
Brown, Emma, 317n58
Brown, Susan, xi, xiii, 4, 5, 6, 7, 47, 51, 57, 59, 60, 67, 73, 87, 88, 94, 100, 300; aid to soldiers, 95, 96; care of sister, 5; financial issues, 8, 68, 70, 71, 78, 79; letters to Ann Waldo, 68–69, 70–71, 77–78, 79–80, 94–96, 100–102; photographs, 95; postwar life, 293; teachers exam, 71, 73, 78, 79–80, 101; Teachers' Institute, 101; teaching, 5, 52, 57. *See also* Waldo, Ann: letters to Morris
Brown, Waldo (Susan's husband), 6, 47, 50, 51, 53, 57, 59, 60, 61, 63, 64, 65, 69, 70–71, 78, 79, 94, 95, 101, 293. *See also* Brown, Susan: letters to Ann Waldo; Waldo, Ann: letters to Morris
Brown, Willis (Will; Susan's son), 6, 60, 61, 69, 87, 94, 101, 293. *See also*

Brown, Susan: letters to Ann Waldo; Waldo, Ann: letters to Morris
bullet-proof vests, 87, 309n11
Burchard, George W., 148, 315n25
burial practices, 157, 158, 187, 298–99
Burnside, Ambrose, 316n44
Burwell, Andrew (Mary's husband), 6, 205, 322n46; as cook for officers, 219–20, 225, 231, 241; postwar life, 297, 298; wounded at Petersburg, 281. *See also* Burwell, Mary: letters to Andrew; Wisconsin Regiments: 5th Infantry
Burwell, Carrie E. (Hume; Mary's daughter), 297
Burwell, Emma (Mary's sister-in-law), 222, 232, 241, 272, 297
Burwell, Lucy (Mary's daughter), 6, 205, 206, 297; eating, 225, 227, 244–45; language development, 221, 234, 244, 246, 257, 263; playing, 214, 227, 234, 244, 249, 275, 284; recognizing papa, 210, 225, 249, 263; teething, 208, 215, 225, 234, 238, 242; walking, 225, 229, 230, 234, 244–45, 265. *See also* Burwell, Mary: letters to Andrew
Burwell, Mary (Swannell), xi, xiii, 4, 6, 7, 298, 300; cooking advice, 219; fall of Richmond, 284, 285, 286, 322n46; farming, 205, 206, 207, 209, 211, 212, 218, 234, 244; financial concerns, 206, 207–8, 211, 212, 214, 232, 236–37, 241–42, 244, 247, 248, 257, 262, 266–67, 269–70, 274, 286; hiring help, 211, 213, 221, 241; letters to Andrew, 205–21, 222–39, 239–43, 243–50, 257–63, 264–67, 269–72, 274–75, 283; loneliness, 216–17, 240, 271, 283; mail, issues receiving, 206, 209, 214, 222, 229, 247, 249; photographs, 208, 210, 212, 214, 215, 217, 222, 225, 249; poetry, 229, 233, 260, 267; postwar life, 296, 297; presidential election of 1864, 205, 225, 319n15; temperance, 270, 275; worries about Andrew, 205, 208, 215, 216, 222, 224, 227, 232, 243, 257–58, 283, 285
Burwell, Mr. (Mary's father-in-law), 207, 217, 218
Burwell, Nellie Winifred (Bartels; Mary's daughter), 297
Burwell, Robert Andrew (Mary's son), 297
Burwell, William Henry (Mary's son), 297
Bushnell, Matthias, 95, 310n20
Butler, Benjamin F., 240, 314n14, 320n23

Cairo, Illinois, 136, 165–66, 319n7
Campbell, John A., 259, 321n33
Campbell, Mr. (Emily's friend), 54, 84, 89, 98, 99, 112, 135, 167, 170
Camp Harvey (Kenosha), 37
Camp Randall (Madison): conditions, 33, 67, 105, 191; Confederate prisoners, 73, 82, 83; conversion of fairgrounds, 15, 16; events for soldiers, 21, 32, 304n30, 304n31, 310n22; hospital, 173; Masonic Lodge, 19; Ozaukee rioters, 312n40; religious services, 34; visits to, 18, 19, 20, 21, 35, 44, 46, 73, 74, 98, 301n22
Camp Washburn (Milwaukee), 312n40
Canadian Pacific Railroad. *See* railroads: transcontinental
Cantwell, Michael J., 146, 147, 315n23
Cape Girardeau, Missouri, 86, 94, 96
capitol building. *See* Wisconsin State Capitol
Carey family, 7, 9, 14, 15, 17, 18, 19, 21, 22, 27, 29, 30, 33, 34, 42, 43
Carr, Mrs. Dr., 121, 317n58
Case, J. I., 306n47
cemeteries, garden, 298. *See also* Elmwood Cemetery
Central Pacific Railroad. *See* railroads: transcontinental

Chadbourne, Paul, 292
Chapel, Stephen, 224, 272, 322n41
Chapman, Jennie, 135, 143, 159, 161, 163, 170, 172, 173
Charleston, South Carolina, 144, 148, 314n20
Chase, Salmon P., 310n13
Chicago, Illinois, 73, 188, 222, 313n4, 317n58, 319n13; schools, 292
Chicago Times, 172, 316n44
Chicago Zouaves, 20
Chittenden, Richard, 57, 59, 307n55
Christmas, 48, 112, 234; soldiers away for, 224, 226, 233, 235, 306n48
Clark, Giles, 40, 41, 45, 51, 53, 56, 59, 63
Clark, William, 141, 143, 147
Clawson, Phineas J., 106, 311n39
Clayton, George, 183, 184, 192, 193, 203, 251, 252, 268, 317n51
Colt, Henrietta (Mrs. J. S.), 295, 317n58
Columbus, Kentucky, 136, 165, 168
Conderman, John, 78, 308n79
Confederate States of America, 49, 63, 66, 100, 144; army, 13, 26, 27, 28–29, 49, 67, 76, 87, 94, 96, 105, 120, 138, 139, 143, 149, 195, 196, 239, 243, 281, 287, 304n35, 307n58, 308n69, 310n24, 314n12, 314n15, 315n15, 316n41, 317n54; deserters, 266; food shortages, 239, 321n34; government, 9, 105–6, 119, 322n46; prison camps, 299, 320–21n30, 321n31; as prisoners, 73, 79, 82, 83, 195, 288, 308n63
Confederate sympathizers, 16, 20, 152, 198, 319n13. *See also* Copperheads
Conger, Henry A., 223, 319n14
Conscription Act, 110, 312n40, 313n7, 315n21. *See also* draft; soldiers: recruitment
Copperheads, 188, 192, 225, 312n40, 313n6, 317n55. *See also* Allen, Gideon Winans; Confederate sympathizers;

Smith, George B.; Vallandingham, Clement
cotton as crop, 161, 162, 164
Cox, Michael (Annie's stepfather), 5, 111, 171, 312n45
Cox, Annie (Poad), xi, xii, xiii, 4, 5, 7, 106, 111, 170, 300, 318n68; advice to Gideon Allen, 106, 109, 120, 121, 171, 189; art, 174, 182; birth name, 124; desire for education, 111, 114, 291; engagement, 120; financial concerns, 179–80, 188, 318n64; lakeshore sketch, 174; letters to Gideon Allen, 106–9, 110–11, 113–14, 120–21, 124, 128–29, 170–71, 172–73, 173–74, 175–76, 179–80, 182, 186–87, 187–88, 189, 190–92, 193–94, 287; political beliefs, 107–8, 108–9, 120, 128–29, 175, 186–87, 187–88, 188, 189, 190–91, 193–94, 317n54; postwar life, 292–93; views on religion, 124, 171, 176, 292; women's role, 107, 108, 128, 188, 318n60
Cox, Elizabeth Baker Poad (Annie's mother), 5, 111
Cox, Florance (Annie's sister), 5
Craig, A. J., 11, 22, 23, 25, 26, 29, 30, 39, 44, 46, 54, 58, 69, 74, 83, 88, 89, 104, 134, 135, 168, 169, 172, 303n12; Teacher's Association, 27, 90, 91, 93; temperance, 35
Cross Plains, Wisconsin, 84, 97, 98, 102
Curtis, Joseph, 167, 316n42
Cutler, Lysander, 196, 318n2

Daniels, Edward, 95, 310n20
Danning family (Emily's friends), 14, 20, 29, 31, 43, 104
Davis, Jefferson, 3, 105, 138, 195, 287, 321n34
days of fasting, 32, 119, 305n38
deaths of soldiers, 4, 157, 291, 298, 299, 308–9n72

Democratic State Register, 5
Democrats, 5, 10, 107, 108, 186, 188, 189, 221, 304n28, 312n40, 313n7, 317n54
Denver, Colorado, 292
deserters and desertions, 82, 243, 266, 299
disability discharge, 268, 320n22, 320n25, 322n47
diseases, 100; ague, 138, 148; consumption, 53, 77, 87; diarrhea, 138, 141, 146, 288, 314n18; malaria, 157; typhoid, 147, 304n28
divorce, 5, 296–97
domestic roles, 3, 9, 82, 294, 300; cooking, 44, 146, 207, 209; housekeeping, 39, 42, 54, 55, 207, 216; knitting, 52, 65, 232; sewing, 38, 51, 78; washing and washing machines, 37, 43, 45, 46, 86, 117, 122, 216, 245. *See also* relief work; soldiers mittens
Douglas, Stephen A., 24, 304n28
draft, 27, 92, 95, 109, 110, 129, 145, 182, 187, 191, 205, 216, 217, 220, 238, 240, 319n14; draft resistance, 313n7; draft riots, 145, 312n40, 315n21; status of draftees, 263, 321n35. *See also* Conscription Act; soldiers: recruitment
Drakely, Pauline, 170
Dunmore, George W., 95, 310n20

Eastman, Adelbert, 285, 322n45
Ellsworth, Elmer, 20, 303n25, 322n42
Elmwood Cemetery (Memphis), 153, 298, 316n30
Emancipation Proclamation, 83, 100, 105–6
Endeavor, Wisconsin, 6, 297, 298
Everett, Edward, 85, 187, 309n10
Ewell, Richard S., 314n12

Fairchild, Lucius, 305n39
Fairchild, Sally Blair, 33, 42, 305n39

farms and farming: beekeeping, 163, 295; cattle, 204, 212, 214; corn, 199, 200, 201, 205, 206, 209, 212, 213, 218, 313n4; currants, 25, 88, 131, 132, 133; hired help, 68, 142, 201, 204, 211, 221, 241; hogs, 118, 209, 210, 211, 212; horses, 122, 125, 200, 212; mechanization, 47, 87, 142, 306n47; milk cows, 21, 205, 207, 212, 225, 261, 272, 274, 286; photographs of, 226, 296; postwar changes, 295–96; potatoes, 204, 206, 212, 213; Southern farms, 119; strawberries, 125, 132; wheat, 119, 122, 125, 142, 200, 201, 209, 211, 234, 248, 295, 313n4; women's responsibilities, 4, 6, 109, 306n47; wool, 125, 132. *See also* Burwell, Mary; Patchin, Margaret; Powers, Sarah
Farnham, Ralph, 12, 303n14
Farr, H. Levander, 231, 320n18
Farrell, James, 147, 157, 315n27
financial issues. *See* Burwell, Mary; Cox, Annie; Patchin, Margaret; Powers, Sarah
Fish, Gilbert, 78, 308n70
Fisher, Mrs. L., 317n58
flag making, 4, 9, 13, 15, 16, 19, 20, 21, 22, 24, 294
Fond Du Lac, Wisconsin, 6
Fort Donelson, 67, 307n58
Fort Pickens, 13, 303n17
Fort Pillow, 137, 164; massacre, 316n31
Fort Scott, 317n54
Fort Sumter, 3, 7, 9, 10
Fourth of July. *See* Independence Day
Fox Lake, Wisconsin, xi, 4, 6, 129, 297
Franklin, William B., 310n13
freedom of the press, 172, 316n44
fundraising. *See* relief work
funeral practices, 298–99
furloughs: inequity in, 116, 123–24, 155, 206, 232, 243, 244; injured soldiers, 87, 138, 141, 152, 159, 160, 161. *See also* Patchin, Margaret; Waldo, Ann

Gage, George Leroy (Mary's brother-in-law), 297, 320n25; advice on soldiering, 225; draft, 217, 219, 223, 246, 258; farming, 205, 206; finances, 208, 225, 236, 242. *See also* Burwell, Mary: letters to Andrew

Gage, Matilda (Mary's sister), 297; farming, 205, 206; illness, 223; Leroy drafted, 246. *See also* Burwell, Mary: letters to Andrew

Gage, Mr. and Mrs. (Matilda Gage's in-laws), 206, 216, 258; finances, 208, 212, 236, 248, 270, 287; storekeeping, 225, 227, 229. *See also* Burwell, Mary: letters to Andrew

Gates, Phineas (Sarah's brother), 143, 144, 314n19

Gayoso Hotel (Memphis), 139, 146, 314n16. *See also* hospitals, military

General Order No. 100, 119

Gettysburg, Battle of, 3, 120, 138, 143, 149, 305n39, 314n12, 315n21

Gettysburg Address, 187, 309n10

Gifford, Sidney, 223, 319n14

Governor's Guard, 13

Grant, U. S., 81, 195; Appomattox, 287, 288; Belmont, 314n13; Fort Donelson, 307n58; Richmond, 260, 283, 286; Vicksburg, 119, 120

Great Northern Railroad. *See* railroads: transcontinental

Greeley, Horace, 315n21

guerilla warfare, 222–23, 227, 319n13

habeas corpus, 189, 312n40, 313n7

Halleck, Henry, 81

Hartson, Frederick, 264, 322n37

Harvey, Cordelia, 74, 81, 317n58

Harvey, Louis Powell, 44, 67, 76; death, 73–74, 81, 82, 306n51, 309n1; funeral, 83

Harvey Hospital, 74, 191

Hastings, Samuel D., 12, 28, 70, 76, 306n51

Hazelton, Gerry W., 54, 307n61

Henry, William I., 152, 315n28

High, James., 12, 13, 14, 20, 22, 25, 26, 32, 34, 35, 36, 104

Hill, Elias, 78, 308n70

Historical Rooms (Wisconsin Historical Society), 61, 103, 104, 180; photograph of, 181

Hodges, James, 159, 316n37

home, importance of, 176

Home Guards, 15

Homestead Act, 295

Hooker, Joseph, 119, 139

Hopkins, Mrs. B. F., 317n58

hospitals, military, 74, 96, 138, 154, 318–19n5; description of wards, 139; field hospitals, 74, 310–11n24; inspection, 147. *See also* Memphis hospitals; Quiner, Emily

hospital stewards, 316n38, 316n42

Hotchkiss, Florentine A., 266, 322n388

Howe, James H., 146–47, 147–48, 150, 315n23

Hoyt, Mrs. Dr., 317n58

Hubbell, Mrs. Judge, 317n58

Hunter, Robert M. T., 259, 321n33

Hutchinson, John G. and family, 89, 310n13

Ilsey, Lottie, 317n58

Independence Day, 24–25, 89, 133, 137, 304n30

Indians: fear of, 206, 209; 1862 uprising, 310n23. *See also* Native peoples of Wisconsin; Winnebago

Irish: bias toward, 189; draft resistance, 315n21; regiment, 308n69

Iron Brigade, 3, 310–11n24, 314n12. *See also* Wisconsin Regiments

Island No. 10, 73, 81, 137

Jackson, Andrew, statues of, 138, 314n14

Jackson, James, 20, 303n25

Jackson, Stonewall, 81

Janesville, Wisconsin, 89, 90–91, 103, 104, 112, 135
Johnson, Andrew, 221
Johnson, Thomas W., 52, 53, 57, 86, 306n50
Johnston, Albert Sidney, 307n58, 308n69
Jones, Homer S., 159, 316n37

Kansas, 49, 59, 317n54
Kearny, Philip, 310n13
Kendall, Charles, 130–31, 313–14n10
Kenosha, Wisconsin, 37, 49, 67–68, 303n25. *See also* Waldo, Ann
Kent, Alfred, 141, 143, 144
"Kingdom Coming" (song), 309n8
Kribbs, Harmon S., 236, 320n16

Ladies Aid Societies. *See* relief work
Ladies Temperance Alliance, 294
Ladies Union League, 113, 114, 120–21, 312n44
LaGrange, Wallace W., 41, 306n46
Lane, James Henry, 49; Lane's Expedition, 51, 63
Lawrence, Oscar, 153, 313–14n10
Lee, Robert E., 9, 120, 138–39, 143, 149, 283, 286, 287, 288, 314n12, 314n15
Lewis, James T., 243, 306n51
Libby Prison. *See* prisons and prisoners
Libscomb, David, 175, 317n48
Lincoln, Abraham: assassination, 288, 290; blockades Southern ports, 10; call for troops, 3, 82, 92, 302n5, 313n6; day of fasting, 119, 305n38; death of Elmer Ellsworth, 303n25; election, 1864, 221, 251, 319n15; Emancipation Proclamation, 100, 105; General Order No. 100, 119; Gettysburg Address, 187, 309n10; Hutchinson singers, 310n13; inauguration, 1865, 267; interaction with McClellan, 49, 66; military hospitals, 74, 82; offer to Lee, 9–10; peace talks, 321n33; State of the Union address, 1861, 306n45; State of the Union address, 1863, 105; Thanksgiving, 305–6n44, 311n30, 318n59
Lincoln, Mary, 66
Lyon, Nathaniel, 28, 304n35

Macaulay's *History of England*, 103, 311n28
MacDonald, Mary (Margaret's niece), 125, 128, 132, 142, 199, 200, 204
Madison, Wisconsin, 5, 9, 15, 92, 112, 294, 312n44; City Guard, 191; City Hall, 13, 14, 24, 88, 89, 172; First Ward Grammar School, 85, 304n27; Forest Hill Cemetery, 73, 292; Lake Mendota, McBride's Point, 23, 93, 97; lakeshore, sketch of, 174; picnic point, 23, 90, 96, 97, 168. *See also* Camp Randall; Harvey Hospital; Ladies Temperance Alliance; Ladies Union League; University of Wisconsin; Wisconsin State Capitol
mail, issues receiving, xiii. *See also* Burwell, Mary; Patchin, Margaret; Powers, Sarah; Sleeper, Belle
Manassas. *See* battles: Bull Run
marriage, 21, 155, 197, 296–98
Marsh, M. M., 268–69, 273
Marshall House (Arlington), 303n25
Maryland, 303n16, 319n15
Massachusetts, 6th Infantry, 303n16
Mazomanie, Wisconsin, 74, 82, 83; photograph of, 75
McClellan, George, 28, 49, 66, 221, 310n13
McRaven, David Olando and Amanda Nantz, 321n31
Meade, George C., 314n15
medical treatment of soldiers: amputation, 130, 152, 157, 308–9n72; mental illness, 239, 297; opium, 157. *See also* hospitals, military; Memphis hospitals; nurses and nursing
Memphis, Tennessee, 105, 137–38, 145, 147, 160, 164, 293; Andrew Jackson

340 Index

Memphis, Tennessee (*continued*) statue, 314n14; Catholic Cemetery, 160–61. *See also* Elmwood Cemetery; Gayoso Hotel; Memphis hospitals
Memphis hospitals, 130–31, 139; Adams, 143, 146; Gayoso, 139, 146, 314n16; Jackson, 139; Officers, 152; Regimental, 147; Small Pox, 160, 161; Union, 139
Mielz, Mark and wife, 232, 320n19
Militia Act, 92, 302n5
Milwaukee, Wisconsin, 11, 40, 56, 222, 312n40, 313n4, 319n13, 319n42
Milwaukee Mitten Society, 305n42
Milwaukee Sentinel, 60
Milwaukee Soldier's Aid Society, 295
Milwaukee Typographical Union, 182. *See also* typesetting
Minnesota, 209, 272, 293, 295
Mississippi River, 12, 73, 119; riverboat trip, 136, 137; union control of, 120, 195
Morrill Act, 292
mourning practices, 74, 81, 82, 280–81, 322n43
Mullin, Mr. (Hiram's fellow prisoner), 288–89
Myrmidons Society, 36, 305n43

National Conscription Act. *See* Conscription Act
Native peoples of Wisconsin, xii, 6–7. *See also* Winnebago
Nell (Nellie; Belle's friend), 184, 203, 251, 253, 255–56, 268, 273, 276, 277, 279, 281, 282, 299
Nelson, Dr. (Emily's supervisor), 139, 143, 145, 150, 161, 162, 163, 164
New Lisbon, Wisconsin, 310n23
New Orleans, Louisiana, 81, 314n14
newspapers, 7, 41, 50, 71, 311n29. *See also Berlin Courant*; *Chicago Times*; *Milwaukee Sentinel*; *New York Tribune*; *Richmond Examiner*; *Sheboygan Diary*

New York City, 145, 315n21, 319n13
New York Tribune, 252, 256, 307n54, 315n21, 320–21n30
Nineteenth Amendment, US Constitution, 295
Northern Pacific Railroad. *See* railroads: transcontinental
Northwestern Soldiers Fair. *See* sanitary fairs
nurses and nursing, 139, 146, 161, 300, 314n7; male nurses, 314n17; photograph of, 140. *See also* Chapman, Jennie; Drakely, Pauline; Quiner, Emily; Quiner, Fannie; Richardson, Louise

"Old Southern Gentleman" (song), 84, 309n8
Oxford, Wisconsin, 6, 274
Ozaukee, Wisconsin, 107, 312n40

Pacific Railroad Act of 1862, 293. *See also* railroads
Packwaukee, Wisconsin, 213, 240, 248
Palmer, Charles Bennett, 6, 182, 183, 277; nickname, 318n69; promotion to lieutenant, 202. *See also* Sleeper, Belle: letters to Charles Bennett Palmer; Wisconsin Regiments: 1st Heavy Artillery
Patchin, Amelia (Margaret's daughter), 116, 312n46
Patchin, Augustus (Margaret's husband), 6, 8, 109; postwar life, 295; prisoner, 120, 198, 201. *See also* Patchin, Margaret: letters to Augustus; Patchin, Margaret: letters to James; Wisconsin Regiments: 10th Infantry
Patchin, Elbert (Margaret's son), 6, 117, 118, 119, 122, 125, 131, 132, 133, 142, 156, 163, 200, 201, 204, 323n19. *See also* Patchin, Margaret: letters to Augustus; Patchin, Margaret: letters to James

Patchin, Herbert (Margaret's son), 110, 117, 118, 119, 122, 124, 125, 127, 131, 132, 142, 151, 154, 163, 199, 201, 204, 295. *See also* Patchin, Margaret: letters to Augustus; Patchin, Margaret: letters to James

Patchin, Horatio (Margaret's son), 116, 312n46

Patchin, James (Margaret's son), 6, 115, 117, 118, 119, 122, 125, 126, 127, 131, 132, 133, 142, 151, 155, 156, 163, 198, 201, 204. *See also* Patchin, Margaret: letters to Augustus; Patchin, Margaret: letters to James

Patchin, John (Margaret's son), 6, 117, 118, 119, 122, 123, 125, 131, 132, 155, 156, 163, 199, 201, 204

Patchin, Margaret (MacNish), xi, xiii, 4, 6, 7, 8, 109–10, 120, 198, 300, 313n5; advice to James, 199; beekeeping, 163, 295; challenge of writing, 115, 118, 122; farming, 119, 125, 131–32, 155, 200, 201, 204, 296; financial concerns, 115, 119, 122–23, 125, 128, 132, 133, 151–52, 156; furloughs, 123, 155; illness, 110, 118, 124, 126, 142, 156, 200, 201; letters to Augustus, 110, 115–16, 116–19, 122–24, 125–28, 131–33, 141–42, 150–52, 154–57, 163; letters to James, 198–201, 204–5; loneliness, 110, 116, 123, 127, 142, 155, 204; mail, issues receiving, 115, 123, 131, 154, 163; photographs, 110, 151; postwar life, 295; religious beliefs, 199; urges Augustus to resign, 110, 116, 123, 125; war widow, 117; worries about Augustus, 115, 120, 150, 151, 154, 198, 201

Patchin, Nancy (Margaret's daughter), 116, 312n46

Patchin, Orlo (Margaret's son), 6, 117, 118, 119, 122, 125, 131, 132, 142, 151, 155, 156, 163, 199, 201, 204, 295, 323n19. *See also* Patchin, Margaret: letters to Augustus; Patchin, Margaret: letters to James

Patchin family farm, 296

peace: desire for, 25, 108, 187, 190, 229, 246, 267, 283, 311n30; negotiations, 195, 259, 262, 321n33

Pease, Oliver D., 78, 308n71

pensions: National Pension Act, 82; difficulty in receiving, 155; for widows, 296–97

Petersburg, Battle of, 203, 239, 250, 257, 281, 316n37, 319n6, 320n20, 322n46

Phillips, Wendell, 73, 307–8n62

photography, 184; photograph painting, 103, 182, 268. *See also* Brown, Susan; Burwell, Mary; Patchin, Margaret; Waldo, Ann

Pickard, Josiah L., 29, 99, 306n51

picnics, 7, 23, 85, 161; school picnic, 29; soldiers' picnics, 21, 26, 32, 98, 304n31

Pierce, Mortimer B., 162, 316n39

Pierson, William, 239, 320n22

Pillow, Gideon Johnson, 67, 307n58

Pitman, William G., 150, 315n27

Pittsburg Landing, Battle of, 73, 76, 78, 81, 87, 308n69, 308n70, 308n71, 308–9n72, 309–10n12, 315–16n29, 318–19n5

Poad, Annie. *See* Cox, Annie

Poad, Elizabeth. *See* Cox, Elizabeth Baker Poad

Poad, Michael, 5, 114, 312n45

Pope, John, 173, 174

Pors, William, 312n40

Portage, Wisconsin, 17, 36, 125, 126–27, 215, 225, 274; photograph of, 212

Port Washington, Wisconsin, 312n40

Powers, Georgie (Sarah's son), 6, 154. *See also* Powers, Sarah: letters to Norman

Powers, Milton (Sarah's son), 6, 148, 154. *See also* Powers, Sarah: letters to Norman

Powers, Norman (Sarah's husband), 6, 8, 12; death, 157–58. *See also* Powers, Sarah: letters to Norman; Wisconsin Regiments: 29th Infantry

Powers, Sarah, xi, xiii, xiv, 6, 8, 129, 157, 300, 306n47; correspondence with J. G. Dunning, 157, 158; letters to Norman, 129–31, 138–39, 142–43, 144–45, 148–49, 153–54; farming, 142–43, 153; furloughs, 138; mail, issues receiving, 129, 148, 154, 157, 158; postwar life, 296–97, 299; war news, 138–39, 143, 144, 145, 148; worries about Norman, 130–31, 138, 148

Powers, Sarah Adelaide (Sarah's daughter), 6, 148, 154. *See also* Powers, Sarah: letters to Norman

presidential election (1864), 205, 217, 221; fears of violence, 225, 319n15

President's Hymn, 188, 318n59

Price, Sterling, 304n35

prisons and prisoners, 27, 67, 76, 79, 138, 143, 149, 195, 252, 288, 299, 304n34, 308n63, 310n20, 315n25, 318n5, 320–21n30, 321n31; Libby Prison, 120, 252, 288. *See also* Blackmer, Luke; Camp Randall; Confederate States of America: prison camps; Mullin, Mr.; Patchin, Augustus; Patchin, Margaret; Richardson, A. D.; Salisbury Prison; Sleeper, Hiram

"privates" messages in letters, 66, 307n57

Purman, David G., 55, 62, 69, 70, 78, 307n60, 308n71

Quiner, Alice (Emily's sister), 5, 166

Quiner, Charles (Charley; Emily's brother), 5, 62, 112, 166

Quiner, E. B. (Emily's father), 5, 13, 15, 24, 34, 83, 103, 112; with 6th Infantry, 28, 37; boating, 171; Civil War history and scrapbooks, 82, 92, 175; Emily's trip to Memphis, 135, 166, 168, 174, 175, 176; *Military History of Wisconsin*, 300; relief work, 36, 48; visits to Camp Randall, 46. *See also* Quiner, Emily: diary entries

Quiner, Ellen (Emily's sister), 5

Quiner, Emily, xi, xii, 4, 5, 9, 26, 38, 73, 82, 99, 120; appreciation of nature, 18, 24, 37; baptism, 116; boating, 20, 22, 26, 27, 29, 84, 90, 93, 96–97, 97; chess, 39, 42, 46, 48, 54, 72, 76, 78, 83, 84, 92, 104; death, 291; diary, xii, 7, 9, 11, 99, 112, 134, 177–78; diary entries, 10–26, 27–37, 39–40, 42–44, 46, 48–49, 52, 54–55, 58, 61–63, 64, 67, 69–70, 72–73, 74–77, 78, 81, 83–86, 88–93, 96–99, 102–4, 112–13, 114–15, 116, 133–38, 139–41, 143–44, 145–48, 149–50, 152–53, 157, 158–63, 163–70, 173, 174–75, 177–78; fishing, 85, 86, 88, 89; flag making, 4, 9, 13, 15, 16, 19, 20, 22, 24; fundraising, 13, 52, 54; housekeeping, 55, 84; Ladies Aid Society, 34, 35; lectures and exhibitions, 24, 32, 36, 49, 55, 61, 64, 67, 70, 73, 85, 89, 104; marriage proposal, 153; Memphis trip, 135–37, 164–69; normal school, 111, 112; nursing, 139–41, 143–44, 145–48, 149–50, 152–53, 157, 159–62, 162–63; patients, 141, 143, 144, 146, 147, 149, 157; photographs, 72, 99; plans to return, 167, 169, 170, 173, 174; reading, 28, 48, 49, 54, 55, 72, 76; relief work, 13, 21, 36, 42, 46, 48–49, 62, 67; sewing for soldiers, 11, 12, 16, 17, 19, 20, 22, 32, 34, 36, 42, 48, 55, 103, 104; Teachers' Association, 27, 89, 90–91; teachers examination, 29, 89, 91; teachers meeting, 85, 86, 88, 89, 90; teaching, 14, 17, 29, 85, 291; Temperance Lodge activities, 18, 35, 55, 62, 69, 72, 76, 84; travels to other towns, 74, 83, 90–92, 102–3, 104,

112, 112–13; Union League, 113, 114; university studies, 72, 76, 83, 84, 85, 99, 104, 168, 176, 291; visits to Camp Randall, 18, 21, 32, 33, 34, 35, 44, 46, 79, 98; visits to legislature, 10; war rallies, 12, 14, 93; washing, 37, 42, 46; Young Ladies Relief Society, 33, 36, 37, 46, 49, 52, 58, 62, 64, 67

Quiner, Fannie (Emily's sister), 5, 11, 14, 18, 20, 25, 26, 29, 30, 38, 44, 55, 89, 99, 112, 167; boating, 20, 22, 90, 96–97, 168, 169; chess, 39, 42, 46, 48, 54, 72; fishing, 88, 89; lectures, 64, 73, 172; Memphis, 135, 139, 141, 146, 147, 172; sewing for soldiers, 17; Teachers' Association, 91; teaching, 22, 25, 27, 36, 85, 304n27; Temperance Lodge activities, 28, 104; work on Civil War history, 97. *See also* Quiner, Emily: diary entries

Quiner, Jane (Emily's mother), 5, 21, 93, 103, 112, 169, 171; boating, 27; church, 13; Emily's trip to Memphis, 177; housekeeping, 55, 84; lectures, 73, 172; reading, 39; sewing for soldiers, 16, 17, 64; visits to Camp Randall, 46; visits to legislature, 62. *See also* Quiner, Emily: diary entries

Quiner, Joseph (Emily's cousin), 62, 79, 308n72

Quiner, Kate (Emily's sister), 5. *See also* Quiner, Emily: diary entries

Quiner, Maria (Emily's sister), 5, 11, 12, 13, 19, 25, 31, 55, 61, 79, 104, 112, 291; boating, 20, 22, 96–97; fishing, 23; fundraising, 13, 52, 54; housekeeping, 84; normal school, 111, 112; photographs, 72, 99; picnic, 23; reading, 39; relief work, 62, 98; sewing for soldiers, 16, 32; teaching, 84, 85, 93, 97, 99, 102; temperance, 11; washing, 37, 46; Young Ladies Relief Society, 64. *See also* Quiner, Emily: diary entries

Quiner scrapbooks, 82, 104, 311n29

railroads, 13, 152, 294, 295, 321n34; attacks on, 222, 257; photograph of, 102; strategic importance, 81, 196, 222, 321n34; transcontinental, 293–94. *See also* Pacific Railroad Act of 1862

Randall, Alexander, 3, 5, 9, 10, 16, 18, 23, 44, 305–6n44

Randall Guards, 14, 18, 19, 303n19. *See also* Wisconsin Regiments: 2nd Infantry

Reed, D. B., 24, 85, 99

Reed, John, 159, 316n37

relief work, 294; flags, 4, 9, 13, 15, 16, 19, 20, 294; fundraising, 12, 34, 52, 84, 93; knitting for soldiers, 52, 65, 294, 305n42; Ladies Aid (Janesville), 317n58; Ladies Aid (Madison), 34, 35, 310n22, 317n58; Ladies Aid (Wisconsin), 243, 294, 300; shirts for soldiers, 16, 17, 18, 32, 294, 305n37; Young Ladies Relief Society (Madison), 33, 34, 37, 48–49, 52, 58, 61, 62, 64, 67, 72, 305n40. *See also* domestic roles; Quiner, Emily; sanitary fairs; seton; soldiers mittens; United States Sanitary Commission

religious faith, 176, 178, 253–54; baptism, 116, 124

Republicans, 10, 66, 107, 108, 186, 187, 190–91

Richardson, A. D., 252, 256, 269, 320–21n30

Richardson, George Lovejoy (Belle's third husband), 298

Richardson, Louise (Lou), 135, 139, 143, 145, 149, 152, 158, 159, 160, 161–62, 163, 167, 169, 170, 172, 173, 177; death of brother, 149–50

Richardson, William, 149–50, 315n26

Richmond, Virginia, 138, 144, 196, 198, 239, 260, 266, 284–85, 320n23; railroads, 293; surrender, 285–86, 322n46

Richmond Examiner, 190

Rood, William, 210, 249, 263
Roxy (Belle's friend), 183, 184, 194, 195, 203, 253, 277, 279
rumors and false reports, 12, 49, 138–39, 142, 230, 303n15, 319n13
Rusk, Jeremiah M., 152, 165, 166, 315n28
Russell, Oliver N., 268, 322n40

Salisbury Prison, 250, 252, 279–80, 288, 299, 320–21n30, 321n31
Salomon, Edward, 74, 82, 83, 92, 105, 111, 167, 173, 174, 187, 306n51, 309n1, 311n30
Salomon, Mrs. Edward, 317n58
sanitary fairs, 188, 294, 317n58
Saukville, Wisconsin, 312n40
Savannah, Georgia, 81, 239, 269
Scott, Winfred, 28
Seattle, Washington, 293
Second Confiscation Act, 83
seton, 34, 305n41
Seventh Day Adventists, 171, 172
Seward, William, 321n33
sewing machines, 16, 17
Sexton, Bell. *See* Sleeper, Belle
Sheboygan Diary, 312n40
Sherman, William Tecumseh, 195, 233, 239; march to the sea, 321n34
slavery, 7, 49, 105, 107–8, 109, 188, 300, 310n13; emancipation, 83, 100, 105, 190
Sleeper, Belle (Arnold), xi, xii, 4, 6, 8, 197, 250, 288, 300; attitude toward voting, 251; awaiting Hiram's return, 273, 274; care of Hiram's mother, 250–51, 253, 254; correspondence with others, 252, 256, 269, 273; despair, 276, 279; fears about Hiram's fate, 252, 276, 279, 280–81, 321n31; illness, 193, 255, 263–64; letters from Hiram, 252; letters to Charles Bennett Palmer, 182–86, 192–93, 194–95, 197–98, 202–4, 250–56, 263–64, 267–69, 272–74, 275–81, 281–82, 288–90; mail, issues receiving, 192, 194, 197; marriage to Hiram, 197; news of Hiram's death, 288–89; postwar life, 296, 297–99; religious faith, 263–64; residences, 198, 255, 263–64; social activities, 184, 268, 277, 282; work at *Berlin Courant*, 183, 184, 192, 202
Sleeper, Charles A. (Al; Belle's brother-in-law), 251, 320n29
Sleeper, Father (Belle's father-in-law), 268, 272, 276, 281, 299
Sleeper, Henry (Belle's brother-in-law), 251
Sleeper, Hiram (Belle's husband), 6, 8, 183, 184, 195, 268, 317n53; burial, 298–99; capture and imprisonment, 250, 252, 256, 274, 280–81, 320–21n30, 321n31; death at Salisbury Prison, 288–89, 298; desertion, 299; enlistment, 197, 198; letters to Belle, 252; marriage to Belle, 197; military service, 198, 203. *See also* Sleeper, Belle: letters to Charles Bennett Palmer; Wisconsin Regiments: 38th Infantry
Sleeper, Nancy (Belle's mother-in-law), 250–51, 253, 254, 272, 276, 281, 299, 320n28
Sleeper, Rosabella Augusta Arnold. *See* Sleeper, Belle
sleighing, 38, 52, 58, 60, 62, 65, 70, 76, 233–34, 247, 268
Smith, George B., 186, 317n55
Smith, George C. (Emily's friend), 10, 21, 46, 48, 58, 61, 99, 102, 103; illness, 168, 170, 172, 173; trip to Memphis, 135, 138, 139, 141, 143, 145, 146, 147, 149, 152, 153, 158, 162, 164, 166
Smith, William, 315n25
Smith, Winfield, 306n51
sociables: Belle Sleeper, 277; Emily Quiner, 11, 12, 19, 20, 22, 34, 36, 42, 48, 55, 103, 104, 114

Index   345

soldiers: 1864 election presidential vote, 221; attitudes toward, 193–94; events for, 21, 26, 32, 98, 304n31; identification discs, 222, 298, 319n12; recruitment, 56, 59, 60, 81, 82, 92, 205, 302n5; temperance, 4, 18, 35, 273, 275, 306n48; weather, impact on, 33, 163. *See also* African Americans; Brown, Susan; Burwell, Mary; Christmas; deaths of soldiers; disability discharges; draft; furloughs; medical treatment of soldiers; Patchin, Margaret; Powers, Sarah; Sleeper, Belle; Waldo, Ann

soldiers mittens, 35, 294, 305n42. *See also* relief work

spirituality, 298–99

Spooner, Judge, 10, 302n9

Springfield, Missouri, 28, 105, 304n35

Stacy, John, 47, 50, 51, 59, 95, 307n56

St. Albans, Vermont, 319n13

Stanton, Elizabeth Cady, 295

Star Spangled Banner, 12, 13, 14, 15, 21, 303n14

State Fair Grounds, 15

State of the Union address: 1861, 105; 1863, 306n45

Stephens, Alexander H., 259, 321n33

Stevens, Julius, 87, 309–10n12

Stewart, Mr. (Gideon's friend), 171, 179–80, 187, 188

Streight, Abel, 119

Sturgeon Bay, Wisconsin, 292–93

Sturgis, Samuel Davis, 304n35

suffrage, women's, 295

Swannell, Ellen (Mary's sister), 297

Swannell, Mary. *See* Burwell, Mary

Swannell, Richard (Mary's brother), 297, 320n25

Sweetland, Dr., 143, 146

Swem, Maggie, 56, 63, 64, 100. *See also* Burwell, Mary: letters to Andrew

Swisshelm, Jane, 67, 307n59

Taft, Benjamin A., 173, 316n45

Taylor, Bayard, 55, 307n54

teachers and teaching, 305n38; normal school, 95, 111, 112–13, 304n29; university courses, 113. *See also* Brown, Susan; Quiner, Emily

teachers association, 27, 89, 90–91

teachers examination, 29, 68, 71, 79–80, 83, 91, 101, 303n26

Teachers' Institute, 101

teachers meeting, 85, 86, 88, 89, 90

temperance, 35, 76, 137, 159, 169, 174, 294, 306n48. *See also* Ladies Temperance Alliance; Quiner, Emily; Quiner, Fannie; Quiner, Maria; soldiers

Tenney, H. A., 14, 15, 24, 30, 31, 33, 36, 42, 43, 44, 303n21

Thanksgiving, 36, 104, 188, 223, 231; proclamations, 187, 305n38, 305–6n44, 311n30, 318n59

Third Volunteer Corp. *See* Wisconsin Regiments: 3rd Infantry

Thumb, Tom, 56, 306–7n53

tobacco use, 169, 235, 238, 240, 263, 265

Townsend, William H. H., 153, 315–16n29

Turner, Mrs. J. H., 317n59

typesetting, 6, 182, 184, 282, 317n51; image of, 185. *See also* Milwaukee Typographical Union

Tyrell, Mrs. Truman, 130, 148

Tyrell, Truman, 148, 315n25

Union Army, xii, 6, 10, 12, 26, 49, 73, 81, 83, 105, 120, 153, 195, 196, 239, 287, 297, 299, 304n35, 306n48, 307n58, 308n63, 308n69, 310n13, 310n24, 314n12, 314n13, 314n15, 314n18, 315n21, 316n41, 322n46; command, 9–10, 81. *See also* battles; Wisconsin Regiments

Union League. *See* Ladies Union League

Union Pacific Railroad. *See* railroads: transcontinental
Union sympathizers, 320–21n30
United States Colored Troops. *See* African Americans
United States Sanitary Commission, 294, 305n37, 308n69
United States Supreme Court, 189, 313n7
University Guards, 89, 313n6. *See also* Wisconsin Regiments: 40th Infantry
University of Michigan, 106, 170, 188–89
University of Wisconsin, 106, 111, 121, 168; admission of women, 109, 111, 291–92, 292, 304n29; Athenian and Hesperian Societies, 99, 172; baccalaureate address, 23, 88; commencement, 24, 88, 134, 313n6; courses, 112–13; exhibitions, 36, 104; Main Hall (now Bascom Hall), 85, 309n9. *See also* Myrmidions Society; teachers and teaching

Vallandingham, Clement, 188–89, 313n7
VanNorman, Ransom, 193, 318n66
Veterans Reserve Corps, 318–19n5
Vicksburg Campaign, 105, 119, 120, 136, 153–54, 315n24; surrender, 143, 148, 158
Vilas, William, 173, 316–17n46

Waldo, Ann, xi, xii, xiii, 4, 5–6, 7, 37–38, 49, 67–68, 71, 73, 86, 300; cavalry disbanding, 39, 40–41, 56–57, 64; death, 102; financial concerns, 37–38, 45, 47, 49, 52, 53, 56, 57, 58, 59, 60–61; furloughs, 41, 47, 49; illness, 100; letters to Morris, 38–39, 40–42, 44–45, 46–48, 50–52, 53–54, 56–58, 58–61, 62–63, 64–66, 86–88; Lincoln, Abraham, 66; Lincoln, Mary, 66; mail, issues receiving, 40, 44, 49, 59, 60, 66; McClellan, George C., 56; photographs, 50, 51, 63; sewing, 41, 51, 53, 57, 65; traitors, 63; trip to Cape Girardeau, Missouri, 94, 100; trip to Kenosha, 49, 51, 52, 53, 54, 56, 61, 67–68; Winneconne, 47, 86; worries about Morris, 39, 47, 53, 54, 86. *See also* Brown, Susan: letters to Ann Waldo
Waldo, Della (Ann's daughter), 5, 37–38, 41, 45; father's letters, 66; illness, 65, 88; learning, 50, 51, 57, 61; locket, 50, 51; missing father, 48, 87; missing mother, 96; religion, 87, 94. *See also* Brown, Susan: letters to Ann Waldo; Waldo, Ann: letters to Morris
Waldo, Morris (Ann's husband), 5–6, 7, 37–38, 49, 68, 309–10n12; finances, 47, 71; illness, 53, 94, 100; service in Missouri, 73, 86, 94, 100. *See also* Brown, Susan: letters to Ann Waldo; Waldo, Ann: letters to Morris; Wisconsin Regiments: 1st Cavalry
Wardrobe, Frederick, 159, 316n38
Wayne, Mr. (Emily's friend), 137, 143
Welch, William, 159, 316n37
Wheelock, Eugene, 204, 319n6
Whetten, Harriett: photograph of, 140
Wick, George, 163, 316n40
widowhood, 296–98
wife's role, 188, 202, 318n60
Winnebago (Ho-Chunk, Hoocąągra), 7, 145, 310n23, 315n22
Winneconne, Wisconsin, 6, 47, 49, 94, 308n70
Wisconsin Civil War Expenditures, 3, 243, 302n10
Wisconsin Historical Society. *See* Historical Rooms
Wisconsin Regiments: 1st Artillery, 105; 1st Cavalry, 37, 86, 94, 306n46, 306n50, 307n56, 309–10n12, 310n21 (*see also* Waldo, Morris); 1st Heavy Artillery, 182, 243, 318n67, 319n14

(*see also* Palmer, Charles Bennett); 1st Infantry, 13, 30, 303n18, 305n36, 307n60; 2nd Cavalry, 35, 315n24; 2nd Infantry, 16, 27, 120, 196, 268, 303n19, 303n24, 304n34, 314n12, 316n40 (*see also* Iron Brigade); 3rd Cavalry, 306n52, 322n38; 3rd Infantry, 13, 120, 305n58, 307n58, 314n12, 315n21, 320n25; 4th Cavalry, 307n55, 320n29; 4th Light Artillery, 82; 5th Infantry, 24, 25, 27, 82, 120, 193, 196, 205, 258, 264–65, 281, 314n12, 318n66, 320n16, 320n18, 322n38, 322n41, 322n46 (*see also* Burwell, Andrew); 5th Light Artillery, 73; 6th Infantry, 25, 27, 28, 82, 120, 196, 322n46 (*see also* Iron Brigade); 6th Light Artillery, 73; 7th Infantry, 31, 32, 82, 120, 191, 196, 322n46; 7th Light Artillery, 73; 8th Infantry, 31, 34, 73, 315–16n29; 10th Infantry, 76–77, 105, 142, 308n70 (*see also* Patchin, Augustus); 11th Infantry, 149–50, 315n26, 316n37; 12th Infantry, 44, 315n23, 316n42; 13th Infantry, 96; 14th Infantry, 78, 308n69, 308n70, 309–10n12, 315n24, 315n28; 15th Infantry, 73; 16th Infantry, 69, 72, 76, 78, 308n69, 315–16n29, 320n17; 17th Infantry, 145, 308n69; 18th Infantry, 308n69, 308n70, 318–19n5; 19th Infantry, 82, 83, 319n14, 322n45, 322n46; 20th Infantry, 93, 311n39; 21st Infantry, 95, 101, 311n27; 22nd Infantry, 319n14; 23rd Infantry, 98, 310n18, 315n27, 316n46; 25th Infantry, 152, 165, 316n41; 26th Infantry, 120, 314n12, 315n28; 27th Infantry, 315n24; 28th Infantry, 312n40, 316n38; 29th Infantry, 98, 129, 130, 148, 314n11, 315n25, 315n29, 316n37 (*see also* Powers, Norman); 32nd Infantry, 146, 315n23, 316n39, 317n50, 322n47 (*see also* Arnold, Wiley); 36th Infantry, 82, 196, 268, 320n22, 322n40, 322n46; 37th Infantry, 82, 319n6, 322n45, 322n46; 38th Infantry, 82, 197, 256, 298, 317n53, 318–19n5, 320n20, 322n46 (*see also* Sleeper, Hiram); 39th Infantry, 204; 41st Infantry, 307n60, 316n43, 320n29; 42nd Infantry, 209, 319n7; 49th Infantry, 251, 320n29

Wisconsin State Capitol, 14, 44, 52, 81, 309n9; Assembly Chamber, 10, 12, 16, 17, 18, 30, 39, 52, 62, 67, 76; photograph of, 11; Senate Chamber, 61, 67, 73

Wisconsin State Legislature, 3, 5, 10, 12, 62, 82, 98, 191, 291–92, 297, 310n23; Assembly, 10, 11, 62, 105, 192, 293, 297; Senate, 10, 105

Wisconsin Supreme Court, 312n40

Wisconsin training camps. *See* Camp Harvey; Camp Randall; Camp Washburn

Wisconsin Women's Suffrage Association, 295

women, civic engagement, 294–95

women's education, 292, 304n29

Woodworth, Sidney D., 203, 318–19n5

Wright, Ebenezer (Ebb), 227, 320n17

Wright, Joseph A., 307n62

Wright, Nancy, 227

Wyocena, Wisconsin, 6, 152, 295; photograph of, 296

"Yankee Doodle" (song), 10, 13, 18

Zouave Drill, 276, 322n42

Wisconsin Studies in Autobiography
WILLIAM L. ANDREWS, SERIES EDITOR

The Examined Self: Benjamin Franklin, Henry Adams, Henry James
ROBERT F. SAYRE

Spiritual Autobiography in Early America
DANIEL B. SHEA

The Education of a WASP
LOIS MARK STALVEY

Forbidden Family: A Wartime Memoir of the Philippines, 1941–1945
MARGARET SAMS
Edited with an introduction by LYNN Z. BLOOM

Journeys in New Worlds: Early American Women's Narratives
Edited by WILLIAM L. ANDREWS, SARGENT BUSH, JR.,
ANNETTE KOLODNY, AMY SCHRAGER LANG, and DANIEL B. SHEA

The Living of Charlotte Perkins Gilman: An Autobiography
CHARLOTTE PERKINS GILMAN
Introduction by ANN J. LANE

*Mark Twain's Own Autobiography:
The Chapters from the "North American Review"*
MARK TWAIN
Edited by MICHAEL J. KISKIS

American Autobiography: Retrospect and Prospect
Edited by PAUL JOHN EAKIN

The Diary of Caroline Seabury, 1854–1863
CAROLINE SEABURY
Edited with an introduction by SUZANNE L. BUNKERS

*A Woman's Civil War:
A Diary with Reminiscences of the War, from March 1862*
CORNELIA PEAKE MCDONALD
Edited with an introduction by MINROSE C. GWIN

My Lord, What a Morning
MARIAN ANDERSON
Introduction by NELLIE Y. MCKAY

American Women's Autobiography: Fea(s)ts of Memory
Edited with an introduction by MARGO CULLEY

Livin' the Blues: Memoirs of a Black Journalist and Poet
FRANK MARSHALL DAVIS
Edited with an introduction by JOHN EDGAR TIDWELL

Authority and Alliance in the Letters of Henry Adams
JOANNE JACOBSON

The Zea Mexican Diary: 7 September 1926–7 September 1986
KAMAU BRATHWAITE

My History, Not Yours: The Formation of Mexican American Autobiography
GENARO M. PADILLA

Witnessing Slavery: The Development of Ante-bellum Slave Narratives
FRANCES SMITH FOSTER

Native American Autobiography: An Anthology
Edited by ARNOLD KRUPAT

American Lives: An Anthology of Autobiographical Writing
Edited by ROBERT F. SAYRE

*Intensely Family:
The Inheritance of Family Shame and the Autobiographies of Henry James*
CAROL HOLLY

People of the Book: Thirty Scholars Reflect on Their Jewish Identity
Edited by JEFFREY RUBIN-DORSKY and SHELLEY FISHER FISHKIN

Recovering Bodies: Illness, Disability, and Life Writing
G. THOMAS COUSER

My Generation: Collective Autobiography and Identity Politics
JOHN DOWNTON HAZLETT

Jumping the Line: The Adventures and Misadventures of an American Radical
WILLIAM HERRICK

Women, Autobiography, Theory: A Reader
Edited by SIDONIE SMITH and JULIA WATSON

The Making of a Chicano Militant: Lessons from Cristal
JOSÉ ANGEL GUTIÉRREZ

Rosa: The Life of an Italian Immigrant
MARIE HALL ETS

Illumination and Night Glare:
The Unfinished Autobiography of Carson McCullers
CARSON MCCULLERS
Edited with an introduction by CARLOS L. DEWS

Who Am I? An Autobiography of Emotion, Mind, and Spirit
YI-FU TUAN

The Life and Adventures of Henry Bibb: An American Slave
HENRY BIBB
With a new introduction by CHARLES J. HEGLAR

Diaries of Girls and Women: A Midwestern American Sampler
Edited by SUZANNE L. BUNKERS

The Autobiographical Documentary in America
JIM LANE

Caribbean Autobiography: Cultural Identity and Self-Representation
SANDRA POUCHET PAQUET

How I Became a Human Being: A Disabled Man's Quest for Independence
MARK O'BRIEN, with GILLIAN KENDALL

Campaigns of Curiosity:
Journalistic Adventures of an American Girl in Late Victorian London
ELIZABETH L. BANKS
Introduction by MARY SUZANNE SCHRIBER and ABBEY L. ZINK

The Text Is Myself: Women's Life Writing and Catastrophe
MIRIAM FUCHS

Harriet Tubman: The Life and the Life Stories
JEAN M. HUMEZ

Voices Made Flesh: Performing Women's Autobiography
Edited by LYNN C. MILLER, JACQUELINE TAYLOR, and M. HEATHER CARVER

The Woman in Battle:
The Civil War Narrative of Loreta Janeta Velazquez,
Cuban Woman and Confederate Soldier
LORETA JANETA VELAZQUEZ
Introduction by JESSE ALEMÁN

Maverick Autobiographies:
Women Writers and the American West, 1900–1936
CATHRYN HALVERSON

The Blind African Slave:
Or Memoirs of Boyrereau Brinch, Nicknamed Jeffrey Brace
JEFFREY BRACE
as told to BENJAMIN F. PRENTISS, Esq.
Edited and with an introduction by KARI J. WINTER

The Secret of M. Dulong: A Memoir
COLETTE INEZ

Before They Could Vote:
American Women's Autobiographical Writing, 1819–1919
Edited by SIDONIE SMITH and JULIA WATSON

Writing Desire: Sixty Years of Gay Autobiography
BERTRAM J. COHLER

Autobiography and Decolonization:
Modernity, Masculinity, and the Nation-State
PHILIP HOLDEN

When "I" Was Born: Women's Autobiography in Modern China
JING M. WANG

Conjoined Twins in Black and White:
The Lives of Millie-Christine McKoy and Daisy and Violet Hilton
Edited by LINDA FROST

Four Russian Serf Narratives
Translated, edited, and with an introduction by JOHN MACKAY

Mark Twain's Own Autobiography:
The Chapters from the "North American Review," second edition
MARK TWAIN
Edited by MICHAEL J. KISKIS

Graphic Subjects: Critical Essays on Autobiography and Graphic Novels
Edited by MICHAEL A. CHANEY

A Muslim American Slave: The Life of Omar Ibn Said
OMAR IBN SAID
Translated from the Arabic, edited, and with an introduction
by ALA ALRYYES

Sister: An African American Life in Search of Justice
SYLVIA BELL WHITE and JODY LEPAGE

Identity Technologies: Constructing the Self Online
Edited by ANNA POLETTI and JULIE RAK

Masked: The Life of Anna Leonowens, Schoolmistress at the Court of Siam
ALFRED HABEGGER

We Shall Bear Witness: Life Narratives and Human Rights
Edited by MEG JENSEN and MARGARETTA JOLLY

Dear World: Contemporary Uses of the Diary
KYLIE CARDELL

Words of Witness: Black Women's Autobiography in the Post-"Brown" Era
ANGELA A. ARDS

A Mysterious Life and Calling: From Slavery to Ministry in South Carolina
Reverend Mrs. CHARLOTTE S. RILEY
Edited with an introduction by CRYSTAL J. LUCKY

American Autobiography after 9/11
MEGAN BROWN

*Reading African American Autobiography:
Twenty-First-Century Contexts and Criticism*
Edited by ERIC D. LAMORE

*Whispers of Cruel Wrongs:
The Correspondence of Louisa Jacobs and Her Circle, 1879–1917*
Edited by MARY MAILLARD

Such Anxious Hours: Wisconsin Women's Voices from the Civil War
Edited by JO ANN DALY CARR

www.ingramcontent.com/pod-product-compliance
Lightning Source LLC
Chambersburg PA
CBHW070403100426
42812CB00005B/1619